LUCAS

LUCAS

HIS HOLLYWOOD LEGACY

Edited by Richard Ravalli

UNIVERSITY PRESS OF KENTUCKY

Copyright © 2024 by The University Press of Kentucky

Scholarly publisher for the Commonwealth, serving Bellarmine University, Berea College, Centre College of Kentucky, Eastern Kentucky University, The Filson Historical Society, Georgetown College, Kentucky Historical Society, Kentucky State University, Morehead State University, Murray State University, Northern Kentucky University, Spalding University, Transylvania University, University of Kentucky, University of Louisville, University of Pikeville, and Western Kentucky University.
All rights reserved.

Editorial and Sales Offices: The University Press of Kentucky
663 South Limestone Street, Lexington, Kentucky 40508-4008
www.kentuckypress.com

Cataloging-in-Publication data available from the Library of Congress

ISBN 978-0-8131-9878-1 (hardcover)
ISBN 978-0-8131-9939-9 (paperback)
ISBN 978-1-9859-0009-7 (pdf)
ISBN 978-1-9859-0008-0 (epub)

This book is printed on acid-free paper meeting
the requirements of the American National Standard
for Permanence in Paper for Printed Library Materials.

Manufactured in the United States of America.

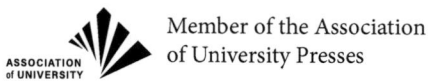 Member of the Association
of University Presses

Contents

Introduction

RICHARD RAVALLI

My research on George Lucas started in 2005 when I was a humanities doctoral student at University of California, Merced. As a historian born and raised in the filmmaker and entrepreneur's hometown of Modesto in California's Central Valley, I was intrigued by the associations that I had been periodically reminded of in my youth, and I decided to learn more about his biographical story. I discovered that opportunities to explore local historical and cultural connections to Lucas and his Hollywood career had been missed. While preparing an article on the subject for the historical society journal *Stanislaus Stepping Stones*, I organized a symposium featuring several speakers, including biographer Dale Pollock, to examine these aspects of Modesto's heritage. Held at Lucas's alma mater Modesto Junior College in June 2006, the event, though lightly attended, helped to stimulate community dialogue and academic interest for a number of years. A 2007 event honoring the thirtieth anniversary of *Star Wars* brought a larger audience and featured several more speakers, including film scholars Peter Krämer and Patti McCarthy. The following year saw a film screening and celebration for the thirty-fifth anniversary of *American Graffiti*, the movie that Lucas made in tribute to his valley roots.

After completing my PhD and relocating from the Central Valley, I was invited to contribute to a walking tour exhibit in downtown Modesto dedicated to the city's car culture and film history heritage. Overall, it was a pleasure to play a small part in the community's deepening involvement in preserving and interpreting its relationship to Lucas, which culminated in a parade in his honor in 2013 and which currently lives on in the building of a Modesto classic car museum. Yet as I continued researching and began teaching an undergraduate course in the history of contemporary American cinema, I remained struck by how little academic attention had been paid to Lucas's

1

Filmmaker George Lucas.
(courtesy Everett Collection)

Hollywood legacy despite a wave of volumes since the mid-2000s devoted to analyzing the *Star Wars* franchise he created. This anthology hopes to encourage a broader dialogue in Lucas studies. It does so by featuring contributors from a variety of academic disciplines, including film, history, art, literature, and museology. Chapters are balanced between Lucas's space fantasy creations and other innovations in American cinema with which he is often associated yet in relation to which he is rarely analyzed. Contributing to but moving beyond standard biographical treatments, *Lucas: His Hollywood Legacy* is the first collected volume to examine the historical contexts and industrial developments that helped make George Lucas one of the most important and influential figures in film history.

Researching Lucas today poses several challenges. Since he has not participated in an independent project since the publication of Pollock's *Skywalking: The Life and Films of George Lucas* in 1983, there are significant gaps that make understandings of him and his associations—particularly for the period following the completion of the original *Star Wars* saga—difficult for historians.

Introduction

Pollock's original interview tapes remain his personal property. Lucas's papers and his former company's archival holdings are also private collections with only limited access for non-Lucasfilm researchers. There are some accessible options for scholars. In San Rafael, the Marin County Library's Anne T. Kent California Room holds Lucasfilm clipping files that offer local press coverage of the company's various divisions and projects into the early 2000s, providing material that is otherwise still unavailable on newspaper databases. Digitized copies of the *Modesto Bee* prior to 1989 can be searched via NewsBank, and a small biographical clipping file exists at the Stanislaus County Library's Special Collections room. Whenever possible, these and other collections have been consulted by authors in this anthology. Despite the opportunities that such sources offer for analysis, accessing original data on Lucas and Lucasfilm will likely remain a significant obstacle for researchers for some time to come. Questions of collections and access at the forthcoming Lucas Museum of Narrative Art in Los Angeles remain unresolved as of this writing.

If gaining intimate knowledge of Lucas and the products of his film industry career is a difficult undertaking, issues of interpretation also hamper careful scrutiny. Lucas, in conjunction with fellow blockbuster filmmaker Steven Spielberg, has often been presented in accounts of the New Hollywood of the 1960s and 1970s as having "ruined cinema," a culprit in turning the industry away from the more challenging, politically engaged films of the era and toward big-budget, corporate products of the late twentieth century. Alternatively, his legacy is swept up in histories that offer more positive portrayals of contemporary Hollywood, with his success as an independent, visionary Northern California artist and entrepreneur being linked to broader commercial and industrial revitalizations of American cinema. This volume is an attempt to move beyond generalized dichotomies that often obscure closer, more nuanced evaluations of Lucas's contributions. In particular, it draws attention to topics that have received less focus from researchers and historians, such as Lucas's ex-wife, Marcia Griffin; Skywalker Ranch; LucasArts; and his work as a producer. The period of time between the completion of the original *Star Wars* trilogy and Lucas's efforts at digitally enhancing the films for theatrical rerelease in the 1990s is an especially intriguing one for the scholar, inviting new avenues for investigation and counterfactual perspective that help make possible more careful understandings of his importance. It is a period that I have been personally interested in since it draws focus to subjects other than *Star Wars* and brings to the foreground crucial questions involving Hollywood business history that I find particularly intriguing. This is not to say that the franchise is undeserving of more inquiry, and contributions to *Star Wars* studies are made in this book. Yet our collection is intentional in framing analyses of Lucas across various eras of his career and not privileging more oft-cited significances. *Lucas: His Hollywood Legacy* errs on the side of well-rounded historical inquiry.

Naturally, not all relevant topics can receive the attention they deserve in any one effort. For example, Lucas's University of Southern California student films have relatively brief mentions in this collection. Other specific works that he either directed or was associated with (*Tucker: The Man and His Dream* [1988], *Radioland Murders* [1994], and *Red Tails* [2012]) are unanalyzed, as are certain aspects of his entrepreneurial activity, such as the educational organization he founded, Edutopia. Hence, this volume is just the start of a continuing dialogue on the importance of Lucas. We begin in Modesto, where Pollock delivered an address some twenty-five years after completing his classic account of Lucas's life and career. Chapter 1 is the text of this talk, which reflects back on his detailed look at the filmmaker's upbringing and the ways Lucas's small-town youth shaped his sensibilities as an artist and businessman. Similarly, in chapter 2, Michael Kaminski returns to his authoritative biographical essay on Marcia Lucas, originally published online. Though ignored in official Lucasfilm histories, she made crucial contributions to Lucas's success as a filmmaker before the couple's divorce in 1983–1984. Lucas's first feature film in 1971, *THX 1138*, offers an opportunity to explore his abstract and politically engaged sentiments, contradicting eventual criticism of him as a reactionary conservative. In chapter 3, John C. McDowell synthesizes scholarship on the dystopian science fiction production and underscores the director's early commitments to nonconformity and social resistance.

Lucas's follow-up film, *American Graffiti*, is examined by Christine Sprengler in chapter 4. Her analysis emphasizes the legacies of *American Graffiti* and its 1979 sequel, *More American Graffiti*, as nostalgia and the productions' complex engagements with the past. The success of the original film was due in large measure to Lucas's conscious move away from his earlier experimental and pessimistic work. In chapter 5, Peter Krämer analyzes how this career trend formed in light of several personal and industrial contexts in the early 1970s and continued through the middle of the decade with the production of the first *Star Wars* movie. In chapter 6, Andrew Howe traces how the original *Star Wars* trilogy has produced a mountain of critical and academic literature since 1977. His historiographical survey discusses the evolution of analyses since the films were first released, from interpretations of the trilogy in relation to the New Hollywood movement toward a great variety of frameworks used by authors to examine the films and the broader *Star Wars* franchise. With *Raiders of the Lost Ark* in 1981, Lucas began a collaboration with Spielberg that flowered into another commercially successful cinematic endeavor. In chapter 7, Janice Liedl demonstrates how the Indiana Jones franchise drew upon the history of Western archaeological practice and how Lucas's cocreation continues to shape perceptions of the discipline today. The following chapter offers an investigation of the role of women in Lucas's early blockbuster productions. Valerie Estelle Frankel considers how the second-wave feminist characters of Princess Leia and Marion Ravenwood ultimately gave way to postfeminist trends as Lucas's women moved from independence to objectivity.

The period following Lucas's Hollywood height in the early 1980s has received less attention from film historians. In chapter 9, Julie Turnock dives deeper into this era, using an archival collection of Lucasfilm yearbooks to examine the history of the company into the early 1990s. She chronicles Lucasfilm's evolving corporate culture during a roughly ten-year period, from a Northern California Bay Area "work as fun" mentality to malaise after high-profile failure and internal reorganization. Chapter 10 explores how Lucas and Spielberg were increasingly vilified by critics and academics as Reagan-era retrogrades and viewed as conjunctively responsible for the era's hypercommercialized Hollywood productions. Jim Kendrick follows the "Lucas-Spielberg syndrome" from its official coining in 1986 to its varied applications into the twenty-first century. In chapter 11, Kenneth Hough takes us to Skywalker Ranch to examine the role of the Northern California location in Lucas's evolving identity as a late century cinema empresario. The chapter draws from Marin County history collections to detail the industrial contributions and missed opportunities that emerge from the ranch's localized past. In the following chapter, Christopher Holliday and Chris Pallant focus on one particular group of company employees working in computer graphics research and development who, over time, established a separately owned animation studio. They discuss the complex history of the highly successful Pixar Animation Studios and emphasize how its various achievements in film were owed in large measure to its years of being within Lucasfilm's corporate structure.

With divorce and company reorganization, success was mollified by loss during Lucas's midcareer years. Yet into the 1990s, distinct significances to American film history and culture emerged that, like Pixar, were pioneered within and existed beyond the confines of his Marin County business. In chapter 13, Stephen Andriano-Moore details the filmmaker's contributions to sound design and the commitments of Lucasfilm engineers to movie theater quality control with the development of the THX system. The following chapter by Stefan Hall demonstrates how Lucasfilm Games, later known as LucasArts, developed innovative, experiential video games as part of a Hollywoodization of the rapidly expanding industry in the late twentieth century. Joseph J. Darowski, in chapter 15, considers Lucas's early television productions, showing in particular how the series *The Young Indiana Jones Chronicles* illustrated his broadening commitments to edutainment transmedia in the 1990s. Lucas's work as an executive producer is further explored by Kathy Merlock Jackson in chapter 16, as she compares his efforts on two successful dinosaur features, *The Land Before Time* (1988) and *Jurassic Park* (1993).

The turn of the millennium saw a long-awaited return to the *Star Wars* universe, which proved to be highly controversial with critics and fans. As Patti McCarthy explains in chapter 17, the *Star Wars: Special Edition* films, released in 1997, called into question issues of authorship and the circulation of meaning within fan culture, as Lucas made significant changes to the original trilogy. In chapter 18, Shanti Fader-Whitesides summarizes the reception of Lucas's prequel films to highlight an evolving attitude toward them in recent online discourse following the release of Disney's *Star Wars* sequels in the 2010s. The last two chapters in this volume explore both the historic and contemporary resonances of Lucas's relationship to Disney and his investments in parks and museums. In chapter 19, Craig Svonkin traces the trajectories of two movie moguls, emphasizing how Walt Disney and Lucas both began as outsiders and evolved into icons of Hollywood's corporate culture. He reflects on the Lucasfilm-Disney relationship and the quasi-religious attitudes fans of both entertainment empires express about them. Finally, Kim Munson examines the history of Lucasfilm exhibits of movie props and costumes, showing how curators, fans, and critics have responded to various museum exhibitions and the company's attempts to legitimize Lucas's artistic visions, culminating in Lucas's forthcoming private art venue.

1

Reflections on George Lucas and Modesto

Dale Pollock

This chapter is adapted from Dale Pollock's address to a symposium in Modesto, California, on June 24, 2006, more than twenty years after the publication of Skywalking, *his classic account of Lucas's life and career.*

What is it about George Lucas that has us speaking about him more than sixty years after he was born, celebrating him, honoring his unique contribution to our culture, our world, and very specifically, the city of Modesto?

I have not been to Modesto since I did my research here in 1982. It's a very different place now: bigger, busier, more racially and ethnically diverse. It's not the 1950s cocoon with a total population of twenty thousand that surrounded young George Walton Lucas Jr., and it's no longer the world he conjured up in *American Graffiti*. One can just imagine Candy Clark, the illustrious Debbie of the blond beehive and spaghetti-strap dress, transported to today's Modesto and saying her version of "Toto, we're not in Kansas anymore."

I have thought about what I could say that could possibly be of interest in this reexamination Richard has begun of George Lucas's roots and their symbolic representation in his work and popular American culture in general. Most of what I had to say I said in the book *Skywalking*, which was published twenty-two years ago and is still in print, having sold more than 150,000 copies.

So I thought I would let George Lucas speak some more, and since he wouldn't share the same stage with me if his life depended on it, I went back and listened to some of the more than seventy hours of taped interviews I did with him. I listened only to the first three tapes, but that was almost six hours.

So I will give a little recap of George Lucas growing up in Modesto in the late 1940s and early 1950s, in George's own words.

George Lucas was a builder. It shouldn't be surprising that he has created the largest franchise in movie history, the largest independent company ever run by a filmmaker, or the largest workspaces a filmmaker ever created for himself, Skywalker Ranch and the new Presidio complex. It all started out in the back alleys of 1950s Modesto, behind the house at 530 Ramona (I know, Richard, that we disagree on that address, but the guy who lived there seemed pretty sure about it).[1]

George Lucas was very proud of the elaborate small environments he created. They transplanted weeds for crops and vegetation and built small cities, which were invaded by soldiers and transformed into battle zones. He had the prototypical boys' clubhouse, a shingled shed in his backyard that was the province of boys only: no girls allowed. Some people believe that the same philosophy still permeates Lucasfilm, a male-dominated company that has never had a woman as a chief corporate officer.

"I liked building; it was very satisfying," Lucas said. He built structures complete with concrete foundations and rebars; he built soapbox derby cars that he and his friends would take around the block; he built anything his fertile imagination could provide. He found building models to be therapeutic, and in a sign of things to come, he would ignore the directions and try to figure out how they went together by himself. He became a fixture with a neighbor across the alley who had woodworking equipment, until Lucas knew how to use every saw, lathe, and sander.

Lucas recalls that this postwar era was a "world of kids"—he had friends like John Plummer, Michael Walker, and George Frankenstein who spent time at his house or in the back alley creating little boy worlds. "I had a *LOT* of friends," he said proudly. Together, they put on elaborate backyard carnivals, evoking a 1930s era that Lucas never formally knew but somehow sensed.

To the scrawny, pint-sized Lucas, Modesto was a very big city. "Going downtown was a big deal," he recalled, remembering shopping trips to the biggest department store downtown, J. C. Penney. When the Lucas family moved out of town to a ranch house on five acres with a walnut grove and a dry creek bed, he sobbed. He loved the little Ramona Street house, and the new location was too far away for his friends to bicycle to visit. In his new environment, Lucas had too much time on his hands.

So he began to tinker, to immerse himself in what he called "a mechanical reality." He learned how engines worked and became seriously interested in car culture. He described himself as a strange mixture of "curious and shy," an appellation that still seems apt.

Lucas prided himself on his broad base of friends and his ability to move between cliques and groups, from the "smart kids" to the "sleazy JDs" the Faros, who were later immortalized by Bo Hopkins and company in *American Graffiti* (with the modified spelling *Pharaohs*, as seen on a gang member's jacket). Known as the "guy who hung out," Lucas described himself as "sort of a likeable kid," proud of his ability to cross between social groups and fascinated by the way each group perceived itself. This ability to place oneself in varying situations turns out to be perfect training for a filmmaker, who must develop characters who inhabit varying worlds and must understand the dynamic of each of those worlds. The cantina sequence in *Star Wars* is a subtle evocation of Burge's Drive-In on Ninth, where the Faros would hang out and challenge anyone who entered their domain. It also served as the direct model for Mel's Drive-In in *American Graffiti*.

Lucas hung out with all these different kinds of kids, but he never really said anything. "I didn't really talk too much until I got to college," he remembered. "If you don't talk very much, people think you are a lot smarter than you are. I'd sit and listen and comment once in a while, but I never thought of myself as a very smart person. I always felt I never knew very much. I was always afraid I'd say something completely wrong. I just wasn't as bright as the other guys. I was very private in public."

Again, some things don't change. Lucas could still be described as very private in public. But can he really still feel dumb? This kind of inferiority complex has defined all of Lucas's public dealings with the film industry; he has distrusted people he thought were more sophisticated than he was in business terms, so rather than compete on their level, he set up his own game. Only in a world of his own creation does he feel smart, on top of it, and in control. There's no one to second-guess him at Lucasfilm, which may ultimately be as much of a bad thing as a good thing.

Because Lucas did not feel as big, as strong, or as smart as the other kids, he retreated increasingly into an interior world. "I spent a lot more time thinking about things," he admits. "I was always trying to figure out how things work and what is reality. How do we fit into a grand scheme that makes sense?" Lucas never liked accepting other people's explanations of how and why things worked; he had a nativist distrust of outside experts. "I couldn't go on just faith. There has to be some logic to all this," he said.

Thinking was about all Lucas could do as a child, along with reading comic books, watching TV shows, eating candy bars by the carton, and drinking sodas. He hated to read, which is why comic books appealed to him so strongly. He picked up weird trivia, loved the exotic locales and bizarre settings of many comics, and worshipped Scrooge McDuck, which he insists was not a metaphor for his incipient wealth. "That kind of greed attracts all young kids," Lucas maintained. He also loved the Superman and Batman comics (What if he had directed one of these franchises?) and loved the comic strips in the newspaper. A rare moment of closeness with his stern father came when George Sr. read his son the Sunday funny papers.

"I feel fortunate that I grew up when all this was a big influence," Lucas said, actually making the point that he had had a better time growing up when there were no big movie franchises. There was very little pressure to accede to the popular culture demands of the 1950s, although Lucas made an obligatory trek to see Elvis Presley perform on tour after his *Ed Sullivan Show* appearance, and he watched all the popular TV shows. Lucas let the culture of the 1950s wash over him.

The Lucas family was one of the last in their neighborhood to get a TV set, but when they finally did, he was hooked. His favorite show was *Adventure Theater*, a daily screening of old movie serials broadcast by KRON from San Francisco. Airing nightly at 5:00 p.m., each episode would feature a twenty-minute serial from Universal or Republic, followed by a *Crusader Rabbit* cartoon. "I watched everything," Lucas said proudly. He called the serials $10,000 versions of *Raiders of the Lost Ark*. When he was ready to make *Star Wars*, he went back and looked at the old *Flash Gordon* serials. "I couldn't believe I was enthralled by something so bad," Lucas recalls. "If I could do it just a little better, wow."

Lucas also fell under the sway of cartoons, really comic books come to life, but he gravitated toward the older, more artistic studio cartoons than the cheap animated shows of the 1950s. He loved Friz Freleng's and Chuck Jones's *Looney Tunes* cartoons for Warner Bros. and the original black-and-white *Felix the Cat* cartoons.

Lucas didn't really go to the movies much until the late 1950s, when the American International Pictures monster-movie craze erupted. Lucas, about eleven years old at the time, remembers the excitement of going to *Godzilla*, *The Blob*, and *Earth vs. the Flying Saucers*. He found them to be scary and dumb, but the good kind of scary and dumb. "That's when I realized you gotta make movies for kids, too," he remembers.

Lucas was also influenced by radio, first in the pretelevision era, with shows like *The Shadow* and *The Whistler*, and then by pop music. "I discovered rock and roll as rock and roll was discovering itself," Lucas remembers. He made the generational transition from 78 rpm discs to the popular 45s that came to symbolize the 1950s and 1960s in pop music.

"As I got older and drifted through college, I came to appreciate the popular arts a lot more," said the man who made film a popular art among an entire generation of moviegoers. "I was never ashamed that I read a lot of comic books and knew all about them. It's a very important thing."

The comic books that John Plummer's father got George Lucas and his friends had a greater impact than just popular culture. Lucas became interested in illustration and graphics and used his natural drawing ability to put his thoughts into images, rather than the words he struggled with, misspelled, and, in a sense, hated. Images are the language Lucas has always felt fluent in; words, whether spoken or in print, intimidate and scare George.

But overall, Lucas recalls his time in Modesto as a "pleasant childhood," even though he can still remember strong feelings that "it wasn't always pleasant." The world that comes to his mind is "frightening," which is not the description you would expect from a coddled, upper-middle-class young man who was showered with presents every Christmas, spoiled by two older sisters and a frequently sick mother, and given a car when he was still fifteen.

Lucas remembers most clearly being the littlest kid on the block, getting picked on for his size and scrawniness, and feeling stupid and out of it. "All kids feel depressed and intimidated," Lucas believes, a statement that Bruno Bettelheim might not disagree with. The fear that Luke Skywalker feels when he leaves Uncle Owen and Aunt Beru's home, the sense that he never really belongs and always has a greater, not quite understood mission, comes directly from Lucas's emotional journey as a child.

"I grew up in, to me, a classic midwestern California existence, about as American as you can get. It's Grant Wood right there in Modesto. The only good thing about the 1950s was to be a kid in the 1950s."

Lucas summarizes this existence in his own terms: "I would come home from school at three, listened to records and read comic books until six, then we would have dinner, then I would eat Hershey bars and drink Cokes and watch TV until bedtime."

"All in all, I was a real average kid," Lucas says, not really accepting that he had any distinguishing characteristics that could have presaged his later success in life. He describes Modesto as feeling very midwestern, even though he has never lived in the Midwest. He describes a childhood of tag football in the park, pickup baseball games, kite flying—but the trials young Luke Skywalker faces are hardly so mundane, and one feels that these events were not mundane for young George Lucas either.

Authority figures brought out feelings of fear and resentment in him, which have continued throughout his life. He has always had trouble expressing emotions and feelings, and his one failed marriage also bears testimony to those enduring issues.

World War II was still a big influence on his childhood, even though his father didn't fight because he didn't weigh enough to get into the army. Lucas played war with tiny plastic soldiers, watched TV shows about famous battles, and came up with battle strategies. "I liked tactical situations," he concedes. "It's just what kids did with the *Star Wars* action figures."

As Lucas looks back, he believes that his talents are a direct product of the way he grew up. "The fact that I'm so ordinary and a lot of people can relate to that. I know what I liked as a kid, and I still like it."

This direct link between childhood desires and adult achievement is rare in today's society. There are so many influences, stimuli, and cues being delivered to contemporary children that it's a wonder they can figure out what they even like. But Lucas credits at least part of his success to the fact that he has a direct emotional line from his childhood to his adult existence.

Lucas still sees himself as a lazy kid only interested in reading comic books, watching TV, and lying in bed, and he may be the only person on the planet to perceive himself in that context. But the lessons his father taught him about commitment and sacrifice, the feelings about a new purpose in life that he had while lying in a hospital bed recovering from a car crash that should have killed him, and a determination to succeed all helped redefine "little Georgie" into a potent creative force who changed the way dreams and visions are presented in contemporary culture.

"Once you commit to something, you can't back out and goof off," Lucas says. "Because I'm not a bright as the next guy and not as talented as the next guy and I don't have the wherewithal that everyone else has that makes it seem so easy, I have to work harder. That's the secret of my success. I work harder than anyone else."

And why has he worked so hard to obliterate Modesto and the rest of his past if it made him what he is today? That's more difficult to understand, and it's probably the hardest part of understanding Lucas, his roots, and his ability to take a relatively undistinguished childhood, hold on to it intact, and somehow transform it into the myth and legend that makes the *Star Wars* series so powerful.

In our interviews, Lucas on several occasions mentioned Thomas Wolfe's *You Can't Go Home Again* as a kind of comment on his leaving his past behind. On a very important level, of course, he hasn't left it behind at all. If there is one message I can leave you with, it's that Thomas Wolfe was only partially right. You may not be able to go home again, but you also take home with you, and whether it's *American Graffiti*, *Star Wars*, or *Raiders of the Lost Ark*, Modesto and its influences have shaped every aspect of George Lucas's life and career.

Note

1 **Editor's note:** The original address of the Lucas home was 230 Ramona Avenue. The street was renumbered in later years.

2

Marcia Lucas

Her Life and Hollywood Legacy

MICHAEL KAMINSKI

Biographer Dale Pollock once wrote that "George had a secret weapon in Marcia."[1] Most admirers of the cinema of George Lucas are aware that he was previously married and that his wife worked in the film industry and edited nearly all of Lucas's early films before their 1983 divorce. But few are aware of the implications her presence brought and the transformations her departure allowed. She was, in many ways, more than just the supportive wife—she was also a logistical and creative partner and the only person Lucas could totally confide in during his early career.

Today, she has been practically erased from the history books at Lucasfilm. In Jonathan Rinzler's *Making of Star Wars* (an authoritative, company-approved volume), she is mentioned only occasionally in passing, a silent extra, absent from any photographs. Other documentaries and books from Lucasfilm fare not much better. Marcia Lucas, the "other" Lucas, has basically become the forgotten Lucas. Nonetheless, Marcia played a role in the shaping of Lucas's scripts and was an instrumental force behind their final form in the editorial stage, where she often cut the pictures herself. But more than that, she had a prolific and successful career of her own as an editor, and she was a key secondary figure in the New Hollywood movement of the 1970s. In fact, the only Oscar the Lucases ever earned was hers, for editing *Star Wars*.

Early Life

Marcia Lou Griffin was born in 1945, making her a year younger than George Lucas. Her date of birth is not quite as significant as the location—Modesto,

14

California. The sleepy town, which was home to about twenty thousand people at that time, also had the closest hospital to Stockton Air Force, where Marcia's father was stationed, and so, as if they were joined by fate, Marcia was born in the far-flung town where Lucas himself lived.

Marcia's father was a career military man, and his relationship with Marcia's mother, Mae, was "off-and-on,"[2] but they finally divorced when Marcia was two. "We had a lot of love and a very supportive family. But economically it was very hard on my mother," Marcia recollected.[3] A boyfriend of the teenage Marcia Griffin worked for a Hollywood museum and wanted to hire her as a librarian there. Unfortunately, librarians had to apply to the California State Employment office to work, and so she was instead sent to the Sandler Film Library, which was looking for an apprentice film librarian without any experience. It only paid fifty dollars a week, but she took it anyway. "That's how I started working in film," she said. "I just walked in off the street."[4]

Verna Fields, one of most respected editors in the industry, had a job for Marcia in 1967. Fields often did business with Hollywood film libraries and asked Sandler Films for an assistant editor to help on a documentary she was putting together. Fields had hired a bunch of film school grads from University of Southern California to cut the picture, and Marcia was assigned to work with one of them, a young man named George Lucas. Locked in a small editing room together, they seemed to be an unlikely pair, Lucas shy and introverted and Marcia bold and outgoing. "Marcia had a lot of disdain for the rest of us," Lucas remembered, "because we were all film students. She was the only real pro there."[5] Eventually, Lucas asked her to go to a screening of a friend's film at the American Film Institute with him. "It wasn't really a date," he said. "But that was the first time we were ever alone together."[6]

Marcia felt that their relationship was kept in check by a very real sense of balance. "I always felt I was an optimist because I'm extroverted," she said. "And I always thought that George was more introverted, quiet, and pessimistic."[7] Pollock concluded that she supplied the aggressiveness that Lucas lacked, while his low-key temperament softened her abrasiveness. "We want to complete ourselves, so we look for someone who is strong where we're weak," he quotes her as saying.[8] Marcia surprised and impressed Lucas's friends as well. "She was a knock-out," John Milius remembered. "We all wondered how little George got this great looking girl. And smart too, obsessed with films. And she was a better editor than he was."[9]

Marcia continued to edit in the commercial world while Lucas became friends with Francis Ford Coppola, who hired him as a documentarian for his next film, *The Rain People*. If Marcia had made her way on her own will-power, it was due to Lucas's connections that she was able to break into the feature-film world. Haskell Wexler, who had known Lucas since he was a teenager in Modesto, wanted to hire Marcia to come to Chicago to edit his directorial debut, *Medium Cool*. But Marcia had a bit of a dilemma: *The Rain People* was in need of her services as well. *Medium Cool* promised not only a better salary but her first credit on a feature; on the other hand, assistant editing *The Rain People* in Nebraska would let her see Lucas. "I'm really going to have to think about this," she told him. "Don't you want to be with me? Don't you love me?" he asked. Finally, she bit the bullet and went to Nebraska. Marcia reflected: "I was poor, right? Financial security was very important to me. I wanted to make it my own way. But we were engaged, we were terribly in love, so I decided to go."[10]

Making *Graffiti*

When *The Rain People* was done, Lucas had miles of footage that he had shot for his documentary, called *Filmmaker*, for which Marcia had acted as assistant editor, a small project for them to do together as they planned their wedding. On February 22, 1969, Marcia Griffin became Marcia Lucas. They had a modest honeymoon in Northern California, where they visited Marin County; it seemed to be the perfect place for them to settle down. Coppola was founding American Zoetrope in nearby San Francisco, and a lot of his and Lucas's buddies, such as Walter Murch and John Milius, were joining them there. Marcia's friends and family were still in Southern California, and she began to grow worried as time went by and she remained unemployed and homesick.

Before American Zoetrope collapsed, Lucas made his first film—*THX 1138*. When the shoot was over, he got to work cutting the film, with Marcia assistant editing. However, *THX* was outside of her tastes; she didn't go for the strange, abstract style Lucas was so fond of, and this is the essential difference in approaches between the two Lucases. "I like to become emotionally involved in a movie," she said. "I want to be scared, I want to cry, and I never cared for *THX* because it left me cold. When the studio didn't like the film, I wasn't surprised."[11]

Lucas had been searching for another project to put food on the table, but he wanted it to be on his own terms, even as Marcia was supporting them both. Seeking a more commercial vehicle, Lucas decided to do a coming-of-age story about young teens in Modesto with a rock and roll soundtrack. Many of his friends thought the idea was silly, but Marcia was one of the few who had full faith in Lucas and encouraged him to do a more emotional, character-oriented piece.

She said: "After *THX* went down the toilet, I never said, 'I told you so,' but I reminded George that I warned him it hadn't involved the audience emotionally. . . . He always said, 'Emotionally involving the audience is easy. Anybody can do it blindfolded, get a little kitten and have some guy wring its neck.' All he wanted to do was abstract filmmaking, tone poems, collections of images. So finally, George said to me, 'I'm gonna show you how easy it is. I'll make a film that emotionally involves the audience.'"[12]

American Graffiti told a simple human drama that relied on editing to interweave the four stories in the narrative. Marcia stepped up to the plate, working alongside Verna Fields herself. It was, in fact, Universal executive Ned Tanen who insisted Fields be on the picture, since he feared that Lucas was just using Marcia as an excuse to cut it himself. Given Fields's status as one of the great editors of the time, everyone assumed she was the genius behind the film's masterful editing, yet Fields only was on board for half of the film's editorial life span.

Lucas looked at *Graffiti* footage every day and explained what he wanted from Marcia and Fields—the only time he ever spoke to his wife during the hectic postproduction schedule. Walter Murch came on board as sound editor, and they collaborated on the difficult task of cutting the music to fit the scene. Marcia argued Lucas out of his original approach to the structure of the film, which depended on a more rigid construction of crosscutting, and she also was crucial in giving scenes longer time to breathe.[13] Fields left once the rough cut had been assembled, since she had another job lined up, but the film was almost an hour too long, so for the next six months Marcia, along with Lucas and Murch, cut the film down. Because of the interlocking narrative structures, the film could not simply be trimmed up in a conventional sense: removing one scene, or part of a scene, affected the next narrative thread and threw off the pacing. Now it was Marcia's turn—she took over and recut the film on her own this time, while Lucas worked with Murch on the sound design.

By January 1973, Marcia had assembled the film for a test screening. The release would be controversial—test audiences adored the film, yet the studio considered it dreadful. But Marcia believed in *American Graffiti*, and when it was released, it became a powerhouse hit that grossed over $100 million and turned Lucas and Marcia into overnight millionaires. In 1974, the film was nominated at the Oscars for Best Picture, Best Director, and Best Screenplay—as well as Best Editing. Marcia desperately wanted to win, but the picture failed to nab any of the above. Lucas didn't really care; producer Gary Kurtz was disappointed; Marcia cried. It would be another four years before she would get her dream.

From Scorsese to *Star Wars*

Even before Marcia Lucas was an Oscar-nominated editor, her career was taking off. Michael Ritchie had been impressed with the young woman when she worked on *The Candidate*, and he recommended her to his friend Martin Scorsese, who was looking for someone to edit his feminist road movie, *Alice Doesn't Live Here Anymore*. Once again, Lucas's connections had given Marcia a crucial stepping stone, and she felt it was important for her to work for someone other than her husband.

Meanwhile, Lucas was writing his next project, *The Star Wars*. As production on *Alice Doesn't Live Here Anymore* stretched on, Marcia had to relocate to Tucson, Arizona, to begin cutting the footage. Lucas didn't like being separated, and so he packed his things and joined her, trying to hash out the first draft of his screenplay.

As far as evidence suggests, Marcia stayed out of Lucas's way when he first started writing the space epic. Like many of Lucas's friends, she didn't quite know what to make of the first draft of *Star Wars* when he showed it to her in 1974; she wasn't a fan of the action serials as Lucas was, and she found a lot of it too bizarre and disliked the lack of strong characters or dialogue. Soon, Marcia landed another high-profile gig, editing *Taxi Driver* for Scorsese. She received a BAFTA (British Academy of Film and Television Arts) nomination for her editing work on the film and was later featured, at Steven Spielberg's recommendation, in an ad by Kodak hailing women in the film industry.

As Milius recalled: "She was a stunning editor. . . . Maybe the best editor I've ever known, in many ways. She'd come in and look at the films we'd made—like *The Wind and the Lion*, for instance—and she'd say, 'Take this scene and move it over here,' and it worked. And it did what I wanted the film to do, and I would have never thought of it. And she did that to everybody's films: to George's, to Steven [Spielberg]'s, to mine, and Scorsese in particular."[14]

Marcia's rising career did not come without its troubles. For one, she had to work in Los Angeles, and the Lucas family tradition had also never allowed a woman to have an independent career. Lucas hated cooking and cleaning, and he hired a housekeeper while Marcia was away. Meanwhile, *The Star Wars* had still not been green-lit, frustrating him further.

Lucas had reconfigured much of *Star Wars* for his second draft, completed in January 1975. Marcia, along with many of Lucas's friends, critiqued which characters worked, which ones didn't, and which scenes were good, and Lucas composed the script in this way.

Marcia was always critical of *Star Wars*, but she was one of the few people Lucas listened to, knowing she had a skill for carving out strong characters. She kept her husband down to earth and reminded him of the need to have an emotional through line in the film. As Mark Hamill commented, "She was really the warmth and heart of those films, a good person he could talk to, bounce ideas off of."[15] When Lucas was having difficulty coming up with ideas or ways of solving scenes and characters, he would talk about it with her; she even suggested killing off Ben Kenobi while Lucas was filming, as Kenobi was originally scripted to survive.[16]

Often, Marcia reeled in Lucas's ego. She encouraged him to do interviews as a way of raising his spirits but was also irritated by the auteur theory of critics, which credited every element of Lucas's films to him alone. Hamill noted in 2005 how her sensibilities influenced the content and structure of his films:

> You can see a huge difference in the films that he does now and
> the films that he did when he was married. I know for a fact that
> Marcia Lucas was responsible for convincing him to keep that little
> "kiss for luck" before Carrie [Fisher] and I swing across the chasm
> in the first film: "Oh, I don't like it, people laugh in the previews,"
> and she said, "George, they're laughing because it's so sweet and
> unexpected"—and her influence was such that if she wanted to
> keep it, it was in. When the little mouse robot comes up when
> Harrison and I are delivering Chewbacca to the prison and he roars
> at it and it screams, sort of, and runs away, George wanted to cut
> that and Marcia insisted that he keep it.[17]

Pollock provided an anecdote that demonstrates how Marcia's presence in her husband's life influenced his films in subtle but significant ways, changing the ending of *Raiders of the Lost Ark*:

> [Marcia] was instrumental in changing the ending of *Raiders*, in
> which Indiana delivers the ark to Washington. Marion is nowhere

to be seen, presumably stranded on an island with a submarine and a lot of melted Nazis. Marcia watched the rough cut in silence and then levelled the boom. She said there was no emotional resolution to the ending, because the girl disappears. "Everyone was feeling really good until she said that," Dunham recalls. "It was one of those, 'Oh no we lost sight of that.'" Spielberg reshot the scene in downtown San Francisco, having Marion wait for Indiana on the steps on the government building. Marcia, once again, had come to the rescue.[18]

Star Wars commenced production in 1976, and upon returning home, Lucas was exhausted and disappointed in his film, and Marcia had to rush him to the Marin General Hospital because of stress-induced chest pains. Lucas had hired a UK editor, John Jympson, to cut the film while they were in England, but after Lucas had seen the rough assembly, he was horrified. The film was dull and without any of the kinetic energy he had envisioned. Jympson was fired, and Marcia took his place, starting over from scratch. "He asked Marcia to work on the final battle sequence, so ILM [Industrial Light & Magic] could start, but he needed someone else to start at the beginning," said coeditor Richard Chew, who was hired not long after Marcia began cutting.[19] With the entire Jympson cut junked wholesale, the film needed to be reordered back into dailies so that Marcia and Chew could start over. "It turned out to be even more of a tremendous job than we thought it was going to be," Lucas said in *The Making of "Star Wars."* "We were running against a terrible time problem, so we hired [another] editor, Richard Chew. He and my wife Marcia, who was also an editor, raced to get a first rough cut of the movie ready by Thanksgiving."[20] A third editor, Paul Hirsch, was later hired.

The Death Star trench run was originally scripted entirely differently, with Luke having two runs at the exhaust port. Marcia had reordered the shots almost from the ground up, trying to build tension lacking in the original scripted sequence. She warned Lucas, "If the audience doesn't cheer when Han Solo comes in at the last second in the *Millennium Falcon* to help Luke when he's being chased by Darth Vader, the picture doesn't work."[21] In the final crunch, the three editors began to trade off scenes as a trio. "We put it all together and spent about three or four days as a tag team," Hirsch said. "George, Richard, Marcia and I would sit at the machine each for a couple of hours, taking turns and making suggestions. The last day, we did this for about twelve hours."[22]

As Marcia continued to rework sequences as late as December 1976, Scorsese called her up. His editor of *New York, New York* had died, and he needed her to finish the film. Marcia was, frankly, sick of working on *Star Wars*. Lucas had another two editors, and the film was on its way to being finished. Even still, he was not pleased. "For George the whole thing was that Marcia was going off to this den of iniquity," Willard Huyck explained. "Marty was wild and he took a lot of drugs and he stayed up all night, had lots of girlfriends. George was a family homebody. He couldn't believe the stories that Marcia told him. George would fume because Marcia was running with these people. She loved being with Marty."[23] Marcia would later confide in Lucasfilm marketing's Charles Lippincott that if she ever had to work with her husband on a film again, "it would be the end of their marriage."[24]

It goes without saying how shocking the film's triumphant release was for all involved. For Marcia, the success of *Star Wars* in 1977 meant something else—they could finally settle down. Lucas was planning to retire. Marcia was planning to have a baby. Finally, it seemed as if they could have a real life.

The Beginning of the End

Marcia is quoted in a summer 1977 article in *People* magazine as saying: "Getting our private life together and having a baby. That is the project for the rest of the year."[25] After trying to get pregnant, the Lucases got some bad news: Lucas was infertile. Adoption was not something the two of them were ready to jump into just yet. And Lucas, despite claiming to be ready to retire, was about to embark on his most ambitious project to date.

"The idea for [Skywalker Ranch] came out of filmschool," Lucas explained in 1980. "It was a great environment; a lot of people exchanging ideas, watching movies, helping each other out. I wondered why we couldn't have a professional environment like that."[26] With *Star Wars* becoming the most successful film of all time by 1977's close, Lucas saw the opportunity he had been given and decided to turn *Star Wars* into a franchise intended to support the costly facility. Marcia was supposed to take a vacation to Mexico with him in 1978, but with screenwriter Leigh Brackett unexpectedly passing away, Lucas spent much of the trip in his hotel room writing *The Empire Strikes Back*. He also began spearheading *Raiders of the Lost Ark* into production. Things weren't as simple as they had anticipated.

A peak of joy finally appeared for Marcia amid their increasingly hectic lifestyle. On April 3, 1978, the fiftieth Academy Awards ceremony was held, with *Star Wars* drawing a wealth of nominations, including Best Picture, Best Director, Best Screenplay, and Best Editing. Lucas was unsurprised that he walked away empty-handed, but *Star Wars* won the Best Editing award, and Marcia and fellow coeditors Chew and Hirsch were all awarded the golden statues. For Marcia, it was the culmination of a constant uphill struggle since she entered Sandler Films in the 1960s and her proudest professional moment.

Lucas coaxed Marcia into sorting out the split-screen edits on *More American Graffiti*, but she did so begrudgingly; Eleanor Coppola asked her to edit her documentary *Hearts of Darkness*, but Marcia said she was "too busy putting her house in order."[27] Scorsese made *Raging Bull* in 1980, but to edit the picture, he went with Thelma Schoonmaker, whom he has hired for virtually every film he has made since. Offers apparently continued to roll in for Marcia to edit, and even to produce and direct, but she continued waiting for her workaholic husband to settle down. "She worked so hard for so many years without stopping that she just wanted to stay home for a while," Eleanor Coppola remarked.[28] *Empire* later opened to much success in 1980, but instead of slowing down, Lucas went straight into production of *Raiders of the Lost Ark* and then began construction of the massive Skywalker Ranch, an involved and stressful undertaking that left him perpetually distant and exhausted.

Marcia tried to find some kind of creative outlet by involving herself in the ranch's design. "Marcia has sort of put her editorial career on hold," Lucas said in 1981, "and is now working as an interior designer. I don't really know if she'll go back to editing—and she's a good editor. Usually the offers are to go to New York or to go to Los Angeles, and that's no fun for us."[29] Lucas commented around this time that he only spent a couple of hours a night at home, "and I'm always real tired and cranky and feeling like, 'Gee, I should be doing something else.' . . . It's been very hard on Marcia, living with someone who constantly is in agony; uptight and worried, off in never-never land."[30] His contract with Fox was for three *Star Wars* films, and so that's what he would deliver. His next *Star Wars* sequel would be the last, his final ace in the hole to pay off the ranch, which he vowed would be his final megaproject before settling down and enjoying the fruits of his labor.

In 1981, Marcia and Lucas adopted a daughter, Amanda. Hoping to clear the table for family life, Lucas hired Lawrence Kasdan to finish writing *Return of the Jedi*; Richard Marquand was brought in to direct; and producer Howard Kazanjian ensured a smooth production.

Marcia recalled with fondness this one brief glimpse of domestic happiness: "I make everyone leave at six o'clock so that when George comes home, it's just the two of us and Amanda. Now that we have Amanda we actually have dinner at the table. I cook, I do the dishes, and we give Amanda a bath together. George sometimes feeds her a bottle in the TV room. We just decided to try to keep our lives as normal as possible."[31]

Yet it was not to last. Lucas became a permanent figure on the set of *Return of the Jedi* in England. He supervised each day's filming and became a full-time second-unit director, while in his spare moments he was busy prepping the much-anticipated Indiana Jones sequel, to be filmed in Sri Lanka. Instead, Marcia was left behind in their empty mansions and hotel rooms. "I think some of the striving has been taken out of my life," she mused to Pollock around this time. "I was a great achiever, a self-made girl who started from nothing and worked hard and got rewarded. In a way, I regret having those obstacles removed."[32] She would later remark, "I felt that we had paid our dues, fought our battles, worked eight days a week, 25 hours a day. I wanted to stop and smell the flowers. I wanted joy in my life. And George just didn't. He was very emotionally blocked."[33] Things did not improve over the months, and although they now shared a child, the emotional coldness only grew.

Richard Walter, who saw the Lucases at a party at Randal Kleiser's house just before their eventual divorce, recalled: "I ended up in the corner with Marcia, chatting with her, and what she told me underscored a sense I'd always had that [intimacy] was not a gigantic part of George's life. . . . She just sort of blurted it out that it was extremely isolating; it was like Fortress Lucas. I'd heard this from people who worked with him at that time. They would say, 'I can't stand it. He's brilliant, but it's so cold. I feel like I'm suffocating. I've got to get out of here.' Marcia told me she 'just couldn't stand the darkness any longer.'"[34]

While Lucas was away shooting *Return of the Jedi* in 1982, Marcia was overseeing the interior design of Skywalker Ranch as it underwent its final phases of construction, with a staff of twenty-five working under her. The facility had a great library, which was capped with an elaborate stained-glass dome. A local artist named Tom Rodrigues was hired to create the elaborate piece, and at some point in that time, Marcia fell in love with him.

The event shocked Lucas, traumatized him even, but in reality it was simply the culmination of a separation that was already long underway. Lucas, however, had come from a conservative family that did not get divorced. Perhaps it is because of this that Marcia edited *Return of the Jedi*—a last-ditch attempt to bring them closer together, a project to collaborate on. Journalist Denise Worrell reported that Lucas said she was "great with emotions and characters, the dying and crying scenes," and that Marcia edited Yoda's and Darth Vader's death scenes and the film's space battles as well. "George listens to her very carefully," Worrell observed.[35]

In early June 1983, Lucas called his staff into his office, and as he and Marcia held hands, they announced they were divorcing after fourteen years of marriage.[36] The news was made public soon after.

Aftermath

Both Marcia and Lucas sought to escape the spotlight subsequently, and by the close of the decade, he would be regarded as a recluse. In the divorce, Lucas lost much of his fortune. With Marcia owning half of Lucasfilm, she walked away with between $35 and $50 million (numbers differ depending on the source).[37] Though she had 50 percent shared custody of Amanda, Lucas methodically ostracized her from their mutual social circle. "It's not enough that I'm erased from his life, he wants to blackball me too, with people who were my friends," she remarked. "It's like I never existed."[38] She looked back in the late 1990s on the state of the company she cofounded:

> By the time George could afford to have a film facility, he no longer wanted to direct. After *Star Wars*, he insisted, "I'm never going to direct another establishment-type movie again." I used to say, "For someone who wants to be an experimental filmmaker, why are you spending this fortune on a facility to make Hollywood movies? We edited *THX* in our attic, we edited *American Graffiti* over Francis' garage, I just don't get it, George." The Lucasfilm empire—the computer division, ILM, the licensing and lawyers—seemed to me to be this inverted triangle sitting on a pea, which was the *Star Wars* trilogy. But he wasn't going to make any more *Star Wars*, and the pea was going to dry up and crumble, and then he was going to be left with this huge facility with its enormous overhead. And why did he want to do that if he wasn't going to make movies? I still don't get it.[39]

Marcia legally kept the last name Lucas, since she had no attachment to her father's name. "But I did have a professional name, the name on all my film credits," she told me privately. "I am proud of the work I did as Marcia Lucas. I was part of an amazing era in American cinema."

John Milius once mused, "One of the great losses is that Marcia never became a filmmaker and continued as an editor."[40] Sadly, her work as editor did not continue either. After beginning family life, the idea of directing or editing lost its appeal; her number one interest, it seems, was being a mom. She has recently emerged in the public again, contributing to Jonathan Rinzler's 2021 biography of producer Howard Kazanjian, a lifelong friend of hers. "For more than forty years, I've stayed in the background, letting George do his thing and tell his stories," she wrote in the foreword. "I never wanted to come out. I never wanted to do an interview. . . . What could I say that people wouldn't interpret as the words of some bitter ex-wife?"[41] She appeared in a featured on-camera interview for the 2022 VICE TV series *Icons Unearthed: Star Wars*, recounting the making of the film. She admits of Lucas's Oscar loss, "If ever there was somebody who deserved a directing award, it was George Lucas for *Star Wars*."[42] Her legacy endures at Lucas's alma mater University of Southern California, where the Marcia Lucas Post-production Building serves as the premier editing facility of the esteemed cinema school. But beyond this, her legacy endures not only in *Star Wars* but in all the early films of George Lucas and those of the Lucases' circle, where her touch helped shape them into the classics we know.

Notes

1. Dale Pollock, *Skywalking: The Life and Films of George Lucas* (New York: Harmony Books, 1983), 228.

2. Ibid., 63.

3. Ibid., 64.

4. Ibid.

5. Ibid., 61.

6. Ibid., 62.

7. Ibid., 67.

8. Ibid., 65.

9. Ibid., 64.

10. Ibid., 83.

11. Peter Biskind, *Easy Riders, Raging Bulls* (New York: Simon and Shuster, 1998), 100.

12. Ibid., 235.

13. Brian Volk-Weiss, creator, *Icons Unearthed: "Star Wars,"* season 1, episode 2, "A New Hope, Part II," July 19, 2022, Nacelle Company, https://www.vicetv.com/en_us/video/a-new-hope-part-ii/62bcca084e24513f31103bf9.

14. John Baxter, *Mythmaker: The Life and Work of George Lucas* (New York: Spike/Avon Books, 1999), 66.

15. Walter Chaw, "Mark Hamill Walks down Memory Lane with Film Freak Central," Film Freak Central, March 20, 2005, http://filmfreakcentral.net/notes /mhamillinterview.htm.

16. Paul Scanlon, "The Force behind *Star Wars*," *Rolling Stone*, August 25, 1977, 41–51.

17. Chaw, "Mark Hamill Walks Down Memory Lane."

18. Pollock, *Skywalking*, 228.

19. Jonathan Rinzler, *The Making of "Star Wars"* (New York: Ballantine Books, 2007), 220.

20. Ibid., 220.

21. Baxter, *Mythmaker*, 233.

22. Rinzler, *Making of "Star Wars,"* 230.

23. Biskind, *Easy Riders, Raging Bulls*, 330.

24. Baxter, *Mythmaker*, 216.

25. "Off the Screen," *People*, July 18, 1977.

26. Jean Vallely, "The Empire Strikes Back and so Does Filmmaker George Lucas with His Sequel to *Star Wars*," *Rolling Stone*, June 12, 1980, https://www.rollingstone .com/movies/movie-news/the-empire-strikes-back-and-so-does-george-lucas-52767/.

27. Baxter, *Mythmaker*, 277.

28. Ibid., 277.

29. Mitch Tuchman and Anne Thompson, "I'm the Boss," *Film Comment*, July/ August 1981, 57.

30. Baxter, *Mythmaker*, 333.

31. Denise Worrell, *Icons: Intimate Portraits* (New York: Atlantic Monthly Press, 1989), 192.

32. Pollock, *Skywalking*, 240.

33. Biskind, *Easy Riders, Raging Bulls*, 422.

34. Baxter, *Mythmaker*, 333–334.

35. Worrell, *Icons*, 191.

36. Baxter, *Mythmaker*, 335.

37. Chris Taylor, *How "Star Wars" Conquered the Universe* (New York: Basic Books, 2014), 275. For the broader effect that the Lucas divorce had on blockbuster film history, see Richard Ravalli, "George Lucas Out of Love: Divorce, Darkness, and Reception in the Origin of PG-13," *Historian* 78, no. 4 (2016): 690–709.

38. Biskind, *Easy Riders, Raging Bulls*, 423.

39. Ibid., 381.

40. Baxter, *Mythmaker*, 70.

41. J. W. Rinzler, foreword to *Howard Kazanjian: A Producer's Life* (Petaluma: Cameron+, 2021).

42. Volk-Weiss, *Icons Unearthed*.

3

"Are You Now, or Have You Ever Been?"

The Alienation of the Administered Society,
Running to Freedom, and the Dystopianism
of George Lucas's THX 1138

JOHN C. McDOWELL

Introduction

Early in George Lucas's debut feature, *THX 1138*, a calm voice audibly articulates, "Are you now, or have you ever been?" The incomplete, and therefore
seemingly arbitrary, question derives from the interrogations by Senator Joseph
McCarthy for the House Un-American Activities Committee associated with
the anticommunist examinations of the late 1940s and 1950s.[1] The movie may
well be set in some indefinable future, but the allusion clearly places it in the
second half of the twentieth century. The image that accompanies it is framed
as a piece of video surveillance, and while at this stage in the film the context is
a little difficult to comprehend, baton-armed police officers restrain a bleeding
man. That image, combined with the ominous score, indicates that the theme
is one of political repression. The image, moreover, channels the spirit of the
government crackdown on anti–Vietnam War student protests. The director
termed this his uncompromising "message" movie, an aesthetically stylized
metaphor for or "an abstraction of [America in] 1970."[2] Whereas the initial
effort, *THX 1138 4EB*, was set on May 15, 2187, Lucas's feature expansion
purposely removed the temporal reference. "*THX* really is Buck Rogers in
the 20th century, rather than Buck Rogers in the future."[3] Whether or not
it was conscious on the part of Lucas and his script cowriter, Walter Murch,

the fingerprints of prominent critical theorists such as Herbert Marcuse and their "damning indictment of contemporary Western societies, capitalist and communist," are all over the movie.[4] The result suggests that the politics of production and consumption are not the means of freedom but are, instead, the very conditions for dehumanizing servitude.

The movie is also significant for understanding Lucas's work more broadly. In 1988, a well-known book claimed that the self-confessed auteur's *Star Wars* (1977) was a feature of, and cultural contribution to, a society becoming politically reactionary. Their study did not, however, pay sufficient attention to the way both *The Empire Strikes Back* (1980) and *Return of the Jedi* (1983) complicate the themes of their predecessor in the saga, to the antiauthoritarian theme of freedom running through Lucas's work more broadly, or to his own interpretation of his space opera as expressing serious concern with America's violent involvement in Vietnam.[5] It is *THX 1138* that can shed some light on the politics of freedom that permeates Lucas's filmmaking, and his confessed "basic dislike of authority figures."[6]

"Propaganda Film for Freedom"

Three of Lucas's early student works at University of Southern California provide a useful backdrop for *THX 1138*: *Look at Life* (1965), *Freiheit* (1966), and *THX 1138 4EB* (1967).

The title of the multi-award-winning *Look at Life* is a play on words. The film of under one minute in length provides a disorienting "rapid-cut barrage of . . . images" progressing from oppression, racial violence, America's intensifying military presence in Vietnam, and political corruption to the word *Love* and consequent images of peace and affection from both *Look* and *Life* magazines.[7] A concluding question placed in uppercase lettering asks, "Anyone for survival?" Even though the theme is rather heavy-handedly purveyed, as one would expect from an early student assignment, the attempt at offering some sociopolitical critique is evident.

Freiheit is the expression of a Lucas "getting involved in all the causes."[8] Accordingly, Randal Kleiser, the film's principal actor, claimed that with the Vietnam draft hanging over the students, "George wanted to make a statement about how easy it is to say that ['I will defend democracy'] but how in reality people were getting killed." Its conclusion to two minutes of a man attempting a break for freedom from East Germany to the West is provocative. A voice-over asserts that "freedom is definitely worth dying for . . . the only thing worth dying for. . . . Because without freedom we're dead." This "angry polemic" directs the critical context not so much to communism, despite the theme of escape from the Soviet-controlled East Berlin, but to the blithe appeal to freedom by Americans that is denied to the Vietnamese.[9] Lucas himself reflected: "It was a propaganda film for freedom. . . . We all knew that it [the Vietnam conflict] wasn't about anything. It was a lie to help the colonials continue their empire. It had nothing to do with us, and it didn't have anything to do with the Vietnamese—all they wanted was freedom."[10]

Based on Matthew Robbins's two-page script "Breakout," Lucas's fifteen-minute long *THX 1138 4EB* would win the National Student Festival drama prize.[11] Set on May 14, 2187, in an emotionless and endlessly surveilled society constructed underground, THX 1138 evades capture by demi-cyborg police officers for sex crimes with his roommate YYO 7117.[12] Intriguingly, where Robbins wrote of the protagonist's yelling for joy on his eventual escape, Lucas tones that down to a long shot of THX silhouetted against the dimming light of a sunset and the use of a complex and brooding organ piece from J. S. Bach's *Passacaglia in C Minor*.

"You Rate Very High in Sanitation" (SEN): Happiness, Social Hygiene, and Solitude

Conducting "Visual Exercises"

With Walter Murch's help on the script, Lucas's feature-length expansion, *THX 1138*, was able to realize a conjunction between form and matter, medium and message, and to do so with a distinctly restricted budget ($777,777.77) and production schedule. Despite the obvious resource limitations, the product was an artistically imaginative and expressive movie, "a kind of *cinema verité* film of the future," that refused to follow the narrative and dramatic conventions of the Hollywood cinema of the time, aesthetically borrowing in some measure from *2001: A Space Odyssey* (dir. Stanley Kubrick, 1968).[13] In a revealing interview with film critic Gene Youngblood in 1971, Lucas described *THX 1138* in predominantly formal terms.[14] This "technically oriented" "visual exercises" movie was even reduced at one point to being "a lighting test."

When the interview turned to more material issues, Lucas, generalizing, admitted a strong connection with two literary dystopias that are vastly different from each other, Aldous Huxley's *Brave New World* and George Orwell's *Nineteen Eighty-Four*. Later, however, he more appropriately narrowed it: "I

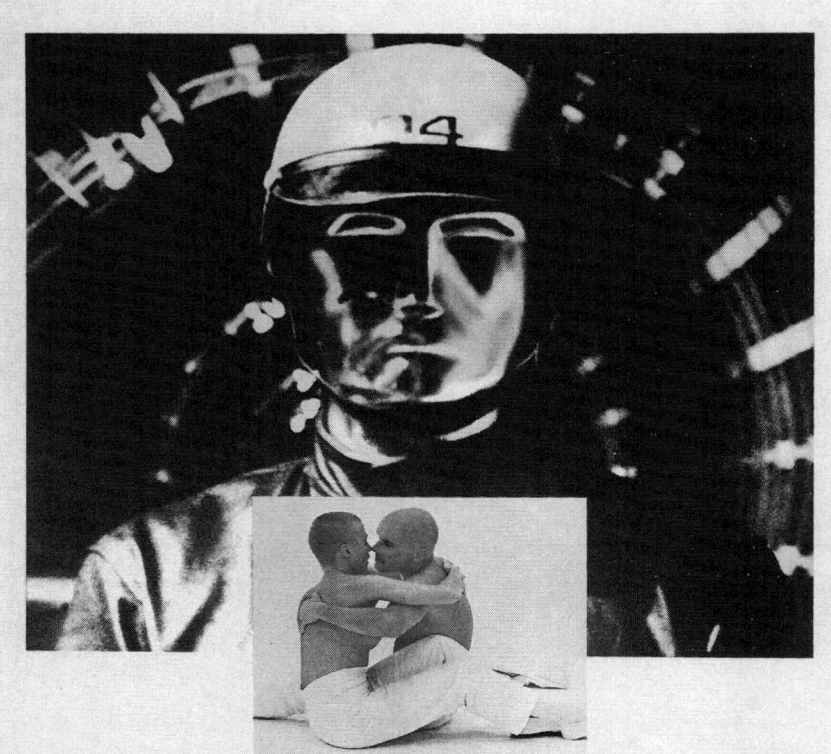

Poster for George Lucas's dystopian film, *THX 1138*. (courtesy Everett Collection)

liked the idea of a futuristic, brave new world."[15] The reference, at least, is broadly to a vision of social bondage, an administered society that constitutes dehumanizing disrepair. On several occasions, Lucas railed against the domination of filmmaking by the Hollywood studios in a way that allowed him to expand his observations more broadly: "The dollar is above the individual." The consequence of this mindset is a form of power that diminishes real talent and creative individuality.

Happiness in an "Immaculate Reality"

That *THX 1138* is set in a dystopian, "repressive," and freedom-denying society is not immediately evident in some ways, however.[16] As Lucas conceded, certain utopian qualities are in evidence.[17] For instance, the environment is brightly illuminated and in good repair, even if a police android malfunctions on one occasion. Using a phrase from Kurosawa, Lucas spoke of this as an "immaculate reality."[18] There is no war, criminal violence, homelessness, or unemployment. Even personal anxiety is managed through state-provided sedation. Violent competition and ruthless acquisitiveness are long gone. In fact, there are no power-accumulating profiteers, whether economic or political, and no elite class subjugating others for personal gain. Instead, in an image likely to have been inspired by Jean-Luc Godard's *Alphaville* (1965), the system is fully automated, with the central computer, OMM 0000, serving as the governing sociopolitical regulator. The technologically mediated (civil) religion is equally nondivisive. The content of its therapeutically consoling platitudes intensifies the system's anesthetization of the consumptive self.[19] On one occasion, OMM urges, "Let us be thankful we have commerce. Buy more. Buy more now. Buy. And be happy." The automated governing system evidently even exercises a paternal form of care, so when THX opens up his medicine cabinet for pills, a voice courteously asks, "Is everything all right? I hope everything is all right." Crucially, happiness is urged on all those who visit the confession booth. Given his narcotically induced somnolent condition, it is noteworthy that on two occasions THX claims that he had been "happy" prior to LUH 3417's illegal decreasing of his drug dosage. When THX briefly switches holographic home-entertainment channels, one character is heard to proclaim, "Never before have we been so contented."

"We Share Nothing but Space"

The film does not locate the sociocultural dehumanization in the dearth of artistic creativity, with the reinvigoration of this creativity providing a source for social change, as Marcuse does, even if the subterranean environment displays little imagination among its citizens. Where it locates the source of the problems, though, is consequential.

First, as well as being fleeting, according to Lucas the hedonistic form of happiness is "purely self-centered" since it is about you.[20] This focus on relationality is important since, second, while the characters are happy in some existentially banal way, their agency has been reduced to the most trivial of consumer choices in what amounts to "consumption as a way of life."[21] Lucas makes a point about social fragmentation, isolation, and alienation within late industrial society through the pervasive signs of dehumanizing alienation. For instance, there is the homogenizing indistinctiveness of the uniform clothing, citizens' shaved heads, the bureaucratic allocation of a letter-number identifier in place of a personal name, and the city environment's sterile decorative minimalism, against which citizens' clothing reduces any uniqueness of visual presence. The city computer even determines living arrangements and allocates roommates. At one point the protagonist rhetorically asks in an OMM confessional, "What am I to her [LUH], she to me? Nothing. She's just an ordinary roommate. . . . Our relationship is normal, conforming. We share nothing but space." Relationships are not mutually engaging, but instead are predicated on an individualism of peaceful coexistence "in indifference."[22] This is exemplified in the way language has been diminished to a bureaucratic function. No real conversation takes place, and yet words pervade the material, predominantly from those who conduct the monitoring processes. When not discussing techniques or iterating consumerist slogans, words occur in monologues, directive statements, incoherent conjunctions of random sentences, and even syntax-disconnected wording. Such a society without meaningful human interaction and relationality seemingly cannot tolerate the intimacy of sexual relations. The alienation from mutually fulfilling sexual engagement is signified in the techno-masturbatory scene when THX's decadently objectifying gaze focuses on a holographic image of a Black exotic dancer. The mundanity of THX's sociopolitically compliant life is expressed through a thin and slow-paced drama that symbolizes the thinning out of persons. Persons' lives have been unmistakably instrumentalized by their own technologies, and THX even manufactures police androids, an intensive metaphor for the literal alienation of workers from the products of their labor. Moreover, as one scene depicts, his labor is eminently dangerous since an unfazed computer announcer reveals in a matter-of-fact manner on the occasion of a fatal accident that Red Sector L had lost "another 63 personnel, giving them a total of 242 lost to our 195."

The disposability of persons, moreover, is ultimately metaphorically manifested in the "the harvesting of organs, the ultimate reduction of the human to a commodity."[23]

Third, while the policing is evidently conducted with a soft and light touch and is accompanied by a pacifying and reassuring tone of voice, the surveillance system monitors everyone. Chillingly, nonconformity carries deadly penalties, as an important sequence of scenes indicates. At one point, when THX is engaged in his work with dangerous radioactive materials, a surveillant observes that he is "exhibiting erratic behavior," while others announce fluctuations in brain-wave and respiratory patterns. A further voice concludes that THX is "suffering severe sedation depletion," and screened text states, "Accusation: illegal programming." The mechanistic language here is telling, and the result of the analysis indicates that the protagonist "requires mind-block and arrest." The consequent external application of the "mind-block" disrupts his cognitive functioning and freezes him to the point of almost causing a nuclear catastrophe.

Following his arrest, THX is, according to another information screen, placed in a "Research cell" to await his trial. The camera cuts to a severely bleeding THX and a baton-possessing police officer binding the wounded protagonist's wrists. When on trial, THX 5752 is described as a malfunctioning machine. The charges are "drug evasion, malicious sexual perversion, and transgression." The last of these is seemingly arbitrary, although it perhaps refers to the fact that the other two criminal actions are contrary to the social order of the state and indicate incompliance due to faulty bio functioning. He is given no opportunity to speak, plead a case, or defend himself. The prosecution lawyer requests "immediate destruction" on the basis of "a totally incurable chemical imbalance with socially deteriorating consequences," a further reference to the mechanistic reduction of lives. The defense counsel objects only to declare this to be a "totally unwarranted destruction. . . . Defendant used, not destroyed." The outcome is that THX is pronounced "incurable, and shall be conditioned and held in detention." The subsequent scene involves him being tortured by three security officers with electric cattle prod–like stun sticks. The punishment being meted out appears arbitrary, with its purposelessness indicated by the dominant officer's announcement, "That's enough," at which point the trio simply departs, leaving a seated THX rocking in clear distress on the floor.

Fourth, even though all lives are regulated for conformity to the social system of production-consumption and are rendered precarious, the subterranean society is nonetheless entirely composed of white persons. Black persons are holographic, nothing more than surface figures constructed for the instrumentalizing gaze of the white society for erotic or comedic entertainment purposes. The hologram who manifests himself in physical form and appears in the prison scene, SRT 5752, however, subverts this bio-racial normativity by willing himself into reality (an agency of self-freeing from the slavery of the white gaze). He disrupts what Gregory Claeys, when reflecting on Huxley, terms the "eugenic super-state."[24]

"Cages with Open Doors": The "Escape" to Freedom

"Illegal Sexual Activity"

In many ways, then, in *THX 1138* it is society itself that generates the conditions for dehumanization and alienation.

It is tempting to focus thoughts of radical resistance on the illicit sexual activity engaged in by those committing drug evasion offences since, after all, YYO, THX's partner in *THX 1138 4EB*, is being interrogated about her possible involvement in a "sexacte." Similarly, early in *THX 1138* a voice identifies the engagement of a couple as "illegal sexual activity." Lucas's dystopia is certainly less Huxleyan at this point. While in *Brave New World* sexual activity is state mandated, its performance is simply for pure hedonistic self-pleasuring. Sexual partners have to be promiscuously interchanged. In Marcuse's terms, this reduces sex to "the realm of commodity production and exchange," which satisfies "in a way which generates submission and weakens the rationality of protest."[25] The sex act in *THX 1138* fails as a potential mode of resistance, albeit for a different reason from Huxley's reduction of the sexual partner to a commodity to be used, discarded, and replaced by another. LUH worries that her activity with THX is being monitored and, consequently, will be punished. These concerns are entirely justified, since both lovers are soon arrested, THX is subjected to bizarre medical experimentation, and LUH is destroyed and her letter-number classification reallocated to fetus 66691, who is being grown in a bottle.

More significantly, the LUH-THX relationship indicates the nature of difference and responsibility: theirs is a meaningful engagement of two persons who intentionally and mutually expose themselves, in the process becoming entirely vulnerable to each other. Erich Fromm argues that "*love is union* with somebody, or something, outside oneself. . . . Productive love always implies a syndrome of attitudes; that of *care, responsibility, respect* and *knowledge*."[26] It is in discovering each other that they discover themselves, and here the movie follows mid-twentieth-century dystopian literature with its theme of a "sexual relationship [that] gradually engenders revolutionary notions of social and personal responsibility."[27] In other words, *THX 1138* at this point construes freedom as considerably more than the freedom of consumer choice. The sexual act is free not because it is chosen as much as because persons give themselves to the other, an act of vulnerability and care for the other, who is not reduced to an instrument or a means to one's own gratification.

To signify what is at stake, the film tenderly depicts two sex scenes using a variety of techniques. The movie's characteristic framing of the sterile visuals through the detachment-inducing documentary-style long camera shots is replaced here by starkly contrasting close-up camera shots. The typically artificial environment's monochromatic color scheme is here countered by the vibrant display of elemental flesh tones that allow for a more contoured depth and visual perspective. Likewise, the couple's engagement in intimate communication diverges from the usually sparse dialogue. Finally, the scenes are accompanied by a delicate and lilting flute score that musically demarcates these moments from the score's pervasive synthesized themes.

It is the relationship that is aberrant more than the simple notion of the nonconforming sexual act itself since, as Huxley's dystopia indicates, sex is itself hardly free of dehumanizingly consumerist potential. Crucially, the relationship is initiated by LUH, and the role of the woman (significantly expanded from the character YYO in the student movie version) in THX's discovery of otherness is depicted as necessary to self-knowledge, understanding, and responsibility. This marks her as something of an Eve character, compelling THX to sin against the system. The system's eventual destruction of LUH serves not as a step in the titular protagonist's self-realization and a politics of libertarianism but as a significant loss that contributes to the uncathartic ambiguity of the climactic scene.

Intriguingly, the movie provides another character, SEN 5241, with some agency. He first appears in the movie as one of those engaged in the surveillance process, but later he manipulates the computer system to remove LUH from THX's room and install himself in her place. There may even be a sexual undertone since, as Murch explained in the Director's Cut commentary, there is a suggestion of desire for THX, something that Lucas, though, denies. Nonetheless, it is clear that he is ideologically dependent on the system in a way that LUH and THX, once free from their state sedatives, are not. For this reason, once separated from THX in his escape, SEN helps a child reattach its sedation device, returns to the city, and confesses his "sin" (SEN's name may signify "sin") to the electronic image of OMM.

"O Lamm Gottes, unschuldig" (O Lamb of God, innocent)

During a moment of concern that their illicit activity has been discovered, LUH distinguishes her agency from that of SEN by exhorting THX to flee with her from the city. In many ways, freedom as involving an escape from the confines of the social arrangements runs through Lucas's work. Soon after his arrest, the bloody THX is informed by a security android (twice for emphatic effect), "You have nowhere to go. You have nowhere to go." In resistance to this message, the central theme of *Freiheit* prominently reappears.

This works itself out in *THX 1138* when the titular protagonist simply leaves, thereby actively realizing his freedom. According to Lucas, "The plot was a vehicle for the . . . importance of self and being able to step out of whatever you're in and move forward rather than being stuck in your little rut. . . . They're people in cages with open doors."[28] Lucas here appears to echo a sentiment that was "the reigning philosophy on college campuses in the late 1960s."[29] Biographers like Dale Pollock relate this idea to the filmmaker's attitude to his strict paternal authority as well as what he regarded as the confines of small-town California, Modesto. It also intensifies the deep cultural value (the American dream) of the self-reliant individual. Nonetheless, it displays an exceptionally glib, bourgeois, and irresponsible assessment of what freedom involves. It certainly neglects to account for the emancipatory failures of both Huxley's and Orwell's protagonists, who are simply not free to successfully break their chains within their governing systems. Lucas's account of freedom is negative and reactionary, a bare freedom from the confines of social systems. It is, in other words, the reactionary mirror image of consumerism's individualism, and it suggests that social problems are only solved with a self-generated rather than socially manufactured solipsism. As Jayson Baker recognizes, "The Hollywood mode of production reformulates, using the hero-myth," the individualistic ideological message "which reflects a culture long accustomed to splitting and dividing its population into isolated, productive units."[30] Moreover, Lucas's claims are distinctly naive since they fail to recognize the irreducible situational and conditioning factors without which there would be no human being at all. In fact, his assertions are "the tell-tale indication of . . . limited experience and of . . . [an] inability to imagine anything outside" the self.[31]

While Michael Ryan and Douglas Kellner remark that "the film valorizes the differentiated individual," *THX 1138* is, nonetheless, considerably more interesting than the filmmaker's self-help "power of positive thinking" would suggest.[32] To begin with, THX's dependency on LUH for his awakening and for relational purposefulness is crucial to the movie's second and third acts. There may well even be something significant in the fact that Lucas's female character is the instigator of the liaison, the author of desire, rather than the passive object of the male's eroticized gaze and agency. Moreover, he is beholden to the agency of SRT for his prison break and discovery of the fateful disposal of his beloved. The racializing of the metaphor of otherness is integral to the plot here. "Since the hologram is an outsider, it seems able to see things that THX and the others cannot: not only the potential for escape, but also the paralyzing condition of its human counterparts."[33] Yet once this semiotic code is in play, as with the character of LUH, Lucas dispenses with the character, who, thereby, only briefly serves as an aid for THX's flight.

Moreover, THX's reluctance to flee is overcome only by a moment of pure and simple instinct rather than by the premeditated planning of a rational agent. On learning of LUH's disposal and bio-recycling, he simply runs until he has managed to evade his pursuers and escaped through a hatch into the surface world.

Finally, the climactic scene requires a reading that acknowledges its complicated ambiguity. Ryan and Kellner are correct that the sun "strikingly isolates . . . and literally singularizes THX by giving him a distinguishing boundary."[34] But it does so as a setting rather than a rising sun, and this descending light not only isolates him but frames him within a form of visual capture. Given the lack of visual markers other than the use of light (natural light, no less), there is nothing to visually locate the silhouetted individual. The escape, then, is into nothingness, an empty space. This is not the escape into freedom that some readers imagine it is.[35] In addition, where Robbins's "Breakout" ended with the escaped protagonist "yelling for joy," *THX 1138* immobilizes the protagonist with a score taken from the opening movement of Bach's *St Matthew Passion*, "O Lamm Gottes, unschuldig" (O Lamb of God, innocent).[36] This is hardly the bombastic harmony of effective action and a success-filled future. Even though THX manages to evade capture, he is now on a surface that the movie has suggested is severely contaminated and uninhabitable. Two birds that fly past certainly suggest hope, but that is a distinctly slender matter. The protagonist has no resources, no tools, and no knowledge of how to survive and flourish in such conditions. If, as Lucas imagined, THX is a Buck Rogers–like character, he is so only as a parody of the very ideology of heroically American self-reliant personhood. Christopher Wydler observes that "the extreme long shot capturing THX succumbing to the desolate landscape practically disappearing into the sun is a frightening image because our hero is alone with nowhere to go."[37]

Conclusion

Lucas's *dus topos* (the diseased or faulty place) has been accused of being emotionally arid and uninvolving. This criticism was most stinging when it came from his wife, Marcia. Lucas's caustic response reveals the kind of social expectations the movie was designed to question: "Emotionally involving the audience is easy. . . . Anybody can do it blindfolded. Get a little kitten and have some guy wring its neck."[38] In this vein, it is hardly surprising that the film's critical trajectory, and its relatively undramatic and experimental art-house style, both irked the Hollywood production company that had financed the picture and also failed to compel cinemagoers through the theater's doors. In a moment of self-consciousness, Lucas reflected, "I realized after *THX* that people don't care about how the country's being ruined. All that did was to make people more pessimistic, more depressed, and less willing to get involved in trying to make the world better."[39]

However, it would be seriously misleading to describe *THX 1138* as having "a bleak message."[40] Once they consider it "as a warning," viewers can hope to escape its dehumanizing future.[41] Lucas himself thought of THX as an unwitting Buck Rogers–like figure who is forced by circumstances into heroic action. "I truly believe in this country," Lucas announces, "that you can do anything if you apply yourself."[42] Despite the glibness of this self-help pop psychology, it is appropriate to say that the film is importantly less interested in any dramatically entertaining conflict with a threatening other from beyond than in the threat to human freedom that is generated by the very values of capitalism's one-dimensional society. In fact, the obvious antagonist is the set of social arrangements that construct persons in a way that reduces them to bare, monotonous, and precarious lives. By this means, *THX 1138*'s analysis echoes that of Marcuse, for whom "the problems confronting the emerging radical movement were not simply the Vietnam War, racism or inequality, but the system itself, and that solving a wide range of social problems required fundamental social restructuring."[43] Lucas combines the eugenic preconditioning of Huxley's *Brave New World* with the disciplinary messages of Orwell's *Nineteen Eighty-Four* to cast a critical lens on the self-deception of a conformist society that imagines itself to be free. Yet this is "the administered life" that conditions persons through modes of soft repression and that produces compliance among those for whom it is "the comfortable and even the 'good' life."[44] Of course, the influence of the Vietnam conflict would harden in Lucas's later work in the *Star Wars* saga. The technologically superior forces of the politically totalitarian Empire are resisted, and defeated, by the guerrilla tactics of the more democratic Rebel Alliance and the colonized Ewoks.[45] Yet in *THX 1138*, what it means to be a free and spontaneous agent in this socially conformist and person-diminishing myth of the free self is a matter for which the text has no answers, although the theme of relational interdependence is a promising start. This theme is fleshed out in *Star Wars* in terms of the Rebel Alliance's collective resistance against the Empire, interspecies cooperation, a democratic political system, and themes of friendship.

Notes

1. Later in the movie, some of SEN's monologues are lifted verbatim from Richard Nixon's 1968 campaign speeches.

2. Citations from George Lucas, in Dale Pollock, *Skywalking: The Life and Films of George Lucas* (Hollywood: Samuel French, 1990), 93; Herbert Marcuse, *One-Dimensional Man: Studies in the Ideology of Advanced Industrial Society*, 2nd ed. (London: Routledge, 2002), xlv; George Lucas, in Sally Kline, ed., *George Lucas: Interviews* (Jackson: University Press of Mississippi, 1999), 4.

3. George Lucas, cited in Chris Taylor, *How "Star Wars" Conquered the Universe: The Past, Present, and Future of a Multibillion Dollar Franchise* (New York: Basic Books, 2014), 74.

4. Douglas Kellner, "Introduction to the Second Edition," in Marcuse, *One-Dimensional Man*, xi–xxxviii (xii).

5. Michael Ryan and Douglas Kellner, *Camera Politica: The Politics and Ideology of Contemporary Hollywood Film* (Bloomington: Indiana University Press, 1988), 11. For more on the political ethos of the saga, see John C. McDowell, *Identity Politics in George Lucas' "Star Wars"* (Jefferson, NC: McFarland, 2016).

6. Lucas, in Pollock, *Skywalking*, 36.

7. Marcus Hearn, *The Cinema of George Lucas* (New York: Harry M. Abrams, 2005), 18.

8. George Lucas, in Brian Jay Jones, *George Lucas: A Life* (London: Headline, 2017), 65.

9. Hearn, *Cinema of George Lucas*, 19.

10. George Lucas, in Paul Duncan, *The "Star Wars" Archives: Episodes IV–VI, 1977–1983* (Cologne: Taschen, 2018), 13.

11. The title was later lengthened to *Electronic Labyrinth: THX 1138 4EB* by University of Southern California.

12. The year is a reference to Arthur Lipsett's *21-87* (1964).

13. Lucas, in Kline, *George Lucas*, 10.

14. *George Lucas: Maker of Films*, directed by Jerry Hughes (1971).

15. Lucas, in Duncan, *"Star Wars" Archives*, 14.

16. Pollock, *Skywalking*, 94.

17. Lucas, in Kline, *George Lucas*, 5.

18. Lucas, in Hearn, *Cinema of George Lucas*, 37.

19. The dominatingly proportioned image of OMM in the confession booth is based on Hans Memling's painting *Christ Giving His Blessing* (1478).

20. Lucas, in Taylor, *How "Star Wars" Conquered the Universe*, 72.

21. Christopher Lasch, *The Culture of Narcissism: American Life in an Age of Diminishing Expectations* (New York: W. W. Norton, 1979), 72.

22. Marcuse, *One-Dimensional Man*, 64.

23. J. P. Telotte, *Science Fiction Film* (Cambridge: Cambridge University Press, 2001), 137.

24. Gregory Claeys, *Dystopia: A Natural History; A Study of Modern Despotism, Its Antecedents, and Its Literary Diffractions* (Oxford: Oxford University Press, 2017), 116.

25. Marcuse, *One-Dimensional Man*, 78.

26. Erich Fromm, *The Sane Society* (London: Routledge and Kegan Paul, 1956), 31, 33.

27. Thomas Horan, *Desire and Empathy in Twentieth-Century Dystopian Fiction* (London: Palgrave Macmillan, 2018), 1.

28. Lucas, in Kline, *George Lucas*, 4.

29. Pollock, *Skywalking*, 93.

30. Jayson Baker, "Waking Up the Mythic American Neo," in *Heroes of Film, Comics and American Culture: Essays on Real and Fictional Defenders of Homes*, ed. Lisa M. Detora (Jefferson, NC: McFarland, 2009), 268–80 (269).

31. Frederic Jameson, *Archaeologies of the Future: The Desire Called Utopia and Other Science Fictions* (London: Verso, 2005), 170–71.

32. Ryan and Kellner, *Camera Politica*, 247; Lucas, cited in Taylor, *How "Star Wars" Conquered the Universe*, 54.

33. Telotte, *Science Fiction Film*, 136–37.

34. Ryan and Kellner, *Camera Politica*, 247.

35. See, e.g., Raymond Cormier, "A Closed Society and Its Friends: Plato's Republic and Lucas's *THX-1138*," *Literature/Film Quarterly* 18, no. 3 (1990): 193–97 (194).

36. Matthew Robbins, "Breakout," in Duncan, *"Star Wars" Archives*, 13.

37. Christopher Wydler, "The Failed Probability of Love over Labor in *THX 1138* (1971)," *Linguaculture* 1 (2016): 7–15 (13–14).

38. Jones, *George Lucas*, 126, citing Lucas from Peter Biskind, *Easy Riders, Raging Bulls: How the Sex 'n' Drugs 'n' Rock 'n' Roll Generation Saved Hollywood* (London: Bloomsbury, 1998), 235.

39. Lucas, in Kline, *George Lucas*, 42.

40. Garry Jenkins, *Empire Building: The Remarkable Real Life Story of "Star Wars"* (London: Simon and Schuster, 1997), 28.

41. Raffaella Baccolini and Tom Moylan, "Introduction: Dystopia and Histories," in *Dark Horizons: Science Fiction and the Dystopian Imagination*, ed. Raffaella Baccolini and Tom Moylan (London: Routledge, 2003), 1–12 (7).

42. Lucas, in Jones, *George Lucas*, 10.

43. Kellner, "Introduction to the Second Edition," xxxv.

44. Marcuse, *One-Dimensional Man*, 49.

45. For more on this, see McDowell, *Identity Politics in George Lucas' "Star Wars."*

4

American Graffiti and More

The Scholarly and Aesthetic Legacies of an Inaugural Nostalgia Film

CHRISTINE SPRENGLER

Scene: Exterior, day. January 2022 (−10 degrees Fahrenheit). Location: Active logging road, Algonquin Highlands, Ontario. I had just set off for home after a weekend escape to my cabin, nestled deep in the woods in an area where I can go days without encountering another human. Moose, wolves, and bears are another matter. I turned off my driveway onto a narrow, single-lane, winding stretch of ice-covered "road" (I use that term very loosely). Suddenly, a pickup truck shuttling loggers to their remote worksite rounded a bend, heading straight for me. With four-foot snowbanks lining the road, there was nowhere for either of us to turn to avoid a head-on collision. We both slammed on the brakes. I stopped; they—on a downhill—couldn't. They slid straight toward me at a good speed. I could see the passenger bracing for impact. I threw my vehicle into reverse, spun the tires a bit, and sped backward, navigating the icy turns with the loggers' truck a foot away from my front bumper until I reversed into a pull off. They drove on by and gave me an enthusiastic round of applause. It wasn't luck that enabled me to avoid a collision but skill, and of a special kind acquired during my teenage years thanks to *American Graffiti* (1973).

My skills were honed "cruising" city streets from the age of (ahem) fourteen until about eighteen. If I'm being fully honest, cruising was also supplemented with a bit of racing. Now, of course, I'm horrified by such recklessness and shudder at the thought of the consequences of my actions. But back then, my friends and I would spend Friday and Saturday evenings driving up and down Yonge Street, radio blaring, following a procession of other friends doing the same, all of us in little old rusty sedans. This was Toronto in the late 1980s and early 1990s and not Modesto in the 1950s, so naturally there were some pretty marked differences. Perhaps the greatest difference was that the inspiration for a bunch of Canadian teenagers originated in film.[1] We may not have known about the postwar habits of our Californian compatriots, but we all had seen *American Graffiti*.

This chapter is about *American Graffiti*'s legacy, though from here on out less in terms of its impact on my own driving record.[2] Specifically, I focus on how the film did much to initiate historiographical debates concerning filmic representations of the past as well as instantiate a particular visual conception of recent history, one heavily reliant on a cinematographic aesthetics of pastness. This chapter therefore touches on *American Graffiti*'s reception in the 1970s nostalgia economy, tracks its mobilization by scholars invested in the concept of nostalgia, and considers the ways in which recent analyses foreground the complexity inherent in its approach to the past. In doing so, I examine how Lucas and "visual consultant" Haskell Wexler accomplished the look of the film and how *American Graffiti*'s aesthetic innovations were realized to rather extreme ends in its sequel, *More American Graffiti* (1979). Lucas's pioneering aesthetic approach may have prompted some initial criticism, but it has also been the source of critical reevaluations and thus a key component of the film's legacy (both scholarly and artistic).

For George Lucas, *American Graffiti* aimed to document "cruising" for posterity, examining it as a specifically American sociocultural phenomenon of the postwar years. Using a vignette structure and observational style, the film follows the exploits of several teenagers over the course of one night: Curt (Richard Dreyfuss), Laurie (Cindy Williams), Steve (Ron Howard), John (Paul Le Mat), Terry the Toad (Charles Martin Smith), Debbie (Candy Clark), Carol (Mackenzie Phillips), and those they encounter along the way, including Bob (Harrison Ford) and the mysterious "Blonde in T-bird," as Suzanne Somers is credited. As much as the film captures the end of an era, the fifties, thus enforcing the common perception that the 1950s really ended with the assassination of John F. Kennedy in 1963, it is also autobiographical. Lucas explains that Terry, Steve, John, and Curt chart his own evolution from a hopeless nerd to a popular high schooler, hot-rodder, and intellectual who escapes small-town California via college.[3] *American Graffiti* is thus invested in tracking a kind of personal and collective evolution and leaving the past behind. It is also about the affective forces that attend significant change: hope, melancholy, optimism, fear, excitement, and, of course, nostalgia.

This developmental trajectory, one that underlies a film ostensibly about people circling in place, led critics to suggest that *American Graffiti* offered a more complex engagement with the past it recreated than other products of fifties nostalgia culture. Writing upon the film's release, Joseph Kanon observes that it "lures its audience with the easy pleasures of nostalgia, then twists that nostalgia into something richer and more interesting—a look into the pop sensibility that drew people to the movie in the first place."[4] Specifically, Kanon commends *American Graffiti* for transforming the nostalgia genre by supplying "the details"—that is, the conventional signifiers of fifties nostalgia—but then manages to "step quickly beyond them." That is, to take the usual "peep-show-of-artifacts" approach so common in the 1970s nostalgia economy and render them private, inscribed with memories of personal experience rather than mass-produced commodity objects.[5] Likewise, Michael Dempsey acknowledges that Lucas's film is more than "a checklist of fifties memorabilia" but is a "trenchant criticism of nostalgia as well."[6] It generates a temporal awareness and an acute sense of the passage of time as extraordinarily rapid when marked by disposable pop culture. It shows how distant even eleven years can seem, laying bare the economies of postwar planned obsolescence and the way in which its objects became fodder for later nostalgia booms.[7] According to Tom Symmonds, this acclaim was not extended to other titles equally invested in fifties nostalgia, thus setting Lucas's film apart from the "less subtle and complex" cinematic investments in the past.[8]

But while Kanon and Dempsey articulate how *American Graffiti*'s approach to the past enabled a more complex rendering of nostalgic impulses, other critics identified ways in which the film simply reproduced fifties nostalgia's typical failings. Writing in the *New Yorker*, Pauline Kael noted its celebration of the white middle-class male experience at the expense of women and other marginalized constituencies through outright exclusion or troubling stereotypes, a charge Lucas accepted as "valid, intelligent, and rational."[9] But whereas Kael praised Lucas's filmmaking, several years later *American Graffiti*'s cinematographic reconstruction of the past became subject to a now-foundational critique of nostalgia itself: Fredric Jameson's argument (originally published in 1984) that it—and other nostalgia films like it—substituted "History" with a history of aesthetic styles, severing meaningful connections to the lived realities of former periods. For Jameson, cinema exchanged the 1950s for "1950s-ness," generating a sense of pastness that is ahistorical and depthless.[10] Jameson's mobilization of *American Graffiti* to demonstrate this trend has led to two enduring consequences: the instantiation of the fifties as a privileged object in nostalgic discourse, including in attempts to define nostalgia, and the conflation of the nostalgic experience with its object. But there is one further consequence borne by *American Graffiti* as a result of these tendencies. As scholars enter into discussions about Jameson's postmodern conceptualization of nostalgia, they too continue to evoke *American Graffiti*, sustaining its legacy as a privileged object in debates about cultural memory, historiography, nostalgia, and the nostalgia film. With this, we find persuasive reevaluations of the film that pay nuanced attention to the source of its complexities as celebrated in initial reviews. But we also see clear evidence of how the meaning of a film is continually recalibrated by its circulations through new contexts.

According to Lucas, *American Graffiti* is a nostalgia film, at least to a point. Like John Ford's westerns or Raoul Walsh's gangster films, which Lucas deems part of a "nostalgia genre," his own film's navigation of the recent past qualifies it for such categorization. However, it is also a film about "moving forward."[11] It is a film about teenagers on the cusp of adulthood, faced with decisions that will orient the direction of their respective futures. But whereas Lucas classifies *American Graffiti* on the basis of its narrative content, Jameson's condemnation of its nostalgic impulse was based on aesthetics, namely its approach to "the 'past' through stylistic connotation, conveying 'pastness' by the glossy qualities of the image."[12] What is more, Jameson cites Lucas's film as inaugurating a trend in this regard by opening up other generational periods for what he terms "aesthetic colonization."[13] That is, he sees *American Graffiti* as innovating the practice of representing the past with recourse to the visual culture of the era in question. This is a practice with enduring popularity. Consider the following: *L.A. Confidential*'s (1997) noir pastiche, *Pleasantville*'s (1998) replication of postwar domestic sitcoms, *Far from Heaven*'s (2002) Sirkian palette, *Good Night, and Good Luck*'s (2005) newscast-inspired monochrome, *Carol*'s (2015) street-photography aesthetic, *Hail, Caesar*'s (2016) recreation of myriad Hollywood genres, *Lovecraft Country*'s (2020) cataloging of horror subgenres, and *Sylvie's Love*'s (2020) visual homage to melodrama. And these are only a few of the many 1950s-set titles showcasing this tendency. Other decades have also been colonized in this way: the 1920s and 1930s in *The Aviator* (2004) and *Hugo* (2011), the 1940s in *The Good German* (2006), and a spate of 1970s- and 1980s-set films. While Jameson finds fault with *American Graffiti*'s legacy in this respect, other scholars locate critical and, specifically, historiographical potential in this type of visual approach to the past.[14]

American Graffiti's visual pastness was generated not only through canonical fifties signifiers (tail-finned cars, diners, fashion, etc.) but through the

1973's *American Graffiti* was George Lucas's nostalgic look at baby boomer life in the 1950s and 1960s. (courtesy Everett Collection)

ways these objects were filmed. As such, its pastness owes much to Haskell Wexler's innovative cinematography and its "jukebox" aesthetic. Lucas explains that Wexler accomplished the look of the film by shooting at night with two cameras, an Arriflex and an Éclair, to achieve different focal lengths, using Eastman Color 5254 rated at 100 ASA and pushed one stop in processing.[15] He also used a mixture of warm and cold lights. As he explains: "The existing lights were very blue (Mercury Vapor), so instead of compensating and overwhelming the blue light, he used it, played with it—used the blue and the red, the cold and the warm lights."[16] The result, according to Vera Dika, is an image that "has a shimmering reflective surface reminiscent of hard-shine paint of the automobiles it so prominently features."[17] The film was also shot in Techniscope, a decision that, for Symmonds, heightens its "self-reflexive thrust." Techniscope rendered *American Graffiti* visually similar to earlier low-budget productions, "recalling a range of beach party films and others that foregrounded rock and roll music and coming of age experience."[18] In other words, *American Graffiti* looked like a certain kind of youth-focused 1950s film.[19]

Another way to conceptualize this strategy is through Marc LeSueur's term "deliberate archaism," defined in relation to *American Graffiti* in his 1977 article on the nostalgia film.[20] Meant to encapsulate the practice of replicating—or pastiching—the look of old media forms (e.g., sepia, Technicolor, monochrome), it prefigures Jameson's discussion of visual pastness in focus but not in intent. For LeSueur, deliberate archaism, and specifically Wexler's jukebox aesthetic, can either "result in a stylistic calcification" or "entail a healthy re-examination of old techniques and formats."[21] By admitting the critical possibilities of deliberate archaism—and in relation to *American Graffiti*—LeSueur ultimately inaugurates an approach to cinematic nostalgia that surfaces through reexaminations of Jameson's argument, one that sparked reexaminations of *American Graffiti* itself.[22] But whereas Lucas's 1973 film continues to enjoy a privileged status in the scholarly analysis of nostalgia and the deliberately archaic tactics that have now become commonplace in cinema, a far more extreme example of deliberate archaism has been all but forgotten: *More American Graffiti*.[23]

Although *More American Graffiti*'s replication of past cinematic aesthetics may indeed veer more toward stylistic calcification than healthy reexamination, it is worth briefly considering here as an important waypoint in the evolution of this visual strategy and thus very much a part of the legacy of *American Graffiti*. *More American Graffiti* was consistently faulted by critics and virtually ignored by film scholars. Dale Pollock summarized the general sentiment among reviewers, acknowledging its attempt at aesthetic innovation but inability to reconcile technical experimentation with narrative concerns, rendering the former "ultimately pointless."[24] Janet Maslin thought it was "grotesquely misconceived" and found its structure of "calculated monotony" to be "gruelling."[25] A handful of critics were a little more forgiving on the grounds of the film's ambitions, as in Roger Ebert's case, or subject matter—the sixties—as in Charles Champlin's estimation.[26] Much of the distaste expressed seemed grounded in its overt "film school" approach, its citation of past media forms to frame the different storylines. My interest here, however, is not in how successfully—by whatever metric—*More American Graffiti* managed to reconcile its aesthetic innovations with other elements of the film but rather in how well these innovations not only continue the visual legacy inaugurated by *American Graffiti* but open up a template for subsequent cinematic experiments with "deliberate archaism."

Like *American Graffiti*, its sequel is also episodic, but in a mathematically structured way. Four storylines, each taking place on a New Year's Eve in

More American Graffiti was a less well-received sequel that focused on 1960s experiences such as the war in Vietnam. (© Universal Pictures/courtesy Everett Collection)

subsequent years during the mid-1960s, involve the following: John Milner's final race before his death in 1964; Terry the Toad's attempt to be sent home from Vietnam in 1965; Debbie's adventures through hippie culture in 1966; and Steve and Laurie's marital woes and flirtation with antiwar demonstrations in 1967. Each scene lasts approximately two minutes and thus the length of the song that accompanies it. Thus, the sequel privileges music as much as the original but uses it differently, as a much more rigid structuring force. Precise aesthetic templates were also devised to frame each character's scenes: John Milner's sequences were shot in wide-screen and Technicolor, in a way that resembled Hollywood of yesteryear and made a direct link to the westerns and epics that underpinned the mythologies of the West intimated by *American Graffiti*.[27] Terry the Toad's footage was shot with handheld 16 mm to resemble Vietnam War newsreel footage. Debbie's foray into psychedelia was underscored by multiple split-screen experiments. Steve and Laurie's marital dysfunction was shot with a long lens to resemble television commercials and the filming strategies of postwar domestic sitcoms. Thus, each segment mobilized cinematographic and televisual practices already deeply coded in ways that framed the events depicted in a self-conscious way. With this, *More*

American Graffiti laid bare the possibilities of self-reflexive aesthetic experimentation to prompt questions about representations and mediations of the past and the extent to which cinematographic strategies accrue the affective resonances of the content with which they are aligned. Put another way, it enables us to consider precisely what can be carried along cinematography's aesthetic vectors.

The deliberate archaism pioneered by *American Graffiti* (and expanded by its sequel) has been mobilized in scholarly attempts to recuperate fifties nostalgia and indeed even nostalgia itself. For instance, Dika argues that *American Graffiti* offers a "direct confrontation" with nostalgia, "indict[ing] the historical or society conditions" of the era represented through its cinematographic approach to representing the past.[28] For her, the "jukebox aesthetic" operates as a "simulacral image, referring to a lost time, to past images, and to its own status as a commodity sign," producing a degree of instability with regard to the affective charge of the film and its negotiation of the relationship between past and present, style and history.[29] Likewise, Michael Dwyer locates the film's complexity in its aesthetic sensibilities and, with recourse to Richard Dyer's reevaluation of pastiche, explores how its "knowing imitation" enables critical reflection.[30] Part of this complexity, for Dwyer, is the result of how *American Graffiti* signals the multiple and diverse political ends to which fifties nostalgia has been used.

Frances Smith's analysis of *American Graffiti* locates its complexity in the way it negotiates between what Paul Grainge identifies as a nostalgia mood and a nostalgia mode, the latter closely aligned with deliberate archaism.[31] By paying close attention to the nuanced way in which Lucas navigates this divide through narrative and stylistic engagements, Smith suggests that the film "draws attention to, and disputes, the tacit belief that gender roles were ever clear and undisputed."[32] She is not arguing that *American Graffiti* is a feminist text, a feat that even the most flexible hermeneutic gymnastics could not accomplish, but rather that the film contains moments that undermine early criticisms that it is structured by a deep and abiding nostalgia for unfettered patriarchy.[33] Locating these moments at the intersection of the film's narrative and visual investments in nostalgia, Smith finds the possibility of more critical perspectives on gender and "moribund models of masculinity" and thus sees *American Graffiti* as a model for reconsidering "other nostalgia texts that have been similarly maligned."[34] In this regard, Smith is securing the film's continued legacy in prompting critical reevaluations of cinematic investments in nostalgia that appeal to both a certain mood and an aesthetic mode.

But as much as *American Graffiti* has occupied a central role in scholarly reconsiderations of nostalgia, there are some voices who temper this enthusiasm. David Shumway found it to be "fundamentally a conservative film that offered its post-Vietnam, post-1960s audience a glimpse of the America it would rather see," a common refrain to be sure.[35] For Lesley Speed, the film's privileging of an adult perspective on the past, one evidently structured by hindsight, contributes to a conservative concealment of ideology, a process that in *American Graffiti*'s case "emphasizes personal trauma over social and ideological factors."[36] Personal trauma here is of a very specific kind, mostly existential and affiliated with white middle-class teenagers. Indeed, even at the time of the film's release, much was made of its depiction of the loss of "innocence," one blamed on "Vietnam, Oswald, hard drugs, birth control pills, Nixon—the whole spectrum of sixties shake-ups."[37] This innocence, however, did not extend to historically disenfranchised communities, to Black Americans dispossessed by Jim Crow laws and subject to continual racist violence throughout the 1950s. Indeed, public discourse then (and still) problematically frames the gains of racialized and gendered communities during the "sixties shake-ups" as white middle-class male "losses." What enables reviewers to speak about a "loss of innocence" and refer to the 1950s as a "pre-trauma" era in this regard from a collective (white) standpoint is the erasure of marginalized constituencies from the film and thus the elision of much deeper traumas.

Issues of gender, class, and race have surfaced in how commentators, Lucas included, have since talked about the film. For instance, although he describes this film as one about change, including the shift from the fifties to the sixties, with the observation that "the fifties can't live," there are also elements of the fifties that, for Lucas, warrant revival.[38] Lucas locates a degree of optimism—as opposed to complacency—in the fifties and attributes that in part to Martin Luther King Jr. His interest lies in the possibilities for change opened up by King and the nascent Kennedy era more broadly.[39] However such opportunities are only figured in terms of Curt's escape, that of a white middle-class budding intellectual who dodges the draft, moves to Canada, and becomes a writer. They are not figured in ways that acknowledge King's advocacy or engage with racialized causes. The film's only narrative acknowledgment of race is through Carol's speculation that Wolfman Jack might "be a Negro," the reason her mother won't let her listen to him. Carol, though, thinks "he's terrific." But while this offhand comment is ostensibly used to confirm a generational divide, it also serves to other this mythical figure even further. As Lucas explains: "He was wild, he had these crazy phone calls, and he drifted out of nowhere. And it was an outlaw station. He was an outlaw, which of course made him extremely attractive to kids."[40] It also confirms the whiteness of the town and world inhabited by the protagonists and, therefore, the highly segregated nature of small postwar Californian enclaves.

However much *American Graffiti* is ostensibly about the insularity of the world navigated by a few teenagers, films move through time and into new contexts, ones enriched and challenged by ever more representations, and thus cannot escape the consequences of their exclusions. They become part of larger fields that rework the signifiers they offer (e.g., tail-finned cars), the aesthetics they innovate (e.g., jukebox aesthetics), and the worlds they define (e.g., youth culture in small-town postwar America). And this is especially true of films that benefit from sustained and popular legacies. As Dwyer rightly points out, the nostalgic meaning of a film, especially one like *American Graffiti*, is reconfigured by its circulations and reception and thus "subject to change over time."[41] In some instances, as certain reevaluations of *American Graffiti*—or nostalgia itself—have shown, this can be critical and self-reflexive, leading to nuanced and analytically minded engagements with history, representation, and practices of mediation. But it can also retrench what were identified as initial problems with both the film and mobilizations of the fifties more generally.

Consider, for instance, how other films or, more recently, television series either reaffirm or undercut *American Graffiti*'s vision of postwar America, thereby necessarily inflecting its role and position in the broader visual register that is "the fifties."[42] While early on *Grease* (1978) and *Happy Days* (1974–1984) bolstered the significance of popular music or sites of youth socialization, *The Reflecting Skin*'s (1990) focus on a 1958 El Dorado as a harbinger of death challenges the significatory thrust of gleaming tail-finned cars. Likewise, when a slow-driving, gleaming tail-finned car is subject to a white scrutinizing gaze because it carries the first Black family into an all-white 1950s neighborhood in *Them* (2021), its significatory power is inflected once again. Images of groups of teenagers cruising in customized vehicles can elicit dating rituals either innocent or predatory. Within cinema and beyond, such images can signal teenage comradery or the threat of racist violence, depending on where and to what ends groups of white teenagers jump into their cars for an evening of aimless driving. It can also evoke modes of resistance as a "spatial practice" and articulation of Latinx class subjectivity, as in the context of one of its offshoots: lowrider cruising.[43]

This is to say that the legacies of a film like *American Graffiti*—with its complex engagements with nostalgia that have enabled multiple readings as well as its entrenchment of now-iconic images of cruising, for example—are eminently dynamic and ever evolving. In this regard, the title of the film could not be more apt. Its title is typically explained through recourse to "graffiti" as a kind of public discourse, the signs left by ordinary people as evidence of their fears and desires, marks of lives past. As Lucas's father (an energetic promotor of his son's films) explains, *graffiti* refers to "inscriptions of a past culture or era."[44] Graffiti is often layered, resulting in accumulations of traces and voices from different times. In this way, the title not only captures a sense of the historiographic work the film does but also presages its own future. It reminds us of the way the film has been mobilized to define the concept of nostalgia, account for the changing sociopolitical significance of the fifties, and showcase the complex and creative ways that pasts can be visually inscribed into celluloid to both critical and emotional effect. All three are central to *American Graffiti*'s enduring legacy.

Notes

1. That said, however much *American Graffiti* sought to capture Californian cruising culture, commentators at the time remarked on the film's subsequent popularization of the pastime, observing that "Modesto—thanks to the film *American Graffiti*—is to cruising what Cooperstown is to baseball, a kind of shrine." See "Cruising: It Holds the Bright Promise of Adventure," *Modesto Bee*, April 10, 1974, 43.

2. *American Graffiti*'s legacies are multiple. My concern here is not with its impact on subsequent filmmaking practices, blockbuster economies, its integration of popular music, its place within New Hollywood, or its advancement of themes explored in Lucas's first film, *THX 1138*, and subsequent *Star Wars* franchise. For detailed accounts of these types of legacies, see Justin Wyatt, *High Concept: Movies and Marketing in Hollywood* (Austin: University of Texas Press, 1994); David A. Cook, *History of the American Cinema: Lost Illusions* (New York: Charles Scribner, 1999); James M. Curtis, "From *American Graffiti* to *Star Wars*," *Journal of Popular Culture* 13, no. 4 (1980): 590–601; Mark T. Decker, "They Want Unfreedom and One-Dimensional Thought? I'll Give Them Unfreedom and One-Dimensional Thought: George Lucas, *THX-1138*, and the Persistence of Marcusian Social Critique in *American Graffiti* and the *Star Wars* Films," *Extrapolation* 50, no. 3 (2009): 417–41.

3. George Lucas, "The Making of *American Graffiti*," *American Graffiti*, DVD, directed by George Lucas (Lucasfilm, 1973).

4. Joseph Kanon, "Movies: On the Strip," *Atlantic Monthly*, October 1973, 125.

5. Ibid. Arguably the film accomplishes even more, especially through its careful selection of cars. Each is invested with cultural meanings that underscore the character with which it is aligned. See Jack DeWitt, "Cars and Culture: The Cars of *American*

Graffiti," *American Poetry Review*, September–October 2010, 47–50. These cars occupy the center of yet another (paratextual) legacy of the film. As DeWitt explains: "The cars of *American Graffiti* have become as big as the stars who drove them. In addition to the millions of posters and models that have been sold, hundreds of imitations of the Chevy Impala and, especially, the Milner coupe have been built in the last thirty years" (50).

6. Michael Dempsey, "*American Graffiti,"* *Film Quarterly* 27, no. 1 (Autumn 1973): 58–59.

7. Ibid. This ambiguity is also highlighted by Stephen Farber, who describes *American Graffiti* as a "comedy with an unexpected resonance," one with the capacity to "summon up the deeply conflicting feelings that we all have when contemplating our own youth." See "George Lucas: The Stinky Kid Hits the Bigtime," *Film Quarterly* 27, no. 3 (Spring 1974): 2.

8. Tom Symmonds, *The New Hollywood Historical Film: 1967–78* (London: Palgrave Macmillan, 2016), 165. Symmonds provides a comprehensive account of the critical response to the film at the time of its release (172–74).

9. See Pauline Kael, "Current Cinema," *New Yorker*, October 29, 1973, 154–55; Larry Sturhahn, "The Filming of *American Graffiti*: An Interview with Director George Lucas," *Filmmakers Newsletter* 7, no. 5 (1974): 22. Local Modesto residents interviewed about the veracity of the film noted that "it only showed one group—it was only based on one type or group of kids hanging around together." See "Graffiti Stirs Memories of Downey Class of '62," *Modesto Bee*, February 17, 1974, 37.

10. See Fredric Jameson, *Postmodernism, or the Cultural Logic of Late Capitalism* (Durham, NC: Duke University Press, 1991), 67.

11. Lucas, in Sturhahn, "Filming of *American Graffiti,"* 22.

12. Jameson, *Postmodernism*, 67.

13. Ibid.

14. I make this claim too throughout *Screening Nostalgia: Populuxe Props and Technicolor Aesthetics in Contemporary American Film* (Oxford: Berghahn Books, 2009).

15. Lucas, in Sturhahn, "Filming of *American Graffiti,"* 27.

16. Ibid., 21. Lucas's experimentation in this regard started during film school, where he was "the first to use color in filming a racing film entitled *1:42:08.*" See "Ex-Modestan Is Director," *Modesto Bee*, June 25, 1967, 34.

17. Vera Dika, *Recycled Culture in Contemporary Art and Film: The Uses of Nostalgia* (Cambridge: Cambridge University Press, 2003), 90.

18. Symmonds, *New Hollywood*, 27.

19. However much jukeboxes and the 1950s now seem aligned, their popularity and use were actually on the wane at that time.

20. Marc LeSueur attended to the visual significance of *American Graffiti* through both its "intense surface naturalism," achieved by dress and cars, for instance, and its "deliberate archaism," as generated by its "garish 'juke box' appearance." See "Theory Number Five: Anatomy of Nostalgia Films; Heritage and Methods," *Journal of Popular Film* 6, no. 2 (1977): 193–95.

21. Ibid., 195.

22. Le Sueur isn't entirely alone in this regard. In his 1979 book on nostalgia, which considers the critical potential of the concept, sociologist Fred Davis also identifies *American Graffiti* as evidence of a new "aesthetic modality." See Fred Davis, *Yearning for Yesterday: A Sociology of Nostalgia* (New York: Free Press, 1979), 73.

23. There is the question of Lucas's involvement in *More American Graffiti* and the extent to which the visual innovations can be attributed to him. According to the American Film Institute, "As copyright holder, the studio could proceed without him, but Lucas was willing to guide the project, as executive producer, provided he could create an entirely new theme and style around the same characters, and thus experiment with the notion of a sequel." See "*More American Graffiti*," *AFI Catalogue of Feature Films*, accessed September 15, 2023, https://catalog.afi.com/Catalog/MovieDetails/56929.

24. Dale Pollock, "*More American Graffiti*," *Variety*, July 25, 1979, https://variety.com/1979/film/reviews/more-american-graffiti-1200424567/.

25. Janet Maslin, "Screen: *More American Graffiti* Covers '64–'69," *New York Times*, August 17, 1979, https://www.nytimes.com/1979/08/17/archives/screen-more-american-graffiti-covers-64-to-67where-did-they-all-go.html.

26. Roger Ebert and Gene Siskel debated the merits of *More American Graffiti* in *Sneak Previews*, season 2, episode 5, 1979, https://siskelebert.org/?p=8238. Also see Charles Champlin, "The Line on *Dallas* and *Graffiti II*," *Los Angeles Times*, July 29, 1979, 23.

27. Curtis, "From *American Graffiti*," 595.

28. Dika, *Recycled Culture*, 80.

29. Ibid., 90.

30. Michael Dwyer, *Back to the Fifties: Nostalgia, Hollywood Film, and Popular Music of the Seventies and Eighties* (New York: Oxford University Press, 2015), 51.

31. See Paul Grainge, *Monochrome Memories: Nostalgia and Style in Retro America* (Westport, CT: Praeger, 2002).

32. Frances Smith, "Smoke Gets in Your Eyes: Re-reading Gender in the 'Nostalgia Film,'" *Quarterly Review of Film and Video* 35, no. 5 (2018): 480.

33. Ibid., 466.

34. Ibid., 467.

35. David Shumway, "Rock 'n' Roll Sound Tracks and the Production of Nostalgia," *Cinema Journal* 38, no. 2 (Winter 1999): 42.

36. Lesley Speed, "Tuesday's Gone: The Nostalgic Teen Film," *Journal of Popular Film and Television* 26, no. 1 (1998): 30.

37. Dempsey, "*American Graffiti*," 58.

38. Lucas, in Farber, "George Lucas," 8.

39. Ibid., 8.

40. Ibid., 6.

41. Dwyer, *Back to the Fifties*, 76. As Dwyer explains, "The conditions of watching will continue to shift as new texts are brought into contact with the film, and as a result, our readings of it (and the history it presents) will continue to change" (54).

42. I consider how cinema has both generated and complicated visions of the fifties, splintering it into various types (*Leave It to Beaver* fifties, Cold War fifties, jukebox

fifties, etc.) in *Fractured Fifties: The Cinematic Periodization and Evolution of a Decade* (New York: Oxford University Press, 2023).

43. See Ben Chappell, "Custom Contestations: Low Riders and Urban Space," *City and Society* 22, no. 1 (June 2010): 25–47.

44. "Modesto Boy Makes Good (Film), Again," *Modesto Bee*, August 19, 1973, 26.

5

A New Hope

From American Graffiti *to* Star Wars

PETER KRÄMER

In 1973, the *AFI Report* published an article entitled "Young Directors, New Films," which featured interviews with Terrence Malick, Sydney Pollack, John Hancock, and George Lucas.[1] Lucas—whose latest film, *American Graffiti*, would eventually turn into one of the highest-grossing movies of all time at the US box office and whose next film would change American and indeed world cinema forever—pointed out that he was something of an accidental filmmaker: "Movies had extremely little effect on me when I was growing up. . . . I started out as a graphic artist, then became a photographer. . . . The reason I went to film school was because my father wouldn't pay for art school, he didn't think it was respectable. But he thought USC was, so I went there."

Surely, there was more to it than this, but it is important to note how insistent Lucas was in this interview, going as far as saying that he had gone to the film department at the University of Southern California "to study still photography" and initially was only "fascinated by the technical aspects" of filmmaking. That he eventually "went crazy" over movies and ended up making two features had, in his retrospective view, never been in the cards.

Lucas also pointed out that, once he had decided, in 1967–1968 after three years of making experimental and documentary shorts, to embark on features (this decision being strongly influenced by Francis Ford Coppola and Lucas's USC classmate John Milius), it was not necessarily up to him which films he would actually make: "I developed a project with John Milius on the Vietnam War. . . . No one could get it off the ground." (The project's title was, of course, *Apocalypse Now*, and it would later be realized by Coppola.)

Lucas emphasized that *American Graffiti* and its successor—"I'm working on the screenplay for an outerspace adventure film, *The Star Wars*"—were both inspired by the experiences of his early years: his adolescence (which he spent assembling "a large rock 'n' roll collection" and "cruising in cars") and his childhood (when he loved watching *Flash Gordon* and became "a comic book freak"). In addition, these two projects (and also, presumably, his feature debut, *THX 1138* [1971], which was based on one of his film school shorts) were informed by his early years at college—he studied for two years at Modesto Junior College before going to USC in 1964—when "I was primarily involved in anthropology and sociology; I was interested in how people reacted to things."

According to Lucas, *American Graffiti* was about young people's responses to necessary changes in their lives and in their society: "*American Graffiti* is really a film about change, about teenagers accepting the fact that they have to leave home. It's about the end of an era. How things can't stay the same." And he also said: "*The Star Wars* deals with sci-fi on a sociological level, how technology affects humans." At the same time, he described it as a "fantasy," which, in his view, "is an abandoned area of film, all the romance went out of outerspace movies long ago."

With reference to *American Graffiti, The Star Wars*, and any projects he might realize further in the future, Lucas declared: "My movies are going to be upbeat. I know that's not fashionable, but it's right. I don't think you can change people's attitudes on specific issues, but you can make them more positive about life and then they will work to change things." He set this statement against his observation that "student filmmakers"—including himself during his years at USC (his very first film there, *Look at Life* [1965], ended with three title cards, "Anyone for survival," "End," and "?") and beyond, up to and including the deeply dystopian *THX 1138*—think that the world is a terrible place and that this has to be the subject of their films. However, Lucas added, people are already fully aware of the dismal state of the world. As the above quotation about "upbeat" movies indicates, he believed that films might be able to help people cope emotionally with that awareness and thus enable them to work toward positive change. It is wholly appropriate, then, that Lucas's third feature would eventually acquire the subtitle *A New Hope*.

In what follows, I pick up on some of the points Lucas made in this interview about the unpredictability of his filmmaking career, about pessimism and the life-affirming potential of movies, and about fantasy and attempts to understand contemporary society, and I do so with particular reference to the development and success of *American Graffiti* and *Star Wars*. But I also reflect on my own academic engagement, across the last three decades, with Lucas's oeuvre, which has resulted in numerous publications, including a recent monograph on *American Graffiti*.[2] The present collection is, among other things, an attempt to consolidate what one might call Lucas studies, and as I am one of the few people who have been working within this academic field—or perhaps it is more accurate to say working toward its establishment—for such a long time, it is, I hope, appropriate on this occasion for me to look back.

About Me, *Star Wars*, and Lucas Studies

As a scholar I have long aimed to work primarily on films I love, and I can certainly say that this applies to *American Graffiti*, but it is equally certain that it does *not* apply to *Star Wars*. In fact, as a somewhat snobbish and overly serious teenage German fan of science fiction literature, I stayed away from *Star Wars* upon its release in West Germany in February 1978, engaging with it only via the film's wickedly funny parody in *Mad* magazine. Instead of going to see *Star Wars*, around that time I went to the cinema for rereleases of Stanley Kubrick's *2001: A Space Odyssey* (1968) and *A Clockwork Orange* (1971), which I considered to be the equal of the best science fiction I had read (indeed, I also eagerly devoured Arthur C. Clarke's *2001* novelization and Anthony Burgess's 1962 *Clockwork* novel).

When, in the 1980s, I did film studies in college, first in Germany and then in the UK, it was easy to absorb the message that films like *Star Wars*— and here one was given to understand that this included anything from *Close Encounters of the Third Kind* (1977) to *Raiders of the Lost Ark* (1981) and *E.T. the Extra-Terrestrial* (1982)—either were not worthy of academic attention or, if such attention was paid to them, should be condemned on the grounds of aesthetics or ideology.

When I first embarked on in-depth research as an undergraduate and postgraduate student, I focused on the writings and films of Jean-Luc Godard and on the silent movies of Buster Keaton. However, when I started doing part-time teaching, in adult education and at universities, in the late 1980s, contemporary Hollywood cinema suggested itself as a more attractive subject (for the students). Around 1990, under the influence of the German film historian (and my close friend) Joseph Garncarz, who had embarked on the systematic study of annual box office charts in West Germany,[3] I became very interested in chart-topping films in the United States. Going through film industry trade papers such as *Variety*, I looked for patterns—and quickly found them.

For example, *Variety*'s "Top 100 All-Time Film Rental Champs" from January 1992 featured *E. T.* at number 1, followed by *Star Wars*; the top ten also included two *Star Wars* sequels, *Raiders of the Lost Ark* and one of its sequels, *Batman* (1989), *Ghostbusters* (1984), *Home Alone* (1990), and *Jaws* (1975).[4] With the exception of the last two films, the top ten were thus filled with science fiction and fantasy adventures, and with the exception of *Jaws*, the top ten movies could all be characterized as children's or family entertainment. Most of these films did not primarily function as star vehicles (Harrison Ford's presence in half of the top ten had more to do with the characters he played—Han Solo and Indiana Jones—than with his unique appeal as a performer). Sequels certainly were important (making up three of the top ten), but most important were the names of two filmmakers: George Lucas and Steven Spielberg, who, between them, were chiefly responsible for seven of the top ten.

I started giving lectures and conference papers on these hit patterns in the mid-1990s, much encouraged by Thomas Schatz's 1993 essay "The New Hollywood,"[5] which, among other things, offered a systematic account of changing hit patterns at the US box office from the 1940s to the 1980s, and also by the organizers of, and participants in, the conference "Hollywood since the Fifties: A Post-classical Cinema?" at the University of Kent in July 1995. I first published my analysis of the all-time US box office chart in the proceedings from that conference, which were published in 1998.[6]

At the time it was common (and to some extent it still is today) to identify the release of *Jaws* in 1975 as the beginning of a new era in Hollywood history, but by highlighting the difference between the family orientation of the biggest hits since 1977 and the much less family-friendly nature of *Jaws* and other box office hits in the decade before 1977 (notably *The Godfather* [1972] and *The Exorcist* [1973]), I eventually committed myself to the claim that *Star Wars* was actually *the* decisive turning point in recent Hollywood history.[7]

I agreed with previous studies that 1967 had been an earlier historical turning point.[8] With many of its highest-profile, most highly acclaimed, and most successful productions from 1967 onward, Hollywood had turned away from its traditional commitment to entertainment suitable for the whole family; from 1977 onward, most of its biggest hits once again functioned and were marketed as family entertainment, and for the first time in Hollywood history, these biggest hits tended to belong to the science fiction and fantasy categories.[9]

Most academic and many journalistic critics saw the historical turn in 1977 in a negative light (while judging the one in 1967 positively) and held *Star Wars* in particular, and the so-called Lucasberger more generally, responsible for what was often referred to as the "juvenilization" or "infantilization" of mainstream American cinema, for its apparent privileging of spectacle and special effects over storytelling and characterization, and for its allegedly reactionary worldview.[10]

Much to my own surprise, I found myself mounting a defense by arguing that films like *Star Wars* were catering to an all-encompassing mass audience, including children and their parents as well as the teenagers and young adults who constituted the core audience for cinemas. They did so in particular by drawing on storytelling traditions associated with childhood, by being released during or in the run-up to the summer and Christmas holidays, and by often focusing their stories on emotionally charged relationships between children and parents or parental substitutes, mostly in the context of incomplete or dysfunctional families or quasi-familial groupings. I argued that these hit movies were doing a valuable kind of social and cultural work for their audiences that, among other things, had to do with accepting nontraditional familial configurations rather than recreating perfect nuclear family units.[11]

By drawing on press clippings files I found in various British and American archives, published interviews with George Lucas,[12] a book about the many script drafts for the film,[13] several biographical and making-of books,[14] and a journal essay on the preparatory marketing research carried out for the film,[15] I tried to reconstruct how George Lucas gradually reworked his initial ideas for *Star Wars* into what I called a "family-adventure movie," how the film was presented to the American public, and how it was received, and made use of, by film critics, public figures, and regular audiences.[16] Among other things, I investigated the controversial appropriation of "Star Wars" as a label for Ronald Reagan's Strategic Defense Initiative (a space weapons program) in 1983.[17]

So from 1998 to 2005, I produced quite a few publications that dealt centrally, in some cases even exclusively, with *Star Wars* (and also, to a lesser extent, the other films in the series), and unlike most academics, I was not a hostile critic; instead, by way of extensive empirical research, I explored the film's production, marketing, and reception, as well as its place within, and its impact on, the history of box office hits in the United States, while also analyzing the film's story and themes in a broadly sympathetic manner. This motivated the editor of this collection to invite me to present during a *Star Wars* thirtieth anniversary event at Modesto Junior College in June 2007. In so many ways, my visit to Modesto brought not just the films (including the early shorts, which, with permission from Lucasfilm, were kindly provided to me on a DVD, quite a coup in the days before YouTube took off) but also the life of George Lucas so much closer to me.[18]

My move toward a fuller engagement with Lucas's work and life was dramatically enhanced by Richard Ravalli's decision to invite me back the following year for a presentation at the downtown State Theatre in Modesto to introduce a screening of *American Graffiti* as part of a daylong celebration of the film's thirty-fifth anniversary.[19] In the run-up to this presentation, I started to collect all kinds of material on this film. And when a few years ago I decided to develop my presentation into a short monograph on *American Graffiti*, I expanded my research—at this time published work and paper documents in archives being complemented by numerous online sources.

I am pleased to note that one of the, for the purposes of this collection, most important insights from this research was the realization that, since the beginning of the new millennium, there has been explosive growth in the literature about George Lucas's life and career, his companies, his movies, and, in particular, anything to do with *Star Wars*. There is now a wealth of critical and historical writing, both academic and nonacademic, including dozens of books and countless shorter pieces in the press, scholarly journals and edited collections, and internet content. It looks as if Lucas studies may have finally arrived.

American Graffiti, Star Wars, and America in Crisis

Together with a long journal essay,[20] my book on *American Graffiti* explores Lucas's early career. I detail the unlikely twists and turns in his development as a filmmaker, which Lucas discussed in the 1973 interview cited earlier, and I explore the origins and development, the story and themes, and the marketing, reception, and impact of *American Graffiti*, with extensive references to film-historical and sociocultural developments in 1960s and 1970s America.[21] Lucas came up with the ideas for *American Graffiti* and *Star Wars* in the wake of Warner Bros.' negative response to an in-house screening of *THX 1138* in May 1970, which was a key factor in his turning away from rather avant-garde productions toward commercially promising properties; his development deal with United Artists in 1971 was for both projects, as was the deal he made the following year with Universal. I outline how the development and production of *American Graffiti* from 1970 to 1973 and its enormous box office success during its extremely long run from 1973 to 1976 (with a rerelease in 1978) were informed by the extraordinary nostalgia boom that resulted from the many upheavals of the late 1960s and 1970s in American society, related to lingering fears of nuclear conflict, opposition to the Vietnam War, assassinations, environmental concerns, Watergate, an increasing awareness of the limits of economic growth, the oil crisis, stagflation, the women's movement, ongoing racial conflict, the sexual revolution, and the generation gap.

With reference to opinion polls, I show that Americans were becoming more pessimistic than they had been in the preceding decades—something Lucas captured in the interview cited at the beginning of this chapter—while I also use psychological studies to show that in addition to offering a temporary escape from current problems, nostalgic visions of the past provide people with additional emotional resources for coping with the present, especially where recollections focus on personal challenges that were met successfully in the past. (Once again, this fits in well with Lucas's interview statements in 1973 about the power of positive feelings that movies can generate.)

By analyzing box office (and ratings) charts, I demonstrate that *American Graffiti*—and also *Star Wars*, a film featuring two teenagers that nostalgically evokes entertainment experiences of the past, especially those associated with childhood—both built on and contributed to a series of hugely successful 1970s movies and television series, as well as other cultural phenomena focusing on teenagers (and those a little bit younger and older) or on the fairly recent American past. And I discuss all this with particular reference to the baby boom—that is, the record number of Americans born between the mid-1940s and the mid-1960s, who made up the bulk of the cinema audience in the 1970s and in particular of the audience of *American Graffiti* and *Star Wars*.

With reference to the story and characters of *American Graffiti* as well as to the film's marketing and reception, I show that it functioned not only as both a celebration and a critique of the past but also—especially during the oil crisis of 1973–1974—as a productive engagement with the problems of contemporary America, pointing forward (notably through Lucas's stand-in, Curt) to a way of life less dependent on cars and excessive consumption.

Having outlined the extraordinary nostalgia boom that resulted from the multiple crises of the late 1960s and 1970s in my book, here I want to add another dimension to the analysis of hit patterns at the US box office by asking whether we can detect a cycle of hit movies dealing head-on with the crises of the day. This is relevant for further contextualizing the production and reception of *American Graffiti* and also for understanding the genesis of Lucas's next film; after all, *Star Wars* deals with a society at a moment of ultimate crisis, and Lucas, in the interview discussed at the beginning of this chapter, is curiously insistent on the fact that whether they are set in the past, the future, or an alternative universe, his films are meant to address reality "on a sociological level."

At the outset, it is important to emphasize that I only look at big hits from the late 1960s and 1970s, rather than at the much larger body of countercultural films, political thrillers, dystopian science fiction movies, allegorical westerns, and similar movies that have been the subject of much academic discussion but did not do particularly well at the box office. I am using the top fifty of the (not-inflation-adjusted) all-time US chart from January 1979 as my reference point, a chart that is of course topped by *Star Wars*, with *American Graffiti* at number 13.[22] I should also point out that the very biggest hits in the United States of the period from 1949 to 1966 rarely dealt with contemporary America or with the recent American past but were largely focused on European and biblical history.[23]

As for the years 1967–1978, the big hit that deals most directly (albeit retrospectively) with a contemporary crisis is arguably the Watergate drama *All the President's Men* (1976; at number 41 in the all-time chart from 1979). The Korean War movie *M*A*S*H* (1970; number 31) was widely understood as a darkly comical take on the Vietnam War, and echoes of that war could also be found in the World War II biopic *Patton* (number 45). There are numerous films about social divisions and conflicts in contemporary America along generational, gender, class, ethnic, and racial lines, although these divisions are rarely addressed in explicitly political terms. These films include *The Graduate* (1967; number 19), *Love Story* (1970; number 16), *Billy Jack* (1971; number 36), *Rocky* (1976; number 14), and *Saturday Night Fever* (1977; number 10). One might even include *The Exorcist* (1973; number 5) here, because it can be seen to allegorize generational conflict, and also perhaps films dealing with similar divisions and conflicts in the recent American past, such as *The Godfather* (1972; number 3) and *Grease* (1973; number 4).

Given widespread concerns about environmental damage, globally limited resources, and the fragility of modern economies, as well as fears of nuclear war, it is surprising that there are hardly any major hits about comprehensive catastrophes at the national or global level. *Planet of the Apes* (1968), which depicts a truly devastating future for all of humanity, only comes in at number 140 in the all-time chart (although it is worth noting that this film and its first two sequels had very high ratings, between 29.1 and 35.2, when first shown on television in 1973).[24]

However, there are numerous hits dealing with the challenges and problems arising from contemporary society's complex relationship with the natural environment, especially with the devastating impact of earthquakes, the weather, and (monstrous) animals on communities of varying sizes. These films, most of which are usually categorized as disaster movies, include *Airport* (1970; number 22), *The Poseidon Adventure* (1972; number 25), *Earthquake* (1974; number 33), *Jaws* (1975; number 2), *King Kong* (1976; number 30) and *Jaws II* (1978; number 18).[25] One can also include *The Towering Inferno* (1975; number 16), in which the natural force of fire is unleashed in a skyscraper, and *Young Frankenstein* (1975; number 34), a parody of one of the key texts exploring the possible negative consequences of human meddling with the natural order of things.

These films may have happy endings, usually due to the intervention of dedicated and skilled professionals and to effective teamwork, but there tends to be a lot of death and destruction along the way. It is important to note that most of them deal specifically with modern society's dependence on complex technology and with the physical damage and social breakdown ensuing when this technology fails (often because of human error or corporate greed) in the face of overwhelming natural forces.

The years from 1967 to 1978, then, saw a large number of very big hit movies more or less directly—and by no means always, or even very often, in an explicitly political fashion—addressing problems in contemporary America, including the shortcomings or failure of political and military leadership, social divisions and conflicts, and modern society's vulnerability with regard to technological breakdowns and destructive natural forces. In addition to contextualizing the impact of *American Graffiti* in terms of popular strategies to deal, mostly somewhat indirectly, with the contemporary world, the success of such films about contemporary crises can be seen as one of the contexts informing both the development of *Star Wars* and its huge impact upon its release in 1977–1978.

From the original idea, in 1970–1971,[26] of an updated version of science fiction serials from the 1930s and 1940s, Lucas's project evolved into a film about civil war in a galaxy-spanning republic, the dissolution of its (presumably democratically elected) senate by an autocratic ruler, the deployment of a newly developed weapon to destroy a whole planet, with such destruction serving to intimidate everyone who might consider resisting the new political order, and also the unlikely success of rebel forces against the vastly superior imperial military. One can certainly see echoes here of the Vietnam War,[27] the

Nixon presidency, civil unrest in 1960s and 1970s America,[28] and concerns that nuclear weapons[29] or environmental destruction may make our planet unsuitable for human habitation.

The big hit movies commenting indirectly on the Vietnam War, dealing with Watergate and deep divisions in contemporary American society, or staging massive disasters may well have helped to shape *Star Wars* (and to prepare the ground for its successful release). But they were, of course, only one factor among many. Another was the film work Lucas had done before.

Star Wars and Lucas's Early Films

In many ways, *Star Wars* was simply an extension of Lucas's earlier films, going back all the way to his first short at film school, *Look at Life* (1965; with its focus on violence in contemporary society and its apocalyptic-sounding end titles), and *Freiheit* (1966; with its simple story about a failed attempt to escape from an oppressive society). Most importantly, without much success at the box office and with an ambiguous but overall rather bleak ending, Lucas had dealt with the problems of contemporary America by way of a futuristic setting in his first feature.

The underground society in *THX 1138* (1971) is completely cut off from the natural world, which presumably has been devastated by the deployment of human technology. People live in a wholly human-made environment, in which frequent disastrous accidents kill hundreds. Their religion asks them to "increase production" and to "buy more," whereby, apart from apparently synthetic food, clothes, drugs, and television, consumption focuses on plastic boxes that, soon after their purchase, are placed in the domestic "consumer," which is in effect a garbage can. Clothes and living quarters are designed to reduce people's sense of individuality, constant surveillance drastically reduces their privacy, and drugs take away other key aspects of their humanity: sensuality, sexuality, any kind of strong emotion. The film's final irony is that after the protagonist has broken free from this society, he finds himself in a natural environment that is unlikely to sustain him; without the technological systems of the underground society, he is bound to die.

In the same way that *THX 1138* drew extensively, in terms of story, themes, and imagery, on Lucas's earlier short films, *American Graffiti* drew both on the shorts and on *THX 1138*, and *Star Wars* was intimately connected to Lucas's first two features. All three films tell stories about young men leaving home, featuring climactic vehicular chases/races, the death of key characters, and a tremendous sense of loss. *American Graffiti* and *Star Wars* focus more specifically on teenagers, and both films are in many ways nostalgic for a past way of life or for the popular culture of the past. Even *THX 1138* starts with a *Buck Rogers* trailer in Lucas's original cut, and *Star Wars* playfully echoes the autobiographical nature of *American Graffiti* in that its protagonist is called Luke Skywalker—that is Luke S./Lucas.

And, of course, all three films explored, to quote Lucas's 1973 comment on *The Star Wars* again, "how technology affects humans." In fact, in this respect (as well as in others) *Star Wars* enhances elements from *THX 1138* and *American Graffiti*: the technological devastation of the earth's surface in *THX 1138* is magnified and turns into the destruction of Alderaan by the Death Star; the robot cops and the deindividualized, numbed people in *THX 1138* recur as deindividualized stormtroopers and a dehumanized villain with his metallic mask and breathing mechanism; teenagers' love of cars in *American Graffiti* evolves into Luke's fascination with flying and Han Solo's attachment to the *Millennium Falcon*; and John saving Terry when he gets beaten up by the people who stole Steve's car from him is echoed in Han coming to Luke's rescue during the climactic attack on the Death Star.

There are also significant departures from the earlier two films, which were already suggested in Lucas's reference to "fantasy," "romance," and "upbeat" movies in the 1973 *AFI Report* interview (although at that point in time the story of *Star Wars* was only beginning to take shape). In contrast to his first two movies, his space adventure would not be limited by the conventions of realistic storytelling or the laws of nature as identified by science. The story would be set neither in the present nor in humanity's future or past but in a separate world altogether, which was to be constructed from scratch, and there would be room in it for the impossible and the supernatural, for highly improbable victories and an unambiguously happy ending (although there is a certain lack of resolution as the chief villain escapes death and the story's love triangle—Luke, Leia, and Han—remains unresolved at the end).

In *THX 1138*, oppressive technology is overcome through an escape from the underground society, but this escape is in effect suicidal. In *American Graffiti*, Curt is not as beholden to cars as are his friends, and this detachment appears to be connected to his ability finally to leave town. While this particular escape does not lead to his death, the film emphasizes his separation from the community he knows and does not indicate which new community he might become part of; in fact, the postscript tells us that after going east, he moves even farther away from home to Canada. By contrast, in *Star Wars* Luke becomes a highly valued member of a new community after he has managed to transcend his attachment to technology by putting his faith in "the Force" (a positive counterpart to the materialist religion in *THX 1138*).

What is more, whereas LUH simply dies in *THX 1138* and the deaths of Terry and John are announced at the end of *American Graffiti*, *Star Wars* emphasizes that death can be overcome, insofar as Obi-Wan Kenobi continues to communicate with Luke long after he has been struck down by Darth Vader. Thus, *Star Wars* was as much a departure from Lucas's earlier work as it was a continuation. Something similar could be said about the film's relationship to long-standing hit patterns at the US box office.

Star Wars and Hollywood Blockbuster Traditions

As far as its emphasis on the Force—and, connected with it, a comprehensive belief system, magical or miraculous powers, and life after death—and the creation of a highly complex and detailed alternative universe, *Star Wars* was very much at odds with hit patterns at the US box office from the late 1960s to the late 1970s. While there were, as noted earlier, big hits dealing, like *Star Wars*, with societies in crisis and with spectacular disasters, almost all of them were set in contemporary America or in the recent American past. Furthermore, the top fifty on the all-time US box office chart from January 1979 do not include a single film set in an alternative, fantasy universe, a science fiction movie, or one with any supernatural elements, from 1967 to 1972, the year before Lucas started serious work on *Star Wars*. As noted earlier, *Planet of the Apes* was only at number 140 in the 1979 chart; Stanley Kubrick's two science fiction hits, *2001: A Space Odyssey* and *A Clockwork Orange*, were at numbers 60 and 133 respectively; and the highest-ranked Disney fantasy from these years, *The Jungle Book* (1967), was at number 56.

During the further development and production of *Star Wars* and its extended release in 1977–1978, there were a few big hits dealing with spiritual/ religious matters—*The Exorcist, The Omen* (1976; number 47), *Oh, God* (1977; number 39), and *Heaven Can Wait* (1978; number 24)—and also a massive science fiction hit (*Close Encounters of the Third Kind* [1977; number 8]; in addition, one might count *Young Frankenstein* as science fiction). But there was still no big hit set in a fully fledged fantasy world.

In the 1973 *AFI Report* interview, Lucas acknowledged that with *The Star Wars* he went against contemporary Hollywood's major trends by declaring fantasy to be "an abandoned area of film." It is intriguing that Lucas immersed himself in work on this project—with extensive if fragmentary notes on ideas for the story, characters, and settings, among other details—early in 1973,[30] around the time that he encountered another serious crisis in his career, due to the negative response by Universal's Ned Tanen to the first screening of *American Graffiti* at the end of January. There were doubts whether *American Graffiti* would be given a theatrical release at all. Furthermore, after he sent Gary Kurtz on a location scouting trip for *Apocalypse Now* late in 1972,[31] Lucas's renewed attempt to get funding for this project once again came to nothing.

In this rather desperate situation, he could have turned to another comedy about the fairly recent American past. In 1972, he had come up with an idea for a screwball-comedy murder mystery set at a radio station in the 1930s, for which he wrote a treatment that he then asked the cowriters of *American Graffiti*, Gloria Katz and Willard Huyck, to develop further.[32] But in early 1973, Lucas focused his attention on what was bound to be an expensive movie in a field that Hollywood had "abandoned." Why would he do this? And why would any studio want to get involved in this project (Lucas managed to make a deal with Fox later in 1973)?

These are important film historical questions precisely because *Star Wars* was so unusual in the context of the 1970s and because it turned into such an enormous hit that it became the main reference point for many subsequent developments in Hollywood cinema—notably, as we have seen, the rise to dominance of science fiction and fantasy movies at the US, and indeed the global, box office[33] and the return of family entertainment to the center of Hollywood's operations. After several years of going through numerous primary and secondary sources, I am still puzzled by Lucas's decision to commit to his space adventure in 1973.

Perhaps an important clue is Lucas's statement, in his 1973 interview, about "fantasy" (in the sense of alternative worlds, the supernatural, etc.) having been "abandoned," because it implies that in earlier times Hollywood had taken care of fantasy, that fantasy had had a home in Hollywood, only then to be sidelined or pushed out altogether. Lucas seems to have assumed that there was an ongoing demand for fantasy that the American film industry did not meet anymore, which led him to commit himself to *Star Wars* in 1973 so as to meet this demand. He made statements along these lines in later interviews, as in the following example: "A whole generation was growing up without fairy tales. . . . I wanted to do a modern fairy tale, a myth."[34]

In the same interview, Lucas also said, "I decided I wanted to make a children's movie, to go the Disney route."[35] While the many statements Lucas made between 1973 and 1978 (and later) about *Star Wars*, the traditions it drew on, and the audience it was aimed at pointed in several different directions, there is the overall impression that he gradually became aware that unlike *American Graffiti*, which was specifically aimed at teenagers and young adults, his next film would additionally address, as Disney features did, young children and their parents; this is certainly the way reviewers and other commentators saw the film upon its release in 1977.[36] In fact, there had been a debate throughout the 1970s about the shortage of high-profile Hollywood films suitable for children or for the whole family.[37] Thus, *Star Wars* occupied two important niches and hence was able to meet the otherwise unmet demand not only for fantasy but also for family entertainment.

In this way, Lucas returned to the older Hollywood tradition of making films that were, in principle, suitable for, and ideally appealing to, all age groups. Most of the biggest hits in that tradition had belonged to the following generic categories: epics dealing with important historical events and developments (for example, *Gone with the Wind* [1939; number 9 in the 1979 all-time US box office chart] and *Doctor Zhivago* [1965; number 20]), including biblical epics (e.g., *The Ten Commandments* [1956; number 23]); international adventures about exciting action in a wide range of often spectacular settings (e.g., *Thunderball* [1965; number 43]); musicals (e.g., *The Sound of Music* [1965; number 6], which is also an epic dealing with the rise of the Nazis); and fairy tales (e.g., *Snow White and the Seven Dwarfs* [1937; number 48], which is also a musical).[38]

With *Star Wars*, Lucas in effect managed to combine elements from these older traditions (apart from the musical) with elements from the recent cycle of 1970s disaster movies, which at the time of their release were widely discussed as a return to old-fashioned Hollywood entertainment.[39] He extended the historical epic into the very distant, and imaginary, past ("A long time ago") and focused on a turning point in the history of a vast civilization spanning "a galaxy far, far away," while also introducing a new kind of religion (the Judeo-Christian God making way for the Force). He extended international adventure into interstellar adventure, updated old fairy tales (and myths), and escalated the catastrophes staged in disaster movies into the explosion of a whole planet (while also, in some ways, relegating the forces of nature to a secondary role, eclipsed by the destructiveness of technology; however, ultimately, the film reaffirms the primacy of nature through the Force). In 1973 and 1974, Lucas articulated the convergence of all these trends in *Star Wars* by describing it as "an epic space fantasy,"[40] in which "*2001* meets James Bond."[41]

Drawing on his own childhood and youth, Lucas designed *Star Wars* so that the film would connect with many of the key movie-watching experiences of all age groups, ranging from post–baby boom children to baby boomers and their parents.[42] This made it possible for the film to vastly exceed the success of *American Graffiti*; whereas his second feature had reached mainly baby boomers, *Star Wars* was truly a film for everybody. By 1979, its record-breaking US rentals amounted to $165 million, as compared to *American Graffiti*'s $56 million.[43]

Conclusion

American Graffiti made *Star Wars* possible. Both United Artists and Universal had turned Lucas's space adventure project down in May and June 1973, but when Fox executive Alan Ladd Jr. saw *American Graffiti* during the summer (before the film's release in August), he was so impressed that he was willing to make a bet on Lucas, and a contract for his space adventure was signed in August 1973.[44] Fox's initial funding for script development probably would not have been enough to sustain Lucas during the long period in which he then worked on writing and rewriting the story, but he could continue for a long time because the enormous success of *American Graffiti* at the box office and his profit participation deal for the film made him a rich man. This unexpected box office hit also encouraged Fox, once a suitable script was in place, actually to go ahead with the production of *Star Wars* and to stay on board despite seemingly endless delays and an ever-escalating budget.[45]

American Graffiti, a film about teenagers confronting challenges in their lives, gaining insights, and making important decisions about their personal futures thus allowed Lucas to create, in *Star Wars*, a whole new world in which ultimate threats to societies are met not only with weapons and teamwork but also with a teenager's individual spiritual growth and decisive action. Remarkably, unlike almost all of Hollywood's biggest hits from the 1910s to the 1970s, *American Graffiti* and *Star Wars* were not adaptations (of novels, plays, stage musicals, etc.) or works based on well-known historical figures and events; they were derived from original screenplays based on treatments written by the same person. With the first of these two films, Lucas reflected on his own teenage years and held up a mirror to baby boomers, who made up the largest generation in American history. With the second, he used his childhood fascination with science fiction and fantasy as a starting point for imagining an alternative cinematic universe in which, as it turned out, Americans from all generations as well as people all around the world could see themselves reflected.

Notes

1. "Young Directors, New Films," *AFI Report*, Winter 1973, 45–46.

2. Peter Krämer, *"American Graffiti": George Lucas, the New Hollywood and the Baby Boom Generation* (London: Routledge, 2023).

3. His first English-language publication on this topic was Joseph Garncarz, "Hollywood in Germany: The Role of American Films in Germany 1925–1990," in *Hollywood in Europe: Experiences of a Cultural Hegemony*, ed. David W. Ellwood and Rob Kroes (Amsterdam: VU University Press, 1994), 94–135.

4. "Top 100 All-Time Film Rental Champs," *Variety*, January 6, 1982, 86.

5. Thomas Schatz, "The New Hollywood," in *Film Theory Goes to the Movies*, ed. Jim Collins, Hilary Radner, and Ava Preacher Collins (New York: Routledge, 1993), 8–36.

6. Peter Krämer, "Would You Take Your Child to See This Film? The Cultural and Social Work of the Family-Adventure Movie," in *Contemporary Hollywood Cinema*, ed. Steve Neale and Murray Smith (London: Routledge, 1998), 294–311.

7. Peter Krämer, *The New Hollywood: From "Bonnie and Clyde" to "Star Wars"* (London: Wallflower, 2005). Cf. Peter Krämer, "'She Was the First': The Place of *Jaws* in American Film History," in *The "Jaws" Book: New Perspectives on the Classic Summer Blockbuster*, ed. Ian Hunter and Matthew Melia (New York: Bloomsbury Academic, 2020), 19–32. See also Peter Krämer, "Big Pictures: Studying Contemporary Hollywood Cinema through Its Greatest Hits," in *Screen Methods: Comparative Readings in Film Studies*, ed. Jacqueline Furby and Karen Randell (London: Wallflower, 2005), 124–32.

8. Cf. Peter Krämer, "Post-classical Hollywood," in *The Oxford Guide to Film Studies*, ed. John Hill and Pamela Church Gibson (Oxford: Oxford University Press, 1998), 279–300.

9. Krämer, *New Hollywood*. Also see Peter Krämer, "'The Best Disney Film Disney Never Made': Children's Films and the Family Audience in American Cinema since the 1960s," in *Genre and Contemporary Hollywood*, ed. Steve Neale (London: BFI, 2002), 183–98.

10. Cf. Krämer, "Post-classical Hollywood," 297–305. See also Andrew Gordon, "Science-Fiction and Fantasy Film Criticism: The Case of Lucas and Spielberg," *Journal of the Fantastic in the Arts* 2, no. 2 (1989): 81–94.

11. Krämer, "Would You Take Your Child to See This Film?" For a wide-ranging discussion of critical readings of *Star Wars*, by both academics and other writers, from the late 1970s onward, see Miles Booy, *Interpreting "Star Wars": Reading a Modern Film Franchise* (New York: Bloomsbury Academic, 2021).

12. See especially Sally Kline, ed., *George Lucas: Interviews* (Jackson: University of Mississippi Press, 1999).

13. Laurent Bouzereau, ed., *"Star Wars": The Annotated Screenplays* (New York: Del Rey, 1997). Some script materials could be accessed in public archives, and many eventually found their way onto the internet, but in 1997 Bouzereau's volume provided insights that were almost impossible to gain any other way.

14. The first two prominent examples were Dale Pollock, *Skywalking: The Life and Times of George Lucas* (Hollywood: Samuel French, 1990), and Garry Jenkins, *Empire Building: The Remarkable Real Life Story of "Star Wars"* (New York: Simon and Schuster, 1997).

15. Olen J. Earnest, *"Star Wars*: A Case Study of Motion Picture Marketing," *Current Research in Film* 1 (1985): 7–13.

16. Peter Krämer, "'It's Aimed at Kids—the Kid in Everybody': George Lucas, *Star Wars* and Children's Entertainment," Scope: An Online Journal of Film Studies, December 2001, http://www.nottingham.ac.uk/scope/documents/2001/december-2001/kramer.pdf. It was noticeable at the time that there was a lot of interest in *Star Wars* within the emerging field of media fan studies; see especially Will Brooker, *Using the Force: Creativity, Community and "Star Wars" Fans* (New York: Continuum, 2002).

17. Peter Krämer, *"Star Wars,"* History Today 49, no. 3 (March 1999): 41–47; an expanded version of this essay can be found in Peter Krämer, "Fighting the Evil Empire: *Star Wars*, the Strategic Defense Initiative and the Politics of Science-Fiction," in *Sex, Politics, and Religion in "Star Wars": An Anthology*, ed. Douglas Brode and Leah Deyneka (Lanham, MD: Scarecrow, 2012), 63–76.

18. My presentation at Modesto Junior College was later published online; Peter Krämer, "The Impact of *Star Wars*," Pure Movies, March 16, 2014, http://www.puremovies.co.uk/columns/the-impact-of-star-wars/.

19. See the online manuscript for my talk: Peter Krämer, "'Where Were You in '62?' *American Graffiti*, George Lucas and the Baby Boom Generation," *Kip's "American Graffiti" Blog*, August 2, 2018, http://kipsamericangraffiti.blogspot.com/2018/08/ (scroll down the page).

20. Peter Krämer, "'One More Fine Technician for the Dream Factory'? George Lucas's Early Film Career, 1964–1971," *Film History* 34, no. 2 (2022): 35–63.

21. Krämer, *"American Graffiti."*

22. Cobbett Steinberg, *Film Facts* (New York: Facts on File, 1980), 4–5.

23. Krämer, *New Hollywood*, 19–37, 111–15.

24. Steinberg, *Film Facts*, 32–33.

25. Several disaster movies also achieved high TV ratings in 1973–1974, most notably *Airport* (broadcast in November 1973, with a 42.3 rating, which means that it was watched in over 40% of all American households) and *The Poseidon Adventure* (October 1974, 39.0); indeed, apart from *Love Story*, these two films were the highest-rated movies ever shown on television up to this point. In addition, I am intrigued by the fact that *The Birds* (1963), a classic revenge-of-nature movie if ever there was one, had become the highest-rated movie ever shown on American television when it was first broadcast in January 1968 (with a 38.9 rating).

26. In some interviews, Lucas claims that he was already thinking about a space adventure along the lines of *Buck Rogers* and *Flash Gordon* before writing and shooting

THX 1138 in 1968–1969, but that seems somewhat unlikely in the light of his general orientation toward documentary and experimental films at that time. It also does not fit in with the two feature projects—*THX 1138* and *Apocalypse Now*—he got involved in during the late 1960s; indeed, the use of the trailer for a *Buck Rogers* serial in Lucas's original cut of *THX 1138* suggests an ironic detachment from, rather than passionate embrace of, a beloved childhood favorite. Then again, ironic detachment and passionate embrace may not have been a contradiction for Lucas; after all, as I discuss in my book, *American Graffiti* was initially announced, in May 1971, as a straightforward critique of the Eisenhower era and its "inane" music and then turned into something much more ambiguous, combining celebration and critique. In any case, Lucas did inquire about the rights to *Flash Gordon* in 1971, which is also the year when *The Star Wars* was listed as the title for a future project in contract with United Artists. There appears to be no evidence that he actually did substantial work on his space adventure before 1973. See, for example, J. W. Rinzler, *The Making of "Star Wars": The Definitive Story behind the Original Film* (New York: Ballantine, 2007), 2–8.

27. Indeed, Lucas later said that the Vietnam War and his work on *Apocalypse Now* exerted a strong influence on his space adventure about "a large technological empire going after a small group of freedom fighters." Quoted in Rinzler, *Making of Star Wars*, 8.

28. Social divisions and conflicts in the US in the "long 1960s" (which lasted into the early 1970s) have been conceptualized as a "civil war." See especially Maurice Isserman and Michael Kazin, *America Divided: The Civil War of the 1960s* (New York: Oxford University Press, 2004).

29. Not coincidentally, during the renewed arms race of the late 1970s and early 1980s, the debate about space-based weapons frequently referred to *Star Wars*, well before the "Star Wars" label became attached to Reagan's Strategic Defense Initiative. Krämer, "Fighting the Evil Empire," 71.

30. Rinzler, *Making of "Star Wars,"* 8–11.

31. Ibid., 7.

32. This project was eventually realized as *Radioland Murders* (Mel Smith, 1994). See Bernard Weinraub, "The Ultimate Hollywoodian Lives an Un-Hollywood Life," *New York Times*, October 20, 1994, http://www.nytimes.com/1994/10/20/movies/the-ultimate-hollywoodian-lives-an-anti-hollywood-life.html; John Baxter, *George Lucas: A Biography* (New York: HarperCollins, 1999), 107, 122, 253; Marcus Hearn, *The Cinema of George Lucas* (New York: Harry N. Abrams, 2005), 78–79; Brian Jay Jones, *George Lucas: A Life* (London: Headline, 2016), 176; Wikipedia, s.v. "*Radioland Murders*," accessed September 15, 2023, https://en.wikipedia.org/wiki/Radioland_Murders.

33. On developments at both the domestic and the international box office since the late 1970s, see Peter Krämer, "Hollywood and Its Global Audiences: A Comparative Study of the Biggest Box Office Hits in the United States and outside the United States since the 1970s," in *Explorations in New Cinema History: Approaches and Case Studies*, ed. Richard Maltby, Daniel Biltereyst, and Philippe Meers (Oxford: Wiley-Blackwell, 2011), 171–84. The crucial role of *Star Wars* in domestic and global box office trends is discussed in Peter Krämer, "The Walt Disney Company, Family Entertainment, and

Hollywood's Global Hits," in *The Oxford Handbook of Children's Films*, ed. Noel Brown (Oxford: Oxford University Press, 2022), 569–90.

34. Stephen Zito, "George Lucas Goes Far Out," *American Film*, April 1977, reprinted in Kline, *George Lucas*, 53.

35. Ibid., 47. I discuss the important connection between classic Disney fantasies and *Star Wars* in various publications, see especially Krämer, "Walt Disney Company, Family Entertainment, and Hollywood's Global Hits."

36. See, for example, Krämer, "'It's Aimed at Kids.'"

37. See, for example, Peter Krämer, "Disney and Family Entertainment," in *Contemporary American Cinema*, ed. Michael Hammond and Linda Ruth Williams (Maidenhead: Open University Press, 2006), 267–70.

38. Cf. also the inflation-adjusted all-time chart that I have analyzed elsewhere (Krämer, *New Hollywood*, 19–27) and the very high ratings achieved by historical epics (with *Gone with the Wind* easily breaking all records in 1976), international adventures, musicals, and fairy-tale-like films such as *The Wizard of Oz* in the 1970s (Steinberg, *Film Facts*, 32–36).

39. Krämer, *New Hollywood*, 63–65.

40. Lucas, quoted in Rinzler, *Making of "Star Wars,"* 11.

41. Larry Sturhahn, "The Filming of *American Graffiti*," *Filmmakers Newsletter*, March 1974, reprinted in Kline, *George Lucas*, 32.

42. There is much more to be said about how Lucas's work relates to the parents of the older baby boomers, the so-called Greatest Generation, which was admired for its participation in World War II. The starting point for *Star Wars* was science fiction serials made for theatrical release in the 1930s and 1940s; *Radioland Murders* was set in the 1930s, and *Raiders of the Lost Ark* (which Lucas embarked on immediately after *Star Wars*) focuses on Nazis in the 1930s. *Star Wars* has stormtroopers and is also about the fall of a republic and its replacement by an imperial dictatorship, which echoes not only the transition from the Roman Republic to the Roman Empire but also that from the Weimar Republic to the Third Reich.

43. Steinberg, *Film Facts*, 4–5. In this all-time chart, *Jaws* was in second place with $121 million, only three-quarters of the figure for *Star Wars*.

44. Rinzler, *Making of "Star Wars,"* 11–13.

45. On the long, drawn-out script development and production history of *Star Wars*, see especially Rinzler, *Making of "Star Wars."*

6

Writing about *Star Wars*

A Historiography of the Original Trilogy

ANDREW HOWE

This historiography of the original *Star Wars* trilogy extends from the release of *Star Wars: A New Hope* (1977) through the conclusion of the sequel trilogy (2019). It encompasses works of varying perspectives in different forms, focused partially or exclusively on the original trilogy and tracing over time the evolution of reception as affected by a variety of social, political, and economic factors. Different typologies frame this historiography, including responses by film critics, academic analyses, popular work, and biographies. A wide range of texts are entertained, from coffee-table books to film reviews and from scholarly works to those focused on a highly specific aspect of the universe or lens through which to access it. Throughout this historiography, specific content categories appear, including problematic depictions and elisions of race and gender; LGBTQ+ themes; influence and genealogy; tie-ins and merchandising; and fan culture. The cultural history of the original trilogy is thus explored in an examination of forty-five years of criticism and the various trends in society that have influenced such focus over time.[1]

Movie Critics

The first wave of published criticism on *Star Wars* derived from movie critics of the 1970s publishing opinion pieces in newspapers and magazines. Hundreds if not thousands appeared in local, regional, and national publications, with critics not only responding to the film itself but also understanding that it captured the zeitgeist of the decade. Many such reviews focused on several themes: genealogical influence, science fiction/fantasy elements, and wonder/special effects. Critics included many well-known ones, such as Charles Champlin, Molly Haskell, and Gene Siskel. Gene Shalit not only published his thoughts but also interviewed the cast shortly after the film's release.[2] As these reviews were for general audiences, they were entry-level accessible. Notably absent was a sustained focus on the politics of the film or, by extension, Lucas's own politics. Such criticism would come later.

Many reviews focused strongly on genealogy, citing not only B westerns and *Flash Gordon* and other science fiction serials but also texts that do not appear as frequently in more contemporary discussions. Writing for *Time*, Jay Cocks was among the first to note the film as a combination of *Flash Gordon*, Hollywood westerns, and Errol Flynn's swashbuckling films. He also included in this pastiche of influence *The Wizard of Oz*, *The Hardy Boys*, *Sir Gawain and the Green Knight*, and *The Faerie Queene*. This critic's primary contribution to the success of *Star Wars*, however, came not in this review but during filming, when he helped Brian De Palma rewrite the opening crawl for George Lucas.[3] Vincent Canby, writing for the *New York Times*, also identified *Flash Gordon* and *The Wizard of Oz* as progenitors but noted that the film was also an amalgamation of *Buck Rogers*, *Superman*, Arthurian legend, and Ivanhoe.[4] Lucas himself later entered this aspect of *Star Wars* criticism by acknowledging his indebtedness to Joseph Campbell, author of *The Hero with a Thousand Faces* (1949).[5] This notion recast the film's genealogy within a larger framework of Jungian archetypes, establishing a mythopoetic dimension to the trilogy. The Campbell connection would soon become the predominant stream of *Star Wars* genealogical studies, even prompting two collaborations with Bill Moyers and PBS, filmed at Skywalker Ranch: *The Power of Myth* (1988), an extended interview with Campbell, and *The Mythology of Star Wars* (1999), a discussion with Lucas.[6]

Other critics focused on the wonder they felt when exposed to Lucas's fictional world. A case in point is Roger Ebert, writing for the *Chicago Sun Times*: "Every once in a while I have what I think of as an out-of-the-body experience at a movie." Ebert continues by describing the cantina scene: "I found myself feeling a combination of admiration and delight. *Star Wars* had placed me in the presence of really magical movie invention: Here, all mixed together, were whimsy and fantasy, simple wonderment and quietly sophisticated story-telling."[7] Most critics understood that they had just seen a film that captured the zeitgeist of the 1970s and evidenced a sea change in American filmmaking. Richard Schickel lobbied for *Time* to make *Star Wars* its movie of the year and later directed two documentaries about the film.[8]

Despite realizing its cultural importance, not all critics were so effusive. Richard Corliss was turned off by the world-building, which for many had been a plus: "All these dense factoids about Galactic Empires and Death Stars—it was like some nightmare of a pop quiz in a course I hadn't taken. The sets were Formica, the characters cardboard; the tale had drive but no depth, a tour at warp speed through an antiseptic landscape."[9] No less a figure than Pauline Kael panned the film in the *New Yorker* for its garish storytelling: "The loudness, the smash-and-grab editing, the relentless pacing drive every idea from your head; for young audiences *Star Wars* is like getting a box of Cracker Jack which is all prizes. . . . There's no breather in the picture, no lyricism . . . it has no emotional grip."[10] Writing for the *New Republic*, Stanley Kauffmann would take this criticism even further, focusing on a style of filmmaking that encouraged audience regression to a state of childlike wonder: "This picture was made for those (particularly males) who carry a portable shrine with them of their adolescence, a chalice of a self that was better then, before the world's affairs or—in any complex way—sex intruded."[11] Although more often directed at Steven Spielberg, such criticism would follow Lucas for the rest of his career.

New Hollywood

A limited form of criticism, consumed largely by those interested in Hollywood history, involves situating Lucas within a particular Hollywood era and group of filmmakers. Numerous stand-alone chapters in critical collections address Lucas in this fashion, although there are a few single-author books that do so. Most of these were published later in Lucas's career, after an opportunity came for reflection on the careers of those in his Hollywood cohort—Francis Ford Coppola, Brian De Palma, John Milius, Martin Scorsese, and Steven Spielberg. These works include Ryan Gilbey's *It Don't Worry Me: The Revolutionary American Films of the 1970s* (2003)[12] and Peter Krämer's *The New Hollywood: From "Bonnie and Clyde" to "Star Wars"* (2005).[13] Axel Madsen's *The New Hollywood: American Movies in the '70s* (1975) was prescient, situating Lucas as a key member of this movement on the strength of the pre–*Star Wars* films *THX 1138* and *American Graffiti*.[14] Michael Pye and Lynda Myles's *The Movie Brats: How the Film Generation Took Over Hollywood* (1979) was also an early entry in this category.[15] Robert Kolker, who wrote for *New York Magazine*, published the key director-focused study of the late 1960s and 1970s. *A Cinema of Loneliness: Penn, Kubrick, Coppola, Scorsese, Altman* (1980) was well enough received that it was republished in 2000, with the inclusion of Oliver Stone.[16] Lucas, however, is only referenced in this work on several occasions, very much a missing component along with Peter Bogdanovich and De Palma. Although Lucas's material may not have resonated well with Kolker's thesis, Spielberg receives quite a bit of attention in this study. Regardless of how such works apportioned focus, several narrative streams began to become evident in such director studies: a "New Hollywood" that revolved around film school—in particular, University of Southern California, University of California, Los Angeles, and New York University—and a divide between "entertainers" such as Lucas and Spielberg and more "serious" filmmakers such as Scorsese and De Palma, with Coppola often seen as bridging the gap. The entertainer label of course ignored prior works such as *American Graffiti* for Lucas and *The Sugarland Express* for Spielberg. The latter partially shed such branding with *Schindler's List* and *Saving Private Ryan*, but Lucas was never able to do so. Indeed, criticism involving Lucas and *Star Wars* often intertwines, with the cultural and political sensibilities of the director often viewed to an extra-ordinary degree as synonymous with the content of his films.

Biographies, Interviews, and Histories

As the popularity of *Star Wars* grew, another historiographic stream emerged: historical documentation. This manifested itself in several ways: interviews, biographies, and "making of" exposés. Often, such works blended several of these approaches. Dale Pollock's biography *Skywalking: The Life and Films of George Lucas* (1983) is one of the key texts here. This work is often noted as authorized, but that is not the case; Pollock simply enjoyed unprecedented access to Lucas and his inner circle. Early on, he situates Lucas vis-à-vis his importance to American popular culture: "George Lucas has become one of the most influential persons in the history of mass entertainment, occupying a special galaxy along with the Beatles and Elvis Presley."[17] Lucas biographies always focus on his relationship with Coppola, but this one goes into great detail, dedicating much of an entire chapter—"Coping with Coppola"—to the complex relationship the two shared at American Zoetrope, what in essence was "a combination of friendship and rivalry."[18] As Lucas told Pollock, the two directors "were like two halves of a whole. I was always putting on the brakes and he was always stepping on the gas. It was good for me, because it loosened me up and got me to take more chances."[19] Given Pollock's access to Lucas, the preoccupation with Coppola indicates the importance of this

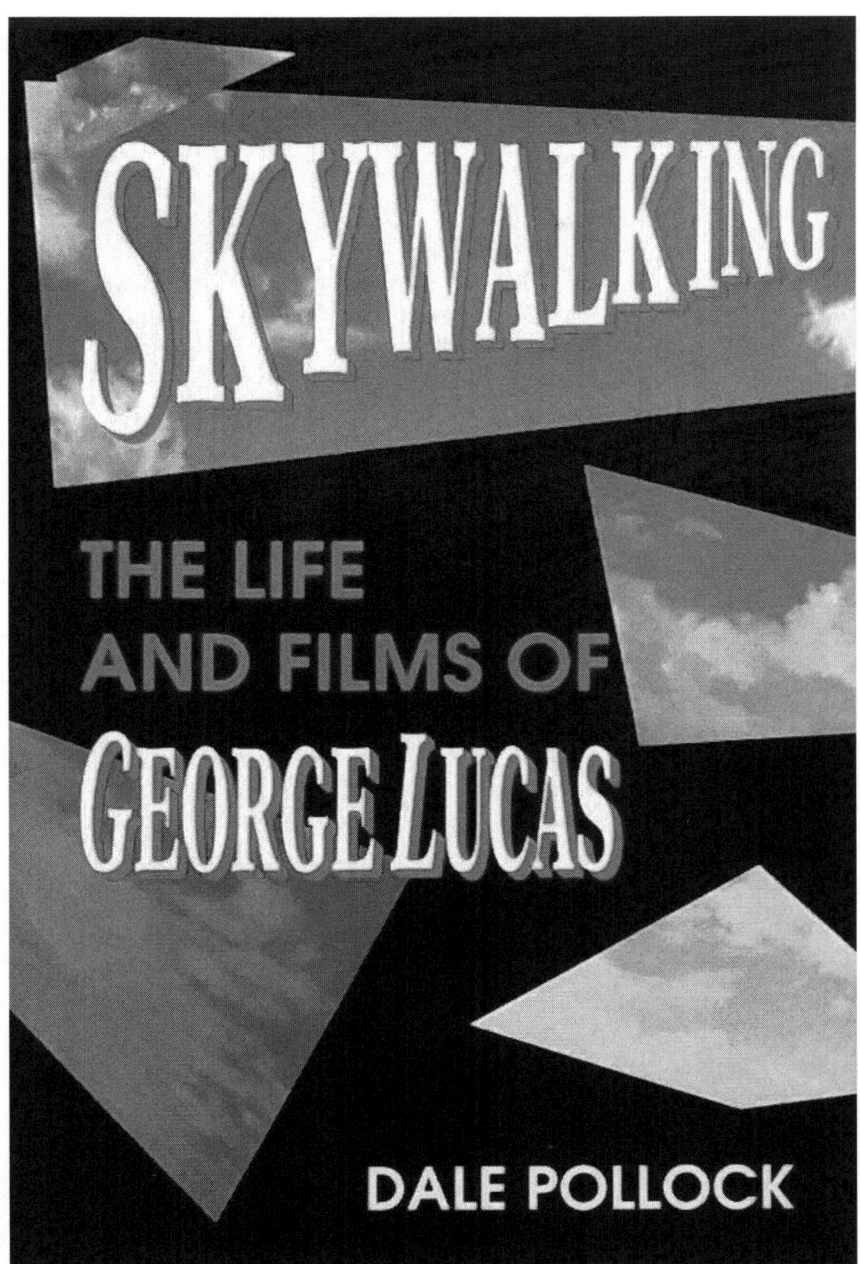

Dale Pollock's *Skywalking: The Life and Films of George Lucas* was a highly influential look at the filmmaker. (courtesy Dale Pollock)

association, even if Lucas did begin to chafe under the burden of being the "younger brother" in the relationship.[20]

Other biographies include John Baxter's *Mythmaker: The Life and Work of George Lucas* (1999) and Brian Jay Jones's *George Lucas: A Life* (2017).[21] These came out later in Lucas's career, allowing them a greater critical distance from the original trilogy. There is even a biography for children, Pam Pollack and Meg Belviso's *Who Is George Lucas?* (2014),[22] part of the Who Is? series chronicling figures such as Martin Luther King Jr. and Eleanor Roosevelt. When it comes to these post-Pollock biographies, Baxter deserves recognition. Although a bit gossip-oriented, *Mythmaker* does not shrink away from noting criticisms of how movies changed, for the worse, because of *Star Wars*. This work also reports on the mixed feelings held by Lucas's friends and supporters from within the film industry; for example, Coppola allegedly referred to the trilogy as "twerp cinema."[23] Baxter himself also criticized Lucas, noting that success made him paranoid and a bit ruthless.[24]

Interviews constitute another subcategory of history. Some books consist largely of interviews; others interweave them throughout larger studies focused on history or criticism. *The Future of the Movies* (1991) comprises three interviews by Roger Ebert and Gene Siskel: George Lucas (Ebert), Steven Spielberg (Siskel), and Martin Scorsese (Siskel and Ebert). The Lucas interview stands out for its greater focus on the technical features of storytelling—sound, light, theaters, color saturation, negatives, copyright issues, and pan and scan, among others[25]—aspects that would grow in importance in his later historiography. Another compilation is the Sally Kline–edited *George Lucas: Interviews*, significant as a volume dedicated exclusively to Lucas and published by an academic press. Part of the Conversations with Filmmakers series, this collection consists of several hundred pages of interviews, many of which involve the original trilogy. In one of these, Lucas notes that he was turned down by several studios and that *Star Wars* was only picked up because of the success of *American Graffiti*.[26] In this same interview, conducted in 1974 and thus three years before the release of *A New Hope*, he also indicated a lack of confidence in the project, planning a slapstick comedy should the film perform poorly.

Other more historically grounded works have examined different aspects of the trilogy. Barry Jenkins's *Empire Building: The Remarkable Real Life Story of Star Wars* (1997) is a standard history, albeit with kitschy chapter titles such as "Wookiee Cookie." Among other stories, he recounts the well-known tale of Lucas and his wife Marcia eating at a Hamburger Hamlet across the street from Mann's Chinese Theatre on the night of the premier, barely believing their eyes when moviegoers began showing up in droves to see the film.[27] Jenkins also discusses Lucas's merchandising acumen—the subject of much focus in the 1980s and 1990s—including a tale not often told involving Lucas nixing a jewelry manufacturer's offer of $500,000 to produce rings and affordable jewelry with the *Star Wars* logo. Apparently, Lucas did not want schlock, finding such artifacts incompatible with his vision of toy tie-ins.[28] In the *George Lucas Companion* (1999), Howard Maxford discusses merchandising fatigue, ironically in the same year it ramped up again with the prequel trilogy.[29] He also focused on Lucas's early collaborations with Disney, not just on Star Tours but also on the short film *Captain EO*, written by Lucas, directed by Francis Ford Coppola, and starring Michael Jackson.

Another history, Chris Salewicz's *George Lucas* (1998), largely consists of generic "making of" fare, albeit with the original *Variety* reviews listed for each of the three films, under the headlines "Outstanding Adventure-Fantasy. All-Age Appeal. Huge Outlook"; "The Force Is Still With It"; and "Great Creatures and Effects Equals Smash B.O. (Box Office) for Trilogy's Finale, but Weak on the Human Side."[30] Michael Rubin's *Droidmaker: George Lucas and the Digital Revolution* (2006) explored Lucas and his placement in the development of digital filmmaking, examining how new technologies and financial models forever changed movies during the 1970s.[31] Michael Kaminski's *The Secret History of "Star Wars": The Art of Storytelling and the Making of a Modern Epic* (2008) is another history that came out in the immediate wake of the prequel trilogy.[32] Chris Taylor's *How "Star Wars" Conquered the Universe: The Past, Present, and Future of a Multibillion Dollar Franchise* (2014) is largely standard fare, although it does note some interesting trivia, including that only a few prior films—including *Fantasia*, *Citizen Kane*, and *West Side Story*—had no opening credits.[33] Taylor's work comes late enough in history to report that *Star Wars* was the first movie to be dubbed in a Native American language. It was screened in Navajo at the rodeo grounds outside Window Rock, Arizona, on July 3, 2013.[34]

Academic Writing—Single-Author Texts

By far the largest portion of *Star Wars* historiography, other than popular magazine articles and the blogosphere, are the hundreds of books and thousands of journal articles in academia that have, in part or in whole, explored various aspects of the original trilogy. Focusing on all of these could fill up an entire book; in the next several pages, a precious few will be treated, especially as they indicate general trends in *Star Wars* criticism. The earliest cultural, social, and political analyses of *Star Wars* did not come from academics but instead from film critics. Molly Haskell and Peter Biskind were the latter, but their books—*From Reverence to Rape* (1973; revised in 1987) and *Easy Riders, Raging Bulls* (1998)—became mainstay texts for academics exploring 1970s cinema. Both subscribed to Kael's view of Lucas; Haskell denoted his "world of eternal adolescence,"[35] while Biskind excoriated the director for "infantilizing the audience, reconstituting the spectator as child, then overwhelming him and her with sound and spectacle, obliterating irony, aesthetic self-consciousness, and critical reflection."[36] Numerous others had already made and have continued to make similar arguments, including Robin Wood, who situated *Star Wars* as part of a "parade of demoralizing 'moral' reactionary movies heralded in the late 1970s,"[37] and Larry Gross, who in *Sight and Sound* laid partial blame at the feet of Lucas for helping introduce a new economic modality that overwhelmed and eventually killed off what remained of the old Hollywood system.[38] As did many, Biskind also read into the original trilogy an allegory of the American imperial project replete with the United States as the Empire, President Nixon as Palpatine, and the Rebels or the Ewoks (or both) as the Vietcong.[39] As the films began to be solidified as cultural phenomena, academics began joining the fray. Not all were from the humanities (e.g., Carl Sagan, one of the first to hold the original film to account for its identity politics). During a 1978 visit to *The Tonight Show*, Sagan noted the predominance of white humans in the text, decrying its "human chauvinism."[40]

Journal articles began to appear in the 1980s, as *Star Wars* became fair game for academic inquiry. Andrew Gordon's "*Star Wars*: A Myth for Our Time," published in *Literature/Film Quarterly* in 1978, was an early outlier.[41] Reception/fan studies and marketing/merchandising became common frameworks for writing about the trilogy. Entire volumes of criticism began to follow with the entry of the *Star Wars* generation into academia, and Peter Krämer and others explored numerous facets of Lucas and his films rather than focusing largely on issues of influence or the changes in the movies during the 1970s.[42] An explosion of such texts occurred during the 2000s, in part because of the rerelease of the trilogy (remastered *Special Editions*) and the prequel films during the late 1990s and early 2000s.

Furthermore, popular-academic presses such as McFarland and Company began publishing such titles with more frequency, attempting to meet the growing demand for texts to be used in popular culture studies. Although McFarland and other presses such as Rowman and Littlefield and John

Wiley and Sons have predominated in this market, universities from both the United States and Great Britain have also published many of these books, as have more mainstream presses such as HarperCollins, Henry Holt, and Palgrave Macmillan. For whatever reason, single-author texts permeated the market first, with edited collections soon following. As in works focused on history, Stephen Miller's *The Seventies Now: Culture as Surveillance* (1999) situates Lucas in 1970s filmmaking but does so through the critical lens of surveillance, a significant area of focus in English departments by the late 1990s.[43] In *Science Fiction Film* (2001), J. P. Telotte positions Lucas within a literary lineage including Mary Shelley, Edgar Allan Poe, Jules Verne, and H. G. Wells, and in cinema George Méliès's *A Trip to the Moon*.[44] Also focused on genealogy, Susan Mackey-Kallis's *The Hero and the Perennial Journey Home in American Film* (2001) suggests a continued critical obsession with Joseph Campbell.[45] A new focus in the arena of influence was typified in Paul McDonald's *The "Star Wars" Heresies: Interpreting the Themes, Symbols and Philosophies of Episodes I, II, and III* (2013), one of many works during this time that reinterpreted the original trilogy on the basis of the prequels. For instance, McDonald recasts Luke throwing down his lightsaber at the end of *Return of the Jedi* as a callback to the violence meted out during Order 66 and Anakin's point-of-no-return killing of the younglings in 2005's *Revenge of the Sith*.[46]

Following the prequels, released during a time of greater sensitivity to depictions of race, gender, and sexuality in cinema, books focused on identity politics became more commonplace. By *Revenge of the Sith* (2005), it was not uncommon to see works focused exclusively on cultural and political topics, such as Kevin J. Wetmore's *The Empire Triumphant: Race, Religion, and Rebellion in the "Star Wars" Films* (2005).[47] Although with a strong focus on colonialism and slavery—introduced in the sublimely titled chapter "Of Fanon and Fanboys"—Wetmore's focus on Asian influences constrains his arguments involving race. Wetmore, incidentally, represents a critic who identifies deeply ingrained problems with the director's racial depictions (and lack thereof), whereas Christopher Deis—whose chapter "May the Force (Not) Be with You: 'Race Critical' Readings and the *Star Wars* Universe" appears in the edited collection *Culture, Identity and Technologies in the "Star Wars" Films: Essays on the Two Trilogies* (2007)[48]—represents one who generally finds such claims to be overstated. In 2009, *Star Wars* was granted a spot in the BFI Classics series, alongside films by directors such as Alfred Hitchcock and John Ford. Among other revelations in Will Booker's analysis is that Chewbacca's iconic sounds were an amalgamation of "cinnamon bear, walrus, seal, and badger," all recorded at the Los Angeles Zoo.[49]

In the mid-2010s, John C. McDowell released two books that explored identity politics in *Star Wars*. The first, *The Politics of Big Fantasy* (2014), included chapters on texts that have captured the zeitgeist of their time, situating *Star Wars* among works such as *The Matrix* and *The Avengers*.[50] The cover of this book features Leia—replete with the side bun hairstyle—posing as Rosie the Riveter. Several years later, McDowell followed up with *Identity Politics in George Lucas' "Star Wars"* (2016), focused exclusively on Lucas. This work seeks to recapture the series from those who see it as a neoconservative text, focusing on violence, gender, patriarchy, and race. For the latter, McDowell concludes that "Lucas presents an environment of human and non-human, white human and colored human co-operation among those not associated with the enforced racial coding of the Imperial system. For the cosmopolitan Jedi Order, the old Republic, the Rebel Alliance, even Jabba's court racial difference does not appear to be an issue that marks out problematic forms of otherness."[51] Such a statement elides the notion that, in choosing largely human characters—and in the original trilogy, largely white human characters—hierarchies and benchmarks of value are established, even when the only overt signs, like statements such as "we don't serve their kind here," are directed not at humanoid beings but instead at droid characters.

Academic Writing: Edited Collections

Edited collections differ significantly from single-author works, unable to cultivate a sustained depth of analysis or unified argument in a single area but benefiting from multiple perspectives across different topics. Such volumes have come a long way since Glenn Kenny's *A Galaxy Not So Far Away: Writers and Artists on Twenty-Five Years of "Star Wars"* (2002),[52] the last twenty years witnessing much work in gender, race, and, especially, LGBTQ+ criticism. By the mid-2000s, edited collections were beginning to feature chapters on the last, joining journal articles that had already begun mapping that terrain. Roger Kaufman's "How the *Star Wars* Saga Evokes the Creative Promise of Homosexual Love: A Gay-Centered Psychological Perspective"—in Matthew Kapell and John Lawrence's *Finding the Force of the "Star Wars" Franchise: Fans, Merchandise, & Critics* (2006)[53]—analyzed examples of male-male social bonding with erotic overtones, troubling easy analysis of a tale usually noted for its heterosexual content. In this same collection, Lincoln Geraghty's contribution on merchandising went beyond the standard arguments by noting the way toy collections and their owners, and most importantly the relationship between the two, evolved with the aging of the collector population.[54]

Although an excellent edited collection, Carl Silvio and Tony Vinci's *Culture, Identity and Technologies in the "Star Wars" Films: Essays on the Two Trilogies* (2007) indicated a growing problem. Now with six films in release—and only nine chapters in this collection—covering any topic in substantial depth was difficult. Douglas Brode and Leah Deyneka solved this problem, releasing two collections in 2012. *Sex, Politics, and Religion in "Star Wars": An Anthology* contains chapters on more standard topics but also includes ones on Emersonian transcendentalism, the Judaic underpinnings of the Jedi, and a highly specific Freudian reading of the anal stage and vaginal fear in *Star Wars* and *THX-1138*. By this point, LGBTQ+ themed contributions were expected, and this collection contained a reexamination, by Ray Merlock and Kathy Merlock Jackson, of Leia as a critical figure in the greater sweep of science fiction and fantasy heroines.[55] The other collection, *Myth, Media, and Culture in "Star Wars": An Anthology*, linked *Star Wars* to more contemporary texts, such as the developing Marvel Cinematic Universe. A chapter by Craig Svonkin on *Star Wars* and Disney was timely; later that year, the latter purchased the former from Lucas.[56]

More collections followed during the next decade, including several of note. Nancy Reagin and Janie Liedl's *Star Wars and History* (2013) constituted a work more singularly focused on politics and history, allowing for a depth of analysis in an oft-ignored area of nontextual genealogy. Topics explored as pertinent to both the original and prequel trilogies included rebellions, civil wars, warrior monks, women freedom fighters, nuclear weapons, slavery, and other historical antecedents. Terrance MacMullan's "'Some Damned-Fool Idealistic Crusade': The Jedi and the Knights Templar" indicated a phenomenon occurring with more frequency: the reinterpretation of information from the original trilogy in light of the prequel films. His chapter is framed by two Obi-Wan quotes from *A New Hope*—the one in the title and "There's no such thing as luck"—but his analysis largely involves the prequels, with the original trilogy appearing only as reinterpreted by the later films.[57] Also, this collection indicated another evolution, one involving the identification of real-world analogues to characters or groups. Arguments from the 1980s and 1990s—for example, the commonplace "the Empire equals British or Nazis" identification—gradually yielded to more specific, sometimes too specific, associations. Although such projects are often reductionist, the parsing of Palpatine and Vader as either Adolf Hitler/Heinrich Himmler (leader of the SS) or Joseph Stalin/Lavrentiy Beria (leader of the NKVD) makes sense.[58] Most of the historical equivalencies throughout the collection were well defended, although perhaps the equation of Qui-Gon Jinn to Abraham Lincoln and Count Dooku to John Calhoun represented a bit of an overreach.[59] Generally, however, this collection is packed with interesting and thought-provoking associations, in part evidence of the migration of criticism involving politics, culture, and history away from generalities.

Similarly, Peter Lee's *A Galaxy Here and Now: Historical and Cultural Readings of "Star Wars"* (2016) represents an edited collection that, although including the standard fare, comes late enough in history that each chapter contains new insights for the critical canon, drawing from but also building on what has gone before. The collection is perhaps a bit light on identity politics, although two chapters focused on race stand out. Paul Charbel offers an interesting study of the "Bedouin Ideal" regarding several cultures on Tatooine, taking his analysis beyond the typical identification of Jawas and Tusken Raiders as tribal groups reminiscent of the Near East.[60] Gregory Rutledge's chapter perceptively explores the way African culture is appropriated in service to the epic genre's resistance motif, disturbingly hijacking aspects of the American civil rights movement to frame the rebellion against the empire.[61]

Popular Audiences

Not all analyses of *Star Wars* have been academically focused. Many works fit into the "coffee-table book" category, generally laudatory and pitched toward a general audience. Although these books rose to prominence in the 2000s, some, such as Thomas G. Smith's *Industrial Light & Magic: The Art of Special Effects* (1986), extend back much further.[62] They are often image heavy, but they also include interviews, features, histories, and even critical analyses. What they lack in depth they make up for in breadth, attracting as wide an audience as possible. Although multiple authors have written more than one such book, Adam Bray, Amy Ratcliffe, Mark Cotta Vaz, and especially J. W. Rinzler have heavily influenced this category. Often, especially for those approved by Lucasfilm, a foreword is included by someone within the *Star Wars*, or at least the filmmaking, community. These contributors have included *Star Wars* sound designer Ben Burtt, actor John Boyega, and directors Brad Bird, Francis Ford Coppola, Ron Howard, Steven Spielberg, and George Lucas himself. Books with no celebrity foreword often include a lead quotation from either George Lucas or Joseph Campbell.

Way too many coffee-table books exist for even a partial historiography; the few noted here are simply included to establish the range of such works. Some, such as Marcus Hearns's *The Cinema of George Lucas* (2005), have focused on early drafts or abandoned storylines, including a cover of "Adventures of the Starkiller"[63] and a scene where Obi-Wan survives and appears on Yavin 4.[64] Replete with photographs, concept sketches, and lots of information about mythology, Mary Henderson's *Star Wars: The Magic of Myth* (1997) was published for the *Star Wars* exhibition at the Smithsonian Institution's National Air and Space Museum.[65] Rinzler's *The Sounds of Star Wars* (2010) explores the auditory dimension of Lucas's universe. This book contains a battery-operated panel that plays 256 sounds as one progresses through the pages; for example, when prompted in the text, the reader can play sound 38 to hear Greedo's taunting of Han Solo and sound 39 for the laser blast that spells doom for the bounty hunter.

Illuminating information is included, such as how some iconic sound effects resulted from limitations faced during filmmaking: "Development of Chewbacca's voice also had to take into account the limitations of the mask worn by actor Peter Mayhew. 'He was restricted to a one-dimensional opening and closing of the mouth,' Burtt says. 'He couldn't shape the lips, so whatever sound I imposed on the face had to be anatomically credible with the movement the viewer saw. Fortunately, the animal sounds were consistent with that. The bear sounds, in particular, were formed in the back of the mouth, without lips or tongue.'"[66]

Pablo Hidalgo's *Star Wars Propaganda: A History of Persuasive Art in the Galaxy* (2016) is more fanciful, consisting of propaganda posters and biographies of the alien artists who produced them. The book never breaks character, including a foreword by Janyor of Bith, who makes the passage from being an imperial apologist to producing propaganda art for the resistance.[67] Examples include a Nazi-inspired reporting poster, with the headline "Report Sedition" and an undercrawl "If you see something, say something" bracketing an image of a human hand shaking a stormtrooper's, with a prisoner being led away in the background. American World War II posters serve as inspirations for several more, including "Loose Lips Bring Down Starships" and a futuristic Rosey the Riveter in the form of Princess Leia with a blaster, with the phrase "We Can Do It!" at the top and "May the force be with you" along the bottom.[68] Tanis Gray's *Knitting the Galaxy: The Official "Star Wars" Knitting Pattern*

Book contains patterns and instructions for how to knit such clothing items as Princess Leia's Hoth snow vest, an Ewok hood, and Lightsaber socks.[69] The fact that a such a book exists suggests something about the depth of the franchise's cultural penetration and the thirst among consumers for ongoing world-building.

Disciplinary Lenses

A final book category emerged in the 2000s and 2010s: a collection of part-popular/semi-academic essays themed around a specific lens, such as psychology, physics, or religion. Much as Rinzler was for the coffee-table book, Kevin S. Decker and Jason T. Eberl have been instrumental figures in this category, producing two different volumes on *Star Wars* and philosophy (as part of the Blackwell series), covering topics such as predestination, stoicism, morality, evil, ethics, slavery, and tyranny and including specific chapters on Aristotle, Hegel, and Heidegger.[70] Their second volume, published after the release of Episode VII, includes chapters arranged under the following headings: "The Philosophical Menace," "Attack of the Morals," "Revenge of the Alliance," "A New Hermeneutic," "Metaphysics Strikes Back," "Return of the Non-human," and "The Fandom Awakens."[71] Not too surprisingly, Travis Langley's *Dark Side of the Mind: "Star Wars" Psychology* (2015) explores the films from a Jungian, rather than Freudian, perspective. Demonstrating how such books can overreach in attempting to generate enough material to sustain an entire collection, the Empire's coercion of Lando at Cloud City is linked to the Stanford Prison Experiment and the destruction of Alderaan to the murder of Kitty Genovese.[72] Although he perhaps reads *Star Wars* as a bit too resonant with Christian heritage, John C. McDowell's *The Gospel according to "Star Wars"* (2007) does not contain the fluff that typifies many books in this category. Perhaps conditioned by his more extensive academic writing on the subject, McDowell successfully demonstrates two arguments: that *Star Wars* is more than just popular, "popcorn" entertainment and that it contains numerous ethical and theological dimensions resonant with both Eastern and Western modalities.[73]

A Rich Historiography

This historiography of literature involving the original trilogy merely provides a basic overview, referencing a very small percentage of a much greater canon of analysis. In general, the development of such criticism over the past forty-five years has indicated an evolution from a focus on influence and the New Hollywood movement of the 1970s to a greater variety of exploratory frameworks, including reception/fan studies, merchandising, and transmedia narratives, the latter finally explored thoroughly in Sean Guynes and Dan Hassler-Forest's edited collection *Star Wars and the History of Transmedia Storytelling* (2017).[74] The focus on identity politics has traveled the road from more general to specific, encompassing new arguments as notions of social justice and equity affect how race, gender, and sexuality are constructed in the films. What societal preoccupations will inform the next generation of *Star Wars* criticism? Disney's continuation of this universe, through new films and television series, has already begun to affect how the original trilogy is viewed. Furthermore, aside from the work of McDowell, not much has been done to explore Lucas's political views as evidenced through his interviews, his films too easy a target for critics in surmising his politics. A problem in Lucas criticism involves his passage, in both the popular and academic imagination, from the counterculture figure of the 1970s to the calculating techno-mogul of later decades. That the prequel trilogy included greater (albeit still problematic) diversity and focused on the rise of a fascist regime troubles easy interpretations of the director's right turn. Hampered by the fact that no biographer has enjoyed comprehensive access since Dale Pollock—whose *Skywalking* was published forty years ago—and by interviews that indicate his political views only in bits and pieces, one is left to wonder about this aspect of his filmmaking. Whatever the next generation of criticism ends up exploring, *Star Wars* will remain relevant, with works such as this edited collection refining old arguments, making new ones, and generally pushing the boundaries of analysis in new directions.

Notes

1. For a previous attempt at a *Star Wars* historiography, see Bruce Isaacs, "A Survey of Popular and Scholarly Receptions of the *Star Wars* Franchise," in *Finding the Force of the "Star Wars" Franchise: Fans, Merchandise, and Critics*, ed. Matthew Wilhelm Kapell and John Shelton Lawrence (New York: Peter Lang, 2006): 265–82. Isaacs restricts his analysis to two typologies—newsprint media and single-author critical works—and selects a few representatives from each. Limiting the focus to fewer works does allow him a depth of analysis, however. Subcategories within the section on newsprint media include "Elite and Influential U.S. Media" (e.g., *New Yorker* and *Village Voice*) and "Popular and Mainstream U.S. Media" (e.g., *Newsweek* and *Rolling Stone*). Subcategories within the section on scholarly analysis include "Cultures and Industries" (impact on

Hollywood and American pop culture), "Politics and Ideology," and "Mythologies." Aside from extending to the present, this chapter covers a larger corpus, not only focusing on newsprint media and single-author scholarly works but also encompassing biographies, purely popular works (e.g., coffee-table books), and edited collections of criticism.

2. "Carrie Fisher, Harrison Ford and Mark Hamill Talk Newfound *Star Wars* Fame," *Today*, December 27, 2016, https://www.today.com/video/carrie-fisher-harrison-ford -and-mark-hamill-talk-newfound-star-wars-fame-42000965510.

3. John Baxter, *Mythmaker: The Life and Work of George Lucas* (New York: Avon, 1999), 230.

4. Vincent Canby, "*Star Wars*: A Trip to a Far Galaxy That's Fun and Funny," *New York Times*, May 26, 1977, https://archive.nytimes.com/www.nytimes.com/books/97/08/24 /reviews/guinness-starwars.html?scp=271&sq=george%2520lucas&st=Search.

5. How much Campbell influenced Lucas, and when exactly that influence developed, has been widely debated by critics. The two did not meet until 1984, after the release of *Return of the Jedi*. An avid reader, Lucas was aware of Campbell and his writings. However, Lucas's designation of the academic as "my Yoda" may have been meant to create a mythology of influence, as during the 1970s Lucas was known to have numerous other inspirations that were not accorded pride of place in the story eventually told.

6. Information on both series can be found at https://billmoyers.com.

7. Roger Ebert, "*Star Wars*," January 1, 1977, https://www.rogerebert.com/reviews /star-wars-1977.

8. Matt Zoller Seitz, "The Art of Entertainment: Richard Schickel, 1933–2017," February 20, 2017, https://www.rogerebert.com/mzs/the-art-of-entertainment-richard -schickel-1931-2017.

9. Baxter, *Mythmaker*, 244.

10. Pauline Kael, "Contrasts," *New Yorker*, September 18, 1977, https://www.newyorker .com/magazine/1977/09/26/contrasts.

11. Baxter, *Mythmaker*, 244.

12. Ryan Gilbey, *It Don't Worry Me: The Revolutionary American Films of the 1970s* (London: Faber and Faber, 2003).

13. Peter Krämer, *The New Hollywood: From "Bonnie and Clyde" to "Star Wars"* (London: Wallflower, 2005).

14. Axel Madsen, *The New Hollywood: American Movies in the '70s* (New York: Thomas Y. Crowell, 1975).

15. Michael Pye and Lynda Myles, *The Movie Brats: How the Film Generation Took Over Hollywood* (New York: Holt, Rinehart and Winston, 1979).

16. Robert Kolker, *A Cinema of Loneliness: Penn, Stone, Kubrick, Scorsese, Spielberg, Altman* (Oxford: Oxford University Press, 2000).

17. Dale Pollock, *Skywalking: The Life and Films of George Lucas* (New York: Harmony, 1983), 3.

18. Ibid., 78.

19. Ibid., 79.

20. Lucas also chafed at this work's foregrounding of his tension with Coppola, perhaps explaining why no subsequent biographer was granted Pollock's access.

21. Brian Jay Jones, *George Lucas: A Life* (New York: Little, Brown, 2017).

22. Pam Pollack and Meg Belviso, *Who Is George Lucas?* (New York: Grosset and Dunlap, 2014).

23. Baxter, *Mythmaker*, 243.

24. Ibid., 245. Baxter's *George Lucas: A Biography* (New York: HarperCollins, 2016) is largely a rerelease of *Mythmaker*.

25. Roger Ebert and Gene Siskel, *The Future of the Movies* (Kansas City: Andrews and McMeel, 1991), 80–82.

26. Sally Kline, ed., *George Lucas: Interviews* (Jackson: Mississippi University Press, 1999), 44.

27. Barry Jenkins, *Empire Building: The Remarkable Real Life Story of Star Wars* (Secaucus, NJ: Citadel, 1997), vii–x.

28. Ibid., 170–71.

29. Howard Maxford, *George Lucas Companion* (London: B. T. Batsford, 1999), 128.

30. Chris Salewicz, *George Lucas* (New York: Thunder's Mouth, 1998), 123, 128, 132.

31. Michael Rubin, *Droidmaker: George Lucas and the Digital Revolution* (Gainesville, FL: Triad, 2006).

32. Michael Kaminski, *The Secret History of "Star Wars": The Art of Storytelling and the Making of a Modern Epic* (Kingston, ON: Legacy, 2008).

33. Chris Taylor, *How "Star Wars" Conquered the Universe: The Past, Present, and Future of a Multibillion Dollar Franchise* (New York: Basic Books, 2014), 171.

34. Ibid., vii.

35. Molly Haskell, *From Reverence to Rape: The Treatment of Women in the Movies* (Chicago: University of Chicago Press, 1973), 377.

36. Peter Biskind, *Easy Riders, Raging Bulls: How the Sex 'n' Drugs 'n' Rock 'n' Roll Generation Saved Hollywood* (London: Bloomsbury, 1998), 343–44.

37. Robin Wood, *Hollywood from Vietnam to Reagan* (New York: Columbia University Press, 1986), 69.

38. Larry Gross, "Big and Loud," *Sight and Sound* 5, no. 8 (August 1995): 7.

39. Biskind, *Easy Riders, Raging Bulls*, 342.

40. Carl Sagan, "Carl Sagan Talks about *Star Wars: A New Hope* Mistakes," YouTube, December 16, 2017, https://www.youtube.com/watch?v=3UsHQEr3A5Q.

41. Andrew Gordon, "*Star Wars*: A Myth for Our Time," *Literature/Film Quarterly* 6, no. 4 (Fall 1978): 314–26.

42. Peter Krämer, "'It's Aimed at Kids—the Kid in Everybody': George Lucas, *Star Wars* and Children's Entertainment," *Scope*, December 2001, https://www.nottingham.ac.uk/scope/documents/2001/december-2001/kramer.pdf.

43. Stephen Paul Miller, *The Seventies Now: Culture as Surveillance* (Durham, NC: Duke University Press, 1999).

44. J. P. Telotte, *Science Fiction Film* (Cambridge: Cambridge University Press, 2001).

45. Susan Mackey-Kallis, *The Hero and the Perennial Journey Home in American Film* (Philadelphia: Pennsylvania University Press, 2001).

46. Paul F. McDonald, *The "Star Wars" Heresies: Interpreting the Themes, Symbols and Philosophies of Episodes I, II, and III* (Jefferson, NC: McFarland, 2013), 130.

47. Kevin J. Wetmore, *The Empire Triumphant: Race, Religion, and Rebellion in the "Star Wars" Films* (Jefferson, NC: McFarland, 2005).

48. Christopher Deis, "May the Force (Not) Be with You: 'Race Critical' Readings and the *Star Wars* Universe," in *Culture, Identity and Technologies in the "Star Wars" Films: Essays on the Two Trilogies*, ed. Carl Silvio and Tony M. Vinci (Jefferson, NC: McFarland, 2007), 77–108.

49. Will Brooker, *Star Wars* (London: Palgrave Macmillan, 2009), 36.

50. John C. McDowell, *The Politics of Big Fantasy* (Jefferson, NC: McFarland, 2014).

51. John C. McDowell, *Identity Politics in George Lucas' "Star Wars"* (Jefferson, NC: McFarland, 2016), 148–49.

52. Glenn Kenny, *A Galaxy Not So Far Away: Writers and Artists on Twenty-Five Years of "Star Wars"* (New York: Henry Holt, 2002).

53. Roger Kaufman, "How the *Star Wars* Saga Evokes the Creative Promise of Homosexual Love: A Gay-Centered Psychological Perspective," in Kapell and Lawrence, *Finding the Force*, 131–58.

54. Lincoln Geraghty, "Aging Toys and Players: Fan Identity and Cultural Capital," in Kapell and Lawrence, *Finding the Force*, 209–26.

55. Ray Merlock and Kathy Merlock Jackson, "Lightsabers, Political Arenas, and Marriages for Princess Leia and Queen Amidala," in *Sex, Politics, and Religion in "Star Wars,"* ed. Douglas Brode and Leah Deyneka (Lanham, MD: Scarecrow, 2012), 77–88.

56. Craig Svonkin, "From Disneyland to Modesto: George Lucas and Walt Disney," in *Myth, Media, and Culture in "Star Wars,"* ed. Douglas Brode and Leah Deyneka (Lanham, MD: Scarecrow, 2012), 21–30.

57. Terrance MacMullan, "Elegant Weapons for Civilized Ages: The Jedi and Warrior-Monks throughout History," in *"Star Wars" and History*, ed. Nancy R. Reagin and Janice Liedl (Hoboken, NJ: John Wiley and Sons, 2013), 67–98.

58. William J. Astore, "Why Rebels Triumph: How 'Insignificant' Rebellions Can Change History," in Reagin and Liedl, *"Star Wars" and History*, 9–40.

59. Paul Horvath and Mark Higbee, "'A House Divided': The Causes and Costs of Civil War," in Reagin and Liedl, *"Star Wars" and History*, 99–122.

60. Paul Charbel, "Deconstructing the Desert: The Bedouin Ideal and the True Children of Tatooine," in *A Galaxy Here and Now: Historical and Cultural Readings of "Star Wars,"* ed. Peter Lee (Jefferson, NC: McFarland, 2016), 138–61. These groups have also been parsed as Indigenous American and Mexican by Gabriel S. Estrada (Nahuatl), "*Star Wars* Episodes I–VI: Coyote and the Force of White Narrative," in *The Persistence of Whiteness: Race and Contemporary Hollywood Cinema*, ed. Daniel Bernardi (London: Routledge, 2007), 69–90.

61. Gregory E. Rutledge, "Jedi Knights and Epic Performance: Is the Force a Form of Western-African Epic Mimicry?," in Lee, *Galaxy Here and Now*, 106–37.

62. Thomas G. Smith, *Industrial Light & Magic: The Art of Special Effects* (New York: Del Rey, 1986).

63. Marcus Hearn, *The Cinema of George Lucas* (New York: Harry N. Abrams, 2005), 84.

64. Ibid., 102.

65. Mary Henderson, *"Star Wars": The Magic of Myth* (New York: Bantom, 1997).

66. J. W. Rinzler, *The Sounds of "Star Wars"* (San Francisco: Chronicle Books, 2010), 75.

67. Pablo Hidalgo, *"Star Wars" Propaganda: A History of Persuasive Art in the Galaxy* (New York: Harper Design, 2016), 8–9.

68. Ibid., 56, 69, 79.

69. Tanis Gray, *"Star Wars": Knitting the Galaxy; The Official "Star Wars" Knitting Pattern Book* (San Rafael, CA: Insight Editions, 2021).

70. Kevin S. Decker and Jason T. Eberl, eds., *"Star Wars" and Philosophy: More Powerful Than You Can Possibly Imagine* (Chicago: Open Court, 2005).

71. Jason T. Eberl and Kevin S. Decker, eds., *The Ultimate "Star Wars" and Philosophy: You Must Unlearn What You Have Learned* (Malden, MA: Wiley Blackwell, 2016).

72. Travis Langley, *Dark Side of the Mind: "Star Wars" Psychology* (New York: Sterling, 2015), 167–71.

73. John C. McDowell, *The Gospel according to "Star Wars": Faith, Hope, and the Force* (Louisville, KY: Westminster John Knox, 2007).

74. Sean Guynes and Dan Hassler-Forest, eds., *"Star Wars" and the History of Transmedia Storytelling* (Amsterdam: Amsterdam University Press, 2017).

7

"Archaeology Is the Search for Fact . . . Not Truth"

How George Lucas and Indiana Jones Redefined Our
Relationship with the Past

JANICE LIEDL

A mysterious lost city was associated with legends of cryptically inscribed monuments and a few artifacts linked to stories of occult magic, all guarded by gigantic crystals. This lore obsessed an explorer who had spent his life traveling the globe in pursuit of rare artifacts and mystical wisdom. Frustrated by the ill-timed outbreak of a world war, he shelved plans to uncover the site and its treasures, which he believed had mysterious powers. Finally, years later, armed with the support of respected professional groups, including the National Geographic Society, and with tantalizing archival details and local corroboration, the explorer set out. Weeks and months passed, but no one returned from this great quest, least of all the man at the center of it all: British surveyor and explorer Percy Fawcett, presumed dead in an ill-fated expedition to discover the Lost City of Z in 1925.[1]

In the century since, many others have attempted to uncover what became of Fawcett and his obsession with a lost city that hid secrets of occult wisdom. Most archaeologists now believe the legendary city to have been invented in an eighteenth-century misinterpretation of eroded limestone ridges underlying South American forests. The artifacts that so enticed Fawcett are thought by most researchers to be nothing but forgeries. However, Percy Fawcett's legacy was more than a debunked city. News of his first expedition helped inspire Arthur Conan Doyle's tale of an intrepid biologist set on uncovering an isolated habitat where dinosaurs still roamed, as chronicled in *The Lost World* (1913).

Its surly academic hero, Professor Challenger, was brought to the screen in several film and television adaptations, including one released in 1960, when a teenage George Lucas was already deeply engaged in film culture even if he had yet to begin his own filmmaking journey.

One could argue that the explorer, Percy Fawcett, and his fictional counterpart, Professor Challenger, inspired the swashbuckling heroics of Indiana Jones, who first appeared on the screen in 1981 in a collaboration between Lucas and Steven Spielberg. However, the character and his context are so much more than this. Through his appearance not only in films but in television, comics, video games, and other media creations, the character of Dr. Henry Walton Jones Jr. defines archaeology and adventure for many. He is less an update of a specific hero than a testament to the way Lucas interwove methods and myths—drawing on his interests in anthropology, archaeology, and storytelling—in his contribution to this key character.

Inspirational possibilities are endless if we look. Howard Carter's discovery of Tutankhamun's tomb rocked the world in 1922, and ten years later came Karl Freund's *The Mummy*, in which archaeology enabled a powerful ancient to meddle with the present.[2] Charlton Heston's adventurer, Harry Steele, comes into bloody conflict with an obsessed archaeologist when they both seek *The Secret of the Incas* (1954). Compare this thrilling tale to the more staid but equally celebrated real-life adventures that occurred in the early twentieth-century expeditions of Hiram Bingham III, future US senator, to uncover the lost Incan city of Machu Picchu.[3] Lucas himself directly referenced classic serials and comic books such as the peripatetic Nazi fighter *Don Winslow of the Navy* when he started developing his character concept in the early 1970s.[4] However, Indiana Jones's adventures were not just a way to draw on the energy of pulp fiction and the power of mythology. They also tied into the twentieth-century emergence of archaeology as a scholarly discipline.

Although no (?) sense of a methodical archaeological fieldwork appears in the films' depictions, Indiana Jones in the classroom and in his conversation with others demonstrates a profound understanding of the stories and mythologies that often become vital clues in his search for artifacts. Lucas harnessed the power of mythology to create characters and even storyworlds in other works, most particularly *Star Wars*.[5] *Raiders of the Lost Ark* (1981) may have shown Indiana Jones inhabiting two contrasting personae of swashbuckling adventurer and harried professor, but what truly defines his character is his deep understanding and reliance on the truths revealed in other ways, particularly through his use of intuition and legend. This combination allowed

George Lucas and Steven Spielberg's influential archaeological hero Indiana Jones, played by Harrison Ford. (© Paramount/courtesy Everett Collection)

Jones to understand meaningful truths about his discoveries that his ruthless rivals overlooked to their doom.

In a 2015 interview, Lucas explained that *"Indiana Jones* was just done for fun to entertain people. And there were some messages in there about archaeology and also what we believe in terms of myths and that sort of thing."[6] It is that combination of entertainment and mythology, particularly regarding how the search for the past can help unlock important knowledge, that defines Indiana Jones. The character, in turn, now defines archaeology in popular culture, so much so that he inspired a National Geographic exhibition in 2015 highlighting his character's impact on the field.[7] The influence of the films did more than create a hero; it drew attention to a discipline and shaped the popular image of archaeology for generations to come.

Indiana Jones as a character, and the linchpin for his multimedia legacy, cannot ever be separated from his cocreator. It was Lucas who shared the concept of this hero in conversations with Spielberg during the spring of 1977. Countering Spielberg's interest in taking on the action-adventure character of James Bond, Lucas offered something different: a hero with the same verve and energy who lived in a world that juxtaposed the mundane realities of academic duty with a sideline of archaeological discovery that occasionally unleashed the supernatural power of legendary artifacts.[8] In films set as early as 1935, along with other media stretching his life forward and backward, we see in Indiana Jones the broad twentieth century of world events and archaeological practice united in a fiction of powerful, dangerous artifacts waiting to be discovered.

Lucas grew up in a postwar California suburbia where his high school and college education introduced him to key insights about societies, myths, and cultures; his film studies added even more to this mix. We get glimpses of the first in his own words and hands, as with a community college paper he wrote for a geography class that detailed the social implications of modified nomadic cultures in North Africa. There, the young Lucas explained how modes of living depended on a complex intermix of environmental and social factors in which cultivation was an important but not always viable option.[9] Lucas had enrolled at Modesto Junior College to study the subjects that mattered to him: sociology, psychology, and anthropology. After obtaining his associate's degree in 1964, Lucas seemed poised to study anthropology further in San Francisco before he turned to nurture his growing passion for film and cinematography at USC.[10] Even though Lucas went no further in the study of anthropology, those years left their mark on his worldview and his creation of Indiana Jones. That archaeologist character represents something of the ideas of anthropology and archaeology, interconnected disciplines throughout this period, which transformed dramatically in the decades leading up to Lucas's undergraduate exposure. Indiana Jones's life also owes a great deal to the sensational stories of archaeological discoveries that dominated the news of the day, from the tomb of Tutankhamun to the treasures of Ur.

Well into the early twentieth century, archaeology was the preserve of well-heeled amateurs or those who could excite the support of groups and individuals willing to underwrite the costs of epic explorations and hopeful excavations. In the 1870s, Heinrich Schliemann destroyed a great part of the ancient city of Troy even as he uncovered some of its secrets. His single-minded pursuit ran counter to new systematic and scientific methods that combined measured excavation with precise description. As Gordon Willey and Jeremy Sabloff note, "The old mold of sheerly speculative thought about the antiquities of the past was broken. Carefully recorded description and classification of the phenomena of the past had begun."[11] By the 1890s, the decade in which Indiana Jones would be born in Princeton, New Jersey, according to the expanded mythos of the franchise, American museums and universities teased out a specialization in archaeology in close alliance with the fields of anthropology and ethnology. Much of this American work focused on the settlements and stories of the Americas. Meanwhile, in Europe, the disciplines had little overlap, and their archaeologists explored the globe. With a Scottish medievalist father, Indiana Jones's upbringing crossed the Atlantic and could draw upon both traditions.

Indy's early international opportunities mirrored the hopes of professional American archaeologists. The Archaeological Institute of America had been founded in 1879 to support the study of the Americas as well as open opportunities for American archaeologists internationally. By the year 1899, this included field schools in Rome, Athens, and Jerusalem.[12] Prominent US archaeologists, such as Frederick Starr, who established the University of Chicago's programs in anthropology and archaeology, defined new methods that became field standards. The Chicago method, as it was known, demanded careful surveying and plotting of a site so that any artifacts discovered could then be precisely placed in context.[13] After World War I, American archaeologists were poised to become the leading forces in the discipline, but they would need to further advance the discipline in theory and practice to make this a reality.

Indiana Jones's own early interest in archaeology, framed in the life and work of his teachers and mentors, relates to further developments of archaeological practice in the first decades of the twentieth century. Abner Ravenwood, Jones's first mentor as well as Marion's father, guided Jones in his early undergraduate studies as a faculty member at the University of Chicago. Many other universities were offering coursework as well as fieldwork options in archaeology, but Chicago was becoming one of the leaders in the field. In 1919, the Oriental Institute opened at the University of Chicago to support work in a dizzying array of subjects dealing with the Middle East. By 1934, it was running excavations in Egypt, Iraq, Palestine, Persia, Syria, and Turkey. The United States Geological Survey was another institution that drew on archaeological expertise as they mapped the nation, present and past. Museums also employed archaeologists to both augment and explain their collections. The renowned University of Pennsylvania Museum was supporting more than a dozen different expeditions around the globe, but even with qualified researchers, resources, and time, they struggled to grab a piece of the archaeological pie, in no small part because many of these expeditions were as focused on spiriting out artifacts for their sponsors as they were on carefully uncovering the secrets of the past.[14]

Marcus Brody, Jones's friend, shows the darker side of this museum-sponsored archaeology with his frequent commissioning of Jones to bring back this or that rare artifact. It is Brody who helps the US government connect with Jones about their search for the Ark of the Covenant in *Raiders of the Lost Ark* (1981). Brody also accepts another recovered artifact, the Cross of Coronado, from his friend in 1938 and then joins forces with him to find the senior Dr. Jones, a medievalist who has gone missing while searching for the Holy Grail in *Indiana Jones and the Last Crusade* (1989). In all of these cases, though, Indiana Jones is far from the only seeker of treasure and knowledge. In fact, he is often in direct competition with less-idealistic archaeologists such as René Belloq, a bitter rival who takes the fertility idol of Pachamama that his American counterpart has retrieved at great personal risk in the opening sequence of *Raiders of the Lost Ark* (1981). Belloq's acquisition, unlike the artifacts that Indiana Jones passes to Brody, heads not to a museum but to a black market of secretive deals. A rescued antiquity, in the words of Jones himself, "belongs in a museum," even if he sometimes chose the exact opposite end, as when he returns the one surviving sacred stone to the villagers in *Indiana Jones and the Temple of Doom* (1984) rather than allowing it to "[collect] dust" in a museum. Such institutions may have been important, if problematic, for archaeologists. They were also only a small part of how the story of archaeology was reaching the public.

Headlines and news reels of the 1920s, 1930s, and 1940s trumpeted high-profile archaeological discoveries, some of which were still very much outside academic formalities. The most notable of these has to be Howard Carter's 1920s expedition that uncovered Tutankhamun's tomb. Carter had no formal archaeological training but had worked as an artist recording ancient Egyptian monuments and from that moved on to briefly serve as the first chief inspector of antiquities in Upper Egypt. Carter lost this plum position, and it wasn't until 1909 when he won the patronage of George Herbert, fifth Earl of Carnarvon, that his fortunes changed substantially. With Carnarvon's support, they won the right to excavate in the Valley of the Kings near Thebes, presumed to be thoroughly emptied and thus of no interest to the better-connected teams. Carter's dogged work paid off in 1922 when he discovered hidden stairs to a heretofore unexplored tomb. Early in 1923, the tomb was opened, revealing funerary riches and the royal mummy of Tutankhamun, a ruler of the New Kingdom era.[15]

These spectacular discoveries fueled a media phenomenon. Archaeological texts—whether penny pamphlets on biblical archaeology put out by religious societies or elegant, prestige editions on ancient languages, artifacts, and architecture—had long been popular with the reading public. Now, old works were hastily reissued with new materials touching on the boy pharaoh. Egyptologist, stage designer, and journalist Arthur Weigall sold more than 1,500 copies of his *Glory of the Pharaohs* before it even reached the bookshops. Another of his volumes, focused on Tutankhamun alone, advised readers that from here on, archaeologists "will have to labour under the eyes of an ever increasing public who will follow him into those regions, and will continuously demand to know what he has found."[16] The periodical press similarly capitalized on the discoveries and achievements of Howard Carter. But his patron's death a few weeks after the tomb was opened fueled more hysterical reporting of a mummy's curse, which overshadowed Carter's carefully orchestrated excavation as well as his own detailed reporting of the find, which was only fully completed in 1932.[17]

Tutankhamun's grave goods, gleaming gold and richly decorated, became a benchmark by which all future archaeological excavations were judged in the popular press. But in the archaeological world, the careful mastery of excavation techniques and robust reporting were what gained admiration. We see this in the career of Leonard Woolley, who had served as assistant to first Arthur Evans and then T. E. Lawrence before gaining the reputation to carry out his own excavations. Even then, Woolley required the deep pockets of an American institution, the University of Pennsylvania Museum, along with his sponsors at the British Museum, to fund a joint exploration of ancient Ur. For twelve seasons from 1922 to 1932, his team excavated and documented the site, showing occupation from the Paleolithic era into the Hellenistic age, over four millennia. Again, Woolley's most reported achievement was his discovery of beautiful, gold artifacts in what were described as the royal tombs of Ur, even if archaeologists might consider his greatest legacy to have been his detailed and timely published reports.[18] This enormous undertaking at Ur also ties into the maturing trends of what Willey and Sabloff termed "the Classificatory-Historical Period" of American archaeology, where professionals sharing detailed observations about stratigraphy, settlement practices, and such, all in pursuit of broader insights about past cultures, were eclipsing the role of enthusiastic but possibly destructive amateurs.[19]

Woolley's Ur excavations had just wrapped up by the time Indiana Jones was on the move in his own big-screen storylines set from 1935, with *Indiana Jones and the Temple of Doom* (1984). In contrast to the staid and methodical approaches carried out under the watchful eyes of museum authorities, the film opens with Jones trading artifacts with a gangster boss in Shanghai. Jones's shady reputation as an archaeologist also comes up in a confrontation at the maharaja's palace. Whatever else the hero is, in 1935 he is clearly operating far outside the expected norms of respectable scholarship. Yet Indiana Jones's knowledge (and occasionally forced pursuit) of legendary artifacts possessed of occult power was not entirely disconnected from the other archaeological activities of the 1930s. The Nazi antagonists of *Raiders of the Lost Ark* (1981) and *Indiana Jones and the Last Crusade* (1989) both seek the Ark of the Covenant and the Holy Grail, two artifacts tied into the long history of Judaism and Christianity. For Jones, this was an important artifact. For the Nazis, it was a source of cultural prestige and possibly an item of supernatural power. This kind of occult interest had been a driving force in the actual Nazi creation of the SS-Ahnenerbe (Ancestor Heritage Society), which Heinrich Himmler commanded to search out antiquities such as the Ark, the Grail, and the Holy Lance or Spear of Destiny (which gained mystical powers after it had pierced Christ on the cross) in the 1930s. Lucas and Spielberg knew about both the Nazi obsession with these artifacts and their occult powers. This information helped to shape Indiana Jones's on-screen activities, which sometimes bore only the slenderest of ties to his claimed profession.[20]

Oftentimes, interest in archaeological sites and artifacts linked to legend, such as the Lost City of Z or the Ark of the Covenant, gets categorized and dismissed as the work of pseudoarchaeology, condemned as the dangerous, anti-science opponent of true archaeology. But what was once respectable scholarship (such as claims of racial classifications that supported white supremacy) was now being debunked as the profession of archaeology tossed out many long-held assumptions.[21] Dismissing unsupported claims and privileging scientific justification became increasingly important to professional archaeology during the years in which Indiana Jones would have operated. The early 1940s saw the spread of a new approach within archaeology: functionalism. This concentrated on both recognizing a wide array of artifacts that were shaped by humans and explaining how all the components on a site helped to reveal the broader context of social and cultural activities. Trained at the University of Chicago at this time, John W. Bennett, through his publications and scholarly leadership, helped to articulate this shift in practice over successive generations, building to "the New Archaeology" that defined the field into the 1960s. This objective dream was later challenged by postprocessual or interpretative archaeology, as epitomized in the work of McGill University's Bruce G. Trigger, which denied that objective conclusions were ever achievable, no matter how exactingly employed were the archaeological techniques.[22]

After World War II, the practice of archaeology expanded not only with new approaches but with researchers from across the globe—some even Soviets. In the new Cold War era, ideological differences popped up everywhere. In the Soviet bloc, doctrinaire Marxism made its way into everything from national politics to academic archaeological boilerplate.[23] Meanwhile, the Red Scare in the United States targeted suspected communists, especially in the worlds of media and academia. *Indiana Jones and the Kingdom of the Crystal Skull* (2008), set in 1957, draws on this context not only with Indiana Jones, who was briefly denounced as a communist sympathizer, but even more so with his chief antagonist, Dr. Irina Spalko, a Soviet scientist obsessed with particular occult artifacts.

However, Spalko was not a fellow archaeologist: she was a psychic researcher who pursued the secrets of Akator or El Dorado only to unlock the mystical powers of telepathy and otherworldly knowledge that the skulls promised. Her hunt, first for the artifact and then for the lost city, was to harness these psychic powers for her personal and her state's benefit. It is only Indiana Jones and his friend, Harold Oxley, who can be said to represent any connection to the academic world of archaeology. Both had studied at the University of Chicago, but Oxley had focused his career largely on the legend of El Dorado, which brought him first to the crystal skull and then to Spalko's interest. We learn that Jones, aside from wartime service with the Office of Strategic Services, has carried on in academia, now as a "tenured professor of archaeology." By the film's end, he has been promoted (or punished) with the position of associate dean: a position of sober leadership in the institution.

By the early 1970s, not only had Lucas been exposed to some of this academic world of archaeology at college but he also knew that the mythologies of archaeology were making their way into popular culture through his own eclectic studies of film and mythology. The year 1968 saw an international popular culture phenomenon rock ideas of archaeology with the work of Erich von Däniken's *Chariots of the Gods: Unsolved Mysteries of the Past*. His writing claimed that many ancient sites and technologies weren't developed by humans but were received as gifts from visiting interplanetary aliens.[24] These themes were eventually interwoven into the *Indiana Jones* franchise. In 1973, another popular paperback, *The Crystal Skull*, reported on the Mitchell-Hedges skull, an artifact purportedly used to will death on others and imbued with unnatural powers, which was claimed to have been uncovered by a British adventurer in the 1920s.[25] A year before, in 1972, Trevor Ravenscroft released a pulp, *The Spear of Destiny*, explaining the power of the Holy Lance and something of how it had been sought by the Nazis.[26] While *Indiana Jones and the Last Crusade* (1989) pursued the Holy Grail and not this other early Christian relic, the parallels between this story and the film's remain obvious. It is even thought that Lucas and Spielberg drew the Ravenwood surname of Indiana Jones's mentor from the author's name.[27] Whether drawing upon medieval mythologies or ancient belief, Indiana Jones's adventures leaned heavily into these fabulist, occult accounts.

News reports on the films noted that the lead not only drew on decades-old movie tropes but also connected to ideas of adventure and travel through the lens of archaeology. Vincent Canby's *New York Times* review of *Raiders of the Lost Ark* (1981) acknowledged the film's clear debt to the movie serials as well as Lucas's interest in myths and folktales, but filtered through a more real-world prospect in the down-to-earth archaeology professor hero.[28] In the *Chicago Tribune*, reporters even offered up a breakdown of how *Raiders of the Lost Ark* drew on the real sites and archaeology of the Nile delta in the film's central storyline.[29] But it was the mystical elements that seemed to be particularly revealing of Lucas's involvement. In his extended discussion of the third film, the *New York Times*' critic observed that Lucas's storytelling interest in the mythic and fabulous still powerfully shaped Indiana Jones's dual life as archaeologist and adventurer.[30]

The films, television, comics, and beyond cemented a new image of archaeology in popular culture. Indiana Jones could be evoked with little more than a dusty fedora, a bullwhip, and a taste for adventure. However, he showed very little engagement with the conventional tools of the discipline. Nevertheless, Meghan Strong showed you could discern an "Indiana Jones Effect" in which his image came to typify archaeology to people both inside and outside the field. This effect was seized upon by other creators of shows trafficking in archaeological topics. They sometime even presented psychologists or religious advocates in the trappings of Indiana Jones to evoke "authentic" archaeology.[31]

Given this hijacking of expertise and academic expectations, some in the field have serious reservations about the impact of Indiana Jones on archaeology. K. Anne Pyburn warned that some archaeologists are tempted to exaggerate the extent or value of what they have uncovered in order to appeal to the media. She worried that the careful preservation focus of community-engaged archaeology disappears behind a depiction that is heavy on treasure-hunting thrill seeking.[32] But even as some decried particular archaeological failings in these depictions, the discipline has largely capitalized on Indiana Jones. His portrayal has been seized upon by many archaeologists as an opportunity. Harrison Ford was elected to the board of the Archaeological Institute of America and also received a prize for positive contributions to the discipline through his portrayal of Indiana Jones.[33]

Some archaeologists celebrate the character as embodying important elements of the field. In 1992, Jean-Pierre Allard suggested that academic archaeology and the films were both compelling fictions pulling together clues about the past. Drawing on Bruce Trigger's call for a holistic archaeology, Allard felt that Indiana Jones embodied some important ideas, recognizing that archaeologists are always telling stories about their discoveries—stories they hope to prove true.[34] Indiana Jones articulates an uncomfortable relation between the pursuit of truth—meaningful insights that drive philosophers and believers—and the pursuit of facts, which can be precisely measured, studied, and managed. Early in *Indiana Jones and the Last Crusade* (1989), he explains that to his class as he intones, "Archaeology is the search for fact . . . not truth." In *Raiders of the Lost Ark* (1981), Jones decries the hocus-pocus surrounding stories of the Ark of the Covenant. But he also knows these legends well, whether from learning them as bedtime stories at his father's side or from searching out tales of artifacts yet to be uncovered. Ryan Staude explains that it is Indiana Jones's synthesis of hardheaded historical insight learned in the library along with hard-won personal wisdom coming from the heart that allows him to formulate the most meaningful truth that guides him to correctly identify the Holy Grail and, ultimately, to release it in favor of life. These connections are what embody his true ethos as an archaeologist and a human.[35] Add to that Indiana Jones's intersection with the enduring popular interest in archaeology as a pathway to ancient treasures, possibly imbued with occult powers, and you have, as Lucas already knew in the 1970s, a compelling archetype that still defines the field.

Notes

1. Anita McConnell, "Fawcett, Percy Harrison (b. 1867, d. in or after 1925), Soldier and Explorer," in *The Oxford Dictionary of National Biography*, ed. H. G. C. Matthew and Brian Harrison (Oxford: Oxford University Press, 2004), 19:182–84.

2. Mark Hall, "Romancing the Stones: Archaeology in Popular Cinema," *European Journal of Archaeology* 7, no. 2 (2004): 161.

3. William E. Kelly, "Bingham, Hiram (1875–1956)," in *Encyclopedia of Anthropology*, ed. H. James Birx (Thousand Oaks, CA: Sage, 2006), 356.

4. J. W. Rinzler, *The Complete Making of Indiana Jones: The Definitive Story behind All Four Films* (New York: Del Rey, 2008), 16–17.

5. See Dale Pollock, *Skywalking: The Life and Films of George Lucas* (London: Elm Tree Books, 1983); Pamela Mason Wagner, dir., *The Mythology of "Star Wars": With George Lucas and Bill Moyers* (1987; Princeton, NJ: Films for the Humanities and Sciences, 2004), DVD.

6. Charlie Rose, *Conversations with George Lucas*, aired December 25, 2015, in broadcast syndication, PBS.

7. Jeremy Berlin, "How Indiana Jones Actually Changed Archaeology," *National Geographic*, May 14, 2015.

8. Ryan Staude, "'You Call This Archaeology?': *Indiana Jones* and Hollywood's View on the Nature of History," in *Excavating "Indiana Jones": Essays on the Films and Franchise*, ed. Randy Laist (Jefferson, NC: McFarland, 2020), 38–47.

9. Images of Lucas's handwritten college paper in economic geography, authenticated by one of his staff at the time they first circulated in 2005, was provided to this author by Richard Ravalli.

10. For more on Lucas's youth and education, see the first two chapters in Brian Jay Jones, *George Lucas: A Life* (New York: Little, Brown, 2017).

11. Gordon R. Willey and Jeremy A. Sabloff, *A History of American Archaeology*, 3rd ed. (New York: W. H. Freeman, 1993), 86.

12. Andrew W. Bell, "Situating Indy: American Archaeologists, Global Ambitions and the Interwar Years," in Laist, *Excavating "Indiana Jones,"* 15.

13. The method owed as much, if not more, to precedents set out of the Peabody Museum, as explained by David Browman, "The Origin of the 'Chicago Method' Excavation Techniques: Contributions of William Nickerson and Frederick Starr," *Bulletin of the History of Archaeology* 23, no. 2 (September 17, 2013): art. 4, 3.

14. Bell, "Situating Indy," 17–18.

15. For the life of Carter, see T. G. H. James, "Carter, Howard (1874–1939), Artist and Archaeologist," in Matthew and Harrison, *Oxford Dictionary of National Biography*, 10:352–53.

16. Amara Thornton, *Archaeologists in Print: Publishing for the People* (London: UCL Press, 2018), 9–11, 120–22.

17. The illustrated London *Sphere* devoted an entire issue on February 24, 1923. This was followed up by another article about "The Strange Death of Lord Carnarvon" on April 14, 1923. For some of the more lurid reporting in American papers, see Bell, "Situating Indy," 16.

18. Christopher Edens, "Woolley, Sir (Charles) Leonard (1880–1960), Archaeologist," in Matthew and Harrison, *Oxford Dictionary of National Biography*, 60:275–77. One example of the contemporary reporting can be found in "Treasures of Mesopotamia," *Sphere*, September 7, 1929, 21.

19. Willey and Sabloff, *History of American Archaeology*, 147–48.

20. Both the historical and cinematic inspirations are discussed in Hall, "Romancing the Stones," 165; as well as in Bettina Arnold, "Pseudoarchaeology and Nationalism: Essentializing Difference," in *Archaeological Fantasies: How Pseudoarchaeology Misrepresents the Past and Misleads the Public*, ed. Garrett G. Fagan (London: Routledge, 2006), 158–60.

21. Robin Derricourt, "Pseudoarchaeology: The Concept and Its Limitations," *Antiquity* 86, no. 332 (June 1, 2012): 524–32.

22. Willey and Sabloff, *History of American Archaeology*, 158–59, 242–53, 298–301.

23. Jan Turek, "Archaeo-Propaganda: The History of Political Engagement in Archaeology in Central Europe," *Archaeologies* 14, no. 1 (April 1, 2018): 154–56.

24. Erich von Däniken, *Chariots of the Gods: Unsolved Mysteries of the Past* (New York: Bantam Books, 1968).

25. Richard M. Garvin, *The Crystal Skull: The Story of the Mystery, Myth and Magic of the Mitchell-Hedges Crystal Skull Discovered in a Lost Mayan City during a Search for Atlantis* (Garden City, NY: Doubleday, 1973).

26. Trevor Ravenscroft, *The Spear of Destiny* (London: Neville Spearman, 1972).

27. Siobhan Lyons, "Indiana Jones and the Crusade for Authenticity," in Laist, *Excavating "Indiana Jones,"* 109.

28. Vincent Canby, "Film Review: *Raiders of the Lost Ark,* Breakneck Pace," *New York Times*, June 12, 1981.

29. Jim, and Shirley Higgins, "Movie Fan's Guide: 'Raiders' Focuses on Archeological Site in Egypt Delta," *Chicago Tribune*, July 19, 1981.

30. Vincent Canby, "Film View: Spielberg's Elixir Shows Signs of Mature Magic," *New York Times*, June 18, 1989.

31. Meghan Strong, "The Indiana Jones Effect" (bachelor's thesis, Lycoming College, Williamsport, PA, 2007), 11–14.

32. K. Anne Pyburn, "Public Archaeology, Indiana Jones, and Honesty," *Archaeologies* 4, no. 2 (August 1, 2008): 201–203.

33. Peter Hiscock, "Cinema, Supernatural Archaeology, and the Hidden Human Past," *Numen* 59, no. 2/3 (2012): 158–59.

34. Jean-Pierre Allard, "Who's Afraid of Indiana Jones? A Search for Fictional Truth in Historical Narrative," *Manitoba Archaeological Journal* 2, no. 1 (1992): 45–46.

35. Staude, "'You Call This Archaeology?,'" 44–46.

8

From Sass to Seduction

The Ambiguously Tough Ladies of
Star Wars *and* Indiana Jones

VALERIE ESTELLE FRANKEL

George Lucas's action women are beloved, though on a closer examination, they get rather sexist treatment. All the heroines have moments as the object of male gaze—especially when they have the inevitable beautiful dress walk-on. Their origin in the highly gender-conventional pulp adventures, with fighting heroes and captured damsels, appears over and over. They are also the only women on their male teams, and they all fall in love—suggesting that the woman's only purpose on the male adventure is to give the hero some romance. Often, she is fought over by two of the men, emphasizing her status as a prize. While *Indiana Jones and the Last Crusade*'s Elsa and *Star Wars*' Princess Leia are powerful professionals, with *Raiders of the Lost Ark*'s Marion tough and holding her own, the women also suffer from an era in which feminism was subsiding into postfeminism, and both trilogy arcs take their heroines from strength to objectification.

Leia the Snarky Princess

Before the release of *Star Wars* in 1977, science fiction had few women and fewer strong ones. As Eliana Dockterman writes, "Without Carrie Fisher's Leia, there may have never been a Xena, an Elsa, or a Daenerys Targaryen. Luckily none of those princesses—or the many to come—have had to wait for a man to come along to save them. They know they can save themselves."[1] Of course, fans adored tough, sassy, blaster-wielding Leia. Many heroines followed in her tradition. Two years later, Ellen Ripley battled through a starship in the *Alien* series, guns blazing. In 1984's *The Terminator*, Sarah Connor joined her.

Selflessly captured so she can send away the Death Star plans, Leia is undaunted. She addresses the monstrous Vader coolly with, "Lord Vader, I should have known. Only you could be so bold. The Imperial Senate will not sit for this, when they hear you've attacked a diplomatic . . ." Even disarmed, she invokes the rule of law to stop Vader. However, the Senate has been dissolved, and she is alone. Next comes a torture scene, though one left off camera, presumably for audience sensibility.

After this, Leia is still sassy and rude, greeting Tarkin with, "I recognized your foul stench when I was brought on board." When she hears she's to be executed, she doesn't back down but retorts, "I'm surprised you had the courage to take the responsibility yourself!"[2] Even as they threaten her beloved home world, she doesn't capitulate but gives up a useless planet. Here, Leia successfully tricks both representatives of the patriarchy. "Because *Star Wars* white women master neither technology nor the Force, they resort to passive resistance against dark masculinity," critic Gabriel S. Estrada explains.[3] However, they cruelly destroy her planet as she screams helplessly. All her power is lost.

Leia then vanishes from the story until the male characters engage in over an hour of adventures and then rescue her. Only her entrancing recording is there to plead for her. This beautiful image, sent to inspire the men, is a clear example of the male gaze. Laura Mulvey, author of the groundbreaking essay "Visual and Other Pleasures," criticizes filmmakers for objectifying women. As she explains, "In a world ordered by sexual imbalance, pleasure in looking has been split between active/male and passive/female. . . . In their traditional exhibitionist role women are simultaneously looked at and displayed, with their appearance coded for strong visual and erotic impact so that they can be said to connote to-be-looked-at-ness."[4] This can be achieved by camera angle, male characters' admiration, costume choices, and dialogue that encourages the audience to look. Luke is indeed spellbound by the princess's appearance.

Moreover, Carrie Fisher described her "no-underwear-in-space look," especially when soaked from the trash compactor.[5] She was given a prim, concealing gown and hairstyle that was iconic rather than glamorous—Fisher recalled "a long white virginal robe with the hair of a seventeenth-century Dutch school matron."[6] Still, there was plenty of emphasis on her looks. Fisher added, "I had so much lip gloss on you might have slid off and broken your own lips if you tried to kiss me."[7] She also was told to lose ten pounds.[8]

As John Paul Pianka observes, "At its core, the first *Star Wars* film is a classic tale about a hero rescuing a princess from an evildoer's 'castle.' In that sense, the film immediately portrays women on a lower plane than men; they require rescuing since they cannot rescue themselves."[9] Luke charges in and stares again. Still, Leia does manage to subvert the moment by snarking, not only sizing up Luke skeptically but objectifying *him* with her famous line "Aren't you a little short for a stormtrooper?"

"This is some rescue. When you came in here, didn't you have a plan for getting out?" she demands of the team. Firmly, she insists she's giving the orders. When Han blusters that he only takes orders from himself, she snaps, "It's a wonder you're still alive."

"Wonderful girl! Either I'm going to kill her or I'm beginning to like her," Han bursts. As such, he's embodying 1970s men's mingled admiration and confusion at the new kind of heroine. "Princess Leia breaks barriers for white women by acting as a spy, a tactical leader, and a gun-wielding Rebel as she consistently defies Han Solo's misogynistic comments," Estrada adds.[10] Down they go into the garbage chute. "Clinging to cleanliness and avoiding filth and whatever loathsome monsters reside in it may be stereotypical feminine mandates but are of less concern to Leia than escaping and getting the operations plans for the Death Star to her allies," Ray Merlock and Kathy Merlock Jackson observe in their essay on Leia.[11] After this, Han disgustedly complains, "If we can just avoid any more female advice, we ought to be able to get out of here." Leia ignores this caveman attitude.

However, even as Leia takes charge and shoots off insults, Luke is the one swinging them to safety and mastering the Force to save the day. In fact, while fighting his space battle, he strands Leia on a planet in even greater jeopardy. They are the heroes, and she is the damsel—and then the prize as she dons a lovely gown and awards them their medals.

Loving the Scruffy Rogue

As the opening crawl of *The Empire Strikes Back* reveals, the freedom fighters have been "led by Luke Skywalker," a commander now. Leia, however, has no military rank. She also stays indoors while Han heroically rescues Luke. After, she kisses Luke to get back at Han, an immature act that fans the flames of their love triangle.

Leia's military snowsuit and wrapped braid are tough and practical. Even as she directs the base evacuation, Han must rescue her and haul her away.

On the ship, their plot is sweetly romantic amid insults and squabbling. Nonetheless, Han is a caveman who corners her and insists, "You could *use* a good kiss." He plants one, and she swoons in the tough man's arms. This is classic but hardly empowering. As Pianka writes, "The implications of this scene are incredibly disturbing. For one, it teaches men that intimidation is a viable way into a woman's heart. For another, it teaches women that men who act this way must truly be in love with them, and that this love justifies borderline violent behavior."[12]

No longer fearless around disgusting things, Leia is horrified by the cave creatures, the Mynocks, so Han volunteers to get rid of them. On board, Han makes the heroic plans, not bothering to share them, while Leia protests and complains unproductively.

On Bespin, swaggering Lando Calrissian provokes a second love triangle. "Hello. What have we here?" he asks, regarding Leia as a possession, a "what." Han reacts by snatching her away. While the men coordinate the repairs, Leia "changes clothes, fixes her hair, frets about the missing Threepio and paces back and forth in her room in the clouds, like an ill-tempered Rapunzel," as critic Jeanne Cavelos puts it.[13] When Leia senses a problem, Han condescendingly kisses her forehead and tells her he'll handle it. "This is not how a person treats his leader. This is not how a person treats his equal. This is how a person treats a misguided inferior."[14] This disrespectful attitude likewise colors the audience's view of the princess.

Leia's red tunic and pants are modestly cut, dressy rather than seductive. Her double-looped braids are fiercer, nodding to those of Mexican *soldadas*. Admiring her superficially, Lando offers her a smarmy, "You look absolutely beautiful. You truly belong here with us among the clouds."

"While Han shoots repeatedly at Vader, and Vader threatens him with death—and then near-fatally freezes him in carbonite—Leia and Chewie are more like pawns."[15] Next, Leia and Han share an epic goodbye and kiss, before Han heroically sacrifices himself. Only when he's been frozen does Leia take agency and finally rescue Luke. She's seen making choices, but they're mostly about falling in love.

Hard-Drinking Marion

Marion Ravenwood is a similarly tough action heroine, if more sexual than Leia. Steven Spielberg explained, "Karen [Allen] was the clear favorite. Because she had spunk and was a firebrand. She reminded me of those thirties women

Karen Allen's tough heroine Marion Ravenwood from 1981's *Raiders of the Lost Ark.*
(© Paramount/courtesy Everett Collection)

[from similar pulp stories]."[16] Allen commented, "I fell in love with Marion; she's Indiana Jones's match. It's a sexy part."[17]

She's introduced in her Tibetan bar, drinking a hefty local under the table. She speaks the local language and collects a hefty pile of cash in the drinking game. In her beige shirt and brown trousers with her hair tightly back and the occasional cigarette, she's not just a 1930s pulp adventurer but a 1980s feminist. She also punches Indy on seeing him again:

MARION: I learned to hate you in the last ten years.
INDY: I never meant to hurt you.
MARION: I was a child! I was in love. It was wrong, and you knew it.
INDY: You knew what you were doing.
MARION: Now I do! This is my place. Get out![18]

In a problematic choice, the film doesn't dwell on Jones's statutory crime, instead only using it to heighten their tension. Jones's excuses here, that he didn't mean to hurt the teenager he seduced and that she was equally knowledgeable, are worrisome. He is written and performed as a character similar to Han—aware he's loutish but relying on outmoded allure to win the modern woman. When he tries a charming smile and adds, "Trust me," she tries to punch him again.

Still, the tough, damaged heroine maintains her agency. Marion tells Jones to leave, so he does, completely unaware that she's wearing the medallion he desires. When Major Toht comes seeking it, she tells him, "No one tells me what to do in my place." Of course, his crowd of Nazi goons outnumber her, and she turns to feminine whimpers when the major menaces her with a hot poker. Jones charges in to rescue her, in a fight so dramatic it destroys her refuge. Nonetheless, she turns the macho destruction into an opportunity, naming herself his "partner."

She's a capable sidekick, though she doesn't use traditional weapons but grabs a more desperate wooden log or frying pan. The pair bicker and flirt amusingly. Allen noted of the fighting in Cairo, "Those scenes were fun. I enjoyed doing those—all the running around in the marketplace and stuff. Any moment where I could join and be useful and resourceful has meaning for me. All of that stuff became part of the character."[19] Still, the kidnapping, in which she's helpless in a basket and lacks agency—her kidnappers switch baskets—is reminiscent of Leia's awaiting male rescuers.

Further, Marion spends her imprisonment in a white lacy gown and high heels. Her captor Belloq spies on her changing, and then she comes out and twirls for his admiration. His desire for her is heightened because of his rivalry with Jones. All this reinforces male gaze and Marion's damsel role. In fact, she dons the dress for a classically feminine seduction, though she flips it as she takes charge. Allen contributed more than acting to the story: with no reason for Marion to be wearing the dress, Spielberg actually had the two actors improvise the scene.[20] When she downs her drink in a shot, Belloq looks startled and apprehensive. He imitates her, but the audience knows he's doomed. Soon enough, she grabs his knife and nearly escapes.

However, the Nazis catch Marion and drop her in the pit with Jones, after dangling her long enough that the audience can see up her skirt. As she gasps in horror at the snakes and climbs on Jones's back, he's soon ripping her skirt off. He saves the day while she shrieks at the snakes and then at the corpses falling on her. With all this, the story has regressed to a more sexist damsel-saving adventure.

Sailing off with the Ark, Marion changes from the battered lace dress into a silky one for a romantic scene with Jones. He looks at it and tells her sincerely "It's lovely," and she's startled into looking in the mirror, in both cases encouraging audience gaze. Soon she's healing him as his nurse in a scene that quickly turns hotter. Still, the comedic intrudes as she whacks him with a mirror and then he falls asleep during her seduction. When he awakes, Jones is back in charge. Though she faces the power of the Ark beside him, he's the one accepting the government's payout and bargaining with them in a male-only meeting.

Now in a Gold Bikini

Of course, the most sexist of Leia's outfits is the gold bikini. While inflicted on her by Jabba, it's a clear statement that she is to be treated as "the girl" in this adventure. (The Ewoks putting her in a pretty dress has a similar message.) With this, feminist films can be seen pulling back. The feisty, powerful woman is fine, they suggest, but the film also needs to show her softer side. Red Sonja, Starfire, and other characters of 1980s films and comics were dressing similarly in a wave of exploitation.[21] Postfeminism, the belief that equality had been achieved so women should return to glamour and acquiescence, was on the rise. As Susan Faludi explains in *Backlash*, her celebrated book on this phenomenon, "In late '80s Hollywood . . . filmmakers once again became preoccupied with toning down independent women and drowning out their voices."[22]

Of course, Jabba's displaying Leia as his slave is the ultimate in male gaze, claiming her as a scantily dressed possession and also inviting the audience to look. Jabba's other slave girls, like Oola the Twi'lek, present a similar image. It is a degrading scene. Fisher noted, "Let's not forget that these movies are basically boys' fantasies. So the other way they made her more female in this one was to have her take off her clothes."[23] It's a weak moment, though the film blessedly moves on. Merlock and Merlock Jackson add, "Whether one agrees or disagrees with creator George Lucas's using Leia in the sequence as a visual homage to the artfully drawn science-fiction pulp magazine covers of the 1930s, her stone-faced reduction to scantily clad decoration is short-lived."[24] She strangles Jabba with the chain he bound her in, reclaiming the power, but the bikini persisted on posters and action figures for decades.

Among the Ewoks, Leia is not seen trying to dismantle the shield generator or gather information, just taking a break from the rebellion as they style her long hair. In Luke's famous moment telling her they are siblings, he doesn't bring her along to fight Vader but leaves her in safety as backup. Just as when her planet was destroyed, she is given no suffering or character growth; she only supports Luke in his pain. Cavelos observes: "Being told that Vader—the archenemy who has pursued her through the trilogy, tortured her twice, killed countless Rebels, frozen her love, tormented and cut off the hand of her other love, and repressed countless planets—is her father ought to trigger the biggest outburst from Leia we've ever seen. It ought to be the climax of an internal conflict that's been building in her throughout."[25] It is not.

In the fight with the stormtroopers, Leia does acceptably but is only seen shooting a few of them. Han's command, Lando's space battle, and Luke's duel with Vader take precedence. Instead, Leia's plot arc involves giving in to love, fittingly for her era. "The plots of some of these films achieve this reverse metamorphosis, from self-willed adult woman to silent (or dead) girl, through coercion, others through the female character's own 'choice,'" Faludi explains.[26] At film's end, she does not even see the Force ghosts or join Luke at their father's pyre—all this arc is left for him.

Willie the Lounge Singer

Jones is a professor. "On the other hand, he's a soldier of fortune. He's a sleazy character right on the edge of legality; Indiana is also a 1930s playboy," Lucas has reflected.[27] The second *Indiana Jones* film begins with his James Bond side, set against a Busby Berkeley–style musical of "Anything Goes" at a nightclub. This required a singer and dancer, whom Lucas and Spielberg found in Kate Capshaw.

Her character, Willie Scott, performs in a stunning gown—original 1920s sequins and beads with a dramatic cutout in back. However, there was a major problem. Capshaw explained, "When I put on that beautiful red dress, it was so tight I couldn't dance. So all the hard work I put into the musical number was for nothing."[28] The tap number happens without her. As a singer, she flirts with the camera, so the tight, glittering dress only enhances her to-be-looked-at-ness, as Mulvey would say. Jones also gropes Willie in the getaway car (with the excuse of getting the antidote) while she shrieks. The sexism is off and rolling.

She is also an incompetent sidekick as she drops the hot gun he has handed her and whines, "I burnt my fingers and I broke a nail!" Dragged along by Jones, Willie boards the plane because Lao Che's gunman opens fire on her, and she wants to leave this now-frightening world. There, she changes into Jones's dress clothes—these let her move for action scenes and are more tomboyish than glamorous, though they also hold the romantic look of the heroine wearing her love interest's jacket (and pants).

As a self-involved opportunist, Willie is something of an antifeminist, insisting that male characters look after her. Capshaw explained, "She has led this pampered life and feels that's what's due her—to be cared for and looked after."[29] While Marion invited herself on the epic quest, Willie, on hearing of a lost sacred stone, cries, "I can't go to Pankot! I'm a singer!" She pours perfume on her riding elephant and bursts into tears when the animal dumps her in the water.

"The biggest trouble with her is the noise," Jones comments as she, wrapped only in a blanket, shrieks about frightening things in the jungle and runs from tree to tree, comically finding something horrid in each. Following Marion, she feels like a comforting regression to a weaker heroine, in a pulling back much like Leia's in *Empire* and *Jedi*. Thus, the postfeminism of the 1980s blended with the historic sexism and pulp stereotypes.

Willie's other memorable outfit is the gold princess gown she wears to the royal banquet. Once more, the young lady on exotic adventures must dress for seduction. In fact, Willie is setting out to marry the king, as she hopes. This turns into a big joke as he is revealed as a child, and Willie's repeated gold digging has fizzled once more. Further, the dinner itself gives her a chance for more horror, while Jones reacts to the snake surprise and monkey brains with a stronger stomach. The camera deliberately pans up Willie's low cleavage to her dismayed face.

"Unfortunately, the female characters in Indy had to go through the most abuse," Kathleen Kennedy commented.[30] Besides the food and the threat of Kali, this film gave Willie the visceral horror of bugs and frightening jungle creatures, over and over. Her reactions became quite predictable. "Hello! Can she do anything else besides scream?" Capshaw asked.[31] It should be noted that Jones shares and exceeds Marion's loathing for snakes, making them equal, while Willie's fears appear more laughable.

When Jones and Short Round shout for help in the room of lowering spikes, Willie fusses about getting "all dirty again." Of course, she encounters corpses, scorpions, and bugs, and screams at them all. "Aw shut, up, Willie," Jones chides, on the edge of death. Granted, as she whimpers at how gross everything is, she does persevere and saves their lives. As Capshaw told it, "All of her earlier life is stripped away from her, and Willie must fall back on her own resources. She discovers that she is a strong woman, a gutsy lady."[32]

Prepared for sacrifice, Willie wears another glittering dress, with an intricate circlet and flower lei. It is exaggerated 1930s glamour as she pants in terror. She is the perfect sacrifice, and as she pleads with him, hypnotized Jones prepares to murder her in the emotionally heightened scene. Of course, Short Round is the one to restore Jones, who uses his strength to save Willie.

She, in turn, is bound so helplessly in the cage descending into a lava pit that she is unconscious. "Woman, then, stands in patriarchal culture as a signifier for the male other, bound by a symbolic order in which man can live out his fantasies and obsessions through linguistic command by imposing them on the silent image of a woman still tied to her place as the bearer of meaning, not maker of meaning," Mulvey writes.[33]

Capshaw, a college-educated feminist, complained of being vilified by the press afterward. "I'm definitely being called on the carpet for creating this female that was like so stereotypically not a feminist with her fingernails and her this and her that and her whining and complaining."[34] She concluded it was supposed to be a fun "ride," not a "statement."[35]

Elsa Never Really Believed

The first draft of Indy III, called *Indiana Jones and the Monkey King* (1984), paired him with a competent female zoologist as well as a female student so the two could fight for his attention. A revision (1986) had more Grail elements, a nun in love with Jones, and the Nazi villainess Greta von Grimm.[36] In the 1987 version, Elsa is a heroic art historian. After a tough heroine and a shrieker, the writers appeared to desire a balance for their third act. "She's in between the two," Elsa's actress, Alison Doody, said. "She's not a screamer, she's a very independent lady. They're actually trying to go more towards the first film again, so I think Elsa is like Karen Allen's character, but she's not as tomboyish as Karen Allen was. She's quite like Indiana Jones in the sense that she goes out and gets what she wants. I would say she is definitely stronger than the second character. She's quite a clever lady."[37] Only in the 1988 revision was she made a villain.[38]

In the released film, Elsa greets Jones and Marcus Brody with flowing blonde hair and lipstick. She and Jones start flirting without pausing for breath.

> ELSA: I knew it was you. You have your father's eyes.
> JONES: And my mother's ears. But the rest belongs to you.
> ELSA: Sounds like all the best parts are already spoken for.[39]

If she wants to be taken seriously as a professional, this is not how to go about it. Considering that the college teaching scene was filled with attractive young women falling all over themselves around the professor, Elsa seems like one more. She introduces herself as "Doctor Elsa Schneider," and Jones gives

Marcus a sidelong glance of surprise. Certainly, this film takes place in an earlier time with far fewer women PhDs. It uses this, in a throwback, to give Jones permission to be surprised that his colleague is female.

In the catacomb of rats, Elsa starts screaming, and Jones has to carry her (making her useless on this adventure). She drives their getaway speedboat well but leaves him to do the fighting. After, in the hotel, Jones bursts in on her in the bathroom, where she is wearing a long silky robe. In the romantic scene that follows, Jones is boorish, but Elsa mirrors his behavior. This makes their aggressive dialogue sound like mutual flirting but also provides a sexist model for less discerning listeners. She turns to leave, and he yanks her around to stop her. As he blurts out all their travails, he finishes, "I'm going to continue to do things the way I think they should be done." He grabs Elsa and aggressively kisses her. She snaps, "How dare you kiss me!" and aggressively kisses him back.[40] On paper, the dialogue is far from consent.

Memorably, when a Nazi holds mussed, terrified-looking Elsa at gunpoint, she shrieks for rescue as Jones's father tells him she's a Nazi. Jones surrenders to save her, and she tells him, taking the Grail diary, "I'm sorry . . . but . . . you should have listened to your father." A few lines later, Jones Sr. reveals that Elsa "talks in her sleep."[41] Sean Connery, as the beloved James Bond actor, added heavy competition. The actor insisted, "Look, anything Indy does in the context of the story, I have done better. When he talks about sleeping with Elsa, you have to write that I slept with her too."[42] Indeed, this increases the men's rivalry. "One wanted the relationship between Indy and his father not to be so harmonious at the beginning," Connery said. "Sleeping with the same woman was a bit of anathema for George, but he eventually came around, because it was possible and funny."[43] Elsa is relegated to their duplicitous prize.

Of course, making the only woman in the film treacherous makes its own point. Spielberg explained, "That character was an homage to a lot of those Alan Ladd [1930s] pictures where you never could trust a woman."[44] Elsa is smart and competent, but these qualities lead to savage ambition. In the Grail room, the great traitress betrays her boss, Donovan. Next, her greed overcomes her, and she takes the Grail, grasping desperately after it until she falls. Enacting their father-son rapprochement and love, Jones abandons greed for family. "Elsa never really believed in the Grail. She thought she'd found a prize," his father says gravely. While Jones never really believed in the Grail either, he learns love and forgiveness, while Elsa fails to grow. She's a regretful but determined traitor from beginning to end.

The character of Elsa Schneider in *Indiana Jones and the Last Crusade* emerged as a treacherous femme fatale. (courtesy Everett Collection)

Conclusion

Leia heralded the second wave of feminism with her 1970s can-do attitude. Likewise, Marion fits well among the male warriors as she drinks and fights. However, both films are followed by a discernable pulling back: Willie is a screaming wimp, and *Empire* sees Leia falling for Han as she lets him take the lead. Further, all the heroines conform to the gender norms of 1930s pulps: treacherous beauty, spunky supportive sidekick, screaming damsel. This deliberate weakening reflects the era, as feminism subsided to postfeminism, and for every step forward, a step back followed.

The early 2000s brought the *Star Wars* prequels, with a wimpier Padmé succeeding Leia as the central action heroine and only woman in the galaxy. Her beautiful gowns made her invisible to the point of being interchangeable—a plot point with her many decoys.[45] This tallied well with 1990s girl power—heroines in gorgeous gowns who kicked butt but prioritized romance. It would take another decade for *Force Awakens* to introduce a spectrum of practically dressed independent women, including Rey, Captain Phasma, Maz Kanata, and a much tougher General Leia.

Indiana Jones and the Crystal Skull (2008) hailed not just Jones's return but Marion's. Valuing the tough heroine instead of replacing her emphasizes how central she is to the franchise and Jones's life. Like General Leia, this older action heroine is delightful. "Marion has a great sense of humor but she's strong, she's up to Indiana, and you believe that she can put him in his place," Lucas said. "They're a real team, so that's always a fun relationship."[46] Indeed, Marion and Leia finally get their chance, after decades, to show their scoundrels who's in charge.

At last, fourth wave feminism had arrived, celebrating women of different ages and backgrounds for more than the romances they could offer the badly behaved hero. Aamir Aziz and Farwa Javed explain in their essay on fourth wave, "The idea is that women's identities are composed of many multi-layered aspects, which present their own difficulties that must be dealt with, and hence, a 'one-size-fits-all approach' does not benefit feminism." As they add, intersectionality is central: "Be inclusive of all types of women within the movement, take into account different types of life experience, show respect for these varying identities and include all women in the debate."[47] This new era acknowledged room on the adventure for all women, including ones who had matured beyond the screaming damsels.

Notes

1. Eliana Dockterman, "*Star Wars* Created the First Truly Kickass Princess," in "*Star Wars*: 40 Years of the Force," special edition, *Time*, November 24, 2017, 38.

2. George Lucas, dir., *Star Wars: Episode IV—A New Hope* (1977; Century City, CA: 20th Century Fox, 2006), DVD.

3. Gabriel S. Estrada, "*Star Wars* Episodes I–VI: Coyote and the Force of White Narrative," in *The Persistence of Whiteness: Race and Contemporary Hollywood Cinema*, ed. Daniel Bernardi (London: Routledge, 2007), 84.

4. Laura Mulvey, "Visual Pleasure and Narrative Cinema," *Screen* 16, no. 3 (Autumn 1975): 6–18, http://www.scribd.com/doc/7758866/laura-mulvey-visual-pleasure-and-narrative-cinema.

5. Carrie Fisher, *The Princess Diarist* (New York: Blue Rider, 2016), 15.

6. Ibid., 34.

7. Ibid., 42.

8. Valerie Estelle Frankel, "*Star Wars*" *Meets the Eras of Feminism* (Lanham, MD: Lexington Press, 2018), 9.

9. John Paul Pianka, *The Power of the Force: Race, Gender, and Colonialism in the "Star Wars" Universe* (master's thesis, Wesleyan University Middletown, 2013), 37, https://www.cdt-pv.org/media/upload/The_Power_of_the_Force-_Race_Gender_and_Colonialism_in_the_Star.pdf.

10. Estrada, "*Star Wars* Episodes I–VI," 85.

11. Ray Merlock and Kathy Merlock Jackson, "Lightsabers, Political Arenas, and Marriages for Princess Leia and Queen Amidala," in *Sex, Politics and Religion in "Star Wars,"* ed. Douglas Brode and Leah Deyneka (Lanham, MD: Scarecrow Press, 2012), 80–81.

12. Pianka, *Power of the Force*, 41.

13. Jeanne Cavelos, "Stop Her, She's Got a Gun!," in *"Star Wars" on Trial: Science Fiction and Fantasy Writers Debate the Most Popular Science Fiction Films of All Time*, ed. David Brin and Matthew Woodring Stover (Dallas: Smart Pop, 2006), 307.

14. Ibid., 310.

15. Frankel, *"Star Wars" Meets the Eras of Feminism*, 19.

16. "Making the Trilogy," *Raiders of the Lost Ark*, directed by George Lucas (1981; Hollywood: Paramount Home Entertainment, 2008), DVD.

17. J. W. Rinzler, *The Complete Making of "Indiana Jones": The Definitive Story behind All Four Films* (New York: Del Rey, 2008), 48.

18. George Lucas, dir., *Raiders of the Lost Ark* (1981; Hollywood: Paramount Home Entertainment, 2008), DVD.

19. "Making the Trilogy," *Raiders*.

20. Ibid.

21. Frankel, *"Star Wars" Meets the Eras of Feminism*, 21.

22. Susan Faludi, *Backlash: The Undeclared War against American Women* (New York: Three Rivers, 2006), 128.

23. Dockterman, "Star Wars Created the First Truly Kickass Princess," 36.

24. Merlock and Merlock Jackson, "Lightsabers, Political Arenas, and Marriages," 83.

25. Cavelos, "Stop Her, She's Got a Gun!," 313.

26. Faludi, *Backlash*, 129.

27. Rinzler, *Complete Making*, 50.

28. Ibid., 156.

29. Thomas McKelvey Cleaver, "Meet Kate Capshaw: Companion in High Adventure," *Starlog* 83 (June 1984): 52.

30. "Making the Trilogy," *Indiana Jones and the Temple of Doom*, directed by George Lucas (1984; Hollywood: Paramount Home Entertainment, 2008), DVD.

31. Ibid.

32. Cleaver, "Meet Kate Capshaw," 52.

33. Mulvey, "Visual Pleasure."

34. "Making the Trilogy," *Temple*.

35. Rinzler, *Complete Making*, 182.

36. Ibid., 188–89.

37. Adam Pirani, "Lady of the Last Crusade," *Starlog* 144 (July 1989): 35.

38. Rinzler, *Complete Making*, 190–91.

39. George Lucas, dir., *Indiana Jones and the Last Crusade* (1989; Hollywood: Paramount Home Entertainment, 2008), DVD.

40. Ibid.

41. Ibid.

42. Rinzler, *Complete Making*, 190.

43. Ibid., 195.

44. Ibid., 197.

45. Frankel, *"Star Wars" Meets the Eras of Feminism*, 52.

46. Rinzler, *Complete Making*, 237.

47. Aamir Aziz and Farwa Javed, "Sci-Fi/Fantasy Movies for Identity Politics in Fourth Wave Feminism," in *Fourth Wave Feminism in Science Fiction and Fantasy*, ed. Valerie Estelle Frankel, vol. 1, *Essays on Film Representations, 2012–2019* (Jefferson, NC: McFarland, 2019), 48.

9

Researching the Lucasfilm Yearbooks

"FAMILY—ONE WIFE, ONE DISCO-BOOGIE BABY, AND 425 FOSTER KIDS"

Julie Turnock

Researching a multibillion-dollar corporation like Lucasfilm is always a challenge, and even more so now that it is owned by an even bigger conglomerate, the Walt Disney Company. Because information about the company is so closely held, it is difficult for both popular and academic accounts to separate public relations from reliable history. Beyond the work of the scholars in this volume, there is very little academic, unauthorized, primary-source historical research on Lucasfilm. *Star Wars* films have been subject to academic fan studies and some limited industrial attention by academics. However, the majority of academic work discussing Lucasfilm and its subsidiaries, like Industrial Light & Magic (ILM), EditDroid, and THX theatrical sound systems, tends to cite Lucasfilm-authorized sources or does not recognize information they are encountering as massaged by public relations.[1]

There is a practical reason for the lack of primary-source documentation on Lucasfilm. Not surprisingly, there has been little upside for Lucasfilm to allow outside academic researchers into its archives. Secondary sources on Lucasfilm are nearly all written or cowritten by former employees. Though vital for certain kinds of information, trade publications such as *Variety* and the *Hollywood Reporter* are likewise subject to the press release and publicity department information provided by Lucasfilm. Therefore, if a Lucasfilm spokesperson makes a statement in an interview, the publication generally must take their word for it. In most cases, reporters did not go to Marin County to see for themselves.

However, researching influential media companies is an important component of holding powerful companies up to scrutiny. That being said, as Patrick Vonderau has asked in his study of the issue of access in media industry research, how can the academic researcher access vital information in the public interest in an era where *information* and *public interest* are redefined by the media companies under scrutiny?[2] What can the researcher do when that information is so closely held by the companies they are researching?

There is no easy answer to that question. However, occasionally one can find research holdings in unexpected places. This chapter will explore an aspect of the only (as far as I am aware) primary-source cache of Lucasfilm information outside of corporate hands: the former ILM general manager Thomas G. Smith's Papers at the Ransom Center at the University of Texas, Austin.[3] Smith's papers include effects storyboards, contracts, and publicity materials. This essay will focus on one subset of those materials, the Lucasfilm yearbooks in Smith's collection. The yearbooks are a little hard to explain since they served a number of purposes. The first and most prominent purpose was similar to a high school yearbook, but they also resembled the old notion of a lowercase face book, as well as a kind of studio-era house organ or in-house magazine. For the researcher, while they cannot be treated as uncut primary data, these yearbooks nevertheless provide a wealth of information for internal use only where we can see the departments, the personnel, and a glimpse into the Lucasfilm self-image. Because every employee and division is included, one can track the configuration and transmutation of the Lucasfilm departments, job descriptions, and personnel over time. There are reports of what each department accomplished (or not) that year, the projects they prioritized, and humorous accounts of what went wrong. Also, unlike in press releases and formal interviews, one occasionally sees glimpses of dissatisfaction and bitterness in the ranks.

Because the yearbooks are not online and require a visit to the Ransom Center to access, this essay will describe in detail the yearbooks in the collection, which I hope will suggest directions for different kinds of histories and case studies the yearbooks might support. In my book *The Empire of Effects: Industrial Light & Magic and the Rendering of Realism* (2022), I used these materials primarily to question the story ILM tells about itself and the self-aggrandizing public relations (PR) material that has passed as unchallenged history.[4] However, the yearbooks have many other stories to tell. This essay will track an employee-focused trajectory of Lucasfilm history, focusing on what the yearbooks in the Ransom's holdings emphasize on a year-by-year basis, which is often at odds with both later histories and PR contemporary with the moment. Different films, different business concerns, and even suppressed histories come to light when one is combing through these materials. As a mark of how conglomerate PR management curtails academic research, this essay cannot reprint images from the yearbooks without submitting the entire volume for unspecified "approval" from Lucasfilm and Disney. Rather than submitting to corporate overseeing, I decided my (impoverished) written descriptions will have to suffice—which is a shame since much of the spirit of the yearbooks is conveyed graphically and iconically.

Media Industries Historiography

First of all, what kind of history do these yearbooks contribute to? By focusing largely on employees, they provide a certain kind of entertainment and creative industry historical ethnography that traces a specific creative industry as it developed from its countercultural roots in the 1970s to a neoliberal powerhouse over the course of the 1990s. The specific form they took provides an example of internal business communication adapted for the management of creative economies. Among many other items of interest to researchers, we also catch a glimpse of a proto–Silicon Valley "tech campus" promoting the values of the "California ideology"—a utopian-tinged live/work space where the worker enjoyed high work satisfaction and was figured as family.[5]

In this way, the yearbooks provide strong examples of what John Caldwell has called the discourse of "production culture," and several kinds of discourses flow from the yearbook's pages.[6] Most prominently, we can see Lucasfilm's promoted image as an early version of Silicon Valley "disrupters" at close range. Former Lucasfilm Computer Group department head and later Pixar founder Ed Catmull has characterized Lucasfilm as "based in Marin County, one hour north of Silicon Valley by car and one hour from Hollywood by plane," drawing suggestive weight from the geographic proximity.[7] Similar to Lucasfilm's rhetoric about itself, Pixar's rhetorical self-description has been characterized by Jordan Gowanlock as "a paradigmatic Silicon Valley tech company," as a group of neoliberal mavericks who remade the movie industry in their image through free and open technology that helped give rise to a more creative and flexible workplace (both neglecting to mention, as Gowanlock points out, both companies' frequent reliance on public university research as well as federal funding and also ignoring Silicon Valley's close relationship to Cold War research and development [R&D]).[8] Nevertheless, like Pixar, though predating it, Lucasfilm took advantage of its geographic relationship to Silicon Valley to make associations with disruptive technological innovation. As Fred Turner has chronicled, Silicon Valley both in its early days and more recently exploits the area's relationship to 1960s counterculture, with their Bohemian work campuses that utopianly blurred the lines between work life and personal life in a "new communalism."[9] Jeff Menne points out the precedent of Francis Ford Coppola's San Francisco–based production company, American Zoetrope, as a configuration that "coarticulated Hollywood and Silicon Valley," with similar "countercultural managerial cultures."[10] Menne uses Pixar as the emblem of the "work as fun" ethos as well as of the contemporary consequences of the 1970s corporatization of counterculture, while I would argue that Lucasfilm serves as an equally good and even earlier example.

To relate this even more to Lucasfilm, I would add the entertainment-business-specific notion of what Menne has characterized as "the economy of genius" and what I have described further as "the romantic image as an artist's dream job where working for an auteur [such as George Lucas] trumps such trivialities as health insurance, overtime pay, and union membership."[11] The yearbooks are powerful primary-source evidence of an intersection of all of these tendencies.

The Yearbooks

The Lucasfilm yearbooks provide the researcher with a rare opportunity to delve into Lucasfilm's early corporate culture. It is worth noting here that Lucasfilm also had a monthly newsletter, the *Lucasfilm Monthly Marquee*. However, it is housed at the Lucasfilm Library (along with a full run of the Lucasfilm yearbooks), which has not been accessible to academic researchers. This essay will cover the 1982–1991 Lucasfilm yearbooks in Thomas G. Smith's Papers in the Ransom holdings. Lucasfilm (LFL) was founded in 1971 by Lucas but was not incorporated until after the success of *Star Wars* in 1977. It seems that 1982 is the first year the yearbooks were produced. Given Lucasfilm's corporate history, it is logical that the yearbooks would start in July 1982, since ILM had only recently opened up to outside business and operations were moving away from exclusively *Star Wars* properties into other services for outside production, including, around 1980, special effects, editing, and sound spaces. Unlike the famously laid-back atmosphere frequently recounted around Lucasfilm and ILM in particular during the production of *Star Wars*, the company at this time was becoming more businesslike. It was now more professionally corporate and diversified, and it was developing a proper R&D division and operations around licensing and marketing. As the business professionalized, the yearbooks helped maintain the illusion that Lucasfilm was as fun, antiestablishment, and irreverent as ever.

The Ransom holdings only cover 1982–1991, but Lucasfilm continued to produce yearbooks in various forms through at least 2011.[12] The yearbooks are typically from forty to sixty pages long, with a few as long as eighty pages. They were reportedly used in-house only and were not given to potential partners or investors.[13]

The yearbooks were most similar in format to a high school yearbook in that they documented the company's varied "student body" over the course of the year. They were designed to forge a sense of workplace unity, within the looser hippie spirit of the 1960s and 1970s. They were distributed at the annual Fourth of July picnic; they had snapshots of the intramural sports teams and events; and people even signed them with messages like high school yearbooks.[14] In this way, the yearbooks forged a kind of corporate version of school spirit. Also, like traditional yearbooks, they include portrait photos of every Lucasfilm employee. Because they appeared yearly, the yearbooks frequently commemorated anniversaries, such as the tenth anniversary of *Star Wars* in 1987 or Lucasfilm's twentieth anniversary in 1991. These anniversaries were often celebrated with lavish themed parties (sock hop) and famous performers (Huey Lewis and the News), pictures of which appeared in the yearbooks, always with George Lucas himself shown in attendance.

The varied Lucasfilm operations were distributed geographically across a wide swath of Marin County. Not all employees ran into one another regularly, and moreover, they were frequently employed for very different kinds of jobs, from R&D to landscaping, marketing, and production. For this reason, the lineup of photos in the yearbooks, separated in most cases by department, were also used like school face books (in the old, lowercase sense). Like university-issued directories listing students with photos and brief biographical data, the volumes allowed people in various departments across Lucasfilm to look up colleagues in other divisions, much as a college freshmen might look up someone from another dormitory.[15] And like face books and perhaps the social media platform those (frequently prep school and elite college-oriented) publications inspired, alongside the pictures of the employees, they usually included short questionnaires that listed personal information such as occupational and educational history, romantic status, and interests. In the earliest Lucasfilm yearbooks, the information included hometown, family (a.k.a. romantic status), schools, interests, (astrological) sign, and employment history. People were clearly not discouraged from providing jokey, lighthearted entries.

Lucas's own questionnaire in 1982 gives a general flavor: "George Lucas, Chairman of the Board. Hometown: Off Hwy 99. Family: growing. Schools: Downey High, Modesto JC, USC. Interests: CBS Evening News, '60 Minutes.' Sign: Taurus. Employment History: 1966: turned down at Hanna Barbera Prod; 1967: Turned down at Cornell Wilde Prod, 1968: first script rejected by United Artists (THX-1138); 1970: second script rejected by every major and minor studio (American Graffiti); 1971: went into business for myself."

Several entries clearly understand the purpose of the questionnaire: finding dates. Jill Sorensen, receptionist, characterized her interests in the proper dating-profile language, as "traveling, wine, sports, antiques, music, dancing, driving, men, and lying in the sun with my Margarita an arm's distance away. Call for an appointment and I'll let you know."[16] Annie Berardini, executive secretary, was even more straightforward. She listed her interests as "men, boys, tennis, dancing, skiing, men, boys, sun surf & sand, men & boys."[17] Others fairly begged for dates, such as later Pixar head John Lasseter, proclaiming his romantic status as "very single, call collect."[18] Into the late 1980s and early 1990s, the questions became more conversational, such as "If money were no object what would you do?" or "Tell a funny story about yourself." That being said, not all employees responded to the questionnaires every year.

The yearbooks also functioned similarly to Hollywood studio-era house organs. These organs, especially the Club News publications produced by Warner Brothers, RKO, MGM, Universal, and others, were employee-authored newsletters published for internal use. These publications at the studios, and then later at Lucasfilm, can be seen as versions of the in-house company magazine, described by JoAnne Yates as developed "to build the worker loyalty that executives learned was necessary for cooperation and efficiency," as part of a twentieth-century process of management systematization.[19] As a "downward communication" managerial tool for controlling a growing business, the in-house magazine was seen as a way to build company esprit de corps through a sense of personalization in the face of an increasingly depersonalized workplace. As Yates put it, the in-house magazines were hardly innocent tools, since they "improved morale and cooperation, thus indirectly reinforcing control."[20]

More specifically, Hollywood studio Club News, like the Lucasfilm yearbooks, covered a great deal of activities and entries. In Club News, generally speaking, each studio department, from camera to editorial, stenography, landscaping, and janitorial, contributed a monthly (or so) chatty-toned entry that included personal anecdotes about work life at the studio, with jokes, cartoons, vacation plans, and other kinds of employee personal details. They included pictures of dinner dances, intramural sports events, and special interest clubs. Similar to these house organs, Lucasfilm yearbooks likewise read like employees speaking to one another rather than the administration talking at them. However, much like the studio Club News publications, the Lucasfilm yearbooks, introduced at exactly the time the company was growing rapidly, are produced and authorized by a higher level of administration to feel informal. Besides the sports teams, group outings and parties, in the many candids, we see people at work, from matte painters with brushes to administrators in their memorabilia-cluttered offices and stained-glass artists installing their work in the Skywalker Ranch main house. We see employee baby pictures, also "production babies" (that is, snapshots of crewmembers' children born over the course of a film production), pets, and other personal attachments. To show how everyone is working for the same thing, the yearbooks included Lucasfilm characters like Yoda, stormtroopers, Ewoks, and Wookiees that appear around the compound in various forms. However, rather than being a monthly social update like many studio Club News publications, the yearbooks only appeared once a year.

This description raises the question of why Lucasfilm began an informal-appearing in-house magazine. The span from 1981 to 1982 was a time of huge expansion for the company, which had moved to Marin County in 1978 and opened to outside business in 1980–1981. The yearbooks, as in-house magazines, helped foster a sense of closeness to a growing team as the company expanded well beyond its original parameters. But why choose the format of a yearbook? While a yearbook might seem like a recruiting tool (Look how fun it is to work here!) or PR, evidence suggests that the yearbooks were for employee consumption only—and therefore were more about employee retention than recruitment. Moreover, the yearbook format personalized the working experience, bringing it within the George Lucas universe. While paging through the yearbooks, one gets a consistent sense that the employees are encouraged to think of themselves as living in the world of *American Graffiti*, making the yearbooks a kind of brand extension of Lucas's own notion of a nostalgic world within an ideal workplace. Although multiple reports of Lucas's personality describe him as hardly warm and communicative, there is clearly an effort to recapture what he saw as the fun of high school days. The white middle-class milieu of *American Graffiti*'s nostalgia (what Paul Monaco, partly in reference to *American Graffiti*, called "memory without pain") is often given as evidence of Lucas's retrograde cinematic politics.[21] Although it is certainly generally unreflective about the racial politics of the milieu, I suggest that Lucasfilm, as *American Graffiti* High School but with working (and largely single) adults, constitutes his utopian work situation. The yearbooks give a picture of life at Lucasfilm as a fun, irreverent, youthful, noncorporate, creative—and a little sexy—place to work, as workers were being paid to be back in (the best parts) of high school.

The Yearbooks Year By Year

Because the Smith collection includes a complete set of yearbooks from 1982 to 1991, it helps us trace a historical trajectory of this formative era in the company. We see the yearbooks directly and indirectly responding to corporate fortunes, big successes, and changing courses. Most yearbooks begin with a letter from the president of Lucasfilm (1982–1985 Robert Greber; 1985–1992 Doug Norby). The yearbooks then break into departmental sections. The administration section starts with an image of Lucas and, until the 1985 yearbook after their divorce, Marcia Lucas, and their children, as well as their personnel questionnaires. They then go (alphabetically) department by department with a brief yearly update essay (sometimes jokey, sometimes more serious in tone), followed by the roster of employees alphabetically by name with pictures and personal information. The strict alphabetization of first the departments and then the employees within the department suggests a leveling of hierarchy. The departments changed names and formations, but in the years covered, Administration, ILM, Sprockets (the editing and sound R&D division that went by various names), Computer Division, Licensing, Games, Production, Business Operations, Skywalker Development (largely construction), and Ranch Operations were the most consistent. After the departmental and personnel roundups, there would be pictures of events that year, such as the employee picnics, parties, and sports teams, as well as other candids around the ranch. The back page varied but usually contained fan cartoons, a bit of nostalgia, or something poking fun at Lucas. The demographics of the employees are overwhelmingly white, although there are some employees of color. Gender distribution is majority male but with a perhaps surprising number of women employees in every department. Sheer numbers of employees increase steadily over the period covered but not dramatically in any given year or department.

Although the first several from 1982 to 1985 were laid out with high school yearbooks as their clear design template, the format frequently changed and was often themed.

The first yearbook, in 1982, set a loose template for the next ten years. The letter from the president, Robert Greber, reads like the speech of a principal at a pep rally, reminding the team that although the company has grown, it is still about how special the people are and how rare it is to work for such a great company:

> We have enjoyed an exciting and prosperous year because of the very real contribution of each and every member of the Lucasfilm "class of 1982."
>
> The size, structure, and activities of the company have changed somewhat, but the major ingredient—the specialness of the Lucasfilm people—has been retained and strengthened. We have in Lucasfilm a unique company that makes all of us very proud to be a part of it. We work and play well together, poke fun at ourselves and each other, have a strong commitment to our jobs, our fellow Lucasfilmers, and to the company itself.
>
> This is a rare and special experience we share and is my hope we can continue to maintain it in the years to come. I wish you the very best in the coming year and all manner of success.

The yearbook begins with a photo-illustrated historical time line of Lucasfilm, alongside candid set photos of Lucas with important collaborators such as Walter Murch, Haskell Wexler, Gary Kurtz, and Marcia Lucas (shown at the editing table and on the set of *American Graffiti*). We see some pre-1982 Lucasfilm company events, like the 1977 Halloween party, previous company picnics, and the "first softball team, 1979." Lucas, Marcia, and baby Amanda preside over the administration section, which includes the questionnaires for all employees. Administration, ILM, Production, Skywalker Development, and Sprocket Systems constitute the 1982 departments. They are followed by the images of the Fourth of July picnic, the softball teams, the sailing club, the Halloween party, the Christmas party, the Academy Awards, and a section called "Old-Timers" with the five current employees who had joined LFL before 1975. These are followed by a "Bulletin Board" section with jokey cartoons about *Star Wars* and work life, with the last page dedicated to "Fan Mail" with images of kids' fan letters to Chewbacca, Indiana Jones, and "Mr Lucas and Mr Spielberg." Finally, to really bring home the yearbook tone, there is a cartoon of the "Yearbook Staff" with one of the team cheerleading "Go team go!" with a megaphone.

While the first yearbook is clearly formatted to evoke school spirit, the second iteration, in 1983, the year of the release of the last film in the original *Star Wars* trilogy, *The Return of the Jedi*, comes as something of a surprise. Clearly the company expects a turn toward a more professionalized future. Production is slick (on higher-quality glossy paper), closer to an annual report to shareholders, albeit still more casual. The 1983 iteration places more emphasis on business activities and suggests a more businesslike atmosphere. It is also one of the longest, with eighty-four pages. Greber's president's letter includes a report on specific business activities from the previous year, recounting the Licensing Department's formation. There is a page of company logos.

Using more corporate lingo than in 1982, the letter states: "The company has undergone a gradual but dramatic evolution in the past six year period. What was once a highly successful film production company has nurtured a number of successful startup businesses and, in Skywalker Ranch, has begun to create an asset of immeasurable value."

In this iteration, lengthy department progress reports (Administration, Computer R&D, General Services, ILM, Licensing Division, Marketing Department, Production, Skywalker Development, Sprocket Systems) appear separate from the employee rosters. The more informal section entitled "R&R" shows candids of the year's events and activities, as well as an employee *Return of the Jedi* screening. Following that, the personnel rosters with questionnaires appear. The back page is a reproduction of Lucas on the cover of *Time* magazine promoting *The Return of the Jedi*, alongside Ewoks and C-3PO.

Apparently that more corporate look and approach rankled, and the format reverted to the high school–style yearbook layouts for the next two years. The 1984 graphic style is almost aggressively juvenile, in that the cover looks like a lined school notebook with workplace candids scattered about. A table of contents divides the book into three sections: "Lucasfilm Ltd 1984 Division Overviews," "Outings," and "Family, the Class of 1984." Instead of the businesslike reports of the previous year, the division overviews have some update information but are much chattier and more flippant. General Services is represented by a Peter Max–style cartoon, bannered "The Clowns That Keep the Ball Rolling." ILM reports on their various high-profile productions, but the section also includes a hectic photo collage with cheeky captions, like "Attack of the giant profits." Outings are the same as the previous year, along with an "Indy [Indiana Jones] screening," the addition of a bowling league, and two pages dedicated to "Lucasfilm Kiddies," or employees' baby pictures. In the "Family" section, Marcia Lucas is now gone after her rancorous divorce, with George "Big Daddy Lucas" and toddler Amanda appearing together. The employees are separated by department, with the same questionnaires as in 1982, which are followed by "Say Cheese" with silly candids and the fan mail "Bulletin Board." The back page is a picture of Lucas and Steven Spielberg putting their hands in concrete together in front of Mann's Chinese Theatre. This edition is clearly a corrective back to the lightly counterculture, *American Graffiti*–style self-image of 1982.

The 1985 edition keeps with the yearbook format, with a "LFL 1985" cover in the USC Trojans (Lucas's alma matter) cardinal and gold colors, with an illustration of an Ewok behind an old-timey camera. A new president (Doug Norby, reportedly brought in to instill corporate discipline) brings a wordier and newsier president's letter, which attempts a "cool corporate" tone that emphasizes Lucasfilm's place among but also apart from other media giants:

> In some ways Lucasfilm has had a boring year compared to many
> of its business associates. Barry Diller left Paramount and moved
> to Fox. Michael Eisner and Jeffrey Katzenberg left Paramount
> and moved to Disney. Marvin Davis sold half of Fox to Rupert
> Murdoch. Capital Cities bought ABC. The Bass Brothers bought a
> substantial piece of Disney. Jack Tramiel bought Atari. Ted Turner
> tried to buy CBS. General Mills tried to sell Kenner. In the midst of
> it all little old Lucasfilm continued to be owned and chaired by the
> same person—you know who. But it's been an exciting year as well.

Unlike those other media companies, with their impersonal grind and turnover, Lucasfilm paternalistically enjoys continuity with its beloved founder.

Despite this more business-oriented start, the 1985 yearbook proceeds much like 1982's, with department updates written and presented in "fun" formats, like the Library Division's *Desk Set* parody or the Marketing collage of gag phone messages. The departments and the employee rosters are once again consolidated, but for the first time they include departmental large group photographs as a signification of group unity. For a family atmosphere, the ILM section has a two-panel set of pregnant employees holding their bellies, next to the same pair holding their newborn babies. This time the picnics and parties are under "Fun and Games." There are a lot of Ewoks. The bulletin board is now dominated by employee cartoons, like "Wicket W Warrick IS Stanley Ewokalski in Lucasfilm's *An Ewok Named Desire*." The back pages are taken up by inside-joke T-shirt designs for Lucasfilm productions, like one with the third *Star Wars*' original title, "The Revenge of the Jedi."

Lucasfilm moved into its fancy new Victorian-style Skywalker Ranch digs in September 1985. This likely encouraged the 1986 yearbook designers to start playing with themed formats. Instead of high school, the designers appear to be going for a combination of a family album and an old-timey studio-era house organ. That year reflected Victoriana with "The Lucasfilm Album 1986" on the leather-looking cover framed in gold filigree. The employee photos are in cameo-like circular mattes. The overall tone is less glib and more sentimental than in previous years. The operations have gotten bigger, and Lucasfilm is clearly now more like a studio than ever. The yearbook documents the big move of many operations to the newly completed Skywalker Ranch, and a more decorous atmosphere prevails. In the candids, employees sedately go about their business. The wild parties and ramshackle intramural sports team pictures of previous years are less prominent. The departments' group pictures are more posed than the year before. The back page, usually the space for cutting loose, instead suggests dignity, with cameoed pictures of Lucas with Akira Kurasawa (who visited the ranch that year) and a candid of president Doug Norby (with, I believe, Jane Mutony of Theater Operations) having lunch on an outside trellised terrace at the new Skywalker complex.

If 1986 was about Lucasfilm's new grandeur, 1987's yearbook looked to its position in the broader media to demonstrate how far they had come. To celebrate "*Star Wars*, the first 10 years," the format ambitiously mimicked the *Time* magazine layout and font, complete with gag ads. The cover looked even further outward, featuring a montage of international *Star Wars* posters. The table of contents lists what look like magazine articles: (1) Divisions; (2) Events: "Hotdogs, eggnog and a sock hop—life after work in the Galaxy of Lucasfilm"; (3) Sports: "Marin fitness craze sweeps through the ranks of LTL . . . or six ways to avoid guilt"; (4) People: "From *Star Wars* to attack of the killer tomatoes, new captions provide new creativity." Howard the Duck (from the film released in August 1986) replaces the Ewoks as the company mascot. Doug Norby's president's letter invokes the theme of "expansion" (amid the first of many *Howard the Duck* puns, "We got our ducks in a row") and foresees the major goals for the year around diversification and development:

expanding production and R&D and growing spatially into new facilities. The as-promised new photos and new captions of employees include favorite films, books, and places. Departmental updates are laid out like image-heavy news articles, containing a mix of newsy items about what is in progress and creative interpretations, such as parody songs, poems, and posters.

The optimistic expansionist mood did not last. After the dismal failure of *Howard the Duck* and its related labor woes stemming from, as ILM's entry reported, "each person [working] an average of 120 hours," which led to the employees asking "for a reorganization of ILM," 1988's yearbook turns its gaze back inward.[22] The theme was "A Year in the Life of Lucasfilm," with the first fifty pages containing uncaptioned black-and-white photography of activity all around the Lucasfilm realm. There is very little text at all over the eighty-one pages. The new topic in the questionnaires is "fondest memory in twenty-five words or less," and only about one in three or four submitted a caption, suggesting employee malaise. There are still many images of parties but no images of sports teams or activity outings. Norby's president's letter states, perhaps with a bit of strain, "This yearbook is a visual record of our company in action during the last year. And it shows that Lucasfilm is a very special place." In the pictures, employees go about their business in both posed and candid-looking pictures of model makers at work, administrative assistants answering phones, families picnicking, trees being planted, meetings in progress, and exercise class. And look out—Lucas might show up anywhere! The self-image of the yearbooks has shifted from informal family fun (with clear parent-child relations) to a slightly new kind of organizational structure, one that wants to look nonhierarchical, with all jobs equally important. Also, on-set pictures from productions (the glamour work) are juxtaposed with day-to-day operations. Although in previous editions it appears to be a natural outgrowth of the work culture, Lucasfilm now has to work to promote an atmosphere of egalitarianism, where the licensing administrator, event coordinator, accounting clerk, landscaper, model maker and sound designers' jobs are of equal importance to the success of the company. Of course, Lucas still always presides over this "level" playing field.

The malaise continues into 1989. That year goes back to a more traditional yearbook format, with no evident theme and a heavy blue cover with a fairly bland design. The Norby president's letter keeps emphasizing how busy they were that year, with a strangely defeatist message: "Our potential is great, but can only be realized if we work together, support each other, and all understand

and contribute to the goals and values embodied in this vision. We have an exciting future ahead of us."

The somewhat short thirty-eight-page book jumps right into the headshots, with this year's theme being "If money were no object," "Tell a funny story," or "Tell us something about your family." While there was much more participation than the previous year, several answers were on the snappish side. Jeff Doran in ILM wrote: "I don't really look like this anymore. There are bags under my eyes, I'm about 20 pounds heavier and my hair is going Gray. God I love this business."[23] Another simply lets the Talking Heads speak for him: "This is not my beautiful house, this is not my beautiful wife. How did I get here?"

The 1990 yearbook reflects a broad reorganization of Lucasfilm. Several departments are combined into "LucasArts." In a further leveling impulse, the primary change to the 1990 yearbook is to dispense with departments as they had been configured in the past and create larger categories: first Lucasfilm (operations and administration), then the newly established LucasArts (production and R&D). The theme is a "contact sheet" design, with negative edge material and sprocket holes visible. There are no stories or questionnaire answers, only names, positions, and departments. There is almost no text, a very brief president's letter, and many candid, uncaptioned pictures of work and events. This yearbook appears to be primarily functioning as an employee directory/face book.

The 1991 yearbook, the last in the Ransom collection, commemorates another anniversary year: Lucasfilm's twentieth. After the doldrums of the late 1980s, the Lucasfilm prospects are once again seeming bright. The format is split between "normal" yearbook expectations and a self-produced history of Lucasfilm. The first eight pages are a pictorial history (with a minimum of text) of George Lucas's journey from film school in 1966 to Lucasfilm, up to 1974. The priority for this year is celebrating company loyalty. The following pages contain headshots of all employees who are still with Lucasfilm in the order in which they were hired, with text narrating "Then" (how they came to work for Lucasfilm) and "Now" (their role in the company as of 1991). After this is Lucas's own account ("Back then . . . Prehistoric, Promising Director/ Greaser . . . Now: Chairman of the Board).[24] Printed employee signatures cover the pictures, mimicking the informal actual signatures collected in the 1982 yearbook. The historical account continues in picture form with images from the old Parkway offices and Kerner optical stages giving way to the grand Victorian buildings constructed on Skywalker Ranch over the course of the 1980s, as well as rare set photos from *Star Wars* and other films, from *Raiders of the Lost Ark* to *Mishima*. It is striking how many employees joined the company in 1981 and 1982 and remained there in 1991, suggesting that employee retention efforts were largely successful. Entries recounting their Lucasfilm work stories are lengthy, with "See how long we've come together" as the theme. There is a return to the spirit of the early 1980s, a mix of "work hard and play hard" attitude, with pictures of people high up the organizational ladder (Lucas, Norby, Dennis Muren) and famous directors and actors (Spielberg, Kurosawa, Harrison Ford) either on set or visiting the complex and mixing with employees. The celebration of twenty years ends with a signed ("May the Force be with you") picture of George Lucas from his own high school yearbook, bringing the nostalgic yearbook theme full circle.

Conclusion

By all accounts, Lucasfilm has long had a reputation in the business of treating their employees well, consistently being one of the best-paying effects houses, and maintaining impressive employee retention. However, the yearbooks demonstrate that even in publications designed to romanticize their workplace, tumult from grumbling to active dissatisfaction can be evidenced at Lucasfilm.

This sketch of the contents and form of the Lucasfilm yearbooks is only the beginning of can be gleaned from not only the yearbooks but indeed the wider materials contained in the Thomas G. Smith collection. Finally, it is incumbent on the researcher, historian, and critic to use whatever materials outside of corporate hands there are so that it is not only conglomerates and their PR teams telling their stories.

Notes

Lucasfilm yearbooks are found in the Thomas G. Smith Papers, Container 20, folders 1–10, at the Ransom Center at the University of Texas, Austin. Lucasfilm Ltd. Yearbook 1983, Thomas G. Smith Papers, 20.4: 38.

1. For a thorough accounting of Lucasfilm publications, see Julie Turnock, *The Empire of Effects: Industrial Light & Magic and the Rendering of Realism* (Austin: University of Texas Press, 2022), 232–33n33.

2. This follows anthropologist Laura Nader's research goals of "linking the perspective of studying down to that of studying up." See Patrick Vonderau, "Access and Mistrust in Media Industries Research," in *Making Media: Production, Practices, and Professions*, ed. Mark Deuze and Mirjam Prenger (Amsterdam: Amsterdam University Press, 2019), 66.

3. Thank you to the 2017–2018 Harry Ransom Center Thomas G. Smith Research Fellowship in the Humanities for providing research funds to make this essay possible.

The Academy of Motion Picture Arts and Sciences Margaret Herrick Library houses clippings files (clipped articles from mass media magazines, industry trades, local newspapers, etc.) on George Lucas, Lucasfilm, and Industrial Light & Magic. The Marin County Library in San Rafael also contains Lucasfilm clippings files from local newspapers and other news sources.

4. See Turnock, *Empire of Effects*, chap. 3.

5. Richard Barbrook and Andy Cameron, "The Californian Ideology," *Science as Culture* 6, no. 1 (1996): 44–72.

6. John Thornton Caldwell, *Production Culture* (Durham, NC: Duke University Press, 2008).

7. Catmull and his Lucasfilm Computer Graphics Group team were sold in 1986 to Steve Jobs and became the core of Pixar Animation Studios. See Ed Catmull and Amy Wallace, *Creativity, Inc.: Overcoming the Unseen Forces That Stand in the Way of True Inspiration* (New York: Random House, 2014), 37.

8. Gowanlock elaborates: "It also neglects the fact the Silicon Valley was a clear product of the Cold War R&D complex, and that letting markets shape the course of research in place of the government does not necessarily produce better outcomes for humanity." Jordan Gowanlock, *Animating Unpredictable Effects: Nonlinearity in Hollywood's R&D Complex* (Berlin: Springer Nature, 2021), 68.

9. Fred Turner, *From Counterculture to Cyberculture* (Chicago: University of Chicago Press, 2010).

10. Jeff Menne, *Post-Fordist Cinema: Hollywood Auteurs and the Corporate Counterculture* (New York: Columbia University Press, 2019), 211.

11. Menne, *Post-Fordist Cinema*, 111; Turnock, *Empire of Effects*, 26.

12. Yearbooks were published under the nomenclature Lucasfilm Ltd, 1982–2007, LucasArts, 1991–1992, Lucas Digital Ltd, 1995–2003. They may not have published every year.

13. Tom Smith, email correspondence with the author, January 2018.

14. Tom Smith's 1982 yearbook was signed by various employees. Lucasfilm Ltd. Yearbook 1982, Thomas G. Smith Papers, 20.3.

15. Tom Smith, email correspondence with the author, January 2018.

16. Lucasfilm Ltd. Yearbook 1983, Thomas G. Smith Papers, 20.4: 47.

17. Ibid., 20.3: 45.

18. Ibid., 20.3: 60.

19. JoAnne Yates, *Control through Communication: The Rise of System in American Management* (Baltimore: Johns Hopkins University Press, 1993), 66.

20. Ibid., 77.

21. See, for example, Peter Lev citing Paul Monaco as a prime example of 1970s nostalgia in *American Films of the 70s: Conflicting Visions* (Austin: University of Texas Press, 2000), xx.

22. Lucasfilm Ltd. Yearbook 1987, Thomas G. Smith Papers, 20.6: 9.

23. Lucasfilm Ltd. Yearbook 1989, Thomas G. Smith Papers, 20.8: 22.

24. Lucasfilm Ltd. Yearbook 1991, Thomas G. Smith Papers, 20.10: 9.

10

Notes on the Lucas-Spielberg Syndrome

Jim Kendrick

"Papering the Cracks: Fantasy and Ideology in the Reagan Era," the eighth chapter in film scholar Robin Wood's seminal 1986 book *Hollywood from Vietnam to Reagan*, begins what is essentially a new section of the book, one that laments the political regression and aesthetic failures of Hollywood cinema in the 1980s after the innovative, transgressive, sometimes incomprehensible, but innately fascinating and politically engaging films of the previous decade, as exemplified by the work discussed in his chapters on Robert Altman, Larry Cohen, George A. Romero, and Brian De Palma. As Wood notes, the book's "unifying principle is the attempt to grasp, in all its complexity, a decisive 'moment,' an ideological shift, in Hollywood cinema and (by implication) in American culture."[1]

For Wood, that decisive shift was a profoundly negative development for the progression of American cinema and culture that was aided and abetted by what he terms "the Lucas-Spielberg syndrome," which appears in bold print as the opening subhead of the chapter. And, while Wood was hardly the first person to lay the blame for commercial and ideological shifts in Hollywood at the feet of George Lucas and Steven Spielberg, the filmmakers behind *Jaws* (1975), *Star Wars* (1977), *Raiders of the Lost Ark* (1981), and *E.T. the Extra-Terrestrial* (1982), he was the first to assign it a medically derived appellation. And, while the term "Lucas-Spielberg syndrome" did not take off into common usage among journalists, critics, and filmgoers, the fundamental idea behind it quickly became part of "common knowledge" regarding Hollywood history of the 1970s and 1980s, much to the detriment of Lucas and Spielberg's combined reputation as film artists. Whatever aesthetic and technological innovations,

138

creative energy, and emotional engagement they poured into their films was set aside in favor of a blame game that assigned to them almost exclusively the burden of having ended the aesthetic and political progress of Hollywood cinema during its vaunted second golden era—variously referred to as "the New Hollywood," "the New American Cinema," or "the Hollywood New Wave"—in favor of conformist, repetitive, and politically dubious blockbuster filmmaking that put profits ahead of artistry and political engagement. The goal of this chapter is to examine and interrogate this discourse around Lucas and Spielberg as purveyors of a simplistic, "high-concept" blockbuster formula, especially as conceptualized in Wood's book, and the manner in which this discourse circulated in mainstream writing about them in the 1980s.

The Lucas-Spielberg Connection

George Lucas and Steven Spielberg had a long history of friendship and collaboration dating back to the third National Student Film Festival, held on January 19, 1968, at Royce Hall on the campus of the University of California, Los Angeles (UCLA). Lucas, who was then a film student at the University of Southern California (USC), had a number of films playing in the festival, including *Electronic Labyrinth THX 1138 4EB* (1967), which he would later adapt as his first feature film, *THX 1138* (1971). Spielberg, who was then a student at California State, Long Beach, and an intern in the editorial department at Universal Studios, was in the audience that night, and he was so impressed by *THX 1138* that he went backstage and sought out Lucas to shake his hand, a seemingly insignificant moment between two aspiring film students that would later blossom into one of the most important collaborative relationships in modern Hollywood, which Lucas biographer Brian Jay Jones describes as "a mixture of good-natured competition and warm admiration."[2]

Lucas and Spielberg stayed in touch as their respective careers grew in the late 1960s and early 1970s—Lucas with *American Graffiti* (1973), a major critical and commercial hit after the disappointment of *THX 1138*, and Spielberg with his made-for-television thriller *Duel* (1971), *The Sugarland Express* (1974), and the defining summer blockbuster *Jaws*. Lucas had initially tried to get Spielberg involved at American Zoetrope, the independent production company founded by his mentor Francis Ford Coppola, for which Lucas initially served as vice president, but Spielberg was considered "too Hollywood" via his association with Universal Studios to be part their outsider revolution.[3] As Spielberg told Peter Biskind, "I was an outsider, I was the establishment.

I was being raised and nurtured at Universal Studios, a very conservative company, and in [Coppola's] eyes, and also in George's, I was working inside the system."[4]

Yet their paths crossed continuously throughout the early 1970s, sometimes via their collaborations with the same people. For example, Matthew Robbins, whom Lucas had met in the mid-1960s at USC and who had become involved with American Zoetrope, cowrote *The Sugarland Express* for Spielberg and worked as an uncredited script doctor on *Jaws*. While Lucas was casting *American Graffiti* in Los Angeles, he slept on the sofa at Robbins's house in Benedict Canyon. At the same time, Spielberg was coming over every evening to discuss the script development of *The Sugarland Express*. These nights at Robbins's house "would cement [Lucas and Spielberg's] blossoming friendship for good."[5]

Their personal and professional interplay helped to shape their early films, as Spielberg recommended that Lucas use John Williams, who composed the music for *The Sugarland Express* and *Jaws*, for *Star Wars*, thus contributing directly to the iconic aural identity of the film that would later displace *Jaws* as the highest-grossing film of all time. Spielberg used Industrial Light & Magic (ILM), the special effects company Lucas founded in 1976 to produce the effects for *Star Wars*, for several of the films he directed or produced, including *E.T.*, *Poltergeist* (1982), *The Goonies* (1985), and *Back to the Future* (1985). They offered criticism and feedback on each other's films, and they were often positioned to see in each other's work what others could not. When Lucas screened a rough cut of *Star Wars* in early 1977, minus any special effects shots or Williams's score, it was a disaster, leaving executives from 20th Century Fox unimpressed and Lucas's wife, Marcia, in tears. Several of Lucas's filmmaker friends, including John Milius and Brian De Palma, were also unenthusiastic, and Lucas was sure that it would be a failure. Spielberg, on the other hand, was prescient enough to see what it could be (and what it turned out to be), saying, "*I* liked it. I think this movie's going to make a hundred million dollars."[6]

Spielberg and Lucas "spoke the same cinematic language"[7] and shared many of the same formative experiences as kids watching movie serials. When Lucas first told Spielberg about his idea for an adventurous, globe-trotting archaeologist searching for the Lost Ark of the Covenant when they were in Hawaii in May 1977, Spielberg immediately jumped at the opportunity to direct it, thus creating the first film to officially combine their box office clout, which the Paramount marketing department was only too happy to exploit:

Steven Spielberg and George Lucas in front of Grauman's Chinese Theatre in Los Angeles in 1984. (courtesy Kobal/Shutterstock)

"Indiana Jones—the new hero from the creators of JAWS and STAR WARS," the initial one-sheet poster announced.

By the time Wood wrote about them, Lucas and Spielberg had collaborated directly on both *Raiders* and its sequel, *Indiana Jones and the Temple of Doom*, while also producing several blockbuster hits individually. For Lucas, there were the two *Star Wars* sequels, *The Empire Strikes Back* (1980) and *Return of the Jedi* (1983), both of which he handed over to other directors (Irvin Kershner and Richard Marquand, respectively) while maintaining creative control as executive producer; for Spielberg, there was *E.T.*, which replaced *Star Wars* as the highest-grossing film of all time. Their names quickly became synonymous with box office success, as one of their films topped the US box office in 1977 (*Star Wars*, with *Close Encounters* coming in second), 1980 (*The Empire Strikes Back*), 1981 (*Raiders of the Lost Ark*), 1982 (*E.T.*), and 1983 (*Return of the Jedi*). In 1984, *Indiana Jones and the Temple of Doom* came in second behind *Ghostbusters*, while 1985 was dominated by the Spielberg-produced *Back to the Future*. Along the way, Spielberg collected Best Director Oscar nominations for *Close Encounters*, *Raiders*, and *E.T.*

141

It wasn't long before journalists and critics started referring to Lucas and Spielberg as a hyphenate entity. Reviewing *Raiders*, critic Stephen Klain referred to it as "another standard-setter from the Lucas-Spielberg camps,"[8] thus demonstrating how, even though this was their first official collaboration, within critical parlance it was already acceptable to think of them as a singular entity. Articles and reviews referred to the "Lucas-Spielberg formula"[9] and "the Lucas-Spielberg juggernaut."[10] By the summer of 1983, *Time* magazine spoke of them as "the mega-hit monopoly of Spielberg-Lucas,"[11] which isolates their cinematic contributions to the financial ("mega-hit"), while also suggesting that their success impeded others ("monopoly"). When it came time for Lucas and Spielberg to immortalize their hand- and footprints in the cement outside Grauman's Chinese Theatre in 1984, they did it side by side.[12]

Reassurance Is the Keynote

As noted earlier, Wood begins "Papering the Cracks" with the subhead "The Lucas-Spielberg Syndrome," which he defines as "films catering to the desire for regression to infantilism, the doublethink phenomenon of fantasy."[13] In discussing the Lucas-Spielberg syndrome, Wood elaborates on both the effect he saw it having on film culture (namely, bland reassurance in the face of mounting cultural contradictions) and the major areas in which these films— predominantly, but not exclusively, Lucas's and Spielberg's—provide reassurance. "Reassurance is the keynote, and one immediately reflects that this is the era of sequels and repetition."[14]

Wood draws heavily on Andrew Britton's 1980 criticism of "Reaganite Entertainment," offering a similar criticism of Hollywood in the 1980s as "the curious and disturbing phenomenon of children's films conceived and marketed largely for adults—films that construct the adult spectator as a child, or more precisely, as a childish adult, an adult who would like to be a child."[15] It is important to note that Wood does not hold himself as being somehow outside of or unaffected by this phenomenon. In fact, he readily admits that he enjoyed the *Star Wars* films and claims, "I enjoy being reconstructed as a child, surrendering to the reactivation of a set of values and structures my adult self has long since repudiated."[16]

Wood then enumerates six major avenues through which these films supply certain "satisfactions" that "diminish, defuse, and render safe all the major radical movements that gained so much impetus, became so threatening in the 1970s: radical feminism, black militancy, gay liberation, the assault on patriarchy."[17] Not surprisingly, the first area on which he focuses is "childishness," which is primarily an evasion of responsibility and complex thought that he blames on filmgoers themselves, as he argues that the "success of the films is only comprehensible when one assumes a widespread *desire* for regression to infantilism."[18] Wood's conception of infantilism is directly tied to the superficial, culturally damaging values of an earlier era—the "good old values" of "racism, sexism, 'democratic' capitalism, and the capitalist myths of freedom of choice and equality of opportunity."[19]

The second major area in which the films create reassurance is through their use of special effects, what Wood calls "the essence of Wonderland Today" and the primary way in which Lucas's and Spielberg's films are distinguished from the old movie serials from which they evolved.[20] The technology of special effects and its ability to generate spectacle works both to blur the lines between "the diegetic wonders within the narrative and the extradiegetic magic of Hollywood" and to provide fundamental reassurance about the state of American capitalism: "If capitalism can still throw out entertainments such as *Star Wars* . . . the system must be basically OK, right?"[21]

In the third area, Wood draws a sharp distinction between "imagination" and "fantasy," which he sees as "fundamentally incompatible," arguing that Lucas's and Spielberg's films fall squarely into the latter category and show no evidence of the former: "If we are to continue using the term *imagination* to apply to a William Blake, we have no business using it of a George Lucas."[22] Wood defines *imagination* as "a force that strives to grasp and transform the world," whereas the fantasy evinced by Lucas and Spielberg attempts to restore "the good old values." Wood finds the fantasy elements of *Star Wars* particularly problematic, arguing that the robots, aliens, and other substitute fantasy figures simply stand in for the racial and ethnic characters of an earlier cinematic era, thus allowing the viewer to engage in "the same indulgence in WASP superiority" and "the same indoctrinated values of patriotism, racism, and militarism" without the overt embarrassment.[23]

The fourth category, which was central to Britton's arguments in "Blissing Out," is "nuclear anxiety," which Wood sees as "one of the main sources of our desire to be constructed as children, to be reassured, to evade responsibility and thought."[24] In fantasy films, this anxiety is manifested in the fight to possess some kind of ultimate weapon (the Death Star in *Star Wars*, the Ark of the Covenant in *Raiders*), which suggests that the enormity of such power is acceptable, if not positive, as long as it is under the control of the right people—that is to say, Americans.

Fifth is "fear of fascism," which Wood notes is not an external fear but an internal one driven by an unconscious anxiety that the forces of democratic capitalism could be turned into a kind of fascist totalitarianism and that there is a thin line between "the American individualist hero and the Fascist hero."[25] These anxieties are heightened by the political turn of the Reagan era, "with the resurgence of an increasingly militant, vociferous, and powerful Right, the Fascist potential forcing itself to recognition."[26] Wood notes that films like *Rocky* (1976) and *Raiders* are not "Fascist films" but rather "precisely the kinds of entertainment that a potentially Fascist culture would be expected to produce and enjoy."[27] Wood here notes the incongruities in the *Star Wars* films, which on their surface appear to unproblematically align heroism against the fascistic Empire. However, just as the United States was founded by people fleeing persecution in England only to enact their own forms of persecution, Wood wonders if the rebels of *Star Wars* would simply create another empire after the defeat of Darth Vader's.

And, finally, Wood notes that the "dominant project" of the reassuring films of the 1980s is the "restoration of the father," which is to be understood "in all senses, symbolic, literal, potential."[28] This return and strengthening of patriarchal authority is deeply intertwined with a regression in women's rights following two decades of progress and liberation, with numerous film plots involving women who are either forced into subordination or removed from the narrative entirely. Within the realm of fantasy exemplified by the films of Lucas and Spielberg, women "are allowed minor feats of heroism and aggression" although "their main function is to be rescued by the men."[29] Taking Princess Leia in the *Star Wars* films, Wood notes that, despite her having "intermittent outbursts of activity," her narrative is ultimately subservient to Luke Skywalker's ("There is never any suggestion that *she* might inherit the Force or have the privilege of being trained and instructed by Obi One [sic] and Yoda").[30] Wood extends the ramifications of renewed patriarchal power to Black and gay characters, noting how they play similarly subservient, supporting, and comical roles. Thus, Wood concludes, "the project of the *Star Wars* films and related works is to put everyone back in his/her place, reconstruct us as dependent children, and reassure us that it will all come right in the end."[31]

Prior to this enumeration of areas in which Hollywood films provide reassurance, Wood offers an important caveat: "I do not want to argue that the films are intrinsically and uniquely harmful: they are no more so than the vast majority of artifacts currently being produced by capitalist enterprise for popular consumption within patriarchal culture."[32] Rather, Wood's concern with the Lucas-Spielberg syndrome is "the enormous importance our society has conferred on the films."[33] As opposed to the old movie serials, which no one took seriously and which therefore played a marginal, minor role in popular culture, Wood worried that the seriousness with which Lucas's and Spielberg's films were taken was already leading to a diminishment of the kinds of films he championed from the previous decade, arguing that it was becoming more and more difficult to get movies that were not like *Star Wars*—that is to say, not reassuring—made on any significant level. He cites as evidence the box office failure of *Heaven's Gate* (1980), *Blade Runner* (1982), and *The King of Comedy* (1983), all challenging, provocative films that failed to find an audience in the post–*Star Wars* era.

And, as it turned out, this aspect of the Lucas-Spielberg Syndrome was the one that was picked up and repeated the most often by critics, journalists, and historians, paving the way to an understanding that Lucas and Spielberg's primary impact on cinema was to limit the kinds of films that could be made within the Hollywood system.

"At the Expense of Others": The Legacy of the Lucas-Spielberg Syndrome

The exact term *Lucas-Spielberg syndrome* never really broke out of academic discourse, although it found its way into a few mainstream publications. For example, in an interview with the *Chicago Tribune* in 1986, the year Wood's book was published, director Roman Polanski, referring to his earlier failed attempts to make his film *Pirates* (1986), said, "The project did not work out for a variety of reasons, the most obvious being the budget involved. That was before the Lucas-Spielberg syndrome took possession of Hollywood."[34] The offhanded manner in which Polanski connects the Lucas-Spielberg syndrome with the idea of possession is telling, since it suggests a kind of hostile and complete takeover that has somehow changed Hollywood from what it previously was, which is precisely Wood's concern. Polanski, who was himself a major figure in the revitalized New Hollywood of the late 1960s and 1970s with his films *Rosemary's Baby* (1968) and *Chinatown* (1974), was clearly aware of the need to distance himself and his own art from that of Lucas and Spielberg, even though the work he was then promoting at the Cannes Film Festival was an action-adventure film with a $30 million budget anchored to his desire to reinvigorate a genre from an earlier cinematic era, in this case pirate films.

145

However, while the phrase *Lucas-Spielberg syndrome* did not take off as a descriptor in mainstream discourse about Hollywood cinema in the 1980s, the fundamental ideas it embodied became the dominant means of understanding what George Lucas and Steven Spielberg represented as filmmakers and what their legacy in Hollywood cinema would be. Simply put, Lucas and Spielberg had changed the industry, and not for the better. In an article reflecting on the publication of Mark Crispin Miller's 1990 anthology *Seeing Through Movies*, *San Diego Union-Tribune* film critic Bill Hagen compiled a list of "what went wrong with the industry over the years, particularly in the 1980s," and the only filmmakers included by name were Lucas and Spielberg, who appear in the middle of the list after "Vietnam" and "Richard Nixon" and just before "Agents" and "Lawyers." Visually and rhetorically, then, Hagen places Lucas and Spielberg in the same category as a disastrous military intervention, a president forced to resign under a cloud of criminal behavior, and the soulless representatives of business. Not surprisingly, Hagen ends the list with "The blockbuster syndrome."[35]

That idea that Lucas and Spielberg were ruining the industry with their success was already thoroughly cemented in the early 1980s, so much so that *Hollywood Reporter* writer Duane Byrge could pen a satirical article about it titled "Lucas, Spielberg to Blame for B.O. Woes." Written as an interview with a fictional chicken farmer named Sampson Herbst who had recently moved to Hollywood from Beaver Junction, Idaho, the article primarily satirizes the practice of relying on "industry observers" in entertainment reporting. In "reporting" on declining box office receipts at the end of 1982, Herbst insists that "George Lucas and Steven Spielberg are to blame for the decline in b.o." When Byrge counters that they are "the ones whose movies are making the bucks," Herbst retorts, "At the expense of others and the industry in general. . . . Lucas and Spielberg are hogging all the revenues."[36]

While Byrge's tone was openly satirical, most of the attacks on Lucas and Spielberg by critics and historians—which essentially boil down to the idea that their success has been "at the expense of others"—have been quite serious. The essence of this vilification can be found most succinctly in the title of film critic David Thomson's debut column in *Esquire* in late 1996: "Who Killed the Movies?," the subtitle of which answers that very question: "How Spielberg and Lucas Ruined American Movies." Thomson minces no words as he writes that "movies are in a very bad state," saying, "I fear the medium has sunk beyond anything we dreamed of, leaving us stranded, a race of dreamers. . . . This is something like the loss of feeling, and I blame Spielberg and Lucas."[37] The rhetoric Thomson uses in assessing why Lucas and Spielberg are to blame for such a precipitous decline in the quality of American cinema largely echoes Wood's, especially in the area of childishness. About *Star Wars*, he writes, "They are films fit for children—a profound commercial strength but a large dramatic limitation."[38] About Spielberg, he writes, "He has become the most successful and famous moviemaker of our time without having to surrender his boyhood."[39] Mirroring Wood's distinction between *imagination* and *fantasy*, Thomson argues that the concept of "youth," which was so central to the explosion of innovation and artistry in 1970s American cinema, has "settled, hardened, and grown into a boisterous armor of immaturity."[40] Thus, *youthfulness*, which Thomson equates with the progressive reinvention of cinematic art, has become *immaturity*, which reflects "lack of character, lack of story, and cheerful incoherence."[41]

More directly, though, Thomson's criticism centers on the way in which Lucas's and Spielberg's massive commercial success altered the film industry, shifting it away from more serious, daring, artistic endeavors toward anything that could appeal to young viewers and be tied to increasingly expansive ancillary markets. Wood's concept of infantilizing the audience is central here, and this thread was picked up by numerous critics and historians, including *New Yorker* critic Pauline Kael, who, in the introduction to her 1985 collection *State of the Art*, refers to "the infantilization of movies in the '80s."[42] In *Easy Riders, Raging Bulls*, his history of American cinema in the 1960s and 1970s, Peter Biskind uses prose that directly reflects (you might even say "cites") some of the major concepts of the Lucas-Spielberg syndrome without naming it or Wood explicitly: "[Lucas and Spielberg] were, as Kael first pointed out, infantilizing the audience, reconstituting the spectator as child, then overwhelming him and her with sound and spectacle, obliterating irony, aesthetic self-consciousness, and critical reflection."[43]

The problem with this supposed infantilization was, as Wood argued, not an issue in and of itself but with how audiences conferred importance on these films and the subsequent effect that had on the kinds the film industry chose to make: "These films did such business that the business itself shifted its focus," writes Thomson. "It developed disdain for 'small' pictures."[44] Looking at the box office charts for 1996, it is not hard to see why Thomson would feel this way, given that the top three highest-grossing films of that year were the alien invasion spectacle *Independence Day*, the tornado-chasing thriller *Twister* (both of which were sold largely on the strength of their computer-generated special effects), and *Mission: Impossible*, a big-screen version of the 1960s television show, anchored by Tom Cruise. Yet, many of the films released that year belie Thomson's lament that "smaller" films were held in disdain in the wake of the Lucas-Spielberg syndrome. Witness the critical and commercial success of Anthony Minghella's *The English Patient*, a throwback to classical Hollywood romantic spectacle; Joel and Ethan Coen's quirky, snow-driven crime thriller *Fargo*; and Billy Bob Thornton's dark character study *Sling Blade*, the latter two of which would have been right at home in theaters in the mid-1970s alongside *The Long Goodbye* (1973) and *Taxi Driver* (1976). Consider also, as an example, 1974, the fabled year of *The Godfather, Part II*; *Chinatown*; *The Conversation*; *The Parallax View*; *Alice Doesn't Live Here Anymore*; *A Woman under the Influence*; and *The Texas Chain Saw Massacre*. Judging from the box office, there is little difference between 1996 and 1974 since the top three highest-grossing films of 1974 were two big-budget, special effects–laden disaster films, *The Towering Inferno* and *Earthquake*, and Mel Brooks's parodic western comedy, *Blazing Saddles*, whose most famous scene involves as much (if not more) flatulence than the 1996 Eddie Murphy remake of *The Nutty Professor*. In other words, there was just as much of a divide between mass-market commercial fare and smaller, more serious art and independent films in the 1970s as there was in the 1990s.

The presence of Lucas and Spielberg may have provided a convenient scapegoat for the perceived decline in film artistry, but they could hardly be blamed for creating a situation that already existed before their greatest hits were produced. Their films may have exacerbated already-existing tendencies within the Hollywood system, but they didn't start the fire. As Joseph McBride has argued, "[Spielberg] and George Lucas have been accused of ruining the film medium with their unprecedented commercial success, by inspiring the 'blockbuster syndrome', an allegation that ignores the prior influence of *The Godfather* and *The Exorcist* and the wider context of changes in film marketing, financing, and demographics."[45] Similarly, the arguments about *Star Wars*, in particular, reflecting a deep, conservative political retrenchment are problematic. As Paula J. Massood notes, "*Star Wars* has often been discussed as anticipating the country's political shift to the right, but the national mood had already been showing signs of a growing conservative shift."[46]

Nevertheless, the received wisdom that the Lucas-Spielberg syndrome is at the heart of Hollywood's inability to properly balance art and commerce persists. In a 2003 article in *Film International*, film historian Jon Lewis argues that "Lucas and Spielberg's initial impact at the box office was unprecedented and remains unmatched. It is ground zero of their importance."[47] Lewis then doubles down on this perspective, arguing about *Star Wars*, "Given the scale of its financial success, questions regarding its artistic merits seemed altogether beside the point."[48] And it is precisely this approach to Lucas and Spielberg—leading with their financial success and treating any of the traditional aesthetic, thematic, and narrative qualities of their films as either simple machinations for fostering reassurance and therefore generating big profits or simply being "beside the point"—that makes it so easy to vilify them. The very idea that an artist can be both artistically *and* financially successful has long been viewed with suspicion within artistic circles ("selling out" being one of the primary sins of any art), and such thinking regularly finds its place in discussions of Lucas and Spielberg. For example, in discussing Lucas's and others' work within the studio system, Thomas Elsaessar suggests that the manner in which they "blended the *auteur* with the entrepreneur . . . may be no recommendation for their artistic integrity."[49]

While Wood grappled with the content of their films in "Papering the Cracks," many of the journalists and critics in his wake simply took the broad outlines of the Lucas-Spielberg syndrome argument and used it as a bludgeon to the filmmakers' collective critical reputation as a convenient means of explaining complex shifts in industry practices, audience behavior, and technological developments they didn't like. Lewis notes that, by the early 2000s, most Hollywood histories regarded Lucas and Spielberg "as turncoats, as industry players who have achieved success by all too willingly accepting and all too deftly accommodating a formula for successful filmmaking."[50]

Part of that formula involves the role of special effects, an issue that Wood discussed at length. In "Who Killed the Movies?," Thomson laments the fact that modern movies rely so much on visual effects as part of the immaturity foisted on the industry by Lucas and Spielberg. Referring to *Independence Day* and *Twister*, he writes, "In other words, what we are seeing is less cinematography than an intricate set of rigged effects."[51] Lewis picks up this same argument, suggesting that "F/X gave gained prominence at the expense of mise-en-scène, performance (of the human kind), and narrative/thematic depth."[52] He goes on to suggest that Lucas and Spielberg's ultimate goal is "the possibility of making movies without human actors, simulating the production phase entirely in a post-production studio. That historians blame Lucas and Spielberg for how bad films have gotten over the past twenty-five years may not just be elitist paranoia. The sky may be falling."[53] And then, to reinforce the paucity of artistry in their work, Lewis makes a distinction between Lucas and Spielberg and what he calls "the first wave" of New Hollywood film auteurs, led by Francis Ford Coppola,

Martin Scorsese, and Robert Altman, by emphasizing their primary focus on mise-en-scène and their "pride in directing actors, set design, and lighting, all things accomplished during the production phase." Lucas and Spielberg, on the other hand, "are almost exclusively post-production directors, experts in sound and special effects and action editing."[54]

At first blush this would appear to be a variation on the argument André Bazin made regarding cinematic realism, which emphasized photography's unique ability to "capture" reality in contrast to the manipulation of montage editing.[55] However, it is also a clear attempt to find a new means of denigrating Lucas's and Spielberg's films by drawing an arbitrary distinction among the phases of production, elevating the production phrase above the postproduction phase. Such an argument is unmoored from film history, as it requires a purposeful ignoring of how filmmakers as disparate as Sergei Eisenstein, Jean-Luc Godard, and Terrence Malick could easily be described as "postproduction directors" whose films were crafted as much—if not more—in the editing room as they were during principal photography. Similarly, it requires one to ignore the enormous impact of visual effects techniques employed by filmmakers like Michael Powell and Emeric Pressburger, whose vision of a convent in the Himalayan Mountains in *Black Narcissus* (1947) was created entirely by optical effects and matte paintings, or Stanley Kubrick, whose *2001: A Space Odyssey* (1968) was one of the first films to employ special effects to create a genuinely convincing visual depiction of interstellar travel. And, most infamously, it would require one to dismiss the works of Alfred Hitchcock, who famously preferred the preproduction aspects of design and storyboarding, bemoaned working with actors, and actively loathed the process of filming.[56]

Conclusion

In the end, what most of these arguments deriving from Wood's concept of the Lucas-Spielberg syndrome have in common is the view that Lucas and Spielberg are more producers than artists. It is true that Spielberg has played an important role as a producer of films by other directors and had a central role in founding DreamWorks SKG alongside Jeffery Katzenberg and David Geffen, while Lucas stepped back from directing for twenty years after *Star Wars* to focus on executive producing the rest of the series and building Lucasfilm and Industrial Light & Magic. And there is truth to the fact that the enormous success of many of their films did influence studio calculus and were part of a larger move toward fewer and fewer expensive tentpole films, a shift that had already begun with the special effects–laden biblical epics of the 1950s and attendant new technologies like wide-screen.[57]

However, while many critics and historians view Lucas and Spielberg's legacy as one that has tainted American cinema, it is also arguable that the critical venom directed at them far outstrips whatever impact they have had on the industry, an exercise in reductive scapegoating that necessarily involves ignoring large swaths of their careers that don't fit the neat trajectory their critics would like to assign to them. This includes, for example, the major role that Lucas played in revitalizing the career of Akira Kurosawa by working with Francis Ford Coppola to convince 20th Century Fox to pay $1.5 million for the international distribution rights for *Kagemusha* (1980), the Japanese auteur's first film in five years and one that otherwise would not have been made. Lucas also served as producer on a number of films that are never associated with the Lucas-Spielberg syndrome, including Lawrence Kasdan's neo-noir *Body Heat* (1981), Paul Schrader's experimental biopic *Mishima: A Life in Four Chapters* (1985), and Anthony Hemingway's *Red Tails* (2012), a rare war film focused on Black pilots. Lucas has donated hundreds of millions of dollars to various film-related endeavors, including his alma mater, USC School of the Cinematic Arts, and the Film Foundation, a nonprofit founded in 1990 by Martin Scorsese along with Lucas, Spielberg, and eight other major American directors that has been instrumental in restoring and preserving major works of international cinema.

It is also possible, of course, to view the very criticisms of the Lucas-Spielberg syndrome in a positive light, seeing innovation, artistry, and commitment to one's vision where critics see simplification, childishness, and reductiveness. In other words, while their critics see Lucas and Spielberg's intense independence as a detriment to the art, they could just as well be held up as not just visionary artists but artists who challenged the system and won. As controversial social critic Camille Paglia has argued, "Only one cultural figure had the pioneering boldness and world impact that we associate with the early masters of avant-garde modernism: George Lucas, an epic filmmaker who turned dazzling new technology into an expressive personal genre." Where critics see infantilization, Paglia sees "novel methods" of cinematic experimentation and bold challenges to conventional camerawork, narrative, and use of color. Where critics see detriment in Lucas's use of digital and visual effects, Paglia sees a closing "of the gap between art and technology" and "significant works of modern kinetic art." Where critics see regressive politics, Paglia sees "a cohesive philosophical system" and "youthful liberalism." And, where critics see the victory of commerce over art, Paglia recognizes "a shrewd businessman" whose financial success "has certainly slowed his recognition as a major artist."[58] Thus, all of the symptoms of the Lucas-Spielberg syndrome are, rather than evidence of a broken system made infinitely worse aesthetically and politically, testament to Lucas's bold vision of the future of cinema.

Notes

1. Robin Wood, *Hollywood from Vietnam to Reagan* (New York: Columbia University Press, 1986), 2.

2. Brian Jay Jones, *George Lucas: A Life* (New York: Little, Brown, 2016), 145.

3. Ibid., 105.

4. Peter Biskind, *Easy Riders, Raging Bulls: How the Sex-Drugs-and-Rock'n'Roll Generation Saved Hollywood* (New York: Simon and Schuster, 1998), 258.

5. Jones, *George Lucas*, 146.

6. Joseph McBride, *Steven Spielberg: A Biography*, 2nd ed. (Jackson: University Press of Mississippi, 2010), 286.

7. Jones, *George Lucas*, 253.

8. Stephen Klain, "Film Review: *Raiders of the Lost Ark*," *Daily Variety*, June 5, 1981, 8.

9. Bob Thomas, "At the Movies: *Indiana Jones and the Temple of Doom*," Associated Press, May 21, 1984.

10. David Elliott, "Hollywood's Summer of Fantasy Bubbles over with Froth," *San Diego Union-Tribune*, July 22, 1984, E-1.

11. "Hot Summer II," *Time*, August 29, 1983, 63.

12. "Briefly: Lucas, Spielberg Leave Their Marks," Associated Press, May 18, 1984.

13. Wood, *Hollywood from Vietnam to Reagan*, 175.

14. Ibid., 162.

15. Ibid., 163.

16. Ibid., 164.

17. Ibid.

18. Ibid., 165.

19. Ibid., 166.

20. Ibid.

21. Ibid.

22. Ibid.

23. Ibid., 167.

24. Ibid., 168.

25. Ibid., 169.

26. Ibid., 169–70.

27. Ibid., 170.

28. Ibid., 172.

29. Ibid.

30. Ibid., 173.

31. Ibid., 174.

32. Ibid., 164–65.

33. Ibid., 165.

34. Dan Fainaru, "Polanski on Swashbuckling," *Chicago Tribune*, May 14, 1986, https://www.chicagotribune.com/news/ct-xpm-1986-05-14-8602030776-story.html.

35. Bill Hagen, "Movie Woes? Blame Ronnie," *San Diego Union-Tribune*, June 20, 1990, Entertainment, C10.

36. Duane Byrge, "Lucas, Spielberg to Blame for B.O. Woes: Industry Observer," *Hollywood Reporter*, January 4, 1982, 3.

37. David Thomson, "Who Killed the Movies? How Spielberg and Lucas Ruined American Movies," *Esquire* 126, no. 6 (December 1, 1996): 56–63.

38. Ibid.

39. Ibid.

40. Ibid.

41. Ibid.

42. Pauline Kael, *State of the Art* (New York: E. P. Dutton, 1985), xi.

43. Biskind, *Easy Riders, Raging Bulls*, 344.

44. Thomson, "Who Killed the Movies?"

45. Joseph McBride, "A Reputation: Steven Spielberg and the Eyes of the World," *New Review of Film and Television Studies* 7, no. 1 (March 2009): 6.

46. Paula J. Massood, "1977: Movies and a Nation in Transformation," in *American Cinema of the 1970s: Themes and Variations* (New Brunswick, NJ: Rutgers University Press, 2007), 188.

47. Jon Lewis, "The Perfect Money Machine(s): George Lucas, Steven Spielberg and Auteurism in the New Hollywood," *Film International (Göteborg, Sweden)* 1, no. 1 (2003): 16, https://doi.org/10.1386/fiin.1.1.12.

48. Ibid., 16.

49. Thomas Elsaessar, *The Persistence of Hollywood* (Florence, KY: Taylor and Francis, 2011), 246, http://ebookcentral.proquest.com/lib/bayloru/detail.action?docID=958043.

50. Lewis, "Perfect Money Machine(s)," 18.

51. Thomson, "Who Killed the Movies?"

52. Lewis, "Perfect Money Machine(s)," 19.

53. Ibid.

54. Ibid.

55. André Bazin, *What Is Cinema?*, vol. 1, trans. Hugh Gray (Berkeley: University of California Press, 1967).

56. Budge Crawley, Fletchers Markle, and Gerald Pratley, "I Wish I Didn't Have to Shoot the Picture: An Interview with Alfred Hitchcock," *Take One* 1, no. 1 (1966), https://the.hitchcock.zone/wiki/Take_One_(1966)_-_I_Wish_I_Didn%27t_Have_to _Shoot_the_Picture:_An_Interview_with_Alfred_Hitchcock.

57. Charles R. Acland, *American Blockbuster: Movies, Technology, and Wonder* (Durham, NC: Duke University Press, 2020).

58. Camille Paglia, "Why George Lucas Is the Greatest Artist of Our Time," *Chronicle of Higher Education* 59, no. 8 (2012), B12–B15.

11

The Dislocations of Skywalker Ranch

KENNETH HOUGH

In the closing moments of George Lucas's first feature, *THX-1138* (1971), a defector slowly scales an enormous concrete air shaft. He is pursued by ominous robotic police officers with featureless chrome faces and blandly saccharine voices—enforcers from the subterranean techno-fascist society that THX seeks to escape. "This is your last chance to return with us," they plead. "You have nowhere to go." Ignoring them, he fixates on the bright glowing exit into the unknown far above and resumes climbing. The film is about an individual awakening to the realization that the walls of his prison are illusory. His difficulty comes in navigating a futuristic built environment, one of the most dislocating ever put on film. The underground cityscape is a confabulation of Southern California's endless rivers of concrete, which USC student Lucas found so dystopic, and elements of Northern Californian futurism, both of the past (Frank Lloyd Wright's Marin County Civic Center becomes a crowded city center) and of the "now" (unfinished Bay Area Rapid Transit [BART] tunnels serve as THX's final escape route).[1] Humans exist here as abstractions, ghosts in the machine. "We share nothing . . . but space," THX confesses about his closest relationship. Heightening the confusion, Lucas and sound designer Walter Murch created a "cubist cinema" land and soundscape at once alien and familiar, oppressive and absurdly comical, technologically precise and malfunctioning. Plato's allegory of the cave meets Buck Rogers, by way of Orwell's *1984* and Becket's *Godot*. Although fans would later see much of *Star Wars*' DNA in the movie, bewildered Warner Brothers studio executives, representing Hollywood's old guard, failed to appreciate the future that *THX* heralded; and so Lucas, like his protagonist, sought an exit.

Nearly a decade later, Lucas surveyed a beautiful green valley near Nicasio, California, evocative of the sunny Garden of Eden we imagine is at the end of THX's escape. Apart from the remnants of an old dairy farm, the pristine 1,700-acre Bulltail Ranch in the coincidentally named Lucas Valley seemed far removed from the twentieth century.[2] In reality, it was only fifty-five miles north of San Francisco, close to where Lucas and Coppola had incorporated American Zoetrope in 1969 in their attempt to build a Northern California film industry. By 1978, *Star Wars* was a worldwide sensation, but its creator was exhausted and still smarting from ill treatment by the studios. Flush with wealth, fired by passion for building, he dreamed of establishing his own film-making domain on this rural spread, free of Hollywood's oppressive influences. "I walked into the valley," recalled Lucas, "and I just said, 'Okay, this is it. I'm buying it.'"[3]

This is part of the origin story for what would become Skywalker Ranch, a pre- and postproduction film facility and the iconic architectural embodiment of Lucasfilm. In a setting out of California's agrarian past, Lucas endeavored to build the future of cinematic arts—a dislocation of space and time worthy of his movie fantasies. Indeed, Lucas has called Skywalker Ranch "my biggest movie."[4] If well-known, the site also has an aura of the vague, which began when Lucas first concealed his role in acquiring the property. An emphasis on security measures and the invisibility of the property outside its gates, as well as his ambiguous goals for the ranch (other than being essentially creative), left even his closest colleagues perplexed. In one of his earliest public statements about the ranch project, Lucas asserted, "I'm trying to develop a place that is designed to stimulate activity, especially among writers."[5] However, for writer-director John Milius, who worked closely with Lucas at USC and during their American Zoetrope days, the ranch failed to live up to such high-minded ideals, becoming Lucas's "private little duchy," whose singular export was "a bunch of pap."[6]

Some may hold Skywalker Ranch in deep reverence, but others came to see it as an expensive distraction or, worse, a self-destructive obsession. The latter impression was particularly acute in the late 1990s among a fan base that had grown impatient during the fifteen-year hiatus between the original *Star Wars* trilogy and the prequels. Despite occasional peeks behind the curtain, the ranch remained off-limits to most, leaving many baffled at Lucas's sequestration there. For instance, two episodes of the animated satire *South Park* disparaged Lucas's CGI alterations of his own beloved movies and courted controversy by depicting Skywalker Ranch as a desecrated temple and the staging ground for criminal predation. Creators Trey Parker and Matt Stone, themselves aging *Star Wars* fans, puzzled over the decline of a filmmaker whom they once idolized, asking, "Is that just what happens when you get old?"[7] There were also Marin County residents whose initial enthusiasm over a famous filmmaker establishing a think tank in their midst had curdled into suspicion. Some came to regard "Lucasland" (their derisive label for Lucas's brainchild) as an unwelcome corporate Trojan horse or "industrial beachhead" threatening the rural character of the valley many had fought to preserve.[8] Mystified observers would be left to debate the various meanings ascribed to the ranch. Is it a studio or a home? Is it truly a place of artistic collaboration and experimentation or just a stylish movie factory? This chapter will attempt to clarify some of these ambiguities by providing a rough time line of Skywalker Ranch's conception, construction, and expansion while also considering the tensions between Lucas's evolving visions of the facility and often more critical popular perceptions.

"To Leave Home to Look for Home"

The impetus to build Skywalker Ranch, like many of Lucas's creations, was rooted in a primal desire to find creative freedom in new horizons. After escaping death in a car crash in 1962, he took his first steps on this journey, choosing to leave his birthplace, Modesto, California, and a comfortable but predictable destiny of becoming a small-town retailer. *American Graffiti*'s (1973) dramatic tension derives from characters risking the abandonment of their established lives or succumbing to indolent willful immaturity. "You just can't stay seventeen forever," says Steve (Ron Howard), contemplating college in another town, while his girlfriend, Laurie (Cindy Williams), muses, "It doesn't make sense to leave home to look for home, to give up a life to look for a new life." Screenwriters Gloria Katz and Willard Huyck initially presented the film's cruising culture as a one-sided purgatorial road to nowhere, but Lucas admonished them to strike a balance between angst and happy nostalgia. "I loved cruising," he admitted, "and I love Modesto."[9]

In 1965, USC's film school and its notoriously dilapidated classrooms became Lucas's new stomping ground. What the environment lacked in style, it made up for in camaraderie and an energetic do-it-yourself ethos that inspired Lucas's early student works, especially *Freiheit* (1966) and *THX 1138 4EB* (1967), with their recurrent thematic struggle for freedom. As he transitioned from pupil to fledgling filmmaker, new father figures emerged, like Francis Ford Coppola, who schooled his new protégé in moviemaking techniques and the artistic necessity of risk-taking for personal evolution. In Lucas's *Filmmaker* (1969), documenting the making of *The Rain People* (1969), a thirty-year-old Coppola advises, "If you're not willing to risk some money when you're young, then you're certainly not going to ever risk anything in the years that follow."[10] Spurred on by the rebellious spirit of the times—and inspirational trips to the Lanterna Films mansion in Denmark and John Korty's barn-based independent studio in Stinson Beach, California (just thirty miles from the future site of Skywalker Ranch)—they sought to establish a filmmaking community of their own far, far away from Hollywood. Both nurtured techno-hippie fantasies of having "a place down in the country" with the latest equipment, where young filmmakers could gather to "discuss the script in the garden and . . . have lunch together." However, economic realities delayed this dream, forcing American Zoetrope into an old warehouse in downtown San Francisco, a "dark building, down in a very kind of rough area," according to Milius.[11] Despite its idealistic atmosphere, Zoetrope's utopian experiment was doomed, largely because of Coppola's profligate spending.[12] "We had the naïve notion that it was the equipment which would give us the means of production," he later admitted. "Of course, we learned much later that it wasn't the equipment, it was the money."[13]

Lucas took these lessons to heart and opted to edit *THX* (with Murch's help) in the cramped attic of his small Mill Valley home, which he shared with his first wife and fellow film editor, Marcia Griffin. "I've always worked out of my house," Lucas subsequently reflected. "It's just a much more friendly atmosphere, more comfortable and calming."[14] Further blurring the distinction between home and workplace, in 1971 the tiny dwelling became the first headquarters of the nascent Lucasfilm, permanently establishing Lucas as a Marin County filmmaker.[15]

After *Graffiti*'s success, Lucas began acquiring real estate, including two San Anselmo, California, houses. At 30 Medway Road, Lucas wrote the initial drafts of *Star Wars*. In the sagging Victorian mansion at 52 Park Way (dubbed "Parkhouse" by Marcia), he built "a little filmmaking complex" that included screening and editing rooms and "Sprocket Systems," a sound department in the basement, which remained there until a flood evicted it in 1982. At Parkhouse, Lucas attempted to recreate the best aspects of USC and Zoetrope, housing close friends and fellow filmmakers, who helped him hone *Star Wars*.[16] Even then, bigger plans were afoot, and Lucas's longtime assistant Jane

Bay remembered him filling legal pads with sketches for what would become Skywalker Ranch.[17]

Star Wars, the story of a despondent young water farmer who saves the universe, was the ultimate expression of 1970s cinematic escapism and brought Lucas closer to realizing his dreams of independent filmmaking. However, he needed more than just a plan and the land to build it on. Lucas's continuation of the *Star Wars* trilogy was largely a means to an end, and much of sequels' proceeds were earmarked for the building of Skywalker Ranch. Hired to direct *The Empire Strikes Back*, Irvin Kershner was amazed by the rough sketches he was shown and marveled at their audacity: "All the billions of dollars ever made in the film business, and no one has ever plowed it back into . . . creating an environment where the love of films could create new dimensions."[18] Yet the pressure was on when Lucas informed him he had literally bet the farm on *Empire*: "If the movie's a success, we'll be able to build all this. If it's a flop, the ranch will never get off the ground."[19]

Skywalker Ranch
A Chronology

1969	Lucas and Coppola form American Zoetrope in San Francisco; Lucas marries Marcia Griffin and moves to Mill Valley in Marin County
1970–1971	Lucas directs and edits his first feature film, *THX 1138*; a critical hit but a box office dud, the movie helps sink American Zoetrope
1971	Seeking debt relief, Lucas founds Lucasfilm in his Mill Valley home, with him and Marcia as the only employees
1973–1974	After *American Graffiti* becomes Lucas's first hit, he uses proceeds to buy and renovate homes in San Anselmo, California; he begins writing *Star Wars* for Fox
1975	Industrial Light & Magic (ILM) Sprocket Systems (later Skywalker Sound) founded
1978	Lucas buys Bulltail Ranch in Nicasio, California, and begins making *The Empire Strikes Back* (1980) to finance construction of Skywalker Ranch; Lucas Research Library collection founded by Deborah Fine, who oversees collection until 1992
1979	Marin County Planners formally approve the construction of Skywalker Ranch

1980	Ranch construction kicks off with first annual Independence Day cookout; Lucas fires Lucasfilm CEO Charlie Webber for wanting to stop ranch construction
1981	Lucasfilm officially relocates to Marin County from Los Angeles
1983	Lucas and Marcia divorce; the $50 million settlement grants Lucas the ranch
1984–1997	Lucas campaigns for an expansion of the ranch onto adjacent Big Rock property
1984	EditDroid, "the first disc-based nonlinear editing system," is developed at the ranch
1985	Douglas Norby becomes president of Lucasfilm (until 1992); in summer Lucas declares Skywalker Ranch open for business
1987	Sprocket Systems becomes Skywalker Sound and moves to ranch's newly completed Technical Building
1988	Debut of *Joseph Campbell and the Power of Myth* miniseries, filmed at the ranch between 1985 and 1986
1991	New climate-controlled Archives Building completed at the ranch
1992	ABC premiers *The Young Indiana Jones Chronicles* series, highlighting the ranch's postproduction and digital SFX abilities
1993	A small-scale ranch expansion approved; ILM's CGI for *Jurassic Park* points to maturation of digital special effects and future of the industry
1994	Lucasfilm president and COO Gordon Radley argues for a "Skywalker Ranch precedent" for environmentally conscious developers; Banned from the Ranch Entertainment founded by former ILM employees
1997	After meeting the demands of county officials and staving off lawsuits, Lucas finally wins approval for an $87 million expansion of Big Rock
1999	MTV hosts a *Phantom Menace* premiere at the ranch; Lucasfilm selected to develop Letterman complex at the Presidio; *Mad TV* parodies Skywalker Ranch
2001	In the low-budget documentary *Starwoids*, despondent fans grapple with Skywalker Ranch security while joking about a break-in
2002	Ranch employee charged with stealing IP related to *Attack of the Clones*; *South Park*'s "Free Hat" episode imagines a comical

	break-in of the ranch; Big Rock Ranch complex opens for business
2003	$350 million Letterman Digital Arts Center groundbreaking; most ranch-based divisions will relocate there, except Skywalker Sound, which remains
2008	"The China Problem," a second, darker parody of the ranch, appears on *South Park*; the Cartoon Network animated series *Star Wars: The Clone Wars* debuts
2009	*Fanboys* released, a Skywalker Ranch break-in comedy misfire with scenes filmed at the ranch's Main House
2012	Lucas announces retirement; sells Lucasfilm to Disney; drops plans for Grady Ranch expansion
2013	George Lucas and Melody Hobson wed at the ranch by Bill Moyers
2019	John Favreau's *The Chef Show* visits Skywalker Ranch; *The Mandalorian* debuts on Disney+

"A Little Mud Hut Outside the Castle"

Completed in the mid-1980s, the Main House is the picturesque centerpiece of Skywalker Ranch. Its intricate yet playful Queen Anne styling speaks to both Lucas's design tastes and his character.[20] "I think my heart lies at about the year 1910," he told *Architectural Digest* in a 2004 survey of the property. "I love that style."[21] Moreover, the cream-white exterior suggests innocence, traditional values, and sturdiness and provides a striking contrast to the surrounding 2,554 acres of greenery and hills. Artfully asymmetrical, the structure's large turrets, picture windows, veranda, and leaded-glass entrance are a balancing act between mechanical precision and Disneyland-like whimsy. "I like being thought of as like a toy maker who makes films," Lucas admits.[22]

His fabricated origin story for the ranch also underscores the Fantasyland parallels. Employees are well versed in the invented legend of a retired ship captain (or was it railroad tycoon?) who, after a lifetime of sailing adventures, supposedly erected a house there in 1869 (the same year, incidentally, as Parkhouse's *actual* construction). To make sense of the interior's jumble of styles—which run the gamut from arts and crafts to art deco—the backstory has the house evolving organically as the fictional patriarch's descendants made their own additions, each representing a new era of design.[23] Conjecturing a disorienting narrative of traditionalism and constant regeneration, Lucas seemed to understand that Skywalker Ranch's true purpose would emerge only later. "I don't know why I'm building the ranch," he told biographer Dale Pol-lock just after construction began. "It's coming up with an idea and just being committed to it without any logical point of view. . . . It's just a feeling I have."[24]

As the Main House and other structures took shape, Walter Murch attempted to pay tribute to the totality of the ranch's visual inventiveness by declaring, "The ultimate vision of the place is just Hearstian."[25] This evocation of William Randolph Hearst, the famously prickly media mogul, is accurate in the sense that both men were independent movie producers who spurned Hollywood's gravitational pull for rural climbs where they exercised ultimate control. While Lucas would joke that his ranch was just "a little mud hut outside the castle," Hearst's "castle" at his San Simeon ranch was fashioned to resemble a seventeenth-century Spanish-Italian Mediterranean village while also boasting plenty of modern amenities just under the surface that allowed him to run a movie business from afar.[26] The obvious downside to the Lucas-Hearst analogy is the impression that Lucas (like the Hearst-inspired title character in Citizen Kane) had traded artistic integrity for money and power, becoming a recluse at "his Xanadu in Marin County."[27]

Collecting is another passion linking Lucas and Hearst, whose estates also functioned as grand display cases. At Skywalker Ranch, props from Lucas's movies share gallery space with works by renowned narrative painters and illustrators like Norman Rockwell, Maxfield Parish, Carl Barks, and Alex Ray-mond. Perhaps the most impressive exhibit is the Main House's Lucas Research Library. Begun in 1978 by Lucasfilm librarian Deborah Fine, it contains more than twenty-seven thousand books, including the former research libraries of Paramount and Universal Studios; hundreds of newspaper and magazine titles; and some seventeen thousand film and video recordings.[28] Lit from above by an enormous, art nouveau orange-and-amber stained-glass mandala, the library's redwood bookshelves ("rescued from a defunct bridge") hide a secret entrance to Lucas's off-limits upper-floor office. According to a ranch brochure, the library is a "full service research department" available to "costume and set designers, hair stylists, makeup artists, directors and producers," and other bookish guests.[29] During the production of The Young Indiana Jones Chronicles TV series, it was inhabited by writers like Carrie Fisher, Frank Darabont, and Jonathan Hales while they researched Lucas's "homework" assignments.[30]

Indeed, a primary aim was to build a place of lively creative collaboration, Zoetrope's lost dream, which Lucas still cherished. Communal spaces abound at the ranch, from volleyball courts to bustling dining areas and serene walking paths around the manufactured Lake Ewok. Attempts at creating a family-like atmosphere even preceded its construction, growing into the annual Independence Day cookouts, once small gatherings that swelled into the thousands as Lucasfilm's fortunes and workforce grew. After Lucas's fruitful collaboration with Spielberg on *Raiders of the Lost Ark* (1981), he hoped the ranch might become a venue for further cooperative efforts. It did, but with mixed success. Some, like Ron Howard, quickly took to the surroundings, spending long periods with Lucas to create the epic fantasy *Willow* (1988). Yet David Lynch, a director like Lucas with a ken for architecture, found the ranch so off-putting that he was racked by headaches—seemingly at the prospect of being under Lucas's control—a negative reaction to the built environment leading him to turn down directing *Return of the Jedi*.[31] Several years later, an overly orchestrated Skywalker Ranch event left Milius similarly nauseated. Perceiving Lucas as a would-be cult leader, he grimly teased fellow attendees Harrison Ford and Francis Ford Coppola not to "drink the cool aid."[32] Fisher, who had roomed at the ranch during writing stints, wryly noted that Skywalker Ranch is "where George makes the rules."[33]

These varying impressions may stem from a confusion over the ranch's primacy, whether business or creativity. Lucas believed the ranch's fusion of art and experimentation was central to his economic success, and in 1980, he fired Lucasfilm CEO Charlie Weber, who deemed the facility a poor business venture. "The ranch is the only thing that counts. That's what everybody is working for," Lucas angrily countered. "And if that's getting lost in the shuffle, then something's terribly wrong here."[34] Douglas Norby, who replaced Weber, was not quite as skeptical as his predecessor, but his tenure was marked by strict cost cutting, especially as the first phase of construction neared completion. Plenty of experimentation still took place at the ranch, especially in the computer division, including the development of EditDroid and SoundDroid technology and the creation of Pixar computer animation, divisions quickly sold off once their technology proved marketable. The Lucasfilm Games Division, once headquartered in the ranch's Stable House, was also populated by exuberant designers developing inventive video games like *Ballblazer*, *Rescue on Fractalus*, and *Maniac Mansion*, which took inspiration from Lucas's pioneering cinema.[35] Yet Norby's severe penny-pinching left some employees convinced the games division was essentially a tax dodge to find novel ways to reinvest in the company. According to Peter Langston, Lucasfilm Games' first employee, Lucas often referred to the games division as "the Lost Patrol"—adventurous but also precarious—and "he needed us to prove that we understood the business."[36]

Those who saw Norby as a corporate outsider uninterested in filmmaking may have bristled at his miserly ways, but he helped to establish Lucasfilm's self-sufficiency.[37] He also served as a lightning rod who could deal with difficult day-to-day people problems at the ranch, shielding Lucas, who most employees in this period still believed was a shy, unsullied, creative genius.[38] Norby's tenure came to an end just as Lucasfilm's successful gamble on computer-generated imaging started upending the movie industry.

The colossal seven-hundred-thousand-square-foot Technical Building is probably the ranch's second most recognizable building, after the Main House, and possibly its most dislocating. Designed by the architectural firm Backen, Arrigoni & Ross (working from Lucas's specifications), its specially distressed red bricks and a vineyard of Merlot and Chardonnay grapes project the look of a turn-of-the-century winery, conforming to the ranch's imaginary history.[39] Yet inside is one of the world's most specialized postproduction facilities, "a Disneyland built for filmmakers," according to Randal Kleiser, Lucas's former USC roommate, who gushed, "It's got everything that you could ever want, every toy, every trick, every cutting-edge tool."[40] The tech building's modularity is another by-product of the push and pull between technological experimentation and Norby's economic austerity, and it was engineered so that all recording, editing, and mixing hardware could be easily swapped out for the latest gear without the need for a total remodeling.[41]

As with other parts of the ranch, the current and classic rub elbows. In the three-hundred-seat Stag Theater, where most of the ranch's screenings take place, the highest-quality sound and projection are contrasted against 1940s art moderne styling, including the ominous art deco statues—props briefly glimpsed in Palpatine's office in *Revenge of the Sith* (2005)—that flank the enormous screen.[42] Opened in 1987, the Technical Building became the permanent home of Skywalker Sound, as Sprocket Systems had been renamed. There, technician Thomas Holman revolutionized movie theater sound by perfecting the THX system. Ever ready to elicit a Wild West mythos, Lucas told Tom Kobayashi, his postproduction head and the general manager of Skywalker Sound until 1992, that the Tech Building was the site of a pioneering adventure: "We're going on a covered wagon West and we're going to be fighting a bunch of Indians."[43] By the early 1990s, just as ranch-produced wines were maturing, so too were the facility's many tech toys, and Lucas found himself once again "getting the itch to play."[44] From this expensive playground sprung *The Young Indiana Jones Chronicles* TV series, whose production served as a blueprint for the long-planned *Star Wars* prequels. If Lucas had finally realized the true purpose of his ranch as the "studio of the future," some of his neighbors were on guard against tomorrow encroaching upon the timeless Lucas Valley.[45]

"If It Wasn't for the Ranch, I Wouldn't Have Made Any More Films"[46]

Continual reinvention is one of the ranch's foremost embedded fantasies—where a calm facade of timelessness contains a riot of technological change. An exception to this narrative is the barnlike two-story, 2,800-square-foot Archives Building, which safeguards tens of thousands of priceless original Lucasfilm artifacts. Completed in 1991, it is among the few places at the ranch as static inside as its surface appearance. A reliquary, like the lost Ark in *Raiders* (which is housed there), epitomizing Lucasfilm's historic memory and cinema's transition from practical to computer effects. Leading this revolution largely from Skywalker Ranch, Lucas believes it will be his most lasting legacy.[47] Yet spearheading a digital future necessitated disrupting the ranch's surface calm. Even before phase 1 of the ranch's construction had been completed, Lucas began gearing up for a major expansion. Silent purchases of several large parcels of land to the east directly adjacent to the existing facilities, ranches Big Rock and Grady, brought Lucas's property holdings in Nicasio to over 5,000 acres. Initially he claimed that these acquisitions were privacy measures blocking a planned housing development.[48] However, in 1985 he began floating the idea of building a major 350,000-square-foot postproduction complex on one the plots, technically a satellite campus to the original Skywalker Ranch.[49] Both Lucas's representatives and contemporary media accounts insinuated the holdings were organic outgrowths of the original property. "A mini Skywalker" is how Lucasfilm attorney Doug Ferguson classified the additions, and necessary upgrades to keep Lucasfilm competitive.[50] Behind this lay a realization that while Lucas might have launched the digital revolution, upstarts were beginning to emerge, like Digital Domain, which was cofounded in 1993 by former ILM general manager Scott Ross.[51] Defections and expulsions became so common that being "banned from the ranch" became a colloquial expression if not a badge of honor in the effects industry. To wit, visual effects specialists Casey Cannon and Van Ling, both former ILM employees, in 1994 founded the special effects company Banned from the Ranch Entertainment.[52] To keep pace, Gordon Radley, who replaced Norby in 1992 as Lucasfilm president and COO argued, "The need to build this [new facility] is inescapable," and predicted, "Sooner or later, it's all going to be digital."[53] Lucasfilm was at a crossroads, but as the second-biggest employer in the region, it hoped to use its economic leverage to win expansion approvals. Radley and other spokespersons threatened to relocate operations away from Marin, which could deal a blow to the local economy and community pride at having "lost" such a unique enterprise as Skywalker Ranch.

Dire predictions like these motivated some to speak up in Lucas's favor. Peter Anderson, a columnist for Marin's *Independent Journal* (and an unabashed Lucas cheerleader), contended that "Skywalker Ranch is not only a magnificent model of work and leisure at perfect juncture; it is also a fitting reflection of Lucas the man—withdrawn, creative, productive in our midst yet barely visible."[54] The *Journal* also reported on the formation of the "Friends of Lucasfilm," purportedly made up of twenty-two local businesses with strong economic ties to Lucasfilm who asked "readers to mail coupons to Marin supervisors voicing their support for Lucas's plans."[55]

Yet the relocation threat also raised suspicions about Lucas's ultimate goals and the impact of bending the county's zoning rules to suit his business needs. Increased traffic along Lucas Valley Road was a central concern of those hoping to preserve the region's "rural character." Even after traffic studies suggested that a ranch expansion would have a smaller impact than the alternative housing development, some remained torn. "My children would kill me if they knew I was saying anything bad about George," admitted area resident Linda Senf, who still felt a "lack of trust" in Lucas's promises to protect the environment.[56] Some guessed Lucas was first and foremost a businessman, who might still decide to pull up stakes at some later date, potentially opening the door to less responsible developers.[57] While applauding Lucasfilm's "unbelievable sensitivity to the land," county supervisor Gary Giacomini chided his perceived self-importance and smirkingly wondered what might happen if "poor George gets run over by a truck or changes his mind." With an almost geological perspective, Giacomini's concern was for securing environmental protections eons past his or Lucas's lifetime. "If we could know George Lucas was immortal and the uses [of the land] would always be put forth by him and ultimately conditioned by us, everything could be wonderful," Giacomini admitted. "But you can't zone personalities. We're all just passing through here, the stewards of this place for just a little while."[58]

Others were less charitable, like *Point Reyes Light* publisher David Mitchell, who declared, "George Lucas is a disaster for this area."[59] Two of the most persistent critics were Ron Marinoff, onetime president of the Lucas Valley Homeowner's Association, and Robert "Bob" Roumiguiere, a Marin County supervisor. Marinoff, who also had a seat on the county's planning commission, complained that county officials had been seduced by "Hollywood glamour crap" when they first approved Skywalker Ranch in 1979—an unforgivable subversion of the countywide plan championed by the preservationists like himself. Skywalker's mission creep from a "rural think-tank retreat" to a corporate headquarters with hundreds of employees was especially galling, and Marinoff concluded, "Lucas has no credibility."[60] As the proposal for Big Rock ballooned from 350,000 to 550,000 square feet, including a "twelve-building complex of sound stages, studios, offices, shops, production areas, and underground parking for 175 employees," Supervisor Roumiguiere balked. "It's so big it's unbelievable. . . . 550,000 is monstrous."[61] Unmoved by a threatened relocation, he vowed, "We're not going to destroy the valley to keep Lucas here."[62]

Eventually, appeals to environmental sensitivity (a mutual concern of both Lucas and his challengers) allowed the Big Rock development to proceeded. Norby at first advanced only the idea of preserving "the rural appearance" of the valley but in time promoted an early corporate sustainability narrative showcasing Lucas's track record of responsible land use, especially his pledge to retain 95 percent of any improved parcel as open space.[63] In 1988, Norby foresaw that corporate attention to environmental protections would be as just as pioneering as the coming digital revolution: "We believe, in fact, that we are creating a model for future development."[64]

Lucas's outreach efforts also evolved, and he learned to employ Skywalker Ranch for better public relations by opening its gates to a select few within the community. In 1992, John Rojas, the president of the Mount Marin Homeowners Association, admitted that tours of the ranch had soothed the fears of many locals.[65] By the mid-1990s, both Marinoff and Roumiguiere had left office, and even former detractors had become more favorable to the expansion. Supervisor Giacomini celebrated Lucas's vast donation of open space, claiming that the preservation of "6,000 acres forever" was his most meaningful accomplishment in Marin government.[66] "A lot of our fears were overblown at the time," admitted a spokesman for Save Our Countywide Plan, a pressure group that had been among the most vociferous opponents of the expansion. "I think there was the feeling we weren't be listened to . . . but it was a matter of us working together. We're proud to have them in Lucas Valley."[67] These experiences lead to not only more frequent use of the ranch as a promotional tool but also moments of important self-reflection. For instance, in 2002 while promoting *Attack of the Clones*, an uncomfortable-looking Lucas guided hip-hop artist and MTV News correspondent Master P around the Technical

Building, and when asked by the rapper to describe his "dark side," Lucas answered candidly, "I think whenever you try to hold on to too much you begin to go to that greedy, self-centered place that gets you into trouble."[68]

However, winning approval for Big Rock's expansion proved somewhat of a pyrrhic victory. It was downsized and delayed for fifteen years, and by the time the project was completed in 2002 (in a Frank Lloyd Wright Prairie style), another home for ILM and most of Lucasfilm's divisions was in the works—the $350 million Letterman Digital Arts Center, an old army hospital at the Presidio in San Francisco that Lucas began renovating in 2003.[69] Although briefly hosting the Lucasfilm Animation division (until that too moved to the Presidio in 2006), Big Rock never became the fully functional studio Lucas envisioned. A 2018 redesign christened "Summit Skywalker Ranch" transformed much of the site into fifty-seven guest accommodations as part of the exclusive Skywalker Retreats real estate rental side business.[70] Community goodwill also seemed to fade over time. A planned third phase of expansion on the Grady Ranch (which in preliminary designs looked strikingly like Hearst's San Simeon estate) met stiff resistance from some residents who feared light pollution from the proposed complex.[71] In 2012, Lucas abruptly called off the project and announced that the site would instead be earmarked for affordable housing.[72] Although desperately needed in Marin County, this too was assailed as opening the door to traffic and crime, and the project remains in stasis today.[73]

Returning to the Cave

In January 2012, George Lucas announced his retirement from feature-film production. At sixty-seven, he was nearly a decade younger than Jack Warner had been when that studio head's departure from Warner Bros. almost literally opened the door for Lucas and Coppola, the "New Hollywood" vanguard who revitalized an ossified film industry.[74] Lucas's exit would also mean handing the baton to a new generation of filmmakers, and like Warner, he would not be walking away empty-handed. In October, he sold Lucasfilm to Disney for more than $4 billion in cash and company stock.[75] Skywalker Ranch figured into this transition, symbolically at first. One of the earliest examples of the nascent Disney-Lucasfilm partnership was an episode of the tween sitcom *A.N.T. Farm* broadcast less than a month after the merger that featured a faux Skywalker Ranch unconvincingly constructed on a soundstage.[76]

The actual ranch would soon be the site of a more personal transition. Almost thirty years to the day after announcing to stunned ranch staff the end of his first marriage, Lucas would wed financier and one-time DreamWorks Animation chairwoman Melody Hobson in a ceremony officiated by ordained Baptist minister Bill Moyers.[77] The ranch-as-home narrative was resurgent in media as well. Two of Lucasfilm's more successful "young Turks," Dave Filoni and Jon Favreau, creators of Disney's popular *The Mandalorian* TV series, appeared together at Skywalker Ranch for an October 2019 episode of Favreau's food travel program, *The Chef Show*.[78] Instead of keeping the public at a distance, as Lucas often had, they welcomed viewers in, feeding them (virtually) on ranch-grown food and behind-the-scenes stories, as if they were preferred house guests. Though Lucas was nowhere to be seen, his presence (like a spectral Obi-Wan Kenobi) still loomed over the occasion, the wizened founder of a schoolhouse-temple, just as Joseph Campbell had once consecrated the ranch. Lucas's lifelong struggle to escape had built this place, but Campbell might also remind him that the beginning and the ending of the hero's journey are fused and that returning to the primordial wellspring of imagination is an essential part of the life cycle. As Campbell once said of the cave, "You feel this is the womb. This is the place from which life comes, and that world up there in the sun. . . . That's the secondary world, this is primary."[79]

Notes

1. Mark Waxman, producer, *George Lucas: Maker of Films* (Los Angeles: KCET, 1971), film.

2. The Lucas Valley was named for a local settler of no relation to George Lucas who received the property as a wedding gift in the 1880s. See Brian Jay Jones, *George Lucas: A Life* (New York: Little, Brown, 2016), 273.

3. Marcus Hearn, *The Cinema of George Lucas* (New York: Harry N. Abrams, 2005), 125.

4. Jones, *George Lucas*, 348.

5. Hearn, *Cinema of George Lucas*, 124.

6. Jones, *George Lucas*, 367.

7. *South Park: The Complete Sixth Season*, season 6, episode 9, "Free Hat," audio commentary by Trey Parker and Matt Stone, aired July 10, 2002, Comedy Central, Paramount Home Entertainment, 2005, DVD; *South Park: The Complete Twelfth Season*, season 12, episode 8, "The China Problem," audio commentary by Trey Parker and Matt Stone, aired October 8, 2008, Comedy Central, Paramount Home Entertainment, 2009, DVD.

8. Paul Liberatore, "Marin's Movie Emperor: George Lucas' Ranch Keeps Getting Bigger," *San Francisco Chronicle*, April 15, 1985, Marin County Library Anne T. Kent

California Room, Moving Pictures: Lucasfilm Clippings 1985–1989 folder, San Rafael, California (hereafter LC 85–89 folder); Jones, *George Lucas*, 334.

9. Hearn, *Cinema of George Lucas*, 46.

10. "Filmmaker," *American Short Films*, directed by George Lucas (1969; Great Britain: Cinema16, 2006), DVD.

11. "A Legacy of Filmmakers: The Early Years of American Zoetrope," written, produced, edited, and directed by Gary Leva, narrated by Richard Dreyfuss, *THX-1138: The George Lucas Director's Cut* (2004; Burbank, CA: Warner Home Video, 2004), special edition DVD.

12. Jones, *George Lucas*, 111.

13. Dale Pollock, *Skywalking: The Life and Films of George Lucas*, updated ed. (New York: Da Capo, 1999), 86.

14. Patricia Leigh Brown, "George Lucas at Skywalker Ranch," *Architectural Digest* 61, no. 3 (March 2004): 129–96, https://global-factiva-com.proxy.library.ucsb.edu:9443 /ga/default.aspx; Pollock, *Skywalking*, 86–87; Jones, *George Lucas*, 103.

15. Jones, *George Lucas*, 125; Pollock, *Skywalking*, 104.

16. Jones, *George Lucas*, 163.

17. Charles Champlin, *George Lucas: The Creative Impulse; Lucasfilm's First Twenty Years* (New York: H. N. Abrams, 1992), 168–71.

18. Pollock, *Skywalking*, 208.

19. Patrick Goldstein, "The Force Never Left Him," *Los Angeles Times*, February 2, 1997.

20. Linda Osband, *Victorian House Style: An Architectural and Interior Design Source* (Newton Abbot: David and Charles, 2001), 9, 13.

21. Brown, "George Lucas at Skywalker Ranch."

22. Waxman, *George Lucas*.

23. John Baxter, *George Lucas: A Biography* (Hammersmith, London: Harper Collins Entertainment, 1999), 3; Goldstein, "Force Never Left Him"; Jones, *George Lucas*, 347; Hearn, *Cinema of George Lucas*, 156.

24. Pollock, *Skywalking*, 242.

25. Baxter, *George Lucas*, 323.

26. Goldstein, "Force Never Left Him"; Michael Cieply, "Turning Point: George Lucas Moves to Produce TV Shows, Movies in Volume," *Wall Street Journal*, January 22, 1986, LC 85–89 folder; Louis Pizzitola, *Hearst over Hollywood: Power, Passion, and Propaganda in the Movies* (New York: Columbia University Press, 2002), 127, 231–32, 267–68.

27. Further entangling the two moguls and their respective estates, in 2019 Lucas's ILM would help to recreate portions of Hearst's San Simeon ranch (including CGI zoo giraffes) for *Mank*, David Fincher's biopic of screenwriter Herman Mankiewicz. Industrial Light and Magic, "Behind the Magic: The Visual Effects of *Mank*," YouTube, March 17, 2021, https://www.youtube.com/watch?v=-kLm1Z6ULkw; Baxter, *George Lucas*, 154.

28. "Lucasfilm Research Library: Interview with Jo Donaldson, Manager, Lucasfilm Research Library & Robyn Stanley, Research Librarian on January 31,

2012," I Love Libraries, February 17, 2012, http://www.ilovelibraries.org/article/lucasfilm-research-library.

29. *Lucas Research Library*, Lucasfilm brochure, undated.

30. Hearn, *Cinema of George Lucas*, 172–73.

31. Jones, *George Lucas*, 304.

32. Ibid., 367; Baxter, *George Lucas*, 12.

33. Jones, *George Lucas*, 386.

34. Pollock, *Skywalking*, 251–52.

35. Jones, *George Lucas*, 347.

36. Ibid.

37. Scott Ross, "Banned from the Ranch," *VFX Business* (blog), May 8, 2011, https://web.archive.org/web/20130303155152/http://scottaross.com/2011/05/08/banned-from-the-ranch/.

38. Jones, *George Lucas*, 341–43.

39. Cieply, "Turning Point"; "Skywalker Ranch, Technical Building," E&S Masonry Corporation, accessed October 5, 2023, https://e-smasonry.com/portfolio/skywalker-ranch-technical-building.

40. *Biography*, season 16, episode 2, "George Lucas: Creating an Empire," aired January 27, 2002, https://www.youtube.com/watch?v=yjDZ6axjhrw.

41. Champlin, *George Lucas*, 179; Beth Ashley, "The Web of Companies inside LucasArts," *Independent Journal*, September 2, 1991, Marin County Library, Anne T. Kent California Room, Moving Pictures: Lucasfilm Clippings 1990–1999 folder, San Rafael, California (hereafter LC 90–99 folder).

42. J. W. Rinzler, *The Making of Star Wars, Revenge of the Sith* (New York: Del Rey Books, 2005), 86–87.

43. Champlin, *George Lucas*, 179.

44. Hearn, *Cinema of George Lucas*, 169.

45. Goldstein, "Force Never Left Him."

46. Pollock, *Skywalking*, 5.

47. Hearn, *Cinema of George Lucas*, 251; Jones, *George Lucas*, 471.

48. Baxter, *George Lucas*, 360.

49. Ken White, "Neighbors v. Lucas: Resentment Building," *Point Reyes Light*, March 24, 1985, LC 85–89 folder.

50. Brad Breithaupt, "Lucasfilm Expansion Targets Another Ranch," *Independent Journal*, March 29, 1990, LC 90–99 folder.

51. Don Clark, "Film Maker Lucas Forced to Change with the Times," *San Francisco Chronicle*, February 24, 1993, LC 90–99 folder; Goldstein, "Force Never Left Him."

52. "Q&A with Van Ling," James Cameron Online, accessed October 5, 2023, https://www.jamescamerononline.com/VanLingQA.htm. See also Moisés Chiullán, "'Banned from the Ranch' (Special Edition) with Drew McWeeny," *Electric Shadow*, podcast episode, aired April 16, 2015, https://esn.fm/electricshadow/23; Drew McWeeny (as "Moriarty"), "HARRY LIME at Skywalker Ranch: An AICN Peek at the EPISODE I DVD," October 1, 2001, https://legacy.aintitcool.com/node/10358; Paul Liberatore,

"Citizen George: Marin's Enigmatic Mogul," *Independent Journal*, May 15, 2005; Scott Ross, "Banned from the Ranch."

53. Martha Groves, "Lucas Hopes to Work His Magic on Wary Marin County Residents," *Los Angeles Times*, October 21, 1994.

54. Peter Anderson, "George Lucas: Citizen of the Year," *Independent Journal*, March 23, 1988, LC 85–89 folder.

55. Brad Breithaupt, "New Twist in Lucas Debate: Coupon Wars," *Independent Journal*, April 26, 1988, LC 85–89 folder.

56. "A Rerun of George Lucas' Wars with Marin's Planners," *San Francisco Chronicle*, June 8, 1987, LC 85–89 folder.

57. Bonnie Bard, "Neighbors Unmoved by Lucas Plea," *Independent Journal*, March 18, 1988, LC 85–89 folder.

58. Joy Zimmerman, "The Supes Won't Budge for Lucas," *Pacific Sun*, April 15, 1988, LC 85–89 folder.

59. Liberatore, "Marin's Movie Emperor."

60. "Rerun of George Lucas' Wars."

61. Torri Minton, "Lucas Expands Expansion Plan," *San Francisco Chronicle*, September 18, 1988, LC 85–89 folder.

62. White, "Neighbors v. Lucas"; Bard, "Neighbors Unmoved."

63. White, "Neighbors v. Lucas."

64. Doug Norby, "Marin Voice: Time to Start Talking," *Independent Journal*, May 17, 1988, LC 85–89 folder; Jim Doyle, "Marin Planning Panel Endorses Lucasfilm Expansion," *San Francisco Chronicle*, October 8, 1996, LC 90–99 folder.

65. Catherine Bowman, "Lucasfilm Projects Faces Tough Fight," *San Francisco Chronicle*, August 24, 1992, LC 90–99 folder.

66. Torri Minton, "Supers OK Lucasfilm Expansion," *San Francisco Chronicle*, October 30, 1996, LC 90–99 folder.

67. Kelly A. Zito, "Lucasfilm's Plans on Track," *Independent Journal*, April 2, 1999, LC 90–99 folder.

68. "Master P Tours the Skywalker Ranch with George Lucas," MTV News, aired 2002, https://www.youtube.com/watch?v=se2A3F1mdNs&list=PL5xmRIR9qq-Iy_OoZf6zjOTpSRK7XdF3G&index=12.

69. Hearn, *Cinema of George Lucas*, 245, 249.

70. Nels Johnson, "George Lucas' Plan: 57 Overnight Guest Rooms at Big Rock Ranch under Review," *Independent Journal*, July 19, 2018; Skywalker Retreats, accessed October 5, 2023, https://www.skywalkerretreats.com/summit-skywalker-ranch.

71. "George Lucas Building Hearst Castle Copycat in Marin, Critics Claim," *Monterey County Herald*, June 15, 2009; Terence Chea, "Lucasfilm Abandons Studio Plan at NorCal Site," *Tribune-Democrat* (Johnstown, PA), April 11, 2012.

72. Norimitsu Onishi, "Lucas and Rich Neighbors Agree to Disagree: Part II," *New York Times*, May 21, 2012.

73. Jonathan Rockwell, "Zoning Out the Poor: Skywalker Ranch Edition," Brookings, July 1, 2015, https://www.brookings.edu/blog/social-mobility-memos/2015/07/01/zoning-out-the-poor-skywalker-ranch-edition/; Emily Fancher, "Is George Lucas'

Affordable Housing Project in Marin Dead?," *San Francisco Business Times*, November 10, 2016.

74. Gene D. Phillips, *Godfather: The Intimate Francis Ford Coppola* (Lexington: University Press of Kentucky, 2004), 45, 51–52; Jones, *George Lucas*, 84.

75. Warner's sale of 1.6 million shares of Warner Brothers stock in 1966 netted $24 million, the equivalent of just over $160 million in 2012 dollars. Bob Thomas, *Clown Prince of Hollywood: The Antic Life and Times of Jack L. Warner* (New York: McGraw-Hill, 1990), 3.

76. *A.N.T. Farm*, season 2, episode 15, "ScavANTger Hunt," aired November 2, 2012, https://www.disneyplus.com/video/b8a54be8-fe20-424c-bf96-597e9db96056.

77. Jones, *George Lucas*, 320; Nels Johnson, "George Lucas Weds Melody Hobson in Skywalker Ranch Ceremony," *Independent Journal*, June 24, 2013.

78. *The Chef Show*, season 1, episode 13, "Skywalker Ranch," aired September 13, 2019, https://www.netflix.com/watch/81061994?source=imdb.

79. Joseph Campbell and Bill D. Moyers, *Joseph Campbell and the Power of Myth, with Bill Moyers* (1988; New York: Mystic Fire Video, in association with Parabola Magazine [distributors], 1988), DVD.

12

Lucas Meets Luxo

Lucasfilm's Computer Graphics Lab (CGL) and the
Development of Pixar Animation Studios

CHRISTOPHER HOLLIDAY AND CHRIS PALLANT

In 2015, Pixar Animation Studios released a two-minute promotional short both to mark the DVD release of its fifteenth computer-animated feature film, *Inside Out* (Pete Docter, 2015), and to commemorate the long-awaited big-screen arrival of *Star Wars: Episode VII—The Force Awakens* (J. J. Abrams, 2015), the latest installment of George Lucas's forty-year *Star Wars* (1977–2019) saga, over a decade since the franchise's previous entry. During the brief sequence that premiered online in October 2015, *Inside Out*'s cast of anthropomorphic emotions Fear, Anger, Joy, Sadness, and Disgust all sit in the control room of eleven-year-old Riley's head, transfixed by teaser footage from the new *Star Wars* film playing on the teenager's computer, while reacting enthusiastically to the return of characters Han Solo and Princess Leia yet lamenting its imminent December release as nonetheless a "long, long way" off. The crossover appeal of this animated advertisement owes a clear debt to the contemporary era of franchised products and transmedia platforming, multiverse narrative crossovers, interconnected storyworlds in service of brand maintenance, and the commercial power of contemporary Hollywood's production logic. By aligning Pixar and Lucasfilm as companies through their iconic products and characters, the short commercial combines intellectual properties to build audience anticipation for the new *Star Wars* film, as even Riley's laptop frustratingly buffers the footage before playing it.

However, this playful collaboration equally bears out the synergistic processes and structures that support conglomerate-era North American cinema, particularly as Walt Disney had already purchased both Pixar (for $7.4 billion) and Lucasfilm (for $4.05 billion) in 2006 and 2012, respectively, meaning that both companies now effectively functioned as Disney subsidiaries. Announcing the deal between Lucasfilm and Disney in the Hollywood trade press, *Variety*'s Marc Graser noted, "The Mouse House shocked the biz Tuesday in unveiling its agreement to buy Lucasfilm Ltd. from Lucas, the company's sole owner," while also pointing to how the contract would allow Disney access to "vfx shop Industrial Light & Magic, audio post house Skywalker Sound, and videogame developer LucasArts" as well as the company's existing multimedia franchises.[1] Graser's article—which emphasized Lucas's imminent retirement as a defining factor in this momentous corporate handover—was appropriately accompanied by an image of the California filmmaker sitting alongside Walt Disney Corporation chairman and CEO Robert Iger as the contract heralding the lucrative deal was signed.

As both a clever marketing ploy and an act of smooth corporate synergy—and in excess of Pixar's and Lucasfilm's roles within the industrial structures of Disney as their parent company—the *Inside Out–Star Wars* intertext also acknowledges a long-standing industrial and creative relationship between Pixar and Lucas that can be traced back to the late 1970s. Lucasfilm is very much a company that has its roots in the postclassical phase of renaissance Hollywood, with Lucas's own role as a creative agent firmly embedded in the breakdown of the studio system and emergence of new blockbuster forms of promotion, marketing, and merchandising. Yet he is also a figure fully entwined with the emergence of 1970s film technology and the arrival of computer graphics, with sanctioned hagiographic accounts of Pixar's early years frequently citing the impact of Lucas on the trajectory of the studio as a digital filmmaking force. This chapter charts the industry narratives and creative collaborations that shaped the emergence and transformation of Pixar from a research and development group into a hugely successful animation studio, and the joint role played by Lucas and Lucasfilm in the solidification of Pixar within the new histories of Hollywood visual effects production. It examines the emergence of the Computer Graphics Lab (CGL) in 1974 at the hands of the New York Institute of Technology (NYIT); the contributions of Ed Catmull, Alvy Ray Smith, and Loren Carpenter to the aesthetics of digital imagery; and the move by the CGL into creative collaboration with Lucas and Industrial Light & Magic (ILM) later in the decade, charting their early video-editing and small-scale digital effects work and subsequent founding as the Graphics Group (constituting one-third of the Computer Division of

Lucasfilm, launched in 1979). By highlighting both the stakes of Lucas's contribution to the trajectory of computer graphics within Hollywood and the critical understanding of his creative (and corporate) presence, this chapter identifies the industrial, technological, and aesthetic importance of the often-forgotten Lucas-era phase to Pixar.

The Computer Graphics Lab

Pixar as an internationally renowned and critically lauded computer-animated film studio is often credited as properly beginning with the entrepreneurial impact of Steve Jobs. It is certainly not hard to find enduring evidence of Jobs's framing as a corporate storyteller within Hollywood's own emergent high-tech computer industry, and his "innovative business strategies" and willingness to experiment with "modes of evaluating new ideas, concepts, and development" fully transformed Pixar from a computer division "for hire" into an award-winning CG facility.[2] The terms and impact of this popular narrative follow a familiar path—one that has its origins as far back as Hollywood studio production—whereby a singular, great inventor and creative genius ushers in a new age of technological progress and innovation. Within the frame of this chapter, there are various individuals alongside Jobs who have received similar hagiographic treatment given their influence on popular Hollywood cinema: Walt Disney, George Lucas, and most recently John Lasseter. However, the professional reality is always more complex than the corporate—and carefully stage-managed—fairy tale. Where the emergence of Pixar is concerned, it is important to question the popular and durable positioning of Jobs within this particular historical moment. Thankfully, Smith's recent book *A Biography of the Pixel* (2021) provides a timely rebalancing of the Pixar story in ways that begin to open up the company's origin story and relationship with Jobs, which began in the 1980s, to alternate industrial forces. It is possible to go further back than the emergence of Pixar, to the earlier phase of Lucas and the labor, creativity, and technologies of this period before the company became newly independent. This formative era stands as a visibly chaotic referendum on what was a new medium in computer-generated imagery. Indeed, a closer look at this Lucas-era phase allows a move away from the kind of "teleological historical writing" within cinema history that is often predicated on "distinct point[s] of rupture and rebirth" and instead embraces a more fractured understanding of the trials and errors with emergent CGI, to which Lucas's contributions, and those made by the CGL during 1979 and 1986, are particularly central.[3]

Lucas first established a computer division at Lucasfilm in 1979, with the aim to develop "a digital video editing system, a digital audio system, and a digital film printer."[4] Lucasfilm already had a visual and optical effects facility in operation at ILM, which had been created during the production of *Star Wars* by the film's Special Visual Effects department to realize the spectacle of its space fantasy. However, ILM was largely a practical effects unit, investing money into the development of motion control cameras (pioneered by ILM's visual effects supervisor, John Dykstra), detailed scale models and miniatures, and optical compositing. Many of these image-making processes involved in the production of the blockbuster cinema of the 1970s and 1980s (including those at ILM but also in the work of Steven Spielberg and Ridley Scott) were, as Julie Turnock has discussed, indebted to the influence of West Coast experimental filmmakers and artists, who taught popular filmmakers "strategies for organizing and mobilizing an elaborately designed composite mise-en-scène."[5] Supported by a broader investment in digital film compositing, Lucas was increasingly interested in integrating computer animation and digital audio mixing and editing, and the founding of the Lucasfilm Computer Graphics Project was an attempt to seamlessly synthesize practical and digital effects traditions, as well as less lofty aspirations, such as developing computer-based accounting processes.[6] Yet despite being "not completely convinced about the future of computer animation," Lucas nonetheless became progressively "fixated on digital postproduction, creating and selling realistic special effects."[7] Lucas hired University of Utah alumnus and computer scientist at NYIT Ed Catmull as vice president of Lucasfilm's new ILM computer graphics division, while a number of creative personnel joined Catmull from the CGL housed at NYIT. These included Alvy Ray Smith, a computer artist who was tasked primarily with digital compositing; David DiFrancesco, who began work at Lucasfilm on a digital film scanner and printer; and Tom Duff, whose 1984 paper "Compositing Digital Images," cowritten with Thomas Porter (who joined Lucasfilm's Computer Research and Development Division in early 1981), prompted the development of key compositing techniques in computer graphics.[8] Other artists such as Bill Reeves (inventor of motion blur algorithms), Ralph Guggenheim (who developed ILM's EditDroid editing system), and James Anderson Moorer (digital audio and computer music engineer) all arrived at Lucasfilm in this formative period too, while John Lasseter would later join as an interface designer in 1983 as part of ILM's contribution to *Young Sherlock Holmes* (Barry Levinson, 1985).[9] It was Reeves, Guggenheim, and Lasseter who would all be credited—alongside Catmull—as central figures in

Pixar's subsequent business move away from computer-animated shorts and contracted commercial work to feature-film production in the mid-1990s.

Speaking in 2020 alongside Hollywood visual effects artist Hank Grebe, digital effects supervisor Theresa Ellis Rygiel, and Smith at the annual SIGGRAPH event, Catmull recalls how the work of the CGL in this period was "important and groundbreaking in many ways" and that many "significant people in the field of computer graphics passed through its doors."[10] Founded by academic and entrepreneur Alexander Schure, the CGL at NYIT was a remarkable proving ground for many animators, artists, and designers who would later go on to give life to Pixar as an animation studio. Adding to Catmull's recollection, Smith notes:

> It was the finest CG lab in the world at the time. It was the origin of the group that eventually became Lucasfilm computer graphics, then Pixar. We made so many advances there that we lost track of them all. It was funded by the first of the three "moneymen" who paved our way to the big screen, but Schure—NYIT's strange president—seldom receives any similar credit to George Lucas and Steve Jobs. He took the first big gamble on us and the idea of an all-digital movie. And, you have to understand, that the place was physically marvelous, too, mansions on large estates. Everything we touched was new. It was exciting to be alive.[11]

In ways that anticipate of framing of Jobs as Pixar's driving force, Schure is overwhelmingly portrayed as a benevolent (if guarded) figure and creative thinker, plowing vast amounts of his own money into the development of computer animation, despite certain industrial narratives having sidelined elements of his influence. Yet such anecdotal evidence regarding Schure's strictness in protecting CGL's—and by extension, NYIT's—proprietary technologies, alongside his marginalized position within popular Pixar histories, not only provides necessary balance to the "Great Man" narrative that has continued to shape the industrial and cultural paradigm of Hollywood technologies but also provides important context to the careful career planning that several members of the CGL undertook when moving from Schure's payroll to Lucas's. Keen to avoid any sharp-eyed litigation or the suggestion of transferring trade secrets, the likes of Smith and DiFrancesco "laundered" themselves by taking up interim employment at the Jet Propulsion Lab (JPL) before moving on to Lucasfilm.[12]

Without doubt, the collective creativity, artistic drive, and technical mastery that coalesced within the CGL was an important point of ignition for what would harden into the US computer animation industry just over a decade later. The extent of the CGL's formative contribution to computer animation can be seen reflected in the responses of Catmull, Grebe, Rygiel, and Smith to the question of which CGL accomplishment they were most proud of. Addressing the SIGGRAPH crowd, Grebe and Rygiel describe their pathfinding work on "geometric modelling" and character design, in particular "jointed characters," while Catmull and Smith offer more expansive summaries of the CGL's accomplishments, with Catmull listing the "alpha channel, extending the fill algorithm to work with anti-aliased lines, the papers with Alvy, the first experimenting with motion blur, the Tween 2D animation system, new 3D rendering algorithms." Smith, in typical fashion, simply notes that they once sat down and tried to list all the firsts they had accomplished at the CGL but that their list got ridiculously long, concluding that basically everything they touched was a first.[13] Fundamentally, the CGL at NYIT played a central role in the story of modern computer graphics as a space of innovation and in the solidification of a group of creative personnel that would eventually become Lucasfilm's computer graphics arm and, later, Pixar.

Moment(s) of Genesis

The innovative qualities fostered at the CGL would quickly extend into the newly established Lucasfilm division, whose industrial infrastructure reaped the benefits of the dissolution of Hollywood's studio system by allowing Lucas to hire "young, untried, but enthusiastic up-and-comers" after "the forced retirement of the old studio effects hands."[14] It was within this industrial context and broader shift away from practical effects imagery that Lucasfilm would cultivate an identity as comprising curious and creative innovators, at least within the Hollywood trade press, though they were not alone among this emergent digital frontier. The New York–based computer technology companies MAGI/SynthaVision and Digital Effects; Pacific Electric Pictures, housed in Los Angeles; Cranston/Csuri Productions (CCP), founded in 1981 by artist Chuck Csuri and investor Robert Cranston Kanuth; Robert Abel and Associates, who specialized in computer graphics for television commercials; and even the NYIT, which continued to advance computer-based rendering, all contributed to computer animation's state of intensified competition. Discussing the exchange between a number of production facilities seeking to introduce "digital computer imaging to the motion picture industry" in the early 1980s, Peter Sørensen teased that "up north of San Francisco in San Rafael, Lucasfilm's Computer Development Division is working on the totally different, hardware approach to image making."[15] Compared to artificial intelligence experiments taking place at the Computer Graphics Research Group at Ohio State University (which would lead to the formation of Cranston/Csuri) and nearby rival company Digital Productions, headed by John Whitney Jr. and Gary Demos, Lucasfilm instead sought to explore the possibilities for "the research and construction of a laser film printer" and the production of cost-effective high-resolution digital images.[16] While such experiments would ultimately galvanize the work of an "independent special effects industry during these years [that] was surprisingly varied and creative" (which occurred largely between Stanley Kubrick's *2001: A Space Odyssey* in 1968 and *Star Wars* in 1977), it was clear from the outset that Lucasfilm was increasingly understood as continuing the "good work" of the CGL through their digital visual effects experimentation.[17]

As Sørensen further explained: "Computer animators in general and the Lucasfilm Computer Development people in particular have a problem with respect to the fears of people in other parts of the special effects industry who feel their livelihoods may be in jeopardy. By the end of the decade that might become a problem except for the fact that by that time most of the conventional special effects people will have long ago gotten involved with digital imaging themselves."[18]

The positioning of Lucasfilm's new computer vision against the grain, not just against the hardware and software of industry competitors but within the production culture of Lucasfilm and ILM too, taps into one of Hollywood VFX's most "enshrined" stories, which has since "hardened into received fact"— namely, that of Lucasfilm's Computer Division and the "triumphalist story of its 'rebel' origins."[19] As Karen Paik argues, "Lucas himself affectionately remembered his Computer Division as the 'rebel unit' of Lucasfilm in the early '80s. [He noted,] 'ILM was saying they didn't need digital technology. But we were building a lot of things ILM didn't understand in the beginning but began to appreciate later.'"[20] Despite recent counters to this narrative and a recognition of influential independent effects studios during the 1960s and early 1970s, the solidification of Lucasfilm's dominant "ILM aesthetic" helped to set the stylistic parameters and formal horizons of early computer graphics while at the same time further qualifying Lucasfilm's dominance over Hollywood's growing special effects industry.[21]

For Turnock, the "ILM aesthetic" is defined through a "perfectly execut-ed, seamless photorealism" alongside "character-based anthropomorphism; palpable, kinetic movement; a flashy, eye-catching graphic quality; and a busy frame, jam-packed with moving elements."[22] Evidence of this aesthetic appears in the famous Genesis sequence from *Star Trek II: The Wrath of Khan* (Nich-olas Meyer, 1982), which Jordan Gowanlock credits as "the product of one of the many early crossovers between military-industrial complex research and the film industry at SIGGRAPH."[23] Coproduced by Jim Veilleux and Ken Ralston (at ILM) as the still-new Lucasfilm special effects division, the Genesis sequence stands as an important collaboration within Hollywood's emer-gent "microelectronic revolution" and also exemplifies how the work of the Graphics Group contributed to the evolution of Lucas's ILM in this period.[24] Sørensen notes in the early 1980s that the Lucasfilm Computer Development Division "did their spectacular 'Genesis' planet terraforming sequence as a sort of teaser, to validate their long term goals," while suggesting that "even George Lucas will get nothing but test images from the team for a few years."[25] As part of an initial demo to Lucasfilm on the aesthetics possibilities of computer graphics, the group animated only the Genesis effect out of its four proposed sequences (the other three included the transformation of a dead planet; a voice recognition sequence; and a retina recognition sequence).[26] Smith dis-cusses the sequence from *The Wrath of Khan* as a molecular transformation "from crystalline inorganic molecules to DNA-type organic molecules," which crucially pioneered some of the division's initial interests in computer graphics and allowed a testing of the expressivity of digital imagery.[27] Yet the signifi-cance of the aptly named Genesis sequence does not stop at the technological. Within this sequence we can also find evidence of the—often de-emphasized—collective human labor of computer animation production and a deep-rooted awareness of cinematographic craft that in turn reveals the Graphics Group's continued desire to become feature-length filmic storytellers.

As part of ILM's celebration of *Star Trek* Day (September 8) in 2021, the company's official website published a lengthy article that celebrated their work over multiple decades crafting the visual escapism of the *Star Trek* franchise.[28] This article is remarkable in its complete absence of detail regarding individual contributions to the Genesis sequence. Instead, it names only effects supervi-sor Veilleux, grouping all other creative labor under the ILM Graphics group umbrella and thereby erasing the work of figures such as Loren Carpenter, whose two-minute short *Vol Libre* (1980), which uses fractal geometry to produce virtual landscapes, prompted an invitation to work with Catmull and Smith at Lucasfilm on *The Wrath of Khan*. Sadly, ILM's discussion of the computer animation process, labor, and history is hardly exceptional. Production hierarchies and influences are narratives always open to cultural analysis, usefully revealing facts about "what happened during production, the local and global politics surrounding that production, and also embedded power structures."[29] In her work on Autodesk Maya, for example, Aylish Wood notes that to examine working practices within Hollywood's multimedia industries is ultimately to reflect on "narratives about poor wages, precarious employment, exploitative practices, reduced status as a creative contributor in an automated pipeline, as well as narratives of great innovation and creative insight."[30] This lack of care when it comes to preserving and communicating the historical micronarratives of screenwork is not necessarily specific to animation's digital era either. Birgitta Hosea cautions that while there may be many anxieties around "the de-skilling of animators and the replacement of their artisanal, tacit knowledge by sophisticated digital processes, the erasure of the animator's individual contribution has been a product of the studio production system since the early days of animation."[31] The occlusion of labor within the industrial contexts of both commercial and independent animation is, ultimately, more far reaching rather than medium specific, as it is "not simply a result of the introduction of new technology, but a product of the way in which the workforce is organised."[32]

It is pleasing, then, to find this exact level of detail in Smith's recent book on the CGL and their connection to Lucasfilm. Serving as a potent corrective to ILM's corporate attempt to tell—or sell—the story of *their* Genesis work (and as a valuable blueprint for all screen historians), Smith recounts how he pitched the sequence before its production and names numerous individuals, including Carpenter, who would help turn this pitch into digital pictures:

Jim Blinn's Voyager spacecraft planetary flybys at JPL were the prime inspiration. The (unseen) spacecraft in my storyboard circled a dead Moon-like planet covered with craters. Loren Carpenter would design the star field and spacecraft trajectory. Tom Duff would make the craters with bump maps. Pat Cole would model the projectile fired from the spacecraft toward the dead planet. The impact of the projectile starts a conflagration. Bill Reeves would implement the fires, using his new particle systems. A wall of fire dramatically engulfs the planet and melts its surface. From the molten surface arise fractal mountains, which Loren would make using the fractal technique described earlier. Seas would form and the mountains would cool and turn green. As the spacecraft speeds away, the dead planet would be newly revealed as living and Earth-like. Tom Porter would oversee this last part with his paint program and texture mapping. The Genesis Effect wouldn't be instantaneous, as desired, but it would take only a minute to explain.[33]

The Wrath of Khan's acclaimed Genesis sequence also reveals the cinematic ambitions of the newly incumbent Lucasfilm Graphics Group. Smith notes that, alongside the spectacular impact that the Graphics Group wanted to make with their computer animation, there was also a keen awareness of wanting to use the digital tools they had created to extend the cinematographic possibilities of the medium. Smith suggests that he knew a secret characteristic of Lucas's viewership, intimating that when Lucas watched a film he was "constantly aware of the camera and the cameraman's decisions" and was impervious to any narrative or emotional manipulation attempted by the filmmakers. Smith recalls how he shared this insider knowledge with his Graphics Group colleagues, explaining: "So, we're going to put a camera move in this shot that no real camera could possibly make. It won't be gratuitous. It'll make perfect narrative sense. But it will blow George's socks off."[34] This strategy worked, and Lucas was quick to visit Smith in his office to commend their work, offering a brief but heartfelt endorsement: "Great camera move!"[35]

Conclusion: A Machine Called Pixar

The rest, as they say, is history. Soon after the release of *The Wrath of Khan* and Lasseter's computer-animated short *The Adventures of André and Wally B* (1984)—which includes in its opening credits the title card "Lucasfilm Computer Graphics Project"—Jobs would acquire Lucasfilm's in-house computer division on February 3, 1986, for a total of $10 million. Of this amount, $5 million would go straight to Lucasfilm, while $5 million would be staked as "guaranteed funding" for the new company now under his control.[36] Allegedly, it was Jobs who renamed the division as the new computer company Pixar (after Lucasfilm's digital compositing computer, the Pixar Image Computer) and shaped the newly formed facility into a developer of graphics hardware and a pioneer of software technology (including its proprietary REYES and RenderMan programs, the latter of which is still used in the Hollywood animation industry today).[37] The first short film made under the Pixar name—Lasseter's *Luxo Jr.* (1986)—would premiere at the SIGGRAPH event that same year, and it would mark the beginning proper of the standalone studio's commercial explorations into three-dimensional computer graphics, digital modeling, and shadow mapping, while functioning as a demonstration of the Pixar Image Computer's capabilities (the short opens and closes with the Pixar machine logo).

However, by revisiting the early configurations of people, places, and processes at both the CGL and Lucasfilm, and by considering the role played by key Pixar personnel within Lucas's speculative orbit (albeit only for a brief passage of time), this chapter prompts a question: What if Lucas had stayed the course and the Pixar pathfinders had remained at Lucasfilm? Of course, we know that the situation at Lucasfilm was untenable, given that Lucas's divorce from Marcia Lucas in 1983 necessitated a budgetary and operational re-profiling of Lucasfilm, with the Computer Graphics team falling outside of what Lucas considered his core business. As part of the research for this chapter, we approached former Pixar animator Steve Segal, who, as well as working on *Toy Story* (John Lasseter, 1995), was part of the computer animation community alongside the likes of Carpenter, Catmull, and Smith, and we posed this very question to him: What if Lucas had retained the Graphics Group? Segal entertained our hypothetical question and offered the following response: "Lucas had the good sense to hire Catmull. So if you have Catmull, and then Lasseter, so you have got one of the top people, maybe *the top* person in Catmull, combined with Lasseter and Smith at Lucasfilm, he [Lucas] had *the* team. They [Lucasfilm's Graphics Group] could have done a lot of great stuff!"[38] While this only takes us so far, when invited to consider the difference between Lucas and Jobs, Segal pinpointed a key quality that Jobs brought to Pixar that Lucas would have struggled to match had he retained the services of the Graphics Group: "Probably the best thing about Jobs: he's a good marketer. So, he could see that 'Lucasfilm Computer Graphics Division,' obviously without 'Lucas' in the name, made for an unwieldy title. So, calling it Pixar, on the other hand, much better. I remember in a meeting that Jobs said: 'we want the name Pixar to be synonymous with quality just like Disney.' Boy, did he do that."[39]

This clarity of vision regarding the potential of computer animation to not just expand the cinematic register but offer a radical new path to quality cinematic storytelling is perhaps the key reason that Jobs, not Lucas, was able to best harness Pixar's digital potential. Indeed, it would not be until March

2003 that Lucasfilm would finally establish its own animation division to compete in a highly lucrative computer-animated film market, ironically one that Pixar had helped to define after its separation from Lucasfilm some twenty years previous. Yet the new "Lucasfilm Animation" subsidiary has tended to focus largely on a number of digitally animated television spin-offs of the *Star Wars* films rather than on feature-film productions. To date, it has produced only two computer-animated films: *Star Wars: The Clone Wars* (Dave Filoni, 2008) and *Strange Magic* (Gary Rydstrom, 2015), the latter directed by sound designer Gary Rydstrom. Rydstrom himself began at Skywalker Sound and provided sound design for *Luxo Jr.* (under the division's original name, Sprocket Systems), before moving to Pixar for *Finding Nemo* (Andrew Stanton, 2003) and later directing the short film *Lifted* (Gary Rydstrom, 2007) and the short *Toy Story* spin-off *Hawaiian Vacation* (Gary Rydstrom, 2011). As a standalone visual effects company, ILM's contribution to computer-animated filmmaking began late too with *Rango* (Gore Verbinski, 2011), its first full-length feature animated film, which signaled a shift by Lucasfilm away from subcontracted work involving animated VFX for big-budget blockbusters. *Variety*'s David S. Cohen reported in 2008 that after its collaboration with Paramount on *Rango*, ILM would finally be "entering the feature animation biz" as "one of a handful of visual effects companies also making high-end motion-capture animated features."[40] Alongside other "vendor for hire" facilities such as Animal Logic and Sony Pictures Imageworks, ILM would follow Lucasfilm Animation in plunging Lucas into a computer-animated film marketplace. Cohen crucially invokes this what-if scenario in which Lucas ultimately kept hold of what would become the Pixar studio. As the journalist explains, "The move represents a second bite at the animation apple: ILM had an opportunity to get into feature animation once before, when staffers in his graphics hardware division proposed setting up an animation shop in the mid-1980s. Lucas . . . disinterested in making toons, instead sold the division. It became famous under its own name: Pixar."[41] It is tempting, then, to view the purchase of ILM by Disney in 2012 as the protracted reunion of Lucas with Pixar nearly thirty years after their separation, by virtue of their close corporate proximity under the ever-growing Disney umbrella. Yet as this chapter has argued, the names of Lucas and the computer graphics division at Lucasfilm should not remain entirely divorced from what would under Jobs become the Pixar studio but rather should be fully entwined as part of a shared, if at times complex, history of the Pixar machine.

Notes

1. Marc Graser, "Disney Buys LucasFilm, New *Star Wars* Planned," *Variety*, October 20, 2012, https://variety.com/2012/film/news/disney-buys-lucasfilm-new-star-wars-planned-1118061434/.

2. Stephen J. Caroll, "Steve Jobs as an Artist," *Journal of Business and Management* 19, no. 1 (2013): 25–26.

3. See Charles Wolfe, "Vitaphone Shorts and *The Jazz Singer*," *Wide Angle* 12, no. 3 (July 1990): 66–67.

4. Karen Paik, *To Infinity and Beyond! The Story of Pixar Animation Studios* (London: Random House, 2007), 20.

5. Julie Turnock, "The True Stars of *Star Wars*? Experimental Filmmakers in the 1970s and 1980s Special Effects Industry," *Film History* 26, no. 4 (2014): 121.

6. Alvy-Ray Smith, *A Biography of the Pixel* (Cambridge, MA: MIT Press, 2021), 382.

7. Richard Neupert, *John Lasseter*, Contemporary Film Directors (Urbana: University of Illinois Press, 2016), 44, 37.

8. Tom Duff and Thomas Porter, "Compositing Digital Images," *Computer Graphics* 18, no. 3 (July 1984): 253–59.

9. Neupert, *John Lasseter*, 50–51.

10. Ed Catmull, speaking as part of the SIGGRAPH 2020 Panel "Pioneering Pixels: The NYIT Computer Graphics Lab Then and Now," August 18, 2020, online, transcription accessed February 22, 2022, https://blog.siggraph.org/2020/08/pioneering-pixels-the-nyit-computer-graphics-lab-then-and-now.html/.

11. Alvy-Ray Smith, speaking as part of the SIGGRAPH 2020 Panel "Pioneering Pixels."

12. Smith, *Biography of the Pixel*, 383.

13. SIGGRAPH 2020 Panel "Pioneering Pixels."

14. Julie Turnock, "Before Industrial Light and Magic: The Independent Hollywood Special Effects Business, 1968–75," *New Review of Film and Television Studies* 7, no. 2 (2009): 133–56.

15. Peter Sørensen, "Movies, Computers and the Future," *American Cinematographer* 64, no. 1 (January 1983): 69–71, 73–78 (71, 73).

16. Ibid., 73.

17. Turnock, "Before Industrial Light and Magic," 134.

18. Sørensen, "Movies, Computers and the Future," 74.

19. Turnock, "Before Industrial Light and Magic," 133.

20. Paik, *To Infinity and Beyond!*, 26.

21. Turnock, "Before Industrial Light and Magic," 135.

22. Ibid.

23. Jordan Gowanlock, *Animating Unpredictable Effects: Nonlinearity in Hollywood's R&D Complex* (London: Palgrave Macmillan, 2021), 149.

24. Sørensen, "Movies, Computers and the Future," 69.

25. Ibid., 74.

26. Alvy-Ray Smith, "The Genesis Demo: Instant Evolution with Computer Graphics," *American Cinematographer* 63, no. 10 (October 1982): 1038–40, 1048, 1050 (1038).

27. Ibid., 1038.

28. "ILM Celebrates *Star Trek* Day," ILM, September 8, 2021, https://www.ilm.com/star-trek-day/.

29. Aylish Wood, *Software, Animation and the Moving Image: What's in the Box?* (London: Palgrave, 2015), 7.

30. Ibid., 7. Mihaela Mihailova similarly describes how the individual labor of animators is typically downplayed in the production of animation processes within motion and performance capture production pipelines that defined digital VFX work during postmillennial Hollywood cinema. See Mihaela Mihailova, "Collaboration without Representation: Labor Issues in Motion and Performance Capture," *Animation: An Interdisciplinary Journal* 11, no. 1 (2016): 40–58.

31. Birgitta Hosea, "Made by Hand," in *The Crafty Animator: Handmade, Craft-Based Animation and Cultural Value*, ed. Caroline Ruddell and Paul Ward (London: Palgrave, 2019): 17–43 (26).

32. Ibid., 26.

33. Smith, *Biography of the Pixel*, 404.

34. Ibid., 405.

35. Lucas, quoted in Smith, *Biography of the Pixel*, 405.

36. Paik, *To Infinity and Beyond!*, 52.

37. While the name Pixar has widely been understood as given to the Graphics Group by Jobs after their transformation into a newly independent studio, the word itself originated years earlier while they were still a division of Lucasfilm's ILM. It was Smith and Carpenter who first coined Pixar in the early 1980s, during Graphics Group's development of a new digital compositing computer, which would go on sale on July 24, 1986, only three months after their acquisition by Jobs. Yet the term was conceived by Smith at least a year earlier while he was working at Lucasfilm, intended as a mock-Spanish verb meaning "*to picture* or *to make pictures*" and later combined with *radar* to produce *Pixar* (initially pronounced as "peeks-Ahr" and then "Pix-ahr"). As Smith puts it, Pixar was "originally the name of a Lucasfilm machine." Smith, *Biography of the Pixel*, 386. See also Brian Jay Jones, *George Lucas: A Life* (New York City: Little, Brown, 2016), 289–90.

38. Steve Segal, Microsoft Teams interview with Chris Pallant, February 25, 2022.

39. Ibid.

40. David S. Cohen, "ILM Makes a Pixel Play," *Variety*, September 15–21, 2008, 4.

41. Ibid.

13

The Audience Is Listening

The Film Sound Legacy of George Lucas

Stephen Andriano-Moore

George Lucas is a significant figure in film history for advancing film sound to a higher status during both production and exhibition for filmmakers, theater owners, and audiences. This chapter discusses Lucas's contributions to film sound from an industrial standpoint that examines filmmaking processes and technological advances fostered by Lucasfilm companies and significant individuals who have influenced the film industry as we know it today. The significances of Lucas's contributions to film sound arise from three registers. The first building block is that Lucas gave film sound, which was often marginalized in the filmmaking process, as high a status as other filmmaking crafts, such as special effects, production design, and editing. The second is his in-house development of technologies and the specialists and creatives he hired to develop and work in a state-of-the-art postproduction sound facility. Lastly, the development of the THX Division provided significant standardizations in postproduction sound, printmaking, and exhibition.

Lucas is a unique figure in film sound as he is a producer, director, editor, writer, and founder of several innovative film companies, including the preeminent film sound company, Skywalker Sound. He has fostered innovative production practices that have led to some of the most significant films in terms of their use of sound, though his contributions have been only marginally examined within film sound scholarship. THX has engaged with significant cases to expand film theory.[1] However, scholarship on sound technology tends to focus on Dolby and surround sound rather than on THX.[2]

Nevertheless, scholarship concerning THX includes Gianluca Sergi's addressing of the historical absence of the listener in film spectator theory to make claims involving active spectators.[3] Michel Chion provides a pessimistic view of THX standardization, arguing that removing the unique aural characteristics of auditoriums contributes to a loss of the collective experience of filmgoing.[4] In opposition to this, Meredith C. Ward theorizes over the aural characteristics of cinema theaters to claim that it is the sounds of the spectators' bodies and breath, rather than the acoustically live characteristics of a theater, that contribute to the collective experience of the cinema and that therefore THX does not hinder the collective experience.[5] Ward argues that the elimination of the surrounding aural space by THX is a significant contributor allowing audiences to become more fully absorbed in a film text and warmly welcomes the technology in the age of the multiplex.[6]

Sound designer scholarship predominantly focuses on the origin story and significance of the work role from the late 1960s through the early 1980s.[7] Jay Beck and Vanessa Theme Ament discuss the more contemporary period of the 1980s and 1990s to argue that "filmmakers and audiences began to take film sound more seriously."[8] Yet throughout sound designer scholarship, there are only limited discussions of Lucas and his company's role. One such case is my own earlier article, which explores the work of sound designers at Skywalker Sound.[9] It is therefore important to examine Lucas, Skywalker Sound, and THX to more adequately place their legacies within the annals of film sound.

Origins: George Lucas's Values for Film Sound

Lucas was one of a handful of young New Hollywood filmmakers in the late 1960s and 1970s who pushed the boundaries of what was possible for film sound. He developed his sense of sound while in a film school graduate program at the University of Southern California. As part of the new film school generation, Lucas, his classmate and collaborator Walter Murch, and many others were trained in all the filmmaking crafts, whereas the previous generation of filmmakers specialized in a single filmmaking craft though union and studio apprenticeships. After graduation, the experimentations and experiences from working on films produced by Francis Coppola's San Francisco–based production company American Zoetrope helped Lucas solidify the idea that producing films in the independent film school style, rather than the traditional compartmentalized Hollywood style, allowed for the creative freedom he desired.[10] Hollywood at that time was working under the studio system of mass production, where each sound task, such as editing and mixing, was conducted by different individuals, the editing and mixing equipment were drastically different, and editors and mixers belonged to different unions. All of this prevented Southern California filmmakers from working in the ways of the Northern California filmmakers.[11]

Under the independent film school style, Lucas and many of the New Hollywood filmmakers worked in several different areas of the filmmaking process. For example, Murch conducted the picture editing, sound editing, and sound mixing on Coppola's *Apocalypse Now* (1979), earning an Academy Award for Best Sound and a nomination for picture editing. This freedom from the compartmentalized structure of Hollywood filmmaking can also be attributed to the unique Northern California union regulations. Rather being based on specific work roles such as picture editing, sound editing, or mixing, Northern California union membership was based on general categories of production and postproduction.[12] This allowed individuals to work in multiple roles on a single film. Lucas's rejection of traditional Hollywood filmmaking practices, along with his film school sensibilities and penchant for the 1950s and 1960s European and Japanese cinema, led him and his contemporaries to develop unconventional production practices, one of which was to hold sound to a higher status than was traditional. As Murch has stated, "From the beginning of American Zoetrope all of us, George, Francis and myself, were interested in pushing sound to be a greater contributor to the story."[13]

Skywalker Sound: Bringing the Sound Designer to Industry

It was through the establishment of a film sound company that Lucas pushed ever more for sound to contribute to storytelling. As *Star Wars: A New Hope* (1977) was going into preproduction in 1975, Lucas established the visual effects company Industrial Light & Magic (ILM) and his postproduction company Sprocket Systems.[14] Sprocket Systems was the editing and sound division of Lucasfilm that eventually housed the original THX mixing studio. In its early years, Sprocket Systems mixers and editors won several Academy Awards, including awards for *Star Wars* in 1978, *The Empire Strikes Back* in 1981, *The Raiders of the Lost Ark* in 1982, and *E. T. the Extra Terrestrial* in 1983. The division quickly established itself as an industry-leading postproduction film sound facility.

Lucas founded Sprocket Systems when he hired Ben Burtt, a recent graduate from the same USC program Lucas had attended, as a "'director of sound' to imagine and implement a creative soundtrack" for the first *Star Wars* film.[15] Rather than using sounds from a sound library, which was the standard practice at the time, Burtt recorded all new sounds and edited and mixed them to create unique effects, alien languages, and the soundscape of a galaxy from far, far away and a long time ago. He produced arguably the most complex and compelling soundscape ever created, earning a Special Achievement Academy Award for Sound Effects for the creation of the alien, creature, and robot voices. According to Burtt, the key to his success was in making sounds that create emotion to "fool the audience into thinking that something is more realistic, scary, or romantic than it really is."[16] Throughout his career, Burtt won four Academy Awards for his work in multiple sound roles.

Sprocket Systems was first located in the small Northern California town of San Anselmo in Marin County. At that time, most of Lucasfilm was located in San Anselmo and was integrated almost inconspicuously into the community. A famous local story tells that in 1979, while "film editors worked upstairs on *Raiders of the Lost Ark* and *The Empire Strikes Back* while sound editors downstairs worked on *Alien* and *E.T.*," Harrison Ford could be spotted in Sprocket's parking lot practicing snapping the Indiana Jones bullwhip, and Kentfield resident Pat Walsh was recording the voice of E.T.[17] According to an undated newspaper article in the local Marin County *Independent Journal*, Burtt and a colleague had heard Walsh talking in a photo shop and thought, "Hey, that's a great voice," and then cast her as the primary contributor to E.T.'s voice.[18]

After an unfortunate flood in 1982, Sprocket Systems moved next door to ILM, just up the road in San Rafael. Sprocket Systems was renamed Skywalker Sound in 1987 when the company moved to the Skywalker Ranch in Nicasio, California.[19] In 2012, Skywalker Sound was acquired by the Walt Disney Company through their purchase of Lucasfilm.[20] Sprocket Systems/Skywalker Sound was as innovative for sound as ILM was for special effects. Skywalker Sound handles all aspects of postproduction film sound, such as effects recording, editing, Foley recording and mixing, mixing, and music recording.[21] Since the release of the first Sprocket Systems film in 1977 through 2022, the company's staff of sound designers, editors, and rerecording mixers have earned sixteen Academy Award wins and fifty-four nominations in the sound categories.

At Sprocket Systems and Skywalker Sound, the people and their unique production practices are the cornerstones of the company's achievements. The most significant production practice applied there is the "Northern California approach" to film sound, which is the original conception of the role of a sound designer. As Lucas has said, "I'm a very strong believer in the approach that one hands-on person should be in charge of the soundtrack from the very beginning to the very end of the picture."[22] With this approach, the sound designer oversees every aspect of the soundtrack, including editing, mixing, and even consulting on the script to help structure the film to use sound in more impactful ways.[23] This is essentially a department head for sound, working similarly to other department heads, such as production designers. However, it is rare in the film industry for someone to work in sound in this fashion, and there is no union job category for a sound designer. Traditionally, the production sound team is only hired at the start of the production phase, and the postproduction sound team begins working toward the end or after production has wrapped.[24] This limits any sound practitioner's ability to contribute to the design and production of a film in ways similar to those of a production designer or director of photography, who begins working during preproduction. According to Murch, the title of sound designer has been appropriated to denote someone who edits and mixes unique sound effects, making that the dominant role of someone designated as a sound designer.[25] At Skywalker Sound, the Northern California approach is one of the key features that draws filmmakers to seek out creatives such as Randy Thom, Gary Rydstrom, and Richard Hymns and contributes largely to the San Francisco Bay Area's reputation as what Larry Blake calls the "virtual center of the film sound world."[26]

Lucas effectively blended the best of the studio system and independent/student filmmaking practices together to produce his films. He built his production company Lucasfilm, the visual effects company ILM, and his postproduction company Sprocket Systems to both work on his films and monetize them to bring the advances in production practices to the rest of the film industry. This is a significant contribution Lucas has made to sound in the film industry. He used innovative techniques and production practices and created companies where such practices could be refined and popularized. Lucas proved there is value in moving the industry beyond the studio-based assembly-line form of filmmaking. As Murch has said, the production practices are very much a "professional extension of the film school idea."[27] Such practices included working with smaller crews in both production and postproduction, increasing collaboration among practitioners and crafts, creating longer preproduction and postproduction schedules, and asking practitioners to work in multiple roles.[28]

Through early 2022, Skywalker Sound has worked on over eight hundred feature films. Numerous film studios have continually sought out Skywalker

Sound, and many directors who give in-depth attention to sound in the filmmaking process use Skywalker Sound for their specific creative talents and unique production practices. These directors include Steven Spielberg, Francis Ford Coppola, Robert Zemeckis, Robert Redford, Kathryn Bigelow, John Lasseter, Tim Burton, Henry Selick, David Fincher, Guillermo del Toro, James Cameron, Michael Bay, Brad Bird, J. J. Abrams, John Favreau, M. Night Shyamalan, Spike Jonze, and Paul Thomas Anderson.

A Selection of Production Companies Who Have Continually Contracted Work with Skywalker Sound and the Number of Films from 1975 to 2022

20th Century Fox: 34	Illumination	Warner Bros.: 19
Amblin Entertainment: 8	Entertainment: 7	Paramount Pictures: 32
American Zoetrope: 3	ImageMovers: 3	Pixar Animation Studios: 24
Blue Sky Studios: 6	Lionsgate: 5	Polygram: 3
Columbia Pictures: 11	Marvel Studios: 19	Touchstone Pictures: 9
Dimension Films: 9	Metro-Goldwyn-Mayer: 9	Universal Pictures: 26
Dreamworks	Miramax Films: 4	Walt Disney Animation
Animation: 11	National Geographic: 3	Studios: 8
Dreamworks SKG: 16	Netflix: 13	Walt Disney Pictures: 21
HBO: 9	New Line Cinema: 4	Walt Disney Studios: 8

Many leading film directors have built up lasting working relationships with Skywalker Sound editors, sound designers, and rerecording mixers and thereby advanced their careers. For example, Skywalker Sound has contributed to every feature film directed by Robert Zemeckis since their relationship started with the award-winning film *Forrest Gump* (1994). For the majority of Zemeckis's films, Randy Thom, Skywalker Sound's two-time Academy Award–winning director of sound design, has applied the Northern California approach by starting early in the filmmaking process, overseeing the sound throughout the entire filmmaking process, and taking on multiple work roles on a single production. Thom, a key figure at Skywalker Sound, got his start in film sound working under Murch on *Apocalypse Now*. According to a Marin County article celebrating Thom's triple Academy Award nomination in 1984 for Best Sound in *Return of the Jedi* (1983), *Never Cry Wolf* (1983), and *The Right Stuff* (1983), he initially worked freelance on several early Sprocket Systems films before he began a permanent position there for the rerecording mix of *Indiana Jones and the Temple of Doom* (1984).[29]

The Zemeckis and Thom collaborations have resulted in five Academy Award nominations in sound categories. The list of their collaborations includes *Welcome to Marwen* (2018), *Allied* (2016), *The Walk* (2015), *Flight* (2012), *A Christmas Carol* (2009), *Beowulf* (2007), *The Polar Express* (2004), *Cast Away* (2000), *What Lies Beneath* (2000), and *Contact* (1997). Another notable director–sound designer collaboration is Spielberg and Skywalker Sound's seven-time Academy Award winner Rydstrom. Rydstrom has worked on numerous Spielberg films using the Northern California approach, including *West Side Story* (2021), *Ready Player One* (2018), *The Post* (2017), *The BFG* (2016), *Bridges of Spies* (2015), *Lincoln* (2012), *War Horse* (2011), *Minority Report* (2002), *A.I. Artificial Intelligence* (2001), *Saving Private Ryan* (1998), *The Lost World: Jurassic Park* (1997), *Jurassic Park* (1993), and *Always* (1989). The creatives at Skywalker Sound have worked on many of the most significant feature films ever made, including James Cameron's *Titanic* (1997) and *Avatar* (2009), Andrew Stanton's *Wall-E* (2008), Lucas's *Star Wars* films, and many of those listed above.

Through fostering innovative production practices, Lucas helped bring the film sound industry from the assembly-line style of the studio system to a more personal mode of filmmaking through the Northern California approach to sound design, for which Skywalker Sound is famous. As Thom has stated, "Good sound requires intense collaboration among director, visual effects supervisor, composer and sound designer—this last being the critical person responsible for blending these disparate ingredients to maximum effect."[30] Through the establishment of Sprocket Systems and Skywalker Sound, Lucas brought innovations to a range of films, including the biggest blockbusters, independent films, and those by first-time feature film directors, such as Benh Zeitlin's *Beasts of the Southern Wild* (2012) and Ryan Coogler's *Fruitvale Station* (2013). In supporting independent and first-time filmmakers, Skywalker Sound hosts the Sundance Music and Sound Design Lab, a collaboration with the Sundance Institute that aims "to educate, develop, and nurture collaboration across filmmakers, composers and sound designers."[31] Josh Lowden, general manager of Skywalker Sound, stated that with the lab, their "goal is to cultivate new relationships between directors, composers and sound designers and encourage collaboration that starts earlier and goes deeper."[32] As a key component of Skywalker Ranch, Skywalker Sound has helped fulfill Lucas's vision of "a colony of artists who come together to collaborate in a unique environment dedicated to filmmaking and storytelling."[33]

THX: Bringing Quality Standards for Sound and Image

Though Lucas and the Sprocket/Skywalker Sound creatives put in great efforts to create the most engaging sound for films, theaters play an important role in the audience experience. In the early 1980s, the advancements in the development of film sound postproduction technologies at Lucasfilm far surpassed the sound systems in theaters. This led a group at Lucasfilm to improve the quality of the theatrical experience in what became Lucasfilm's THX Division. As with so many of the innovations brought on by Lucasfilm, THX has been one of the most expansive, as it has gone beyond the film industry and into home theater, televisions, gaming, computer sound systems, personal stereos and headphones, car audio, concert and live theater, and virtual reality. Everywhere audio or moving images go, THX has gone and provided a system of standards and technologies to ensure that the artist's aural and visual works meet the highest criteria.

THX is most recognizable from its trailer with the metallic THX logo, "The Audience Is Listening" tagline, and accompanying thunderous crescendo of encompassing sound known as the Deep Note, which plays in a theater just before the feature presentation. The THX trailer indicates that the theater, project system, and sound system meet the standards developed by Lucasfilm and adopted worldwide. As with many Lucasfilm creations, the THX trailer and its many iterations, including several "lost" THX trailers, have gained a cult following.[34] The trailer was parodied by *The Simpsons* (1989–) on several occasions, and there have been over twenty-eight different official trailers since the first was shown just prior to the opening scene of *Return of the Jedi* in 1983.[35] The latest THX trailer, titled *Genesis*, was designed in 2019 to celebrate the now-non-Lucasfilm company's thirty-fifth anniversary with a redesigned THX Spatial Audio three-dimensional Deep Note sound.[36] David Allan, author of *Super Sonic Logos: The Power of Audio Branding*, calls the Deep Note one of the "ten most noteworthy sonic logos of all time."[37]

As with many of Lucasfilm's industrial endeavors, the key to innovation and industry transformation lies within the practice of hiring the right people. To develop the most advanced sound-mixing studio, and eventually many initiatives under the THX label, Lucas hired Tomlinson Holman as the corporate

Lucasfilm's THX Division set industry standards for theater sound in the late twentieth century. (courtesy THX Ltd.)

technical director of Lucasfilm. Holman, a significant electrical engineer for sound, revolutionized recording by developing the preamplifier in the 1970s. Lucas hired Holman to "bring a new level of quality to film post-production."[38] Holman was the central figure in the build of the Sprocket Systems mixing studio.

As Holman has stated, "What I did was to consolidate many of the developments made between 1947 and 1980, add a few of my own (which got patented), and make one comprehensive system out of it."[39] The cornerstone to the mixing room was the patented electronic crossovers that Holman created, which separate the high frequency sounds from the low frequencies and sends each range to particular speakers suited to that range. To get the most out of the sound technologies, Holman developed acoustic standards for the mixing studio that specified specific architectural treatments including specialized speaker placement and enclosures, sound baffles, and auditorium sound characteristic guidelines. The combination of the THX crossover, THX certified amplifiers and speakers, and speaker instillation specifications became known as the THX Sound System. That system made the Sprocket Systems mixing theater the most advanced and revolutionary postproduction facility ever developed.[40] The name THX initially stood for Tomlinson Holman Crossover, as the electronic crossover Holman developed was the basis of the THX Sound System, and the name was later changed to stand for Tomlinson Homan eXperience.[41] Adding to the mythical status of THX is the coincidence that Lucas's first feature film was titled *THX 1138* (1971).

A mythologized cinemagoing experience contributed to the development of the THX Theater Alignment Program, which was the first step in improving theater sound. According to James A. Moorer, the creator of the THX Deep Note sound, it all started with preparing for the 1980 debut of *The Empire Strikes Back* at the Coronet Theater in San Francisco.[42] And in another version of the THX origin story, preparation for the 1981 release of *Raiders of the Lost Ark* at the Blumenfeld Theater in San Francisco started it all.[43] In either case, both origin stories place Holman, sound designer Burtt, and sound effects recordist Gary Summers at a theater in San Francisco to set up for a film premiere. As both accounts go, Holman poked his head behind the movie screen and saw that speakers were missing or disconnected and that the surround speakers had been placed in a closed-off balcony.[44] They worked on the sound system, but the result was nowhere close to how the film had sounded in the mixing studio.[45] According to Steve Martz, former THX senior design engineer, "Everything in the auditorium and mix room are well controlled and well defined, going into a commercial cinema, those factors, those sets of controls weren't in place."[46] At that time, theater design and their sound systems had not changed much since the 1950s, when the Altec "Voice of the Theater" sound system was the standard movie theater and mixing studio sound system.[47]

After seeing the state of theater sound systems, the Lucasfilm team embarked on a study of movie theaters because no matter how well a film is made, if the theater cannot reproduce the sound to the film's specifications, then the theater creates a broken link between the filmmakers and the audience. The Lucasfilm study showed that "half of all theaters had their left and right speakers reversed" and that the sound equipment often was not optimally tuned for the room.[48] Furthermore, they found that many theaters had uneven screen illumination and that noise bled through from adjacent theaters. According to THX folklore, in 1982, during the mix for *Return of the Jedi*, Lucas and the postproduction team took a print to a theater in San Francisco, and they found that parts of the soundtrack were inaudible because of the quality of the theater's sound system.[49]

As a result, Lucasfilm, led by the manager of Sprocket Systems, Jim Kessler, and Holman, set out to improve theater exhibition projection and sound.[50] Every theater in the United States receiving 70 mm prints of *Return of the Jedi* would have technicians align and certify the projector for even illumination across the screen and tune up the theater sound system to the proper speci-fications.[51] This became the THX Theater Alignment Program (TAP). With the implementation of standards for projection and sound, TAP ensured that theaters playing 70 mm prints of blockbuster films in the 1980s would have the best projection and sound possible. TAP gained popularity among both filmgoers and filmmakers. Director Sydney Pollack stated in 1985 that "the Lucasfilm TAP program is the first comprehensive, systematic approach to improving standards in the presentation of motion pictures. If enough of us get behind this idea we can change the standards of the industry."[52] The next step in improving film sound was in bringing the THX Sound System, with its specialized amplification, THX crossovers, speakers, speaker layout, and baffling, from the mixing studio into the movie theaters.[53] The patented THX baffling contains the behind-the-screen speakers and "provides reinforcement for low frequencies while absorbing unwanted high frequencies" that reverberate off the screen.[54]

Lucas also found that the quality of film prints for theatrical release was inconsistent. With such large orders for 1980s blockbusters in 70 mm, labs were not checking the prints before sending them to theaters. In one case, a riot almost erupted in San Diego when the sound disappeared forty minutes into *The Empire Strikes Back* because it was not printed on the film beyond the fourth roll.[55] Additionally, with the nature of film stock, once it ran through a projector for the first time, it would start to degrade with scratches, spots, and breaks. The Lucasfilm study showed that by two weeks of running in a theater, three out of four prints were significantly damaged, with much of the damage done to the optical sound track.[56] TAP services, from 1984 until the development of digital cinema projection, included a review of film reels prior to distribution to theaters, post-release evaluations of print conditions, projector and sound system calibration, and a twenty-four-hour technical assistance hotline.[57]

A milestone for TAP was "the adoption of its Criteria and Standards for Quality and Theatre Performance of Indoor Theaters as the industry standard by the National Association of Theatre Owners."[58] According to Lucas, "There will always be a need for a quality control system in the cinematic experience. Because it is highly technical and there are so many variables, you really need to have a way that you can equate what is created on one end with what the viewer sees on the other, and have them match up."[59]

Lucas further stated: "The Theater Alignment Program was dedicated to seeing to it that the quality of the theatrical experience was a good one. That all of the specifications that were required in terms of the light level of the screen, the ambiance of the room, the quality of the theater itself, and the quality of the prints and the quality of the transfer from the master negative to the release prints were all consistent and of the highest quality."[60]

TAP combined with the THX Sound System to become THX theater certification.[61] The key principle of THX certified theaters, including the certified digital cinemas of today, is that they meet the benchmark technical and acoustic standards developed by the THX company, which match those of the THX certified mixing rooms where the qualities of a film's sound are finalized. THX theater certification covered four areas of the theater: the physical structure, projection system, seating arrangement, and the sound system.[62] Within the physical structure, THX regulated that the minimum viewing angle of any seat must be at least twenty-six degrees, with an optimal angle of thirty-six; that there must be no obstructed views; and that the sound must be clear and distinct from any seat.[63] Physical structure requirements included meeting specific acoustic standards for low background noise (such as from air conditioners and projectors), isolation from outside sounds (such as from other theaters and the lobby), specific acoustic reverberation criteria for the shape and volume of the theater, and specific sound absorption qualities.[64] Meeting these acoustic standards meant the dialogue and higher frequency sounds would be more intelligible, there would be no audio distortion, and sounds would not reverberate or echo.[65] Once the room met the structural standards, it was fitted with THX approved equipment, such as the THX crossover, amplifiers, speakers, subwoofers, speaker baffling, screen, and projector. THX certified screen projection included standards for screen luminance, image contrast, color collaboration and accuracy, and focus resolution.[66] Theaters could choose sound and vision equipment from a number of manufacturers, as long as the equipment had been certified by THX, though the crossover sound processor was leased from THX.[67] THX certification requirements could be retrofitted into existing theaters or designed into new theaters. These standards ensured that a movie would sound and look the same across all certified theaters.

During the 1990s, digital sound provided for higher fidelity at a higher volume, and trailers took the opportunity to greatly increase their volume over that of their competition. This led projectionists to contend with overly loud trailers by turning down the volume of the sound system. However, this sometimes led to sounds in the feature films, such as dialogue, becoming unintelligible as the feature film's volume was played lower than intended.[68] In 1999, because of rising complaints of excessively loud film trailers, the National Association of Theater Owners introduced the TASA (Trailer Audio Standards Association) standard with a voluntary sound-level limit of 85 dBA.[69] This level was set to the TAP volume standard. THX is one of two TASA Certified Independent Audio Engineering Firms that certifies film trailer volumes.[70]

While THX's initial concern was to ensure quality image and sound play-back, the company participates in the protection of filmmaker and audience hearing as well.

THX has become the film industry's standardization regulator at both the postproduction and exhibition stages. Today, the company certifies postpro-duction sound facilities, film and digital prints, and movie theaters for sound and image quality. THX certified theaters provide "a faithful representation of the filmmakers' original vision, exactly how they want their movie to be seen."[71] THX split off from Lucasfilm into its own company in 2002, and in 2016 the gaming accessory company Razer purchased it. The development and signif-icance of THX in film history are intertwined with advances in both sound and image, and THX has become a marker of excellence. The advances THX helped usher in led to a new era where filmmakers, theaters, and audiences view sound as integral to the moviegoing experience.

Lucas, Skywalker Sound, THX, and creative workers have raised the status of sound within the industry at production and exhibition levels, for filmmakers as well as for the audiences, through innovations in the quality and significance of sound in the storytelling process and through the stan-dardization of sound quality. Lucas developed companies such as Sprocket Systems, Skywalker Sound, and THX to work on his films with his preferred production practices and standards of quality and made them world-leading companies. Lucas then brought these innovations to the film industry, where other filmmakers can utilize the technologies and state-of-the-art facilities and have the sound supervised, directed, edited, and mixed by highly talented creative sound practitioners specializing in the unique Northern California approach to sound design. Lucas led a revolution in film production and equally influenced film exhibition, where THX brought improved standards to the theater and beyond. By the 1990s, THX had brought their standards and quality controls to the home with THX certified home cinemas.[72] THX has helped popularize audience demand for quality filming experiences. Lucas changed how the industry and audiences perceive film sound through these significant advances and can be understood as a great facilitator in advancing the status of film for filmmakers and audiences.

Notes

1. See Michel Chion, *Audio-Vision: Sound on Screen*, trans. Claudia Gorbman (New York: Columbia University Press, 1990); Paul Grainge, *Brand Hollywood: Selling Entertainment in a Global Media Age* (Oxford: Routledge, 2008); Gianluca Sergi, "The

Sonic Playground: Hollywood Cinema and Its Listeners," Theoretical Film Sound Texts, FilmSound, 1999, http://www.filmsound.org/articles/sergi/index.htm; Meredith C. Ward, "Soundscape of the Cinema Theatre," *Music, Sound, and Moving Image* 10, no. 2 (2016): 132–65; Meredith C. Ward, *Static in the System: Noise and the Soundscape of American Cinema Culture* (Oakland: University of California Press, 2019); William Whittington, *Sound Design and Science Fiction* (Austin: University of Texas Press, 2007).

2. For scholarship on the impacts of Dolby and surround sound technologies, see Jay Beck, *Designing Sound: Audiovisual Aesthetics in 1970s American Cinema* (New Brunswick, NJ: Rutgers University Press, 2016); Kathryn Kalinak, ed., *Sound: Dialogue, Music, and Effects* (New Brunswick, NJ: Rutgers University Press, 2015); Mark Kerins, *Beyond Dolby (Stereo): Cinema in the Digital Sound Age* (Bloomington: Indiana University Press, 2011); Gianluca Sergi, *The Dolby Era: Film Sound in Contemporary Cinema* (Manchester: Manchester University Press, 2004).

3. Sergi, "Sonic Playground."

4. Chion, *Audio-Vision*, 101.

5. Ward, "Soundscape of the Cinema Theatre."

6. Ward, *Static in the System*, 110.

7. Jeff Smith, "The Auteur Renaissance, 1986–1980," in Kalinak, *Sound*, 83–106; William Whittington, "Sound Design: Sound Design in New Hollywood Cinema," in *Sound and Music in Film and Visual Media: A Critical Overview*, ed. Graeme Harper, Ruth Doughty, and Jochen Eisentraut (New York: Bloomsbury Academic, 2009), 555–68; Stephen Keane, "Murch and Burt: Walter Murch and Ben Burtt; The Sound Designer as Composer," in Harper, Doughty, and Eisentraut, *Sound and Music in Film and Visual Media*, 452–62.

8. Jay Beck and Vanessa Theme Ament, "The New Hollywood, 1981–1999," in Kalinak, *Sound*, 177.

9. Stephen Andriano-Moore, "The Rise of the Sound Designer: Northern California Film Sound in the 1960s and 1970s," *Historical Journal of Film, Radio and Television* 38, no. 3 (2018): 536–54.

10. Larry Blake, "George Lucas: Technology and the Art of Filmmaking," Mixonline, November 1, 2004, https://www.mixonline.com/recording/george-lucas-365460

11. Stephen Andriano-Moore, "The Motion Picture Editors Guild Treatment of the Film Sound Membership: Enforcing Status Quo for Hollywood's Post-production Sound Craft," *Labor Studies Journal* 45, no. 3 (2020): 282–83.

12. Andriano-Moore, "Rise of the Sound Designer," 547.

13. Walter Murch, "Chairman of the Edit: Walter Murch," interview by Doniphan Blair, *CineSource Magazine*, May 10, 2010, https://cinesourcemagazine.com/index.php?/site/comments/chairman_of_the_edit_walter_murch/#.Yg22Zi0RpB0.

14. Steve Jennings-X, "In A Galaxy Far from L.A. . . . Bay Area Film Post: A History, Part One," Mixonline, November 1, 2004, https://www.mixonline.com/recording/long-time-ago-371960.

15. "About," Skywalker Sound, accessed March 7, 2022, https://www.skysound.com/about/.

16. "Burtt Captures Sound for Movies," *Independent Journal*, n.d., Marin County Library Anne T. Kent California Room, Moving Pictures: Lucasfilm Clippings 1985–1989 folder, San Rafael, California (hereafter LC 85–89 folder).

17. "Timeline: 1971–Present," San Anselmo Historical Museum, accessed March 7, 2022, https://sananselmohistory.org/timeline/timeline-1971-present/.

18. "Burtt Captures Sound for Movies."

19. Tom Kenny, "Skywalker Sound," Mixonline, November 1, 2004, https://www.mixonline.com/recording/skywalker-sound-367038.

20. "Disney to Acquire Lucasfilm Ltd.," Walt Disney Company, October 30, 2012, https://thewaltdisneycompany.com/disney-to-acquire-lucasfilm-ltd/.

21. Foley is performed sound effects for movements of props and characters, such as footsteps and clothing sounds. See Vanessa Theme Ament, *The Foley Grail: The Art of Performing Sound for Film, Games, and Animation*, 3rd ed. (New York: Routledge, 2022).

22. Lucas in Blake, "George Lucas."

23. Randy Thom, "Designing a Movie for Sound," Randy Thom Articles, FilmSound, 1999, http://www.filmsound.org/articles/designing_for_sound.htm.

24. Stephen Andriano-Moore, "Motion Picture Editors Guild," 274.

25. Walter Murch, "Sound Doctrine: An Interview with Walter Murch," interview by Michael Jarrett, accessed February 17, 2022, http://www2.york.psu.edu/~jmj3/murchfq.htm.

26. Blake, "George Lucas."

27. Walter Murch, in Michael Ondaatje, *The Conversations: Walter Murch and the Art of Editing Film* (New York: Knopf, 2002), 15.

28. Ibid.

29. Gaye Jacobus, "Sounds That Could Win an Oscar," *Independent Journal*, April 4, 1984, Marin County Library Anne T. Kent California Room, Moving Pictures: Lucasfilm Clippings 1980–1984 folder, San Rafael, California.

30. Randy Thom, "Film Hopefuls Feel the Sonic Force at Skywalker Sound," interview by Marco della Cava, *USA Today*, July 31, 2013, https://www.usatoday.com/story/life/movies/2013/07/31/skywalker-sound-sundance-institute-music-and-sound-design-lab/2586705/.

31. "Sundance Music and Sound Design Lab Returns to Skywalker," Skywalker Sound, July 16, 2019, https://www.skysound.com/latest/sundance-music-and-sound-design-lab-returns-to-skywalker/.

32. "Storytelling, Amplified: Sundance Institute and Skywalker Sound Announce Composers, Directors for 2017 Music and Sound Design Labs," Sundance, July 5, 2017, https://www.sundance.org/blogs/news/music-and-sound-design-labs-2017.

33. "About," Skywalker Sound.

34. "The 7 Lost THX 'Tex' Trailers," Fandom, accessed February 17, 2022, https://creepypasta-fanon.fandom.com/wiki/The_7_Lost_THX_%22Tex%22_Trailers.

35. The first *Simpsons* THX trailer parody was aired on May 15, 1994, during the episode "Burns' Heir." For a history of THX Trailers, see https://thx.fandom.com/wiki/THX_Trailers.

36. "THX Unveils New Deep Note Trailer—Genesis," THX, August 22, 2019, https://www.thx.com/blog/thx-unveils-new-deep-note-trailer/.

37. David Allan, *Super Sonic Logos: The Power of Audio Branding* (New York: Business Expert, 2021), 5.

38. George Lucas, cited in Michael Rubin, *Droidmaker: George Lucas and the Digital Revolution* (Gainesville, FL: Triad, 2006), 216.

39. Tomlinson Holman, "An Interview with Tomlinson Holman," interview by Matteo Milani, March 2009, https://www.academia.edu/5707064/An_interview_with_Tomlinson_Holman.

40. Tomlinson Holman, *Sound for Film*, 3rd ed. (Burlington, MA: Focal, 2010), 226.

41. "Lucasfilm Originals: THX," Lucasfilm, August 18, 2021, https://www.lucasfilm.com/news/lucasfilm-originals-thx/.

42. James A. Moorer, "The Deep Story Behind Deep Note—the THX Logo Theme," accessed February 17, 2022, http://www.jamminpower.org/THX.html.

43. Rubin, *Droidmaker*, 223.

44. Ibid.

45. Moorer, "Deep Story."

46. Steve Martz in THX, "THX Certified Cinemas," Soundworks Collection, December 16, 2012, https://soundworkscollection.com/post/thx-certified-cinemas.

47. Jerry Zernicke, in THX, "THX Certified Cinemas," Soundworks Collection, December 16, 2012, https://soundworkscollection.com/post/thx-certified-cinemas; Holman, "An Interview with Tomlinson Holman"; "Altec Library," Great Plains Audio, accessed February 17, 2022, https://greatplainsaudio.com/altec-lansing-library/.

48. Rubin, *Droidmaker*, 224.

49. Zernicke, in THX, "THX Certified Cinemas."

50. Rubin, *Droidmaker*, 279.

51. Holman, "An Interview with Tomlinson Holman."

52. Sydney Pollack, An Open Letter to Film Exhibitors, 1985, cited in Rubin, *Droidmaker*, 231.

53. Lucasfilm, "THX Monitor 3417 Instructions Manual," 1987, http://www.film-tech.com/warehouse/manuals/THX3417.pdf.

54. LucasArts Entertainment Company, THX Division, "THX Architectural Suggestions," 1992, http://www.film-tech.com/warehouse/manuals/THXAS.pdf.

55. Rubin, *Droidmaker*, 232.

56. Ibid.

57. LucasArts, "THX Architectural Suggestions."

58. Ibid.

59. George Lucas, in THX, "The THX Story," Soundworks Collection, April 11, 2015, https://soundworkscollection.com/post/check-out-three-retro-thx-videos-thx-wow-the-thx-story-thx-soundtrack.

60. Ibid.

61. LucasArts, "THX Architectural Suggestions."

62. Lucasfilm Ltd., "Recommended Guidelines for Presentation Quality and Theatre Performance for Indoor Theaters," 2000, http://www.film-tech.com/warehouse /manuals/TAPGUIDELINES.pdf.

63. Ibid.

64. Ibid.

65. Holman, "An Interview with Tomlinson Holman."

66. "FAQ: What Is Projection System Calibration?," THX, accessed February 17, 2022, https://www.thx.com/faq/.

67. Lucasfilm, "Recommended Guidelines for Presentation Quality."

68. Wayne Staab, "Movies Too Loud? Still?," Hearing Health Matters, December 6, 2017, https://hearinghealthmatters.org/waynesworld/2017/movies-loud-still/.

69. "TASA History," TASA, accessed February 17, 2022, https://www.tasatrailers .org/history.html.

70. "TASA Certified Independent Audio Engineering Firms," TASA, accessed February 17, 2022, https://www.tasatrailers.org/engineering.html.

71. "THX Certified Cinemas," THX, accessed February 17, 2022, https://www.thx .com/thx-certified-cinema/.

72. Don Clark, "Lucasfilm Bringing Movie-Quality Sound into Homes," *San Francisco Chronicle*, May 30, 1990, C1, C5.

14

LucasArts and the Hollywoodization of Video Games

Stefan Hall

Introduction

Rebounding after *THX 1138* (1971) with the successful *American Graffiti* (1973) and even more so in the wake of the blockbuster *Star Wars* (1977), George Lucas thought to take the liberating environment of film production he had established with Francis Ford Coppola and the creation of American Zoetrope into other areas of entertainment. In 1979, Lucas created the Lucasfilm Computer Division to research ways in which advances in computer technology could be integrated with film production and intersect with other industries. The division was further divided into one department for video games, known as the Games Group, and another for graphics, known as the Graphics Group.[1] Lucasfilm was not the only film studio joining the ranks of companies looking to expand their properties through video games. 20th Century Fox would establish Fox Video Games after initially licensing a number of games (including *Worm War I*, *Beany Bopper*, *Fast Eddie*, and *Deadly Duck*, all released in 1982) from software company Sirius before turning more fully to adaptations from their film library. The Walt Disney Company, after initial licensing agreements with Atari and Mattel Electronics in the early 1980s, would eventually form their own in-house gaming unit, Walt Disney Computer Software (WDCS), in 1988. The importance of Atari and its market dominance at this time cannot be understated, and it was one of the reasons that Lucas would go on to sign a joint cooperative agreement with Atari.[2]

Although the Games Group was cushioned within several levels of corporate structure—in a sort of contained design environment in what would now be referred to as a "game incubator"—its formalization in May 1982 within the Computer Division necessitated some additional support. Atari in turn invested $1 million into the Games Group.[3] Ed Catmull, who was running the Computer Division, hired Peter Langston to head up the Games Group. In 1971, while at Reed College, Langston had begun designing a popular game called *Empire* inspired by strategy board games that appeared on mainframes through the mid-1970s.[4]

Early Releases

According to Robert Doris, vice president of Lucasfilm and general manager of the Computer Division, the movement into the video game business was a calculated result of the perception of video games, even at this nascent level of hardware capabilities, becoming more and more cinematic. While the deal between Lucasfilm and Atari was mutually beneficial for both companies, it was perhaps more advantageous for Lucasfilm as the Games Group would use Atari as a sort of testing bed for video game development, taking several years to release the first two games, *Rescue on Fractalus!* and *Ballblazer*, for the 5200 and the 7800 game systems. Atari had found strong success in a licensing agreement with Steven Spielberg, with their version of *Raiders of the Lost Ark* (1982), and some notable commercial failure, with *E.T. the Extra-Terrestrial* (1982). Even so, "amid this convergence of technology and entertainment, it was apparent that the core target audiences of special-effects movies and the Atari game platform had significant similarities."[5] The spectacle (or fantastic) aspect of game design pushes it toward certain film franchises as certain types (genres) of narratives lend themselves to game adaptation more readily than others: "A feature like *Star Wars*, full of futuristic, electronic space hardware, might attract an audience more likely to play space games than would, say, *Caligula*."[6] Although this was a tumultuous time for film-to-game adaptations, with over thirty such titles produced between 1982 and 1984, for many years the Games Group would eschew developing their own *Star Wars* games, and Lucasfilm preferred to license out the franchise.[7] Lucas admitted, "I wanted to have a really creative, independent shop. It's not a coincidence that our early video games were *not* based on the *Star Wars* or *Indiana Jones* films."[8]

Before they even began thinking about a game, the Games Group created some very basic 3D, point-of-view (POV) routines as an experiment and then turned to studying the dedicated chips and microprocessor of Atari's computer.[9] Doing this gave the group a very thorough understanding of not only what the architecture was designed to do but also where the technology could be pushed or "how the form might evolve—ultimately, maybe, to meld with movies themselves."[10] In 1983, two early versions of the first games—known at that point as *BallBlaster* and *Rebel Rescue*—were shown to Atari, and final versions of the games were delivered in May 1984 and announced at a press conference that began with the opening sequence from *Star Wars*.[11] *Ballblazer* was essentially a sports-style game where both players carry a ball in a ship called a rotofoil and attempt to carry or shoot the ball through the opponent's goal. The game had three modes—human versus human, human versus AI, and (interestingly) AI versus AI—and featured an algorithmically generated theme programmed by Langston, who was a trained musician. *Rescue on Fractalus!* put the player in control of a Valkyrie space fighter converted to search-and-rescue duty on an alien planet to retrieve stranded Ethercorps pilots. One innovation in the game was the use of fractal geometry algorithms to create the planetary landscape. The Computer Division had previously used fractal technology as the basis for the special effects of the Genesis device in *Star Trek II: The Wrath of Khan* (1982). Loren Carpenter, who was responsible for the terraforming effect, was able to create a fractal generator on an Atari 800 computer, and so he was loaned from the Computer Division to the Games Group to help finish the game.[12] Lucas himself offered an interesting twist on the straightforward rescue premise when he suggested that the team have disguised aliens, known as Jaggis, masquerading as downed pilots; through a combination of sound and visual effects, a player has to make a rather quick decision about whether or not to allow a pilot on board or risk destruction, and this jump-scare experience was noted by several reviewers as a notable feature in addition to the interesting gameplay and graphics.

This time in development enabled Lucasfilm to experience video game industry operations while only committing a small amount of its resources (initially the Games Group was only six men). Conversely, the Games Group borrowed heavily from development procedures in the film production division, including drawing models, making costumes, and writing extensive storylines to more fully develop a narrative underpinning for the games. As Langston explained, "My charter was to figure out where in the entertainment industry to apply the kind of high-tech approaches that were proving so revolutionary in graphics, sound, and editing for movies. . . . It took very little time to settle on pursuing games."[13] In an internal memo written in 1982, game designer David Fox listed some thoughts on game development, in particular what films do well—such as special effects modeling new realities and creating narrative engagement—and where video games lag behind, noting that they were not taking full advantage of the hardware, including video and audio (remarking that the game based on *TRON* [1982] by Bally Midway was an exception); sometimes seemed constrained in game mechanics because of genre; and did not offer a high level of escapism.[14]

Both *Rescue on Fractalus!* and *Ballblazer* were well-received titles even as their release coincided with a serious downturn in the North American video game market during 1984.[15] This also delayed the release of the games for home computers while Warner Communications sold the consumer division of Atari, but ultimately Epyx published both titles for multiple computer systems in 1985. At this point, as merely a developer, the Games Group had to rely on other companies to help publish and distribute their games. This would continue with the next two releases, both in 1985, *Koronis Rift* and *The Eidolon*. Both games incorporated the fractal technology first developed for *Rescue on Fractalus!*, and *Koronis Rift* had an additional innovation with depth cuing, the process by which programmers can make the background slowly appear on the screen and more realistically approximate human vision. *Koronis Rift* continued with the science fiction motif used by the Games Group, with the player controlling a rover on the surface of an alien planet, navigating mazes while fighting robots and saucers left behind by an ancient, vanished civilization known as the Ancients. The game mixed arcade action with some puzzles to provide some variety in play style for the user. The title of *The Eidolon* refers to a strange, nineteenth-century vehicle that the player controls while traversing another dimension after an accidental transportation. Navigating mazes forms the basis of the gameplay here, too, although instead of science fiction antagonists the player must defeat guardian dragons and other fantastic monsters like greps, bottlenecks, and rotoflies. While in some ways a fairly conventional arcade shooter, *The Eidolon* is notable as being one of the progenitors of the first-person shooter (FPS) genre with the levels rendered as pseudo-3D environments.

Adventuring into Cinema with *Labyrinth*

Unlike the initial four games produced by the Games Group, their first foray into adventure games was an adaptation of a film property: *Labyrinth* (1986). As Lucas was a producer on the film, and Lucasfilm itself one of the production companies, along with Hanson Associates, getting the rights was a relatively straightforward endeavor. This would also give the Games Group their first opportunity with a film property, as the ban on anything to do with *Star Wars* was still in effect. Because of the production schedules of both the film and the game, the movie would be playing in theaters before the game was released, so to keep the properties somewhat distinct, the game was officially titled *Labyrinth: The Computer Game* and significantly modified the narrative as told in the film. While key events and locations are represented in the game, players construct their own identity—through a combination of name, gender, and favorite color—and do not play as Sarah, the protagonist from the film.[16] The game begins as a simple text-based adventure, and eventually players enter a movie theater to, in a metanarrative move, watch the movie *Labyrinth*. At this point the game switches to a full-color, 3D environment, and Jareth appears on the movie screen, transporting the player to a prison maze, and a timer of thirteen real-time hours starts.[17] The player must locate and defeat Jareth in this time or lose the game. While timers had been used in many video games before this one—especially arcade games, which needed to motivate the players to complete levels and not endlessly tie up the machines—this usage was rather innovative.

Designer David Fox would be joined by Steve Arnold, and through Jim Henson, both would be sent to England to work on story elements with noted writer Douglas Adams. A focus on exploring the narrative and interacting with characters was privileged over combat elements, and to facilitate this a word-wheel interface was created to allow a player to select two-word commands—one noun, one verb—contextually related to the area of the maze they were in.[18] Most critics and reviewers praised the variety of the puzzles, the detailed graphics, and the user interface while finding the overall design perhaps a little too slow and a little too simple. Despite this, *Labyrinth: The Computer Game* showed that the Games Group could do an extremely respectable job of adapting a film property, and they waited for their next opportunity to further refine their design skills.

Developing and Publishing: *Maniac Mansion*

Buoyed by their success with *Labyrinth: The Computer Game*, the Games Group stayed with the adventure genre for their first self-published video game, *Maniac Mansion* (1987). They took on the dual roles of developer and publisher as a result of increased confidence in their own properties coupled with an interest in increasing control and profitability.[19] First conceived in 1985 by Ron Gilbert and Gary Winnick, the game drew inspiration from the world of cinema, specifically horror film and B-movie clichés; however, the story would be an intentionally comedic adventure following teenage protagonist Dave Miller and his six friends (with the player choosing only two to accompany Dave) as he attempts to rescue his girlfriend, Sandy Pantz, from Dr. Fred, a scientist whose mind has been enslaved by a sentient meteor. Gilbert wanted to avoid the command line interface of earlier adventure titles, such as those popularized by Sierra On-Line, and instead use a completely point-and-click interface for the player to guide characters through the 2D world while solving environmental puzzles.

Another important development to come from *Maniac Mansion* was Gilbert's creation of SCUMM: Script Creation Utility for *Maniac Mansion*.[20] This game engine would be used for the next four adventure games—*Zak McKracken and the Alien Mindbenders* (1988), *Indiana Jones and the Last Crusade: The Graphic Adventure* (1989), *Loom* (1990), and *The Secret of Monkey Island* (1990)—again reflecting the propensity of the Games Group to recycle code and maximize what could be done in programming by improving each iterative design. Gilbert also promoted the idea of cutscenes in the game—noninteractive plot sequences like those used in games such as *Pac-Man* (1980) and *Donkey Kong* (1981), among others—featuring them extensively in the point-and-click adventure *Maniac Mansion* and further popularizing these cinema scenes to tell an elaborate story between the game's action sequences. Game designers began thinking of these in a more cinematic way, using techniques such as different camera angles, wide-screen letterboxing, and subtitles to replicate a movie-like experience. Finally, in a move that had been used occasionally in the entertainment industry, *Maniac Mansion* was adapted into a three-season television show in 1990 (written by comedian Eugene Levy).[21] While there had been some adaptation of games to other visual media before, such as *The Super Mario Bros. Super Show!* (1989), this sort of development was rather new and presaged the often poorly regarded round of adaptations that would begin with *Super Mario Bros.* (1993). Upon release, the game was highly praised, with many reviewers and critics noting numerous movie connections along with the innovative gameplay and engaging story, particularly as told through the cutscenes.

Returning to Cinema with *Indiana Jones and the Last Crusade: The Graphic Adventure*

Designed to coincide with the release of the theatrical film in 1989, *Indiana Jones and the Last Crusade: The Graphic Adventure* had its long name to distinguish it from the more arcade-style *Indiana Jones and the Last Crusade: The Action Game*, coming out in the same year and also published by Lucasfilm Games (although it would be developed by Tiertex Limited, a UK studio and thus an interesting occurrence of a Lucasfilm title being outsourced). Built with SCUMM, *The Graphic Adventure* also introduced the Indy Quotient (IQ) system, which encouraged replayability in the game for those players who wanted the maximum score possible; as with *Labyrinth*, "the trick was to make the game compelling and the challenges engaging for players who had seen the movie."[22] Typically this could only be achieved by thinking and trying nonobvious solutions to the game's puzzles, so as much as the game followed certain plot points of the film while outright deleting others (e.g., no mention of Sallah or the Brotherhood of the Grail), these deviations—done with input from Lucas and Spielberg—created a new narrative experience that differed from the film at certain points as well as crafting three different endings to the game. In a nod to other adventure games, particularly those by Infocom, the game included a modified Grail diary that not only added additional backstory to the narrative but also was required to solve certain puzzles (such as the identity of the true Grail).[23] Upon release, the game became the biggest seller for the Games Group, selling a very respectable 250,000 copies, and it would eventually be followed by a sequel, *Indiana Jones and the Fate of Atlantis* (1992), which told an original Indiana Jones story. Work commenced on a second sequel, *Indiana Jones and the Iron Phoenix*, but the project was ultimately abandoned. However, publisher Dark Horse Comics picked up the rights to the story and turned it into a four-issue miniseries in 1994.

When You Can't Make a Movie, Make a Game: *The Dig*

In 1990, through a reorganization of the Lucas companies, the Games Group of Lucasfilm became part of the newly created LucasArts Entertainment Company, which included Industrial Light & Magic (ILM) and Skywalker Sound, and this would foster an increased level of collaboration between all the groups. Achieving a respectable level of success with Indiana Jones games, and releasing other innovative titles such as *The Secret of Monkey Island* (1990) and *Loom* (1990), Lucasfilm Games finally moved to developing their own *Star Wars* games after the property was with other developers for several years.[24] Although Lucasfilm Games would essentially become synonymous with these *Star Wars* titles—beginning with *X-Wing* (1992)—one final important entry in their output should be acknowledged: *The Dig* (1995).

Beginning with *Star Wars: Rebel Assault* (1993), LucasArts Games had started releasing titles on CD-ROM to take advantage of the medium's increased storage. This was also a time when full motion video (FMV) sequences would increase the fidelity of the cutscenes in games by having actual actors in costumes create narrative clips that often looked more like live action movies. Originally imagining an episode for *Amazing Stories* and then an original film, Spielberg realized that the story he wanted to tell would be prohibitively expensive, and so after the success of *Indiana Jones and the Last Crusade: The Graphic Adventure*, he approached the Games Group with the idea and the possibility of making a game. The premise of the story was actually a rather serious science fiction tale about a five-man team attempting to destroy on an asteroid on a collision course with Earth. The team discovers that the asteroid is actually hollow and contains a device that transports three of them to an alien world, and they must solve puzzles to return home and destroy the asteroid before the extinction-level event. Using professional voice actors—including Robert Patrick and Steve Blum—and a full film score, *The Dig* was extremely ambitious in scope. In fact, *The Dig* was the first LucasArts game to offer its soundtrack for sale as an audio CD.

Unfortunately, the game was released to mixed reviews, with praise for its atmosphere, score, and story but with problems noted with the complexity of puzzles and, perhaps surprisingly, issues with the acting. The problems might be related to the game's extended development period, which ran roughly from 1989 to 1995. Still, LucasArts Games should be proud of this attempt to realize a major cinematic idea in game form, and it is yet another title in a long run of games that had deep digital roots in film. Less than a year after the acquisition of Lucasfilm by the Walt Disney Company in December 2012, Disney announced the shuttering of LucasArts in all but name, essentially transforming it into a division that handled the licensing of Lucasfilm properties to third-party developers, particularly Electronic Arts, and transferring in-house development to Disney Interactive Studios. In 2021, however, Disney reestablished the importance of Lucasfilm Games and moved them back into a place of greater corporate prominence, recognizing the legacy of one of the most significant game development studios in the industry.

Notes

1. Comprising about one-third of the total employees in the Computer Division, in 1982 the graphics department would be spun off into its own corporation and ultimately become Pixar.

2. Michael Ciraolo, "Lucasfilm & Atari," *Antic*, August 1984, https://www.atari magazines.com/v3n4/lucasfilm.html.

3. Russel DeMaria and Johnny L. Wilson, *High Score! The Illustrated History of Electronic Games*, 2nd ed. (New York: McGraw-Hill, 2004), 198.

4. Ibid., 51.

5. Rob Smith, *Rogue Leaders: The Story of LucasArts* (San Francisco: Chronicle Books, 2008), 11.

6. David Shifren, "Video Games: A Burgeoning Industry Provides a New Revenue Source in Theatre Lobbies," *Film Journal*, December 21, 1981, 6.

7. It was board game developer Parker Bros. who initially secured the licensing rights to *Star Wars* games for home consoles, while Atari held the rights to *Star Wars* games for the arcade. Atari's *Star Wars: The Arcade Game* was rather popular with Spielberg, who borrowed the one owned by the Games Group for the sound stage while working on *Indiana Jones and the Temple of Doom* (1984) and eventually bought his own for his Los Angeles office.

8. Smith, *Rogue Leaders*, 7.

9. Peter Langston, "Ten Tips from the Programming Pros: Secrets From Lucasfilm's Games Group," *Atari Connection*, Spring 1984, 34. Since 3D computer modeling was barely in its infancy, the Games Group had Industrial Light & Magic create scale models of the ships in *Ballblazer* and *Rescue on Fractalus!* in the same process used with the *Star Wars* films.

10. Associated Press, "Lucas Looks beyond Film—Will Interactive Movies Try to Eat Your Popcorn?," *Access*, Fall 1984, 12.

11. Jonathan Greer, "*Star Wars* creator teams up with Atari," *San Jose Mercury News*, May 9, 1984, http://www.langston.com/LFGames/SJMN19840509.html. During the playtesting of *Rebel Rescue*, Lucas looked for a fire button on the controls. In the game's fiction, it was explained that the weapons had been removed to make more room for the marooned pilots to be rescued. Lucas asked Fox if that was a part of the game design or a moral choice. See Smith, *Rogue Leaders*, 16. This is an important question to raise, and the introduction of moral choices as part of the play mechanics usually took the form of alternate endings based on what actions the player had or had not done. Offering different narrative outcomes was initially far easier to do on computers and helped to distinguish them from other gaming platforms.

12. Smith, *Rogue Leaders*, 17.

13. Ibid., 12–13.

14. As the title of *Rebel Rescue* had to be changed because of its loose connection to the *Star Wars* universe, Fox also raised a question regarding the licensing agreement of *Star Wars*, wondering if games might be set in the world of the films, referencing

places, vehicles, and weapons while providing new characters and stories, an idea that was truly prescient for its time. See Smith, *Rogue Leaders*, 15.

15. Unfortunately, work-in-progress (WIP) copies sent to Atari wound up being pirated and distributed over early online bulletin board systems. Despite some bugs, the technology was still impressive and caused a serious buzz at the 1984 Consumer Electronics Show (CES).

16. Early in development, the design team screened a rough cut of the film.

17. This idea came from Adams, who said he was inspired by the change from black and white to color in *The Wizard of Oz* (1939).

18. The design of *Labyrinth: The Computer Game* would also influence the Games Group's *Habitat* (1986), the first attempt at a large-scale commercial virtual community and a forerunner of modern massively multiplayer online role-playing games (MMORPGs).

19. It should be noted that before *Maniac Mansion* the Games Group had developed two military vehicle simulation games: *PHM Pegasus* (1986) and *Strike Fleet* (1987), both of which were published by Electronic Arts. The former became, at the time of its release, the biggest hit for the Games Group, selling over one hundred thousand copies, a notable achievement at that time.

20. The Games Group had access to the Unix workstations used by the Graphics Group, and while this aided in game development, both Gilbert and programmer Chip Morningstar recognized the need for a more user- and platform-friendly scripting language. Smith, *Rogue Leaders*, 31.

21. The game would also get a sequel, *The Day of the Tentacle* (1993).

22. Smith, *Rogue Leaders*, 42.

23. Infocom referred to these extra items packaged with a game as "feelies" as they were designed to make the game feel more realistic to the players. It also helped thwart piracy of the games.

24. *Loom* featured a truly innovative musical interface and also included a cassette tape that introduced the complete backstory of the game. This would be incorporated into the CD-ROM rerelease as dialogue modified by science fiction author Orson Scott Card.

15

Franchise and Edutainment in the History of Lucasfilm Television

Joseph J. Darowski

Shortly after the success of *Star Wars*, Lucasfilm began to release projects on television. These specials, made-for-TV films, and series have a checkered history when it comes to critical praise, ratings success, and fan engagement. From the oft-mocked *Star Wars Holiday Special* to the very successful *Mandalorian* series, Lucasfilm Television's productions have ranged from odd relics of pop culture past to fully embraced hit series that are considered core texts within a franchise. With decades of history and disparate goals for the productions from Lucasfilm Television, an eclectic reception is not unexpected. The early period of Lucasfilm's television productions, from the late 1970s through the early 1990s, is particularly interesting in terms of Lucas's vision for the projects and the uneven reception from fans.

The most obvious impulses behind Lucasfilm's television productions are the creative opportunity to tell stories in a different medium and the business opportunity to ensure continued interest in franchises. As Henry Jenkins explains, "In the ideal form of transmedia storytelling, each medium does what it does best—so that a story might be introduced in a film, expanded through television, novels, and comics, and its world might be explored and experienced through gameplay."[1] The Lucasfilm television productions from the 1970s, 1980s, and 1990s were all adaptations of existing franchises, and the goal was likely exactly what Jenkins described. Hoping to play to the strengths of different mediums, the stories expanded the storyverse of existing intellectual property. The presence of a franchise in multiple media forms increased awareness and profit opportunity.

In this era, Lucasfilm Television seemed more intent on reminding the public of the existence of franchises than on creating new core texts for fans to embrace. With made-for-TV specials and Saturday morning cartoons set in the *Star Wars* universe or a sitcom adaptation of a video game developed by Lucasfilm, viewers could watch interesting but unessential chapters in franchise storytelling. However, when transitioning *Indiana Jones* to television, Lucas laid out an entirely different concept and purpose. One of the most intriguing television productions from Lucasfilm is *The Young Indiana Jones Chronicles*, which saw a very hands-on approach from George Lucas as he sought to not only expand the transmedia presence of *Indiana Jones* but deploy a popular entertainment franchise as an educational opportunity for young viewers. In adapting *Indiana Jones* to a new medium, Lucas had a vision that was ahead of his times in terms of how the series could embrace emerging technologies. This series told new Indiana Jones stories, but with specific educational goals Lucas himself saw as an essential purpose of producing *The Young Indiana Jones Chronicles*.

Transmedia *Star Wars*

The first foray of Lucasfilm into television production has taken almost mythological import in *Star Wars* fan lore. *The Star Wars Holiday Special* has become more famous as a curiosity than anything else, and it stands in bizarre contrast to most stories told in the *Star Wars* universe. In part because it was inaccessible for so long, the majority of fans who did not see its single airing on CBS on November 17, 1978, only heard tales of how bad it was. Lucas was busy preparing production on *The Empire Strikes Back*, and after "sitting down with television writer Bruce Vilanch to go over a story treatment that provided only some very vague but ambitious basics," he put the special in the hands of veteran producers Dwight Hemion and Gary Smith.[2] The end result pleased no one. Lucas has famously said that "if he had a hammer and the time, he would track down all existing copies" of the *Holiday Special* and destroy them.[3]

When the result is so famously bad, it may seem like this was a bad idea from the start. But, as Andrew Ferguson argues, "In mid-1978 the *Holiday Special* must have seemed like a no-brainer. *Star Wars* had just returned to theaters nationwide for an encore run; in some locales it had never left the screen since its debut the previous May. . . . As the next installment would not be ready for another year or two, some sort of booster shot seemed necessary to bridge the gap—in particular something that would remind children and parents that there was a whole galaxy of *Star Wars* toys that would make ideal Christmas presents."[4]

While the opening of the special would appear to promise the *Star Wars* action fans loved, featuring repurposed shots from the film that reveal the *Millennium Falcon* being pursued by Star Destroyers and a brief new scene of Han talking to Chewbacca, the program quickly leaves those familiar confines. Ferguson sums up the next sequence: "What follows the credits is one of the most bewildering segments ever to air on network television, almost avant-garde in its refusal to provide any accommodation to the viewer."[5] It consists of Chewbacca's family speaking, growling at one another with no subtitles, as they go through what seems to be a routine morning in a Wookiee household. While the upcoming variety show bits are perhaps understandable in an era of television featuring *The Sonny and Cher Comedy Hour* or *Donny and Marie*, this opening is truly bizarre.

The one bright spot for the special is an animated sequence that features the first appearance of Boba Fett, whose design aesthetic made him immediately visually appealing to fans. The animation was provided by a new production studio based in Canada called Nelvana. While the entire special can easily be tracked down online now, this version is the only portion of the *Holiday Special* that has ever officially been released since the first airing on television. It is now available on Disney+ under the title *The Story of the Faithful Wookiee*.

The disastrous reception of the *Holiday Special* was immediately apparent. Lucas's legendary frustration with the product is understandable in terms of its quality. This was not good *Star Wars*. And it was also potentially incredibly damaging for a young brand. There were books and toys, but for many fans, this was likely the second engagement they ever had with the franchise. As Ferguson argues, the failure of the *Holiday Special* on an aesthetic level is obvious to everyone, but for Lucas, "more acute is the missed opportunity to establish *Star Wars* as a presence on TV and accelerate the transition into the transmedia juggernaut we know today."[6] Lucasfilm would not use television as a means of expanding the *Star Wars* storyworld again until after the original trilogy was completed.

After *The Return of the Jedi* successfully closed out the original trilogy, Lucasfilm revisited television with the made-for-TV movie *The Ewok*

Adventure: Caravan of Courage. Lucas wrote a storyline and was the executive producer. Originally, he was interested in producing a half-hour story for television, but ABC inquired if it could be expanded to be featured in its Sunday night movie of the week time slot. The script was written by Bob Carrau, and it was directed by John Korty.

After being completely hands-off with the production of the *Holiday Special*, Lucas was more involved in the finished product for *Caravan of Courage*. While Korty had directed many television movies previously, "Lucas couldn't leave things alone, rewriting scenes and trying to manage Korty from afar."[7] Korty reports that during filming Lucas repeatedly contacted him with suggestions: "His big thing is 'Let's have more conflict, let's have more fights, let's have more explosions.'"[8] After seeing the footage Korty had shot, Lucas ordered additional reshoots. Korty had moved on to another project, so Lucas directed the reshoots himself. The reshoots would give a couple more moments to the character of Mace and also rework the ending of the film.[9] Lucas would also oversee the final cut of the film before it aired on ABC.

Lucas was motivated in part by the drive to push filmmaking technology forward. For *Caravan of Courage* the production would include "75 or so matte, blue-screen, and other FX shots" that were "extraordinarily ambitious for television."[10] This was especially bold with a nine-month production schedule, as compared with the years the *Star Wars* films had used between installments. The result was an interesting mix of advancing production technology while also looking back. Joe Johnston, who was a production designer on *Caravan of Courage*, recalls, "We did forced perspectives and glass paintings, back-to-basics things that had been around since the 1920s. George just told us to go out there and have some fun."[11] For Lucasfilm, working within budget limitations had always resulted in blending what had been done before with what is still on the horizon to try to create movie magic. ILM's special effects were noted for being above the quality expected for TV movies, and the film was released internationally in cinemas.[12]

The entire premise of the *Caravan of Courage* is a family attempting to be reunited. There are the parents, Jeremitt and Catarine, and two siblings, Mace and Cindel. While the parents leave to get help after a shuttle crash, Mace stays to take care of his little sister. Eventually, when their parents don't return, Mace and Cindel go after them and meet the Ewoks, including Wicket, and eventually the family is reunited for the happy finale. *Caravan of Courage* aired on November 25, 1984, and "65 million viewers tuned in for ABC's second-highest night of the year. The program achieved a 40% share of the time slot and led all network viewings by a wide margin."[13] At the time, there was a positive enough reception to the film—including a nomination for outstanding children's programming and a win for best effects at the Emmys—that a sequel film was quickly put into production. In terms of viewers, the film was a hit, so it was natural ABC would want another *Star Wars* film for the time slot.

Lucas again provided the story for *Ewoks: The Battle for Endor*, but he did not write the screenplay or direct the movie. This film has a much darker opening premise than the first Ewok adventure. Biographer Brian Jay Jones notes that Lucas "apparently never seemed content with a sequel unless it was darker than its forebear," and he reportedly insisted, "I want this to be all about death."[14] While the first film spent two hours on a quest to reunite Cindel with her family, the sequel would do away with those characters in the opening scene. *Ewoks: The Battle for Endor* begins with an attack by marauders who kill Cindel's mom, dad, and brother. Now an orphan, Cindel and Wicket have an adventure together.

These made-for-TV movies demonstrate that Lucas was interested in expanding the *Star Wars* storyverse even after he completed the feature film trilogy. Perhaps because he had some success with ABC's Ewok films, Lucas would continue to work with ABC on two animated series, *Ewoks* and *Droids*. He would also seek out a former collaborator, the Nelvana production house, which had done the animated portion of the *Holiday Special*. Despite his overall negative feelings toward the *Holiday Special*, Lucas must have at least approved of the quality of the animation work in this sequence. Much like the *Holiday Special*, *Ewoks* and *Droids* probably seemed like sure things when they were conceived. But neither series would last long. *Ewoks* lasted two seasons, which was one more than *Droids*, and neither series achieved the significance or popularity of the films.

Released in a period when children's animation was experiencing something of a revolution, the two series appeared like a natural fit for the Saturday morning landscape. *Ewoks* would align with the type of series that networks believed girls would be more interested in, with magical cute animal tales in the vein of *Care Bears* or *The Smurfs*. *Droids* would be produced with a more adventurous science fiction edge, in the vein of *Galactic Guardians*. Unfortunately, this division ended up dissecting the genre blend that is one aspect of what made *Star Wars* such a success. The films were science fiction *and* fantasy. The cartoons moved the science fiction into the *Droids* series and the fantasy into *Ewoks*, and as a result neither ended up feeling quite like a continuation of *Star Wars*.[15]

Droids was canceled after only one season. *Ewoks* would continue for one more, and a *Droids* special was also produced. After this, the two series were available only infrequently as reruns on the Sci-Fi Channel in the early 1990s and videotape releases that edited a few episodes together and presented them as a single movie. Recently, *Ewoks* has been released on Disney+ on a section of the streaming service labeled "Vintage *Star Wars*." But, on the whole, the two series have been treated as unessential curios that only the most die-hard fans would know in any detail.

These early television projects are representative of efforts to expand the *Star Wars* storyworld and also ensure the continued longevity of the brand. There is an undeniable commercial aspect to the projects. The *Ewoks* movies carried on one of the most marketable aspects of *Return of the Jedi* and ensured continued exposure of the furry creatures that overthrew the Empire. Notably, the word Ewok is never said in *Return of the Jedi*, and one reason the name for the creatures is so well known is likely the dual exposure that arose from the Ewok live-action TV movies and the *Ewoks* cartoon. For the cartoon series, toy lines were released and comic book adaptations were produced. While the impact of the TV movies, series, and associated products is minimal in the long-term development of the *Star Wars* franchise, these early steps are evidence of some of Lucas's goals and concerns of maintaining brand awareness, ensuring marketing tie-ins for increased profitability, and—in the case of the Ewoks movies—exploring filmmaking techniques and technologies that attempt to provide film-quality products with television-sized budgets. Lucas was most hands-on with the live-action films, providing the storyline and involving himself in the postproduction in a more direct way than he did with the animated projects. Yet in all of these efforts the results never achieved the large-scale success of the original films.

Maniac Mansion

One of the more forgotten Lucasfilm television series was a coproduction with Atlantis Films titled *Maniac Mansion*. The sitcom was inspired by a video game that had been developed by Lucasfilm Games for the Commodore 64 and Apple II computer systems. It was a series produced in Canada that "came to television from the satiric imaginations of the SCTV comedy troupe" and was developed by Eugene Levy.[16] Despite being based on a Lucasfilm Games product, much of the show's style and tone seem to come more directly from SCTV than from Lucasfilm. *Entertainment Weekly* referred to

George Lucas behind the scenes of *The Young Indiana Jones Chronicles* with director Carl Schultz. (© Lucasfilm Ltd./courtesy Everett Collection)

the series as "packed with veterans of SCTV" and noted, "There are former SCTV actors, writers, directors, key grips—even *Mansion*'s makeup artist is an old *SCTV*er."[17] SCTV alumnus Joe Flaherty starred as the patriarch of the Edison family.

Among the more surreal elements of the series is the family's four-year-old, who, because of a science experiment gone awry, is "the size of a professional wrestler" though he retains the mind of a toddler.[18] On a similar note, Uncle Harry has a human head on the body of a fly and is the size of a fly. The sitcom hijinks revolve around the strange inventions and experiments that occur in the family's mansion, most of which are powered by a strange meteorite in the basement.

The series produced sixty-two episodes across three seasons. In the United States, it aired on cable's Family Channel, and in Canada it aired YTV. While this is an example of corporate synergy as the gaming and television units promoted the same property, the long-term impact of the *Maniac Mansion* franchise is more notable for what the game did to advance video game design than what the TV show did for an ongoing franchise. The first game was released in 1989, and a sequel came out in 1993. The TV show ran from 1990 to 1993. Occasional entertainment journalism pieces that look back on the video game industry will highlight *Maniac Mansion* or its sequel,[19] but as a recognizable piece of popular culture, the *Maniac Mansion* franchise has largely faded from memory outside of nostalgic gaming discussions.

From what reports exist surrounding the show's production, Lucas himself was almost entirely hands-off when it came to *Maniac Mansion*. After he pushed forward when hearing the initial pitch, there is little said of his involvement in this series. While an absence of reports or evidence that Lucas was personally invested in the series is not evidence that he ignored the project, it does stand in stark contrast to the many examples of Lucas's direct interest in the *Ewoks* movies and in the next project from Lucasfilm, *The Young Indiana Jones Chronicles*.

The Young Indiana Jones Chronicles and Edutainment Programming

From all accounts, Lucas was fully invested in guiding *The Young Indiana Jones Chronicles*. The series stands out for its overall ambition, but it is also an odd artifact of popular culture history. It never seemed to find its place when it was produced, and its legacy highlights the significance of the technological evolutions it pushed forward more than its contributions to *Indiana Jones* lore. As has sometimes happened with Lucas's desires to tinker with and perfect his company's productions, there exist multiple versions of episodes from the series as many have been reedited through the years.

The series began with a bold plan, but one rooted more in educational opportunities than in business ventures or artistic endeavors. Lucas pushed to create an educational series that, in his mind, would push the franchise directly into the classroom. Lucas was heavily invested in the idea of entertainment as a tool for education and saw *Indiana Jones* as an ideal property to explore those ideas. As Marcus Hearn explains:

> In 1991, Lucas's frustration with the teaching methods that had failed to engage him as a youngster, coupled with the desire to explore how technology could improve classroom learning, led him to establish the non-profit George Lucas Educational Foundation (GLEF). Inspired by the educational potential in some of the interactive software being produced by the Computer Division, GLEF began exploring ways of enriching public education in the digital age. The philosophy of "edutopia" (an environment where students and teachers can easily access information from beyond

their school building) is promoted through TV programs, videos, CD-ROMS, and, more recently the website www.glef.org.

One of Lucas's earliest aims was to use technology such as videodiscs . . . to present multimedia lessons, accessed via computers in classrooms. The original videodisc project was the title *A Walk through Early Twentieth Century History with Indiana Jones*, but Lucas soon saw the potential to develop the core of the idea as the television series *The Young Indiana Jones Chronicles*.[20]

Lucas specifically saw "the possibilities of the videodisc combining text, sound, and both still and moving graphics, all at the user's command via the computer keyboard or mouse."[21] The goal was for this technology to be readily accessible in classrooms. While this sounds very much like technology that is available today, for the early 1990s it was visionary.

Lucas saw the future of technology and often treated it as the next natural step. In an interview in 1993, he also saw the future many viewers enjoy today, with on-demand viewing being delivered through streaming services. He said, regarding viewer-on-demand video, "If they get it down to the level of $1 an hour there will be an instantaneous revolution that will wipe out the home-video business in a year."[22] He also knew that as computers became a part of television viewing, finding programming would be "infinitely easier" than with the VCRs that were commonly used at the time, and in the end viewers would be able to "tell your TV 'I want to watch *Murphy Brown*' and it would happen automatically."[23] Lucas was speaking of this technology as though it were inevitable and on the horizon, but it would not become commonplace for well more than a decade: Netflix did not begin streaming content until 2007, and there are numerous news articles from 2011 predicting that voice control remotes would eventually become commonplace.[24] Lucas envisioned *The Young Indiana Jones Chronicles* to have the type of interactivity that is possible with computer technology and streaming opportunities in 2022, but the technology simply did not exist in the early 1990s.

Trusting that *Indiana Jones* had the cultural cachet to entice viewers and also incite curiosity, Lucas prepared a time line of Indiana Jones's life. This was inspired, at least in part, by the opening of *Indiana Jones and the Last Crusade*. In that film, River Phoenix plays a young Indiana Jones, and we see the first glimpses into the character's past. Reportedly, Lucas had prepared seventy hours' worth of episodes. What was produced bounces around time and does not present a linear storyline with a clear natural progression. Rather, the episodes hop through time, guided by the narration of an elderly Indiana Jones.

In the end, six episodes were produced for season one. These aired on ABC in March and April 1992. The premiere had 26.2 million viewers, and the season finale had 15.2 million. Twenty-two episodes were produced for a second season. Eighteen were aired between March and July 1993. Four episodes were unaired. ABC canceled the series, but the Family Channel ordered four made-for-TV movies, which aired between 1994 and 1996. Internationally, some episodes of the series were split or combined in reediting. In 1996, after the series was canceled, Lucas hired an editor, T. M. Christopher, to recut the entire series. The result transformed the twenty-eight episodes and four movies into twenty-two feature-length films.

Lucas was always personally invested in *The Young Indiana Jones Chronicles*. Jim Smith notes the hands-on nature of Lucas's involvement with the series: "Of the initial seventeen hours of television that comprised the first production block, every episode was storyline and partially written by Lucas himself. Before the series began its creator stressed that, although it would be an adventure series, there was also a strong educational angle to many episodes, part of the point of the show being to expose American children to history in an involving way."[25]

Depending on the episode, the series might feature a version of Indiana Jones who was a child, played by Corey Carrier, or a young man, played by Sean Patrick Flanery. The series usually had an elderly Indiana Jones, played by George Hall, who would narrate the adventures of his younger self. Because this was an educational project, historical figures abounded in the series. Jones would encounter writers and artists such as Ernest Hemingway, Edward Degas, and Pablo Picasso. He would run into Pancho Villa, Winston Churchill, and Theodore Roosevelt. He would have conversations with Carl Jung, Sigmund Freud, and Albert Schweitzer. In Lucas's vision, children would watch these adventures but be able to pause them and pull up real-world facts and histories about the people and events that were depicted. Of course, this was impossible at the time. In the end, the series aired over traditional television airwaves with no option for the immediate interactivity that was crucial to the educational vision Lucas had for it.

Lucas was still invested in the idea of edutainment, and a series of books were published with young Indiana Jones as the protagonist. Additionally, the company created a *Series Study Guide* that was made available to teachers. The guides included additional information about the historical context of the episode and discussion prompts for the classroom. According to Mimi White, "Similarly, the novels based on the series often include book lists for further reading about the period and historical personages in question. Thus, the television program aggressively proposes itself as the focal point for a series of derivative texts and activities of educational value"[26] Many years after the series was canceled, Lucasfilm was still exploring its potential educational impact. Eventually, in the early 2000s, ninety-four documentaries about the real people and historical events Indiana Jones encountered were produced, to be included as DVD extras with the series. This seems to be as far as Lucas was able to push the educational goals for the series. However, in 2007, Lucas admitted that he still saw "the project as a means of teaching early-20th century history to high school students."[27]

The series had a huge budget for television production. This is, of course, one reason it was canceled. In the economics of Hollywood, an income that exceeds the budget is much more crucial than any potential educational value a series may have. As Howard Maxford writes, "Each episode of *The Young Indiana Jones Chronicles* cost in the region of $4m to make, and the series shot in over 20 countries, among them Africa, India, China, Britain, Spain, France, Turkey, Russia, Czechoslovakia, Italy, Austria and America. The shooting schedule lasted over three years."[28] To help reduce costs, Lucasfilm used the somewhat counterintuitive idea of spending money to save money. For this series, Lucas invested in and helped create new special effects technology that has become standard in the years since it was invented. *The Young Indiana Jones Chronicles* is the first production to use CGI rather than hundreds or thousands of extras to create a crowd scene. That innovation has become commonplace and routinely saves huge amounts of time and money for studios who employ it.[29]

Despite the worthy goals Lucas had and the money that was poured into *The Young Indiana Jones Chronicles*, the series never had the impact that the films achieved. As Smith sees it: "*Young Indiana Jones* is one of the great unknown quantities of 90s television. The history of the series is one of lavish filming, changes of network, changes of format and changes of cast. Additionally, as with the Imperial trilogy, George Lucas has proved incapable of leaving the series alone, producing multiple versions of episodes, incorporating new titles, new effects and even shooting in attempts to iron out problems both perceived and real, and in order to make the series more to his—and audiences'—liking."[30]

The series faltered in the ratings and was canceled before all the stories Lucas had plotted could be filmed. One reason it failed is that different goals for the series pulled the content in different directions. The network wanted a popular series that entertained its audience. Some producers wanted to ensure the continued relevance of *Indiana Jones* as a viable franchise. Lucas clearly wanted this to be a multimedia educational franchise, an early example of cross-technology edutainment. And, with the large budget that had been provided, this was also a series that was pushing the boundaries of technology. The last goal is one where the series succeeded most fully and where its legacy is an undeniable influence on how films and television are made today.

While *The Young Indiana Jones Chronicles* is not entirely forgotten, its significance in popular culture history is not recognized enough. Perhaps this is in part because the educational aims that Lucas had for the project seem to have largely missed the mark. An aspect of any TV production—to draw in viewers and earn money for the network—was also disappointing. But the behind-the-scenes efforts that Lucas had for the series yielded dividends that altered how Hollywood filmmaking has occurred since the early 1990s. Lucas encouraged the development of technology in ways that made the synergies between blockbuster films and prestige television productions more viable than they had been before his too-grandiose-for-the-time vision for *The Young Indiana Jones Chronicles*. Lucas was ahead of his time but helped bring about the very future he saw.

While Lucas is a very successful businessman and storyteller, in *The Young Indiana Jones Chronicles* we find a passion project that was motivated not by business profits or artistic expression but by a desire to improve educational opportunities for children. The pursuit of making history education fun and accessible excited his creative impulse, and he planned a far more extensive series than what was produced in the end. The fact that he has revisited the series and funded reedits and additional documentaries demonstrates that Lucas is not solely a businessman or a storyteller but also someone personally invested in providing children better educational opportunities than he himself had when growing up. Lucas's vision of the future was not limited to predicting what technology will evolve or become available. It was also focused on the children who will grow up to use that technology.

Notes

1. Henry Jenkins, "Transmedia Storytelling," *MIT Technology Review*, January 15, 2003, https://www.technologyreview.com/2003/01/15/234540/transmedia -storytelling/.

2. Brian Jay Jones, *George Lucas: A Life* (New York: Back Bay Books, 2016), 275.

3. Howard Maxford, *George Lucas Companion* (London: BT Batsford, 2000), 76.

4. Andrew Ferguson, "*The Holiday Special* and the Hole in the Archive," in *The Transmedia Franchise of Star Wars TV*, ed. Dominick J. Nardi and Derek R. Sweet (New York: Palgrave MacMillan, 2020), 39.

5. Ibid., 43.

6. Ibid., 48.

7. Jones, *George Lucas*, 338.

8. Jim Smith, *George Lucas* (London: Virgin Books, 2011), 338.

9. Ibid., 152.

10. Ibid.

11. Marcus Hearn, *The Cinema of George Lucas* (New York: Abrams, 2004), 148.

12. Charles Champlin, *George Lucas: The Creative Impulse* (New York: Abrams, 1997), 109.

13. J. Richard Stevens, "The Battle for Endor: Ewok Television Films as Transmedia Brand Extension," in Nardi and Sweet, *Transmedia Franchise of Star Wars TV*, 55.

14. Jones, *George Lucas*, 339.

15. Joseph J. Darowski, "Several Decades Ago in Your Living Room: *Ewoks, Droids*, and *Star Wars* Saturday Morning Cartoons," in Nardi and Sweet, *Transmedia Franchise of Star Wars TV*, 121–37.

16. Champlin, *George Lucas*, 158.

17. Benjamin Svetkey, "'SCTV' Alumni Are Working on the Show," *Entertainment Weekly*, January 17, 1992, https://ew.com/article/1992/01/17/sctv-alumni-are-working-show/.

18. Champlin, *George Lucas*, 158.

19. John Walker, "The Best Games Hidden inside Other Games," Kotaku, December 16, 2021, https://kotaku.com/the-best-games-hidden-inside-other-games-1848227658.

20. Hearn, *Cinema of George Lucas*, 171.

21. Champlin, *George Lucas*, 130.

22. Thomas R. King, "Lucasvision," in *George Lucas: Interviews*, ed. Sally Kline (Jackson: University of Mississippi Press, 1999), 171.

23. Ibid., 172.

24. Peter Burrows and Cliff Edwards, "Voice Control, the End of the TV Remote?," *Bloomberg*, December 8, 2011, https://www.bloomberg.com/news/articles/2011-12-07/voice-control-the-end-of-the-tv-remote.

25. Smith, *George Lucas*, 188–89.

26. Mimi White, "Masculinity and Femininity in Television's Historical Fictions: *Young Indiana Jones Chronicles* and *Dr. Quinn, Medicine Woman*," in *Television Histories: Shaping Collective Memory in the Media Age* (Lexington: University Press of Kentucky, 2003), 54.

27. Brian Lowry, "Lucas Opens Up at Paley Festival," *Variety*, March 4, 2007, https://variety.com/2007/film/news/lucas-opens-up-at-paley-festival-1117960483/.

28. Maxford, *George Lucas Companion*, 139.

29. Scott Mcuire, "Digital Dialectics: The Paradox of Cinema in a Studio without Walls," *Historical Journal of Film, Radio, and Television* 19, no. 3 (1999): 379–97.

30. Smith, *George Lucas*, 188.

16

George and the Dinosaurs

George Lucas's Contributions to The Land Before Time *and* Jurassic Park

KATHY MERLOCK JACKSON

In a 1974 interview, George Lucas quoted classic film director George Cukor as saying, "I'm not a filmmaker. A filmmaker is like a toy-maker, and I'm a director." Lucas believed the opposite, saying, "Well, I am a filmmaker. I'm very much akin to a toymaker. If I wasn't a filmmaker, I'd probably be a toy-maker. I like to make things move, and I like to make them myself. Just give me the tools and I'll make the toys. I can sit forever doodling on my movie."[1] This desire to make things move drove early filmmakers like Winsor McCay, widely regarded as the father of early animation. In his 1914 short, *Gertie the Dinosaur*, he makes a bet that he can make a dinosaur live again through thousands of handmade drawings shown sequentially, and his associates at a Chicago paleontology museum take him on. Not content just to see what a dinosaur looks like, they chide, "McCay, your bet was that you could make it move."[2] McCay does. Gertie raises each foot, sways back and forth, dances, and gives her creator a ride on her back as McCay demonstrates to his audience the joy and awe of bringing a dinosaur to life. George Lucas, who delights in making things move, is cut from the same mold. As a coproducer of *The Land Before Time* (1988) and *Jurassic Park* (1993), he too brings dinosaurs to life. At first blush, these would seem odd projects for the *Star Wars* creator and futurist, who is more linked to high-tech machines moving at warp speed than giant, lumbering reptiles. Closer examination, however, reveals that he is a good fit and that his talents and sensibilities are effective for recreating the prehistoric past, a task that serves him well. Lucas's work on *The Land Before Time* and *Jurassic Park* has been overlooked because he directed neither feature and his other works merit greater attention. Nevertheless, his foray into the land of the dinosaurs proves important for one to better understand the unique talent that is George Lucas as well as the development of two popular films.

Lucas realized while making *Star Wars* (1977) that he disliked the day-to-day stresses of dealing with volatile personalities on the set and preferred creating imaginary worlds through the layering of images and sounds. Thus, in 1978, he bought a large parcel of property in Marin County, California, north of San Francisco, and began building Skywalker Ranch to house Lucasfilm, his own studio specializing in sound mixing, recording, and images to enhance cinematic storytelling. Lucas was committed to developing state-of-the-art technologies to enhance cinematic storytelling, bringing to the table his own mythology, cultural ideology, and cinematic sensibility. Director Steven Spielberg was a big supporter of his venture and approached Lucas to serve as co–executive producer on an animated feature to be directed by Don Bluth about threatened baby dinosaurs finding their way from a barren land to a new, green Great Valley, released in 1988 as *The Land Before Time*.

The Land Before Time had been Spielberg's idea. As Lucas tells it, Spielberg, who had been enamored of things Disney since childhood, wanted to make a Bambi-type animated adventure "about baby dinosaurs, and he wanted me to executive produce it with him."[3] The director they chose for the project, Don Bluth, seemed perfect. In 1955, Bluth had begun animating at Disney, where he worked with John Lounsbery on *Sleeping Beauty* (1959), and he found the place inspiring. As he recalled in an interview, "I think it was mainly because my fixation with those early Disney classics was so strong—the production values, the beautiful things that I saw on the screen when I was a child, the stories themselves, which were so strong. They were full of threat and horror and scary and everything and then they rescued you from that."[4] Although Bluth left a full-time position at Disney after a couple of years to do Mormon missionary work and establish his own theater, he continued to do projects on and off for the studio and respected Walt Disney's vision, saying, "There was a feeling in the building when Walt was there that you were doing all this for him. There was a feeling that he was the paternal figure; he knew what he was doing. You had a pride in the film you were making because he was there."[5] Bluth returned to the Disney Studio full-time in 1971, after Walt had died, and he found it stifling, a changed place. As he worked on features such as *Robin Hood* (1973), *Winnie the Pooh and Tigger Too* (1974), *The Rescuers*

(1977), and *Pete's Dragon* (1977), which he also directed, he tried to recover some of the previous magic, but to no avail.

In *Storming the Magic Kingdom*, John Taylor expresses Bluth's complaint "that the studio was skimping on the production values that made the classics so remarkable. Lakes no longer reflected their surroundings, raindrops no longer glistened when they hit the ground, curls of smoke no longer floated from fires. (So meticulous was the attention to detail in *Snow White* that, for example, the water trickling from a bar of wet soap was slightly filmed with suds and glistened in candlelight.) Bluth also declared that Disney's stories had degenerated into saccharine mush, devoid of the dark undercurrent of fear, loss and death that linked the classics to traditional fairytales."[6]

He walked out of the studio in 1979, taking several other Disney artists with him and prompting Disney executive Ron Miller, who was also Walt's son-in-law, to call him "a son of a bitch."[7] In the words of Disney production chief Tom White, Bluth was "obsessed with recreating the Disney of the Forties."[8] Bluth possessed a passion for detail and darker vision for animation, one that infused his productions with terror and sadness, not just brightness and light.

Spielberg shared Bluth's fondness for 1940s Disney, and in *Close Encounters of the Third Kind* (1977) and *E.T. the Extraterrestrial* (1982), he recreated the deep-blue, starry *Pinocchio* sky, paying homage to Disney's 1941 classic. Bluth set up his own studio and fashioned *The Secret of NIMH* (1982) to capture the old Disney style. Spielberg, working with his own Amblin Entertainment and Universal Pictures, liked it enough to executive produce Bluth's next two films, *An American Tail* (1986) and *The Land Before Time*, bringing Lucas along as an executive producer for the latter. Bluth was in the process of moving his studio from Van Nuys, California, to Dublin, Ireland, to take advantage of business incentives offered by the Industrial Development Authority, and he was glad to have big names like Spielberg and Lucas on board. Spielberg saw animation as primarily a children's medium, which Bluth attempted to dissuade him of, but all involved hoped to tap into children's strong fascination with dinosaurs, which was evident in the popular culture of the time.[9] By this time, both Spielberg and Lucas had become fathers, and their lives had changed. Lucas recalled holding his adopted newborn daughter Amanda just hours after she was born, saying it felt "just like a bolt of lightning had hit [him]."[10] He and Spielberg were enthusiastic about making a movie for the child audience, which they were now relating to in a new way.

From the onset, executive producers Spielberg and Lucas had their own ideas about *The Land Before Time*; they worked cooperatively, bouncing ideas off one another, and it is often difficult to parcel out who contributed what. The setting would be the prehistoric earth in chaos, threatened by climate change. Spielberg wanted the death of the central character's mother to set the action in motion, much as in *Bambi* or many early hero sagas. He and Lucas envisioned a film about baby dinosaurs without any dialogue, analogous to "The Rite of Spring" segment in Disney's *Fantasia* (1940). According to Bluth, Spielberg's rough concept for the film was "a soft picture that does not have any real driving plot. It's about five little dinosaurs and how they grow up and work together as a group."[11] He adds that a *Tyrannosaurus rex* would be the villain, triggering a journey in what "would be more of a pastoral kind of picture . . . symphonic in nature, soft and gentle."[12]

The need for the film to have dialogue and a discernible story quickly became apparent. The producers brought in writers Judy Freudberg and Tony Geiss to create a storyline for a sort of cine-poem. When the material was deemed too childish, producers brought in another writer, Stu Krieger, to flesh out a script, and they suggested a narrative strategy to create conflict. According to Bluth, "As the storyboarding continued . . . we came up with another idea, that none of these dinosaurs get along with each other, they all hate each other. They're taught from the time they were born not to associate with each other, that's racism. They're going to have to be untaught the racist idea and learn to like each other and therein lies the triumph of the movie. They would work together to overcome a common goal or enemy."[13] In a throwback to the early days of the Disney Studio under Walt, the filmmakers approved parts of the script before the whole thing was completed.

In May 1987, executive producers Spielberg and Lucas traveled to London to screen the unfinished film, which was about half complete, to see how it was taking shape. They were generally pleased but felt that character development was still lacking. Lucas stepped in to help. In an interview with *Lucasfilm Fan Club Magazine*, John Pomeroy, a member of Bluth's team who served as producer and directing animator on the project, recalls Lucas's involvement: "While he was in London, we had a two-day marathon story session with George Lucas, and during that time my respect for him went up about 10 decimals. All of us, Don Bluth, [producer] Gary Goldman, George Lucas, and myself sat down, and I won't say we re-wrote the story, but we made major structural changes. We took all the raw material and everything we had done up to that time, and reformed it without taking anything away from the original story writers (Judy Freudberg and Tony Geiss), or script writer (Stu Kreiger [sic]). We were all very happy with the results, and 80% of the finished story came from that meeting."[14] By the end of the session, each of the little dinosaurs had a clearer, more distinctive personality. Littlefoot, a brontosaurus who loses his mother in a battle with a Sharptooth tyrannosaurus as she tries to protect him and his friend, becomes the leader of the "thunder lizards" and spearheads a journey to the Great Valley, the leafy green promised land his mother had told him about. He is accompanied by Cera, a triceratops; Spike, a stegosaurus; and Ducky, an anatosaurus. Along the way, they meet Petrie, an orphaned pterodactyl, who is boisterous and courageous on the outside, masking his deep fear of doing what all other pterodactyls do—fly.[15] Together the dinosaurs set off to find their families and a safe place and help each other overcome personal foibles and insecurities.

Pomeroy credits Lucas with making another key suggestion: changing Cera from a tough little boy to a tough little girl. According to Pomeroy, "Cera is a very bravado, aggressive character. There is really very little that is feminine about her. She is very intolerant of anything or anyone who gets in her way. She is soft inside, but hides it in a cast iron shell. We finally reveal her vulnerability at the end, in soft colors. When she walks up to her father at the end of the film, she is pink rather than orange or yellow. It is one of the many ways we use color to convey emotion."[16] Lucas's feel for color imagery enhanced the production. Color in the film not only reflects characters' personalities but also demonstrates the changing earth, from the muted brown, destroyed land the dinosaurs are leaving to the bright, green lushness of the Great Valley.

Lucas was also influential in the editing of *The Land Before Time*. Although the death of Littlefoot's mother was always part of the original storyline, the filmmakers went as far as to consider eliminating it because it could frighten children but realized its strength as a plot device; still, they differed on how to depict it. Bluth, who had been drawn to the darker, more Gothic elements of classic Disney, preferred a fiercer and more violent portrayal. Lucas and Spielberg wanted to mute it. They sought the advice of child psychologists for advice on how best to show it without making it too intense and scary for young children. One solution, Pomeroy notes, was to add "a sequence with the Rooter character. He is a mole-like reptile that Littlefoot falls into company with just after his mother's death. That sequence softens the blow, showing that death is a reality that Littlefoot, and the audience, have to deal with."[17] This is not unlike the chirpy, coming-of-spring sequence following Bambi's mother's death in the 1942 Disney classic.

Lucas and Spielberg still felt that the production could terrify young children like their own. They insisted that parts of the tyrannosaurus battle scene be cut because they were too frightening and could cause psychological damage in child viewers. In all, ten minutes of material deemed too violent were cut from the final film, leaving a million dollars' worth of footage on the cutting room floor.[18] *Animation* magazine reported that, in all, "nineteen scenes were cut, including front-on scenes portraying the children in severe jeopardy and distress. In addition, the children's screams were replaced by milder exclamations."[19] Excising the footage brought the film's running time down to sixty-nine minutes, making it one of the shorter animated features on record. Not happy with the final cut, Bluth blamed Lucas, who, according to Lucas biographer Brian Jay Jones, "involved himself in the editing process, where he and Spielberg suggested that Bluth tone down some of the film's scarier sequences—this from the two who had delighted in human sacrifice and brain eating in *Temple of Doom*, an irony that was not lost on Bluth."[20] Influenced by their own experiences as fathers, Lucas and Spielberg elevated myth building over action and gore and desired to reach the largest swath of the child audience. They had changed, and their imprint on Bluth's directorial effort was unmistakable.

The Land Before Time opened Thanksgiving weekend in 1988, going head-to-head with another animated feature, Disney's *Oliver and Company*. Although this was Bluth's studio's third picture, following *The Secret of NIMH* and *An American Tail*, much of the film's promotion and critical response centered on Spielberg and Lucas. *Hollywood Reporter* predicted, "With *Oliver* and *Land* competing for the holiday money pot, this Steven Spielberg–George Lucas co-production could well end up with the short end of the box office stick."[21] The same review concluded, "It's surprising that these cute dinosaurs with long eye lashes and pink cheeks yet are the best that Spielberg, Lucas, et al., could come up with for a new animated feature—an idea, one could say, that Uncle Walt first exploited some 40 years ago."[22] *Variety*, characterizing the film as "one of the slowest hours ever to crawl across the screen" with a "two-dimensional story [that] will try the patience of all but the youngest viewers," expressed a similar opinion: "Spielberg-Lucas aegis should lure initial business in 1,400-screen release, but pic faces extinction soon after."[23] In general, though, the film met with a mixed critical response, with many reviewers praising its animation quality and artistic style. John Cawley summarizes the accolades: "*Newsday* called it a 'beautiful, lyric odyssey.' The *Dallas Times-Herald* referred to it as 'a warm family film that's long on charm and excitement.' Siskel and Ebert gave the film 'two thumbs up.'"[24]

Marketed as much as a Spielberg-Lucas film as a Bluth one, *The Land Before Time* opened on 1,400 screens nationwide to huge audiences, earning over $7,526,000 in its opening weekend and going on record as the highest-grossing animated film ever on first release.[25] It beat out *Oliver and Company* at the box office for several weeks before the Disney competitor overtook it, taking in $54 million to *The Land Before Time*'s $46 million. Accompanied by a Pizza Hut promotion, *The Land Before Time*, priced competitively at $24.95, sold well in the video market, exacerbating the dinosaur craze that had spawned it.

Bluth associate Pomeroy, reflecting on *The Land Before Time*, said, "It was fun . . . I would love to work with George Lucas again."[26] However, the opportunity never came. Bluth felt that he had made too many concessions to get along with his executive producers. In the words of one executive insider, throughout the production, "Don's desire to do a forceful, dramatic recreation of prehistoric times often was at odds with other parties' desires to produce 'a cute movie about dinosaur kids.'"[27] Spielberg expressed similar dissatisfaction, even after extensive postproduction work on editing and remixing music and sound effects. The Bluth team, Lucas, and Spielberg parted ways and never made another film together. Although *The Land Before Time* inspired sequels and a cable cartoon, Lucas and Spielberg were not involved, having moved on to other projects.

They were not, however, finished with dinosaurs. In 1990, Spielberg's Amblin Entertainment and Universal Pictures bought the rights to Michael Crichton's best-selling novel *Jurassic Park*, a science fiction tale of scientists cloning dinosaur DNA to bring prehistoric species back to life for a dinosaur theme park on a remote island off the west coast of Costa Rica. Spielberg would direct the big-budget feature. Lucas, by this time, shunned directing and instead concentrated on projects through his various production companies. THX, for example, provided equipment for enhanced digital sound for film and music. Skywalker Sound and Industrial Light & Music, subdivisions of Lucasfilm, specialized in sound and visual special effects. Although Spielberg did not recruit Lucas to be an executive producer on *Jurassic Park* as he had on *The Land Before Time*, he did call on his friend to help in bringing its dinosaurs to life.

Like *The Land Before Time*, *Jurassic Park* was part of a dinosaur mania gripping America. *National Geographic* describes the fascination: "What is it about dinosaurs that enchants us? Is it the joy of searching for and finding a long-dead creature? Is it the thrill of seeing a forgotten species uncovered before our very eyes? Could it be the tragedy of a world lost? Or is it the terror inspired by an animal higher on the food chain?"[28] Child psychologist Sheldon White offered a simpler, three-word explanation for the appeal of dinosaurs: "big, fierce, and extinct."[29] Michael Crichton was caught up in the craze. In 1989, Crichton's wife was expecting the couple's first child, and the soon-to-be father of a daughter could not resist buying stuffed dinosaurs. He recalled, "I was sort of obsessed with dinosaurs; and the whole idea of children and dinosaurs, and the meaning of what that was, was just stuck on my mind a lot during that period."[30] Crichton turned his obsession into a novel. Spielberg and Lucas, who had already dabbled in dinosaurs and even helped fuel the cultural trend, were enthusiastic about making another movie, but this project was different: *The Land Before Time* was fully animated, while *Jurassic Park* would be live-action. As Marcus Hearn writes in *The Cinema of George Lucas*, "The challenge this time was to create digital technology to create creatures that appeared to live, breath, and move in believable ways."[31]

Spielberg felt that filmmaking techniques had progressed to the point that he could make a convincing live-action movie about dinosaurs. Previous dinosaur movies had used stop-motion puppet animation and miniature photography, but he was not sure what form his would take. Spielberg and Crichton agreed that the film adaptation would differ from the book, and they brought in screenwriters, first Malia "Scotch" Marmo and then David Koepp, to collaborate on the project. One of their first decisions, for practical purposes, was to reduce the fifteen species of dinosaurs in the book to just six in the film.[32] Spielberg wanted a realistic look and hired production designer Rick Carter to create storyboards to chart the dinosaurs' movements. Planning to work with models, as he had with the shark in *Jaws* and alien in *E.T. the Extraterrestrial*, Spielberg hired Stan Winston to work with paleontologists to create realistic, life-size, moving dinosaurs made of clay covered with latex and powered with hydraulic technology.[33] According to Rick Carter, Spielberg "wanted to have as much full-scale as he could pull off so that he could convey what it would be like to be in the same time and space as the dinosaur."[34] For the larger dinosaurs, however, he would use miniatures.

Then Lucas and his Industrial Light & Magic (ILM) team appeared on the scene. According to Doug Brode in *The Films of Steven Spielberg*, the timing was crucial: "Dennis Muren, ILM's effects supervisor, brought computer graphics to the mix, having just perfected a concept called 'morphing' for the fluid transition sequences in *Terminator 2: Judgment Day*."[35] Lucas's team constructed the dinosaurs' skeleton and walk cycle in a computer. Spielberg had been wary of computer-generated imagery (CGI) for his project because previous creatures developed with the technology had lacked the realism that he sought for images and movements, and he thought the advanced digital software he needed was still years away. However, a new software program called Matador provided cinematic detail that met Spielberg's standards, allowing for shadows, smudges of mud, sagging skin, and swaying bellies on the dinosaurs.[36] Lucas recalled Spielberg's stunned reaction: "We did a test for Steven . . . and when we put [the dinosaurs] up on the screen, everyone had tears in their eyes. It was like one of those moments in history, like the invention of the lightbulb or the first telephone call. A major gap had been crossed and things were never going to be the same. You just cannot see them as anything but real. It's just impossible."[37] Lucas had just revealed to his friend the future of filmmaking, and Spielberg's amazement at seeing the dinosaurs move was not unlike that of characters Grant and Ellie in the film. As Lucas biographer Brian Jay Jones notes, ILM's CGI "had gone from simply being *a* tool in filmmaking to being *the* tool."[38] Spielberg's plan for the film had changed.

Unlike on *The Land Before Time*, on *Jurassic Park*, Lucas was not involved in the writing or editing, Forever the tinkerer, though, he and his ILM unit continued to refine the film's look and sound. While the cameras were roll-ing on location on the Hawaiian Island of Kauai and the Mojave Desert and on stages at Universal Studios, ILM technology experts at Skywalker Ranch worked on techniques. One challenge was creating a stampede of *Gallimimus*, which traveled in herds and required several wide-angle shots. ILM's Dennis Muren built a skeleton, and then, he says, the team "animated about ten of them running along in a herd. For the backgrounds, we picked some photos out of a book on Africa and scanned them into the computer."[39] The effect was astounding. Muren previewed the shots for the production team at Amblin, and, as he recalls, "everybody went nuts. No one had ever seen anything like it. Even though the gallis were just skeletons, there was so much motion and blur that your mind was filling it in."[40]

Another challenge was executing a walking tyrannosaurus in daylight.[41] Muren explains how he used a still photo of a hill, laid the animal into it, and scanned it onto film, saying, "The shot started out with the T-rex maybe a hundred feet away, about two-thirds the size of the frame. Then it just walked toward camera step by step, and we sort of tilted up at the head as it passed by. Everybody went absolutely crazy. It was like nothing anyone had seen before."[42] Spielberg was so taken with the T-rex that he even reworked the ending of the film so that she would make a return appearance in the climactic scene, placing trust in ILM to deliver the desired effect. Because of the CGI technology used for several key scenes, Spielberg did not have to transport as many large, heavy dinosaur models as he thought he would for on-location shots, saving time, energy, and money.

Filming on *Jurassic Park* wrapped on November 30, 1992, and Spielberg was due on location in Poland a few weeks later to begin shooting his next feature, *Schindler's List*. He placed his coproducer Kathleen Kennedy in charge of *Jurassic Park*'s postproduction.[43] Although uncredited, Lucas was also heavily involved, overseeing the special effects when Spielberg could not be there and, as always, contributing his mythic vision. As Rick Carter said, "From a design standpoint, the stars of *Jurassic Park* are the dinosaurs. That's not to say that the characters are not important, because they are. But on a visual level, the dinosaurs are the stars."[44] Thus, much work remained to be done after the actors went home. ILM continued refining the CGI scenes until just days before the film was released, and Spielberg stayed in close contact with the team, reviewing and approving videotapes each week.

Lucas was also integral to the innovative sound in *Jurassic Park*. According to Don Shay and Jody Duncan in *The Making of Jurassic Park*: "Because of its reputation within the industry, and its history with Steven Spielberg, Skywalker Sound was a prime candidate for the *Jurassic Park* sound assignment. It was an assignment that ranged from the usual—such as producing all of the exotic sounds and vocalizations for the dinosaurs—to the more standard task of replicating lines of dialogue. Additionally, the sound facility would create sound effects not related to the dinosaurs, plus blend all the elements of the film's sound—including the musical score—into a satisfying final mix."[45]

While many moviegoers assume that sounds are simply recorded on the set while shooting, that is not the case, especially for a film such as *Jurassic Park*. Skywalker Sound redubbed about five hundred lines of dialogue that were inaudible and, more importantly, created the aural profile of dinosaurs in their rain forest environment. Supervising sound editor Richard Hymns at Skywalker Sound traveled to the remote rain forests of Australia and spent two months capturing the sounds of animals, birds, insects, and moving foliage, saying, "I was able to record a lot of strange stuff, unusual bird calls and night sounds to create moods that were eerie and scary—the kind of sounds you hear when you know something bad is about to happen."[46] Since no one knows exactly what dinosaurs sound like, the Lucas team had to improvise and mix to create a plausible and moving portrait of the living dinosaur. Sound designer Gary Rydstrom explains how, for example, his team "used a combination of sounds from real animals to create the range of sounds for the T-rex. It was made up of elephant, alligator, penguin, tiger and dog sounds, all layered together. For the roar, we recorded a baby elephant that made a nice trumpet scream. We used that for the mid-range of frequencies, then added a tiger roar and an alligator growling sound."[47] They even had to simulate sounds for dinosaurs breathing. In all, sound editors at Lucas's Skywalker Ranch provided the sound mixing for the production, creating dinosaur vocalizations, replacing lines of dialogue, and integrating John Williams's transcendent musical score, adding to the film's total effect.

All told, Lucas spent two years contributing to his second dinosaur movie. *Jurassic Park* contains fifty-four CGI sequences encompassing six and a half minutes of running time. They include the T-rex in full-body and close-up in the road attack scene, the brachiosaur, various velociraptor shots, and the *Gallimimus* herd. Although these segments make up a small fraction of *Jurassic Park*'s running time of two hours and eight minutes, they are the film's most memorable, creating the visual movement and emotion that enabled audiences to feel the awe of dinosaurs and adrenaline rush of fear. In addition, sound added to the film's immediacy. In the words of sound editor Richard Hymns, "If the audience notices our work, then we've spoiled the illusion; and if we do a really good job, nobody is award of it."[48] Proud of the film and ILM's and Skywalker Sounds' innovations, Lucas declared, "*Jurassic Park* changed everything."[49]

As expected, when *Jurassic Park* was released on June 11, 1993, it broke box office records, earning over $200 million in its opening months and amazing moviegoers. Reviewers were less enthusiastic in their overall praise but acknowledged the film's special effects, with *Rolling Stone*'s Peter Travers calling it "colossal entertainment."[50] As Richard Corliss wrote in *Time*, "No film could be more personal to [Spielberg] than this one, a movie whose subject is its process, a movie about all the complexities of fabricating entertainment in the microchip age. It's a movie in love with technology."[51] The dinosaur film was important to Lucas as well. It functioned as a proving ground for a project of his own, a continuation of his signature *Star Wars* trilogy. As Marcus Hearn observed, "For Lucas, the success of *Jurassic Park* proved that the scenarios and creatures he envisioned for the *Star Wars* prequel trilogy were finally feasible."[52]

In the grand scheme of George Lucas's life and career, his work producing cinematic dinosaurs is just a footnote. However, it is emblematic. Director Ron Howard, in his 2004 foreword to *The Cinema of George Lucas* by Marcus Hearn, characterizes Lucas as a moviemaker, affirming that directing "is not so much fun for George. He's happiest conceptualizing and editing. Nevertheless,

George is a total filmmaker, and he's still pushing the cinematic envelope. Digital filmmaking is a perfect logical step—and I think everyone will soon embrace that logic."[53] Lucas may be linked in the public imagination with *Star Wars*, but he himself has said as much. "I hope," he says, "I'll be remembered as one of the pioneers of digital cinema."[54] Lucas is driven by the desire to create exotic imaginary worlds that no one has ever seen before using devices and software that no one has ever even conceptualized, let alone employed. In *The Land Before Time* and *Jurassic Park*, Lucas realized what he could do: harness futuristic digital technology to travel backward, creating a captivating rendition of life one hundred million years ago and telling stories that engage with life's great questions. This little man who stands at just five and a half feet could do miraculous things: travel through time, design new worlds, and control great beasts. On a more basic level, though, that may not be what intrigued Lucas about dinosaurs. Early on in his career, he revealed what motivated him, saying, "It wasn't *movies* so much as film that moved. I was more fascinated with the medium . . . that real childish image of 'Gosh, look at this thing . . . it moves.' It became a sort of obsession. I was fascinated with the fact that you could take real life and put it onto an image and make it more and you could manipulate it. Play with it."[55] Like Winsor McCay, Lucas was simply enchanted by the ability to breathe life into dinosaurs, making them move.

Notes

1. Michael Rubin, *Droidmaker: George Lucas and the Digital Revolution* (Gainesville, FL: Triad, 2006), 3.

2. Open Culture, *Gertie the Dinosaur (1914)*, YouTube, https://www.youtube.com/watch?v=32pzHWUTcPc.

3. Brian Jay Jones, *George Lucas: A Life* (New York: Little, Brown, 2016), 367.

4. Gerald Duchovnay, *Film Voices: Interviews from Post Script* (Albany: SUNY Press, 2004), 145.

5. Ibid.

6. John Taylor, *Storming the Magic Kingdom: Wall Street, the Raiders, and the Battle for Disney* (New York: Knopf, 1987), 22–23.

7. Andrew Osmond, *100 Animated Features* (London: Palgrave Macmillan, 2010), 183.

8. Ibid.

9. John Cawley, "*The Land before Time*," *The Animated Films of Don Bluth*, November 18, 1988, http://www.cataroo.com/DBland.html.

10. Jones, *George Lucas*, 309.

11. Cawley, "*The Land before Time*," 8.

12. Ibid.

13. Ibid.

14. Lisa Cowan, "Exclusive Interview: John Pomeroy Producing *The Land before Time*," *Lucasfilm Fan Club Official Magazine*, Winter 1989, 8.

15. Lisa Cowan, "Review of *The Land Before Time*," *Lucasfilm Fan Club Official Magazine*, Fall 1988, 7.

16. Cowan, "Exclusive Interview," 8.

17. Ibid.

18. Cawley, "*The Land before Time*," 10.

19. Ibid.

20. Jones, *George Lucas*, 367. Nevertheless, an Amblin memo from 1986 suggests that Lucas's involvement in the production process was not entirely geared toward toning down Bluth's darker inclinations. See Tom Klein, "A Land before Time in a Galaxy Far, Far Away, 1986," Cartoon Research, December 12, 2015, https://cartoonresearch.com/index.php/a-land-before-time-in-a-galaxy-far-far-away-1986/.

21. Cawley, "*The Land before Time*," 11.

22. Ibid.

23. Ibid., 12.

24. Ibid.

25. Ibid., 13.

26. Cowan, "Exclusive Interview," 8.

27. Cawley, "*The Land before Time*," 10.

28. "Our Love Affair with Dinosaurs," *National Geographic 6 Minute Read*, December 19, 2017, https://www.nationalgeographic.com/books/article/our-love-affair-with-dinosaurs.

29. Ibid.

30. Don Shay and Jody Duncan, *The Making of "Jurassic Park"* (New York: Ballantine Books, 1993), 3.

31. Marcus Hearn, *The Cinema of George Lucas* (New York: Abrams, 2005), 174.

32. Douglas Brode, *The Films of Steven Spielberg* (New York: Citadel, 1995), 213.

33. Ibid., 215.

34. Shay and Duncan, *Making of "Jurassic Park*," 16.

35. Brode, *Films of Steven Spielberg*, 215.

36. Ibid., 216.

37. Hearn, *Cinema of George Lucas*, 174.

38. Jones, *George Lucas*, 378.

39. Shay and Duncan, *Making of "Jurassic Park*," 49.

40. Ibid., 50.

41. Brode, *Films of Steven Spielberg*, 216.

42. Shay and Duncan, *Making of "Jurassic Park*," 51.

43. Ibid., 123.

44. Ibid., 45.

45. Ibid., 141.

46. Ibid., 142.

47. Ibid., 143–44.

48. Ibid., 147.
49. Hearn, *Cinema of George Lucas*, 174.
50. Brode, *Films of Steven Spielberg*, 225.
51. Ibid., 225.
52. Hearn, *Cinema of George Lucas*, 174.
53. Ibid., 6.
54. Jones, *George Lucas*.
55. Rubin, *Droidmaker*, 6.

17

Star Wars: Special Editions

Film Ownership and Cultural Implications

Patti McCarthy

Special Editions: Taking Ownership

After twenty years of wishing he could make *Star Wars* better, George Lucas, in 1997, got his wish and released a Director's Cut of his *Star Wars* trilogy, saying it was the version he had always wanted filmgoers to see.[1] Not only was this rerelease of a new film version an unprecedented film history event, but it marked the first time that a filmmaker had made changes to an original film after its theatrical release.[2] After three years and $15 million, the *Star Wars: Special Edition* trilogy was ready for the theaters, and fans were anxious to see it.

Lucas said: "We were hoping to get 200 theatres, maybe 400. . . . But then theatre owners began to get really excited during the summer after we ran some trailers and it started getting standing ovations. We began to say, 'This is going to be more than just a limited event for fans. This is going to be a big thing for everybody.' I realized that maybe there were more people like me that wanted to see it with their kids on the big screen."[3]

The new *Special Edition* trilogy, released over a two-month period in the winter and spring of 1997, made an astounding $35.9 million its opening weekend, the highest ever for a film reissue and the eighth-largest opening weekend of all time.[4] By the end of its run, the reissued *Star Wars: Special Editions* had made over $100 million, taking *Star Wars* alone to a total box office of $461 million domestic by the end of 1997.[5]

Some people argued that Lucas's desire to go back and "fix" the originals was a reaction to the studios who had bought his films and reedited both *THX 1138* and *American Graffiti*.[6] While this explanation may have merit,

241

the reasons Lucas gave for the reissue of a twentieth-anniversary *Star Wars: Special Edition* were threefold: (1) to make improvements to the original films made on a $10 million budget, (2) to give back to *Star Wars* fans, and (3) to provide a large-screen viewing experience for his (at the time) four-year-old son, Jett, to see the movie as originally intended and conceived.[7] Lucas stated: "The most obvious thing that's happened is we've gone back to the original negative, cleaned it up considerably, redone a lot of the optical effects . . . and improved the quality of the film, because it was deteriorating. So that was the primary concern. The audience will get a brand-new print that's . . . better than the original release."[8]

Besides cleaning up the original print, the *Special Editions* made a lot of changes to the original 1977 trilogy filmgoers had seen in theaters. Notably, *Star Wars: A New Hope* had sixty-nine changes from the original, *The Empire Strikes Back* had fifty-five, and *Return of the Jedi* contained thirty-eight. Even after the *Special Editions* were released, changes to the original trilogy occurred with each new distribution of a VHS, laser disc, or DVD.[9] Among the most significant CGI (computer generated image) changes to the trilogy in the *Special Editions* were the expansion of Mos Eisley to make it look like a bustling metropolis; an enhanced scene with Han Solo and Jabba the Hutt; a reinstated Biggs scene; and extended Endor celebrations.[10] More controversial changes were also made to character and story (e.g., the Han and Greedo cantina scene). "You try to make the movie that you wanted to script, and along the way, you have to make a lot of compromises," Lucas said. "There's never enough time, never enough money; some things just aren't possible. So, you have to rewrite, change and you have to cut things out that you planned to have in the movie. Sometimes you cut things out because they don't belong in the movie—because the idea didn't work and the film looks better if you cut it out."[11]

Seeing there was money to be made in reissues, in 1998, other distributors followed Lucas's lead and reissued both *Gone with the Wind* and *The Wizard of Oz*, making a profit. The idea of recutting, deleting, or adding scenes or other important storytelling elements to these classic films might have been considered but never done.

Making Changes: Cultural and Historical Implications

If changes to the *Star Wars: Special Editions* were purely technological, our discussion would end here, but the addition of scenes and actual changes to original characters and narrative storylines requires further examination. Since the release of the *Star Wars: Special Editions*, other filmmakers have decided to go back in and "fix" a film that was produced under tight deadlines, tighter budgets, and running-time pressures. Francis Ford Coppola, for one, did so and changed the title of *Apocalypse Now* to *Apocalypse Now Redux*. Steven Spielberg also made changes to the twentieth-anniversary release of *E.T.* Producer Kathleen Kennedy states, "George went in and he redid whole scenes and sequences. In contrast, *E.T.* is receiving a wide variety of subtle changes."[12] These "subtle" changes included tweaking E.T.'s performance through CGI and eliminating all guns from the film (e.g., the cops carry walkie-talkies instead of guns while chasing E.T. and Elliott), among others. Spielberg regretted all the changes, saying, "I realized that what I had done was robbed the people who loved E.T. of their memories of E.T." As recompense, Spielberg demanded Universal include both the 1982 version of *E.T.* and the digitally enhanced 2002 version in the twentieth-anniversary DVD release. In 2012, both the original version and the digitally enhanced version were fully digitally remastered and included in the thirtieth-anniversary release.[13]

As soon as the *Special Editions* were released on DVD, *Star Wars* fans asked George Lucas to do the same and include the original 1977 version of the film on any subsequent DVD releases. It was clear the fans were attached to the original narrative and images and wanted both back. Originally, George Lucas decided not to rerelease the unaltered *Star Wars* films, but on May 12, 2004, he followed Spielberg's lead and released them on DVD in a two-disc set along with a remastered version. Fans realized that the versions of the original trilogy included in the two-disc set were inferior in quality to the *Special Editions* films.[14] Fans believed this was done to privilege the viewing experience of the *Special Editions* over the 1977 version, and like anything else, if these classic films weren't watched, they'd eventually fade from public memory—erasing them from history.[15] Ironically, the loss of the original print was one of the primary reasons Lucas used to justify a release of the *Special Editions* in the first place.

Lucas argued that the *Special Editions* *were* the originals since they better expressed his auteuristic vision. Fans, however, didn't buy that argument; they regarded the films they had seen in the theaters in 1977 as the definitive versions. Once the films were screened in the theater, the fans claimed, the films no longer belonged to Lucas but to them. A fan posting on savestarwars. com claimed, "Lucas deliberately wanted the original versions to be presented in an inferior format so that they would not have to compete with the *Special Editions*."[16]

In reaction, fans created the website originaltrilogy.com. The site was dedicated to petitioning Lucas to rerelease the "real," unaltered 1977 trilogy in a better format. Interestingly, the website has become a springboard for fan edits, in which fans create their own edited versions of *Star Wars* films. Early theories of popular culture painted fans as passive consumers of commercial goods, but this representation is far from the truth. Rather, fans interact with popular culture products and interpret them in ways that have personal significance for them.

While Lucas defends his films as his own product and reserves the right to alter them as he sees fit, he has not attempted to suppress the right of fans to create their own films. He applauds their entrepreneurial bravado and creative thinking by offering online platforms (starwars.com) where they can express themselves online. Lucas endorsed the work of some filmmakers like USC Cinema Arts alumni Joe Nussbaum and his short film parody, *George Lucas in Love*. Henry Jenkins has stated that fandom is intimately connected to the development of mainstream participatory culture in which the industries increasingly share spaces with their audiences and spur them to become cocreators. This increased dialogue between users and producers has political implications and shapes a new public sphere.[17] Some speculate about the motives the Lucasfilm (now Disney) corporate machine might have for offering this kind of online platform to fans at starwars.com and argue that it is a thinly veiled attempt to regulate and control fan product output and narratives, a Trojan horse that on one hand offers creative freedom while on the other takes it away as fans limit their imaginations by following either explicitly posted rules or implicit corporate expectations to please the powers that be in control of the site. This is important to consider since the media industry profits from the activities of fans and sees fandom as a form of labor to be used to exploit and promote products across a variety of transmedia platforms. However, while this may be true, fans also profit from the entertainment these spaces provide and the sense of ownership they get over the fiction they love.[18] Meanwhile, since 1997, fan videos have multiplied, but they are also conflicted. Some of these texts are critical of Lucas and the changes he made but at the same time also express a deep appreciation for the "original" films he created and the films they grew to love.[19]

As to authorial power hierarchies, Kathleen Kennedy, *E.T.* producer and current Lucasfilm president, said, "It would be a big controversy if the studio was going to make a bunch of changes to movies and then release DVDs, because they felt the movie was better or something. But if a director is releasing a movie and wants to go in and make adjustments, that's entirely up to the vision of the director."[20]

One can only imagine what would happen if one of the studios went back and changed *The Wizard of Oz* or *Casablanca*. These films, these shared cultural artifacts, are as much about our culture as they are about the people who watch them. Movies are products of their times and a part of our cultural history. Countless pre–civil rights films considered American classics feature offensive portrayals of Black characters, and many early James Bond films were sexist. Strong political arguments have been made that these images should be erased like the guns the cops carry in *E. T.* But are we better served as a nation if the blatant racism of D. W. Griffith's *The Birth of a Nation* or tacit racism of Fleming's *Gone with the Wind* were struck from all screenings? Should we simply erase a past we don't like?

Every day our collective memory is jarred and fragmented as history is reworked, revised, and changed on television, in print, and online. As history becomes more fabricated and suspect, it becomes another form of entertainment. In the age of "wag the dog" and "fake news," the potential for a fabricated reality does cause concern. Some people still don't believe that the United States astronauts actually went to the moon, thinking they were filmed on a movie set. "Maybe they could have made it all up" is not an uncommon knee-jerk reaction—because the potential is there. The reissue of *Star Wars*, *E. T.*, and other films helped in a small way to highlight the digital possibility of historical fabrication. Ever since the birth of photography and film, which promised viewers a manipulated reality, people have questioned what is "real." As the death of history as posited by some inches closer, truth and fiction begin to intertwine. CGI and the digital revolution effect not only the film business but also our culture and worldview.

Fandom and Creative Practices

While some *Star Wars* fans were happy with changes Lucas made to the *Special Editions*, others were not. Fandom is usually defined as a community that surrounds a particular TV show, movie, book, or other text and produces different types of narratives and objects to express themselves through play and performances. Through these homages, which are heavily inspired by the existing texts or source texts, fans mediate existing symbols, plotlines, characters, and settings and create new textual relationships. Fandom also refers to the interpretive and creative practices whereby fans can migrate across different media and production contexts.[21] As such, fandom is a community that creates its own subcultures and can occur online or as "lived," in-person experiences (e.g., fan conventions or LARPs [live-action role playing]). For some, fandom is akin to being a member of a religion with its own system of beliefs, values, myths, communal identity, and ritual practices. In fact, many people in the 2001 census in English-speaking countries identified their religion as Jediism[22] or belonged to an online Jedi Church.[23] For many *Star Wars* fans, the original trilogy films are sacred texts to be safeguarded by the faithful.

Any letdown that fans were feeling, Will Brooker contends, was due to how much of an impact the film had made in some of the fans' lives.[24] *Star Wars* had figured in many fans' development as children. They had played it and acted it out at home and at school, keeping it alive while viewing in groups or studying it while watching alone. They had used their own sweat equity to emotionally invest and identify with the *Star Wars* characters, who after so many years had become fully integrated into their lives and, hence, were established as an integral part of their personal identity.[25] The films acted as a social touchstone and icebreaker that had helped people build a sense of community and belonging throughout their lives. *Star Wars* was a "secret password" that enabled fans to make instant connections and, in doing so, share an immediate sense of communal culture.[26] Viewed within this context, it is no wonder that fans would take any changes to the *Star Wars* films personally.

One remarked: "I care about the characters in the SW universe. In a way, I share a sense of fellowship with them. I know the difference between fantasy and reality, and though the characters in SW will never be as precious to me as my "real" friends. . . . Through the years, I have become invested in their lives. From that first moment I felt a bond form with that lonely farm boy on a planet in a galaxy far, far away, I have followed the exploits of the SW family, in their triumphs and sharing their tragedies."[27]

For many, *Star Wars* is more than a movie and the people in them more than movie characters. These characters had, in many ways, become an important part of the fans' real and imagined lives. Not many films can boast this kind of deep identification with the characters. This phenomenon in itself is a true tribute to the storytelling power of Lucas.

On the other hand, *Star Wars* fans, although dedicated to the original text, self-consciously and self-reflexively parody and revise particular scenes, recreating them to make the text their own. This is not new. Fans have been changing the works of storytellers to suit their understanding of the world since our Neanderthal ancestors bragged about a hunt near a campfire. Even when there were no printing machines and the local priest kept the handwritten copies, most stories were transferred from person to person orally. Bad memories and good imaginations embellished these tales to suit the times or current moral code. Story material was just a springboard for further speculation, embellishment, and editing.

Tetina Holubovska explains, "The first modern fandom was centered focused on Sherlock Holmes and included written parodies and pastiches that were written and circulated among fans. After Holmes was killed, fans objected and reacted by writing their own stories of the event which ignored the author's version."[28] Like the early Sherlockians, it is clear that *Star Wars* fans are very emotionally attached to their narratives and want to appropriate them in certain ways instead of others. Affectivity is a crucial "glue" that connects fans to the original text or artifact. In other words, being a fan is an experience that is grounded in a feeling—connected to a story.

Fans Reclaim the Narrative

Star Wars: Special Editions became a cause for detailed comparisons that involved hours of scrutiny between the original films and the reissues. The most controversial change made in the *Special Editions* centered on "who shot first" in the Mos Eisley cantina. In the original *Star Wars*, Han takes out his gun from his holster and points it under the table, while Greedo, a seasoned bounty hunter, tries to collect a debt for Jabba the Hut. The conversation escalates, and Han shoots first, then hightails it out of the cantina. This action establishes Han as a dangerous character. Getting emotionally involved is not part of his makeup. His worldview is intentionally different from that of the idealistic Luke, and because of that difference, Han's change from mercenary to resistance fighter makes his character arc all that more meaningful and rewarding for the audience.

However, in the *Star Wars: A New Hope, Special Edition*, the narrative gets changed. Greedo fires first but misses, justifying Han's retaliation. Some fans not only didn't believe that a seasoned bounty hunter like Greedo could miss at point-blank range but felt that Lucas had gone too far by making Han the "nice guy"—it's antithetical to Han's nature and later motives and downplays his arc from hardened mercenary to a rebel with a cause. What is significant here is that *fans refused to accept Lucas's changes* to the reworked *Star Wars*

George Lucas giving a nod to fan culture in 2007 with a "Han Shot First" shirt. (courtesy ZUMA Press Inc./Alamy)

universe over their own understanding of it—especially when the changes directly flew in the face of what they had determined characters would or would not do. Brooker points out that *Star Wars* "characters and stories have escaped the original text and grown up with the fans, who have developed their own very firm ideas of what *Star Wars* is and is not about."[29]

In 2012, Lucas defended the change and claimed that it had always been the case that Greedo shot first and that Han was responding to defend himself: "It's a movie, just a movie. The controversy over who shot first, Greedo, or Han Solo, in Episode IV, what I did was try to clean up the confusion, but obviously it upset people because they wanted Solo to be a cold-blooded killer, but he actually isn't."[30] It may be just a movie to some, but to others, denying that Han Solo shot first is like finding out you're adopted; it's akin to changing your fundamental understanding of the truth.[31]

Shared Cultural Artifacts: Emotional Affect and Ownership

The strong emotional pushback by *Star Wars* fans over Lucas's tampering of the original films in his *Special Editions* might be explained by how people experience what are called "shared cultural artifacts."[32] Shared cultural artifacts are called "shared" for a reason. The release of the *Star Wars: Special Editions* reinforced the idea that films are not merely stand-alone cultural artifacts like a piece of bone dug up at an archaeology site. Instead, there exists a shared space, between the audience and the creative work, that becomes charged and invested with emotional and psychological reactions, which are filed away into memory and become part of the viewers' personal history and, thus, identity. Rather than *Star Wars* existing as something outside of viewers, it takes root within. *Star Wars* is not only what fans do; it's what they are.[33]

Affect helps construct the identity of the fan, which is grounded in an emotional ownership of media content. This emotional ownership is achieved through creative practices, the purchase of objects and memorabilia, and the establishment of social bonds with like-minded individuals. Thus, fandom is a way of making sense of the world through felt and shared experiences.[34] While the creator (George Lucas, in this case) owns the work (film), the emotionally charged space, which exists and is experienced between the creator and the audience, is shared by both. When changes are made to existing stories and a shared experiential space is challenged, especially one with the cultural and emotional impact of *Star Wars*, some audience members will react favorably, and others, less so. At stake, for some, is nothing less than their childhood memories and sense of personal identity.

Buying and collecting *Star Wars* merchandise can trigger memories of the past. Accessing positive memories and tapping into nostalgia have been shown to be a critical component of forming a meaningful personal narrative, and the simple act of picking up a toy lightsaber can return fans to childhood, to a time when they felt happy and secure. Even those who didn't have the rosiest childhood can still escape to the *Star Wars* universe, creating an alternate reality where cherished friends, caring mentors, and happily-ever-afters await.[35]

Nostalgia plays a big part in a fan's relationship with *Star Wars*. Nostalgia means a "painful return, a longing for something far away or long ago. . . . Homesickness. . . . It takes us to a place where we ache to go again."[36] Situated in an advertising and media landscape that often overpromises and underdelivers, the world of *Star Wars* helps fans create meaning when they might otherwise be unfulfilled.[37] *Star Wars* not only promises a journey into space but, like a time machine, returns us back home again, to a time and place where we are happy and loved. It is no surprise that "returning home" is a major theme that underscores the *Star Wars* narrative.

Making Connections: Cosplaying and Immersive Experiences

"Embodied cognition," Lindsay Portnoy explains, "acknowledges that the mind and body are agents working together to make meaning of our experiences."[38] Embodied play makes it "real." Dan White explains: "My son loves *Star Wars*. He encountered . . . a cosplayer in a Kylo Ren costume . . . he was completely entranced. Seeing Kylo Ren was impactful in a way that Kylo Ren on a screen couldn't touch. Life in the 21st century is increasingly digitally mediated, but our brains are still wired to delineate between first-hand, embodied experiences and digital experiences. While both 'real' and digitally mediated experiences can be impactful, we tend to assign more weight to the former."[39]

While online play offers a sense of community, embodied play goes deeper and affords a powerful degree of presence. People are not so naive to think people disappear into a digital space, but there is a vacancy.[40] Embodied play grounds the world of ideas to physical matter. Practicing embodied mindfulness through immersive experiences is a way to reconnect these fragments of our fractured self and bring them home again.

Making memories is key. Swinging lightsabers and getting a birthday cake with *Star Wars* characters on top while being sung to by loved ones all gets stored away into a psychic cache. Such experiences conflate, and feelings evoked by these different people, experiences, and things become indistinguishable from one another. And so *Star Wars* no longer exists as a story out there in the world but as a feeling that takes root in our blood, our bone, and our heart.

Immersive Experiences and Embodied Play

Disney's new *Star Wars*: Galactic Starcruiser immersive theme park is an embodied-play game changer. It is also the natural extension and end game to the invitation Lucas handed out when he first asked fans to play with *Star Wars* merchandise available in 1977, then again when he pioneered the digital film revolution in 1997 with the introduction of the *Special Editions*. *Star Wars*: Rise of the Resistance immediately positions park-goers as rebels who have been recruited by Rey to fight the First Order (Kylo Ren) and immerses them into the post–Episode VIII narrative, seamlessly blurring the boundaries of traditional conceptions of "queue," "preshow," and "ride" to offer riders a holistic experience "full of rich details and excitement on a cinematic scale."[41] The blend of ride, animatronics, holograms, sounds, special effects, decor, and role-playing cast members who either insult and pester riders before they enter an interrogation chamber (First Order lieutenants) or help them escape (the Resistance), or a confrontation with fifty menacing stormtroopers in an immense hangar bay after stepping off a captured transport, all combine to make this a truly thrilling and memorable experience.[42]

Opened in 2022, the Galactic Starcruiser might be referred to as a "*Star Wars* Hotel," but it's a getaway live-in theme park that is designed to mimic a cruise to space, tucked on the outskirts of Disney's Hollywood Studios. "This is a luxury cruise line with ongoing dinner theatre-style entertainments in an escape room-style setting with amazing theming," Scott Trowbridge, creative executive of Imagineering, explains.[43] In fact, it's a *Star Wars* LARP at its most technologically advanced. The basic immersive storyline involves the guests/players in a battle for control of the ship, known as the *Halcyon*, between the First Order and Resistance rebels. And there are subplots that allow for world play to enter.[44] Since players are embodied in the experience, it becomes contextualized in a way that watching the story unfold on the screen or reading in black and white simply cannot duplicate.[45]

Missions for each guest appear on the Play Disney Parks app, all of them involving tasks and minigames. Trowbridge explains, "Play allows you to try on and model different versions of yourself. We make it okay to try on different versions. It's not, you know, Todd being evil or authoritarian. It's 'Star Wars' Todd, right? It's First Order Todd." He continues, "We built a structure that allows you to try on these different personas and different versions of yourself—to model different kinds of choices and see what fits. That . . . is the power of play. We want to give our guests an opportunity to model behavior that demonstrates to them that change is possible, if we learn how to have the boldness to make these choices."[46] In this space, Luke might be the character you pretend to be, but with time, "playing Luke" helps you become the person you always wanted to be.[47]

People are looking for immersive experiences that allow them to fully engage with their environments. The fact that immersive experiences are enjoyed with others and are shared as memories is a big part of their appeal. People still want to take home a souvenir, something they can play with, but they also want to take home a memory they can relive again. Todd Martens recalls his first LARP experience at Disney World, when he was ten years old. "The Adventurers Club was . . . immersive theatre, all dedicated to a love of exploration . . . I had met Disney characters before, but it was the Adventurers Club that I felt truly *seen* by them."[48] To be seen, to be recognized in the physical world, to be acknowledged in such a way is to *matter*. The glance is not focused on a device or a screen; it is clearly focused on, and reflects, the gaze of another human being—who, with a returned look, acknowledges your presence, your being, your embodied self. And thus, the Galactic Starcruiser, and similar fan-type gatherings, succeed where no ride or internet game ever could. Whether you're learning how to wield a lightsaber with Rey or making friends with a stormtrooper, you are seen, you are connected, and, in a very intimate and personal way, you have found your way back home again.

The *Star Wars* Galactic experience is the culmination and normal progression that started with the digitization of film. George Lucas, the father of the franchise and merchandising, gave permission to tamper with, play with, and change the original trilogy and green-lit the ability for others to do the same. All at once he highlighted the right of the author ("I own this, so I can do what I want") and opened the door to an intermodal space prompting a more personalized relationship with the *Star Wars* narrative. Despite the ongoing debate, fans still love *Star Wars* and base their love on their own personal involvement with the saga.

In many ways, *Star Wars* no longer belongs to Lucas or Disney anymore, not in the literal sense. *Star Wars* characters and stories have escaped the boundaries of the original text and have grown up with the fans, who have developed their own sense of what *Star Wars* is and is not. So, when Lucas revisited the *Star Wars* universe in 1999, he found resistance on the part of the fans, who had created, via play, discussion, and identification, their *own version* of the *Star Wars* epic. Both the fans, who appropriated *Star Wars*, and Lucas, the writer, director, and owner of copyright, can be considered "creators" and co-owners of this shared cultural space.

Notes

1. Patti McCarthy, *The Lucas Effect: George Lucas and the New Hollywood* (New York: Teneo, 2012), 212.

2. Amy Wallace and Marla Matzer, "Lucas Cuts a Deal with Fox for Next *Star Wars*," *Los Angeles Times*, April 3, 1998, https://www.latimes.com/archives/la-xpm-1998-apr-03-fi-35475-story.html. Lucas owns the entire franchise except for the original film, which Fox financed for about $10 million. In exchange for a much-lower-than-usual (likely less than 10%) distribution fee on the films plus the rights to debut Episode I on its Fox TV network, Fox gave Lucas the rights to the original *Star Wars*, making his empire complete. By getting ownership, Lucas also took on the financial responsibility and risk of making new *Star Wars* films. Lucas's ownership of the second and third *Star Wars* films and all subsequent films is unique in Hollywood. Even influential filmmakers such as Steven Spielberg have not been able to wield such clout.

3. Claudia Puig, "*Star Wars* Appeal Is a Surprise Even to Creator Lucas," *Los Angeles Times*, February 4, 1997, F4.

4. In contrast, the original *Star Wars* opened twenty years before and made $1.6 million opening weekend.

5. Puig, "*Star Wars* Appeal," F1, F4.

6. Michael Coate, "Where Were You in '73? Remembering *American Graffiti* on its 40th Anniversary," The Digital Bits, August 1, 2013, https://thedigitalbits.com/columns/history-legacy--showmanship/where-were-you-in-73-american-graffiti-40th. Lucas was very unhappy with the reedits the studios did to both his films, *THX 1138* and *American Graffiti*. His first feature, THX 1138 (1971), had five minutes removed by Warner Bros., and Universal Pictures removed at least two minutes from *American Graffiti* (1973). In 2004, Lucas supervised a director's cut of THX 1138, restoring the picture while adding some modern special effects. John Baxter, in his book *Mythmaker: The Life and Work of George Lucas*, recalled that Lucas felt that the studio's action was best described as "cutting the fingers off his baby" (New York: Avon Books, 1999), 95.

7. Puig, "*Star Wars* Appeal," F1.

8. George Lucas, interview, Star Wars, published January 15, 1997, http://www.starwars.com.

9. "List of Changes in *Star Wars* Releases," Star Wars, accessed May 3, 2022, https://starwars.fandom.com/wiki/List_of_changes_in_Star_Wars_re-releases. Most people don't realize that ever since *Star Wars* was released in 1977, George Lucas has been making changes to his work—original trilogy and prequels included. These changed every time a new VHS, laser disc, DVD, Blu-ray, or theatrical print was released to be screened for the public. The changes vary from minor differences in color timing and take choices to major insertions of new visual effects, additions of characters and dialogue, scene expansions, and the replacement of original cast members with new ones to better support later prequel casting and narratives.

10. Will Brooker, *Using the Force: Creativity, Community and Star Wars Fans* (New York: Continuum, 2002), 63, 65. Other CGI changes included, but were not limited to, an establishing shot of Obi-Wan Kenobi's home on Tatooine; additional TIE fighters placed strategically in the final Battle of Yavin; enhancements to the Wampa Ice Creature and Dew Back; the redecoration of Cloud City: and the addition of Jabba's "Jedi Rocks" band.

11. Constantine Nasr, "George Lucas: Recaptures the Force," *Daily Trojan*, January 29, 1997, 10.

12. Mark Caro, "Spielberg Alters Scenes in *E. T.* for Twentieth Anniversary Release," *Los Angeles Times*, November 5, 2001, F9.

13. Ibid.

14. "#ReleaseTheOriginalTrilogy: The Unaltered Theatrical Version of the Three Classic *Star Wars* Films," Original Trilogy, November 29, 2021, https://originaltrilogy.com/announcement/ReleaseTheOriginalTrilogy-OriginalTrilogy-coms-enduring-goal-How-you-can-help/id/90630.

15. Ibid.

16. "Got GOUT? The 2006 Original Version DVD Bonus Feature Fiasco," Save Star Wars, accessed May 11, 2022, https://savestarwars.com/gout.html. A fan explains, "While bootlegs were sourced from Laserdiscs, to outcompete them all one would have to do is make an official transfer from the laserdisc master—the result would be just a bit better than the bootlegs, which would be enough to put them out of commission. In other words, the least amount of quality possible to still have this as the 'best available version.' A high-quality new transfer is unwanted because it also makes the Special Edition not look as good, so all you have to do is pull that 1993 master tape out of a dust bin in the Lucasfilm archives and you've accomplished your mission of not letting people really enjoy watching the originals: the look rough, crude, the way Lucas wants us to think they look."

17. Henry Jenkins, *Convergence Culture: Where Old and New Media Collide* (New York: NYU Press, 2006), 21–22.

18. John Banks and Sal Humphreys, "The Labour of User Co-creators: Emergent Social Network Markets?," *International Journal of Research into New Media Technologies* 14, no. 4 (2008): 401–18.

19. Alexandre O. Phillippe, dir., *The People vs. George Lucas* (2010; Los Angeles: Lionsgate, 2011), DVD. This film has been described as a "twisted love letter to George Lucas."

20. Caro, "Spielberg Alters Scenes," F9.

21. Nicolle Lamerichs, *Productive Fandom: Intermediality and Affective Reception in Fan Cultures* (Amsterdam: Amsterdam University Press, 2018), 14.

22. Wikipedia, s.v. "Jedi Census Phenomenon," accessed May 4, 2022, https://en.wikipedia.org/wiki/Jedi_census_phenomenon.

23. "Jedi Church: Jedi Religion and Jedi Faith," Jedi Church, accessed May 9, 2022, https://www.jedichurch.org.

24. Brooker, *Using the Force*, 82.

25. McCarthy, *Lucas Effect*, 214.

26. McCarthy, "A Force Awakened: Why So Many Find Meaning in *Star Wars*," The Conversation, December 11, 2015, https://theconversation.com/a-force-awakened-why-so-many-find-meaning-in-star-wars-51853.

27. Brooker, *Using the Force*, 86.

28. Tetina Holubovska, "The Beginning of the Fan Movement: Brief History of the First Fandoms," MedKult, accessed April 15, 2022, http://medkult.upmedia.cz/2016/08/03/the-beginning-of-the-fan-movement-brief-history-of-the-first-fandoms/.

29. Brooker, *Using the Force*, 77.

30. Alex Ben Block, "5 Questions with George Lucas: Controversial *Star Wars* Changes, SOPA and *Indiana Jones 5*," *Hollywood Reporter*, February 9, 2012, http://www.hollywoodreporter.com/heat-vision/george-lucas-star-wars-*interview*-288523.

31. McCarthy, "Force Awakened."

32. McCarthy, *Lucas Effect*, 215.

33. McCarthy, "Force Awakened."

34. Lamerichs, *Productive Fandom*, 18–19.

35. McCarthy, "Force Awakened."

36. Anne Friedberg, *Window Shopping: Cinema and the Postmodern* (Berkeley: University of California Press, 1993), 168.

37. McCarthy, "Force Awakened."

38. Lindsay Portnoy, "Embodied Cognition and the Possibility of Virtual Reality," Digital Culturist, April 4, 2017, https://digitalculturist.com/embodied-cognition-and-the-possibility-of-virtual-reality-ca2ec8fd05ea.

39. Dan White, "How VR Changes Learning," Filament Games, November 14, 2016, https://www.filamentgames.com/blog/how-vr-changes-learning/.

40. During the COVID-19 pandemic, people were required to shift to digitally mediated meetings on Zoom. Even when looking at people face-to-face during an online Zoom meeting, something was missing. A feeling of presence was lost. You could see images of the people in the virtual Zoom room, but seeing and being seen—looking someone directly in the eye—was impossible.

41. Cindy E. Nykamp, "Star Wars: Rise of the Resistance: Our Full Review and What You Need to Know," Disney Lists, November 30, 2021, https://www.disneylists.com/2021/11/news-star-wars-rise-of-the-resistance-now-open-our-full-review-2/.

42. Mick Jones, "Total Immersion and More Make Disney World's Rise of the Resistance Worth the Wait," CinemaBlend, December 5, 2019, https://www.cinemablend.com/news/2486089/total-immersion-and-more-spectacular-features-make-disney

-worlds-star-wars-rise-of-the-resistance-worth-the-wait. As an added note: As a life-long *Star Wars* fan and scholar, riding Star Wars: Rise of the Resistance on January 15, 2023, for the first time was a jaw-dropping and, if I can be totally honest, emotional and highly profound experience that I will never forget.

43. With cabin rates for two starting at around $5,200.00, the cost for most people is prohibitive.

44. Todd Martens, "*Star Wars*: Galactic Starcruiser." Among the many subplots on the Starcruiser are an alien romance, a would-be scoundrel who has items to steal, a droid with sensitive info, and an attempt to rescue Chewbacca, which includes scenes featuring famed droids.

45. White, "How VR Changes Learning."

46. Martens, "*Star Wars*: Galactic Starcruiser."

47. McCarthy, "Force Awakened."

48. Martens, "*Star Wars*: Galactic Starcruiser."

18

Changing Critical and Popular Responses to the *Star Wars* Prequels

Shanti Fader-Whitesides

Few pieces of pop culture media have undergone a roller-coaster ride of popular and critical opinion like the *Star Wars* prequel films. The initial announcement of the films was met by delirious excitement, followed by months of anticipation and an initial excited response when the first of the prequels was released in 1999. However, this excitement quickly gave way to disillusionment and extremely vocal disparagement of the prequel trilogy, followed by a critical reevaluation some ten to twenty years later. To understand these shifting conceptions, one must examine the larger cultural shifts surrounding them, including changes in technology, George Lucas's level of engagement, and changes in fandom itself.

A Good Story Poorly Told

On paper, the story the prequel films tell works beautifully: an enslaved child discovers his lofty destiny, rises to become a war hero with mystical powers, and then is brought low by forbidden love. Meanwhile, a scheming politician undermines both the political structure of the galaxy and the spiritual order tasked with protecting it. The Jedi fall to their own hubris, the Republic falls to authoritarian rule, and both storylines converge as the tyrant takes the destined child under his wing, corrupting a noble spirit into a puppet for evil.

This is the outline of a classic tragedy, tinged with references to the fall of the Roman Republic as well as to the political upheaval in turn-of-the-millennium

America. It has deeply personal stakes in addition to broader ones. So what went wrong? Why did the prequels become the subject of so much derision, disappointment, and bile?

First, it is important to note that the initial negative reaction was neither as immediate nor as complete as it is frequently made out to be. Roger Ebert gave *The Phantom Menace* (TPM) a positive review, praising its visuals and noting that "what [Lucas] does have, in abundance, is exhilaration. There is a sense of discovery in scene after scene of 'The Phantom Menace,' as he tries out new effects and ideas, and seamlessly integrates real characters and digital ones, real landscapes and imaginary places."[1]

While box office does not necessarily translate to quality, all three prequels earned a respectable amount of money, with TPM taking in a worldwide gross of $924,305,084. Even *Attack of the Clones* (AotC), the lowest-earning of the trilogy, took a worldwide gross of $645,256,452 (Box Office Mojo). The people complaining about these movies were spending a fair amount of money on the things they claimed to hate.

In fact, for all their faults, the prequels have many positive aspects. For one thing, they opened the *Star Wars* universe, expanding and enrichening it. Ebert was not the only one to praise their visuals: they boasted gleaming silver starships, elaborate new planetscapes, and thrilling battle sequences, all shot on crisp digital film. They introduced a staggering number of new alien characters and creatures, with stunning costume and makeup/prosthetic work.[2] Longtime fans of the Jedi finally got to see large numbers of the warrior-monks in action, including an entire Council of Jedi masters. The prequels also brought more diversity to the Star Wars universe, with female Jedi and fighter pilots, and Black Jedi masters on the council. Composer John Williams carried off the challenging task of composing memorable new themes such as "Duel of the Fates" (created for the climactic three-way lightsaber battle in TPM) that flow seamlessly into the existing musical world.

While much has been said about the wooden performances in the prequels, there are some notable exceptions. Ian McDiarmid is the real standout, shifting effortlessly between Palpatine the kindly politician and Darth Sidious the scheming Sith lord, until in *Revenge of the Sith* (RotS) he drops all pretense and chews the scenery with abandoned delight, clearly knowing exactly what kind of movie he is in. Ewan McGregor also shines as young Obi-Wan Kenobi. His performance goes beyond a mere imitation of the late Sir Alec Guinness, growing from the impatient Padawan of TPM to the anguished master of RotS, where he infuses genuine heartbreak into his final exchange with Anakin. Liam

Neeson projects a calm, sage presence as Qui-Gon Jinn, and Pernilla August radiates weary grace in her small role as Shmi Skywalker, Anakin's enslaved mother. Finally, the late Christopher Lee infuses the groaningly named Count Dooku with far more gravitas than the character deserves.

These performances, however, are the exceptions. For every Obi-Wan's "You were my brother!" there is an Anakin's "I'm haunted by the kiss." The same can be said of set pieces: for every "Duel of the Fates," there's a pod race.

Perhaps the worst failure is found in AotC, seen by many as the weakest of the trilogy. It hinges on the forbidden romance between Padme and Anakin, but that romance falls miserably flat because of a combination of poor acting, laughable dialogue, and one truly baffling costume choice—why would Padme wear a black leather corset while spurning Anakin's love? If the idea was to imply that she is sending mixed messages, it technically succeeds, but with no nuance or subtlety. For his part, Anakin is meant to seem passionate and conflicted, a brilliant Jedi held back by the timorous council, but he comes across as a petulant brat and a creep.

The prequels are further marred by side characters who personify egregious ethnic stereotypes—this was most likely inadvertent, but it is nonetheless hard to ignore. The worst offenders are Watto, a money-hungry slave trader who reads uncomfortably like antisemitic propaganda, and the Neimoidian Trade Federation leaders, who look and talk like bad Asian stereotypes. Characters designed to be fan favorites, like Jar Jar Binks, fell flat, while highly anticipated villains such as Darth Maul and General Grievous were barely present.[3]

Many baffling story choices made their way into the prequels. Some seem to be attempts at shoehorning in progressive moments—was it really necessary for Padme to be *elected* Queen of Naboo?—while others, like young Anakin building C-3PO, feel like cheap nostalgia grabs. A dry and confusing storyline about trade agreements dragged TPM down, and the introduction of midi-chlorians turned the mystical power of the Force into bland scientific fact, a revision so roundly derided that midi-chlorians vanished from the films aside from a brief reference in RotS.[4] The strong-willed Padme probably would not have given up on life just as her babies were born. Finally, it made no sense that the Jedi would want to fulfill a prophecy bringing "balance to the Force" when they held power throughout the galaxy.

As for the critics, not all of them agreed with Ebert. "The actors are wallpaper, the jokes are juvenile, there's no romance, and the dialogue lands with the thud of a computer-instruction manual"; "This is a fantasy with no poetry in it"; "Drink the Kool-Aid. Wear blinders. Cover your ears. Because that's the only way you can totally enjoy *Revenge of the Sith*."[5]

Anticipation

This all points to a prequel trilogy that is neither an unquestionable masterpiece nor a complete failure. Why, then, was it seen as universally bad for so many years? One reason might be heightened anticipation leading to expectations that could never possibly have been fulfilled, making the sense of letdown that much brutal.

It may be difficult to imagine in our current *Star Wars*–saturated state, but when TPM was released in 1999, there had been no new *Star Wars* movies since 1983. Fans made do with tie-in novels, video games, and the occasional TV offering. Many of them had been spinning fantasy prequels and sequels in their heads for nearly two decades and had grown deeply attached to their stories. Then, in 1997, Lucas rereleased the original trilogy in theaters as the *Special Editions*, restored and with enhanced special effects (along with certain less welcome changes). It was a canny move, whetting appetites right in time for the announcement of the prequels.

The advance publicity for TPM stirred fans up even more. People flocked to movies they had no interest in seeing, just for the trailer (this was before you could easily watch trailers online). A teaser poster with a small boy casting Darth Vader's shadow was not only an effective entice-ment, confirming that the prequels would tell the long-awaited story of the iconic villain, but a striking piece of art in its own right. A similar teaser poster for AotC set up the doomed romance between Anakin and Padme, promising more depth and pathos than the movie would deliver. When it was finally time to buy tickets, lines wound around blocks, with people setting up miniature campsites and striking up conversations with their neighbors while they waited, in some cases for over two weeks. After all that buildup, disappointment was, while certainly not inevitable, a strong possibility.

A few fans even entertained the possibility of disappointment at the time, as demonstrated in a series of *Dork Tower* comics, in which fans watch a TPM trailer and revel in collective delight—until one of them comments, "It could suck."[6] But for the most part, the people waiting in line for tickets or buying movie tickets purely for a trailer had grown up with *Star Wars*, felt its absence keenly in their lives, and wanted more. Some brought their children, hoping

Poster for *Star Wars: Episode I—The Phantom Menace* in 1999. (© 20th Century Fox Film Corp. All rights reserved/courtesy Everett Collection)

to introduce them to the universe they had loved so much. As a result, when the actual prequels fell short, it felt like a personal betrayal.

Being a science fiction fan was not considered "cool" or even mainstream in the 1970s and 1980s. Despite its enormous popularity, fans of *Star Wars* were often imagined as nerds and losers—outsiders to be mocked. In the days before the internet, fans sought one another out in local clubs, distributed self-published fanzines, and met at conventions, seeking assurance they were not alone. This out-group status, and the clannishness it fostered, helps explain why the prequels' shortcomings hit so hard: the bullies who'd sneered at them had been proved right, and the fans looked like fools.

One Man's Vision

"It could suck."

In the *Dork Tower* comic referenced previously, this comment touched off a long, heated debate over whether Lucas could be trusted with his own creation. In fact, even at this high point in *Star Wars* popularity, cracks in Lucas's shiny veneer were already appearing. Critics pointed to the overly cute Ewoks[7] and the redundant Death Star in *Return of the Jedi*, as well as the disastrous *Holiday Special*. Lucas, notorious for constantly changing his movies, also took heat for some of the changes in the *Special Editions*, especially the infamous "Han shot first" kerfuffle.

For the most part, however, at the end of the twentieth century Lucas was widely seen as the genius behind one of the most popular and beloved series in movie history. His references to Joseph Campbell and the global monomyth[8] gave Lucas the added sheen of a modern mythmaker, a creator of stories that went beyond mere entertainment to offer insight into the human condition. Those with a less spiritual bent admired Lucas for his business and marketing acumen. As a result, when it came to the prequels, Lucas essentially had free rein, and everyone knew it: "George Lucas can put whatever he wants on-screen and get away with it. He has become the ruler of the universe, at least the one between his ears; his wish is our command."[9]

For better or for worse, the prequels represent the clearest and most unfiltered expression of Lucas's vision regarding the *Star Wars* universe. The constraints on the original trilogy have been well documented, including a limited budget (especially for the first movie), the technology of the 1970s and 1980s constraining what could appear on-screen, and editors who reshaped his ideas, many of them quite wild, into the story we eventually saw on the screen.[10]

Ironically, without these constraints, *Star Wars* might never have become such a sensation. Harrison Ford famously told Lucas, "You can type this shit, but you can't say it," and much has been written about the influence of Lucas's then wife Marcia, who served as a film editor on the original trilogy. George and Marcia Lucas divorced in 1983 and did not work together on the prequels. In fact, Marcia Lucas is reported to have cried at a screening of TPM.[11]

The prequels had other editors, of course, but by then Lucas was held in such high esteem that few people could tell him no or convince him to change anything he was set on doing. Lucas was widely seen as—and firmly believed himself to be—the sole creator of *Star Wars*. It is hardly surprising that few people were willing to step up and point out flaws, be they weak dialogue, poor pacing, or improbable plots.

Lucas himself has even admitted that dialogue is not his strength, but—tellingly—he decided that was not important for the prequels. In a 1999 interview for *Empire Magazine*, he said: "I'd be the first person to say I can't write dialogue. My dialogue is very utilitarian and is designed to move things forward. . . . After a while of working in the medium, I decided that wasn't ultimately essential to making the movies. So in the last few movies we did not try and be clever with the dialogue."[12] This lack of "clever" dialogue definitely hurt the prequels. The sparkle and wit of the original trilogy were in short order; what humor did land was largely unintentional.

Freedom from technical restraints hurt the prequels as well. Lucas was famously unhappy with the special effects technology of the 1970s and 1980s, hence the updates made to the Special Additions. In the 1990s, CGI emerged as a tool for generating photorealistic images out of thin air that could be added into animation (as in several Disney Renaissance productions) and live-action movies (most notably 1991's *Terminator 2: Judgment Day* and 1993's *Jurassic Park*). Lucas seized the opportunity to realize his artistic vision more completely.

However, where Spielberg used a judicious blend of animatronics and CGI in *Jurassic Park*, Lucas splashed computer-generated aliens, backdrops, and locations all over the prequels. In his review of AotC, Ebert went as far as to say, "It is important to understand that 'Episode II' is essentially an animated film with humans added to it."[13] CGI gave Lucas the power to create aliens with less humanoid appearances, like the insectoid Geonosians or the Kaminoans with their attenuated limbs and necks, without being bound by the limitations of puppets or stop-motion models. CGI also allowed for more depth, detail, and movement in backgrounds; the constant stream of multilevel, multidirectional air traffic on Coruscant, for example, would have been challenging if not impossible without CGI.

But liberal use of CGI had its downside. It made the movies feel weightless and insubstantial, and live-action actors (already burdened with pedestrian dialogue) struggled to give convincing performances when both their scenery and their scene partners were nonexistent. Furthermore, because of rapid and ongoing advances in the technology, the most dazzling CGI work looks dated very quickly, and the prequels are no exception.

The issue with CGI is best illustrated by Yoda. Originally, the small green Jedi master was a puppet whose expressive face and movements rendered him convincingly alive. The puppet was replaced by CGI in the prequels, though Yoda was still voiced by Frank Oz. While this gave the character more freedom to move around and even engage in acrobatic lightsaber duels, many viewers felt that computerized Yoda lacked the "soul" of the original, tangible puppet. As Ebert says: "Yes, it's fun to see the surprise Yoda has up his sleeve, but in the scene itself, he turns from a substantial, detailed, 'realistic' character into a bouncing blob of Yoda-ness, moving too quickly to be perceived in any detail."[14] Notably, when Yoda returned in *The Last Jedi* (TLJ), he was a puppet once more.

It is hardly surprising, then, that much ire was focused on Lucas. Many fans—and certainly the loudest ones—turned from admiring Lucas and defending him from the smallest criticism to savagely attacking him, even going as far as to say he'd "raped their childhood."[15] This melodramatic comment was also used in reference to the poorly received *Indiana Jones and the Crystal Skull* (2008), on which Lucas was an executive producer. If Lucas had not been viewed as the sole creator figure behind *Star Wars*, he might have been spared much of this. It is an abject lesson about putting all-too-human creators on pedestals—and a lesson for Lucas on letting oneself be put there.

History Repeats Itself: The Disney Era and the Sequels

RotS, the third and final prequel, was released on May 19, 2005. Like the first two, RotS received mixed reviews but performed well at the box office, earning a record-breaking $158 million in its opening weekend alone (Box Office Mojo). Many critics and fans alike considered it to be the strongest of the prequels. Interestingly, some viewers criticized it for the exact thing others admired: RotS was a darker movie than the other two, with fewer laughs and fun set pieces, and significantly more body horror and character death. It was not enough to save the overall reputation of the prequels, however, as RotS still shared many flaws with the first two movies.

Disillusioned fans criticized Lucas's appearance and mocked his words. Ahmed Best, who provided the voice for Jar Jar, revealed via Twitter that the constant negative reaction to the character drove him to consider suicide.[16] Not all bullying took place online, of course. As Ron Jonson notes in his 2015 book *So You've Been Publicly Shamed*, online bullying has deep roots in the physical act; they feed off each other. Jake Lloyd, the unfortunate child actor who played Anakin in TPM, was taunted by schoolmates until he gave up acting and destroyed all his *Star Wars* memorabilia.[17] But the internet allowed—even encouraged—widespread anonymous bullying, rewarding cruelty with more attention.[18] Twitter, which first appeared in 2006, sped up the spread of virtual venom and robbed online discourse of nuance.

For around a decade, the fate of the prequels and their creator appeared to be sealed. No new *Star Wars* movies were released or even planned. Lucas tried his hand at a few non–*Star Wars* film projects, with little success. He had better luck bringing *Star Wars* to television. *Star Wars: The Clone Wars*, a CGI animated series launched in 2008,[19] took advantage of television's long-form storytelling possibilities to fill in the gaps between Episodes II and III and flesh out the sketchy characterizations from the movies. But *The Clone Wars* didn't lead fans to reconsider the prequels; they just pointed out how much the movies suffered in comparison.

Then something unexpected happened.

In 2012, Lucas sold the rights to *Star Wars* to the Walt Disney Corporation. The media giant announced an ambitious slate of new movies, including a sequel trilogy that would tie up the Skywalker saga—a project Lucas had wanted to take on himself but had given up after the prequels. Suddenly, *Star Wars* was creating buzz again in a big way. Some saw Disney as a better captain for the ship than Lucas had become. Others were concerned that because of Disney's focus on profit the new films would be bland and "safe," losing much of what made *Star Wars* special. Still others feared that the notoriously litigious corporation would clamp down hard on fan creations—fiction, artwork, even costumes and lightsaber hilt props—which had flourished alongside licensed products for decades.

While some of these fears did come to pass—Disney restricted what fans could make public and sell, and they eliminated much of the Extended Universe lore that had built up over the decades—concerns about the quality and creativity of Disney-helmed movies were somewhat allayed by the trailer for

The Force Awakens (TFA), released in 2014. It had a Black stormtrooper! A mysterious villain with a cool new lightsaber! Han and Chewie on the *Millennium Falcon*! The trailer offered a potent blend of nostalgia and novelty, aided by the widely publicized news that the new movies would return to a greater use of practical effects.

TFA opened in 2015 to primarily positive reviews, and fans raved about it—initially. But that first flush of excitement soon gave way to the feeling that they had consumed the movie equivalent of a hollow chocolate bunny. The more one watched it, the clearer it grew that despite its charismatic new cast and scene-stealing beach-ball droid, the story was a beat-for-beat retread of *A New Hope* that undid all the victories of the original trilogy and rendered its sacrifices moot. If the prequels were a good story poorly told, then the sequels told the same story as the original trilogy, with varying degrees of success.[20]

If this sounds familiar, it should. Popular reaction to the sequel series has thus far followed a trajectory very similar to that of the prequels: excitement, disillusionment, rejection, and a turn back to what preceded it. While the specific reasons may be different, the pattern is startlingly similar.

People who had previously complained bitterly about the prequels' shortcomings now defended those very shortcomings on the grounds that at least they were original ideas. Lucas was praised once again, this time for at least trying something different. His singular vision was also compared favorably against that of J. J. Abrams, director of two of the three sequels, who admitted in a recent interview that he had had no plan going into the project.[21]

Throughout the 2010s, articles and videos defending the prequels began popping up, including a remarkably even-handed essay on the *AV Club*[22] that nonetheless sparked a lengthy, heated argument in its comments section. After the sequels, these takes increased, many of them praising the prequels while acknowledging—even embracing—their faults. Callum Russel called the prequels an "attempt at Shakespearian tragedy that falls charmingly short."[23] Neel Patel pointed out that they were perfect for the internet age: "The internet is a paradise of irreverence, just like George Lucas' scripts. These qualities don't always translate well on the silver screen—they create an oft-disjointed narrative that leaves audiences feeling cold and alienated. But in the digital world, these are the things that bring people together."[24] The recent explosion of memes (amusing snips of pop culture that are shared online, often in an altered state) using images from the prequels supports Patel's argument.

Others explain the shift in discourse as a changing of the generational guard: "The prequels and George Lucas were smart enough to know who their target audience was, and that wasn't necessarily the older generation, but in reality the new one. . . . Thus, it may have made older generations feel a bit alienated at the time. And because they still controlled a lot of the discourse media at the time, it was their voices that were amplified the most."[25]

After all, in the end these are children's movies. Just as children and young teenagers loved the original movie in 1977, their children loved the prequels. The prequels were "their" *Star Wars*, new and fresh and exciting, just as the original trilogy was for their parents. Ewan McGregor sums it up beautifully in a *Vanity Fair* interview: "George Lucas wanted to do something very different with the prequels. That's why people felt cheated. It was upsetting when people would laugh and joke about it. Now, many years later, the prequels meant a lot to the generation that were kids then. So from smirking, cynical opinions, now I'm getting feedback from the kids they were made for. I'm really happy about that."[26] While this sentiment is far from universal, it is no longer anathema to enjoy the prequels.

Conclusion: A Child's First *Star Wars*

As with most cultural phenomena, there is no simple answer to the changing prequel response. The evolving nature of fandom and of fans played a role, as did generational change, the shifting image of Lucas, and simply the presence of something new against which to compare the prequels. Even the political climate of the late 2010s and early 2020s made stories about liberty dying "to thunderous applause" chillingly relevant again. All the factors explored herein play a part and help deepen our understanding of the phenomenon and of the prequels themselves.

Fans continue to shape the *Star Wars* discourse. In fact, some fans are now official creators of new *Star Wars* content, inspiring fans of their own. David Filoni, who worked on the CGI *Clone Wars* series and its follow-ups *Rebels* (2014–2018) and *The Bad Batch* (2021–), tells stories that feel very much like professional fan fiction. Jon Favreau, producer of the Disney live-action TV show *The Mandalorian* (2019–) and director Bryce Dallas Howard refer to themselves as "an after-school club that's making its own *Star Wars* film. With very rich parents."[27] Fan-made films and official parodies have, of course, been a part of *Star Wars* fandom since the beginning, and some people used the medium to express their disappointment with the prequels.[28]

This pattern of enthusiasm, rejection, reclamation, and elaboration is likely to continue with the Disney-era films and TV shows. *Star Wars* may change creators and forms as time passes, but it is unlikely to leave the cultural landscape entirely, so each generation to come will have "their" *Star Wars*. And both worlds—real and fictional—will be richer for it.

Notes

1. Roger Ebert, "*Star Wars—Episode I: The Phantom Menace*," Roger Ebert, 1999, https://www.rogerebert.com/reviews/star-wars-episode-i-the-phantom-menace-1999.

2. I had the good fortune to examine many of these costumes up close at the *Dressing a Galaxy* exhibit at the Fashion Institute of Design & Merchandising (FIDM) in 2005. The construction and detail work, much of which was not visible on-screen, is absolutely breathtaking.

3. There is actually a very good reason for Maul's insignificance, which I explore in my *Parabola* essay on TPM. That doesn't change the fact that his brief screen time and ignominious exit was one of the factors that enraged many viewers. See Shanti Fader, "In Sheep's Clothing," *Parabola: Myth, Tradition, and the Search for Meaning*, 24, no. 4 (1999): 88–90.

4. Midi-chlorians would reemerge in David Filoni's animated *Clone Wars* series and later, albeit obliquely, in *The Mandalorian*. Nonetheless, the concept remains wildly unpopular. One fan theory contends that midi-chlorians represented a flawed attempt to understand and quantify the Force, made by late-Republic Jedi who had lost much of their wisdom.

5. Peter Travers, "*Star Wars—Episode I: The Phantom Menace*," *Rolling Stone*, May 19, 1999, https://www.rollingstone.com/movies/movie-reviews/star-wars-episode-i-the-phantom-menace-101886/; Stephanie Zacharek, "In Space, No One Can Hear You Groan," *Salon*, May 16, 2002, https://www.salon.com/2002/05/16/attack_clones/.

6. John Kovalik, "The Force Is Strong in This Trailer," *Muskrat Ramblings*, November 12, 2000, http://www.dorktower.com/2015/11/12/the-force-is-strong-in-this-trailer/.

7. I personally would argue that while the Ewoks were cute, they were also ferocious, highly intelligent little carnivores that don't deserve their negative reputation. Furthermore, I see their battle pitting sticks and stones against the high-tech Empire as one of the clearest examples of Lucas's "man vs. machine" theme.

8. See Joseph Campbell, *The Hero with a Thousand Faces* (San Francisco: New World Library, 1949); Bill Moyers et al., *The Power of Myth* (PBS, 1988).

9. Zacharek, "In Space."

10. Michael Kaminski, *The Secret History of "Star Wars"* (2007), https://drbeat.li/album/Bücher/The_Secret_History_of_Star_Wars.pdf.

11. J. W. Rinzler, *Howard Kazanjian: A Producer's Life* (New York: Harry N. Abrams, 2021), 316–17.

12. Ian Freer, "George Lucas: The *Star Wars* Prequels Interview," *Empire Magazine*, September 1999, https://www.empireonline.com/movies/features/star-wars-archive-george-lucas-1999-interview/.

13. Roger Ebert, "Lucas Demonstrates Potential of Digital Video with *Attack of the Clones*," Roger Ebert, May 14, 2002, https://www.rogerebert.com/roger-ebert/lucas-demonstrates-potential-of-digital-video-with-attack-of-the-clones.

14. Ibid.

15. As with many an internet-era trope or meme, it is extremely difficult to pin down the original source of this phrase. An online user with the handle Robogeek claimed to be its originator in a comment on a 2006 Ain't It Cool website post (http://legacy .aintitcool.com/node/30307), but I have not been able to verify this.

16. Camille Augustin, "*Star Wars* Actor Considered Suicide after Relentless Jar Jar Binks Criticism," *Vibe*, July 5, 2018, https://www.vibe.com/news/movies-tv /star-wars-ahmed-best-suicide-jar-jar-binks-criticism-594996/.

17. Sean O'Neal, "*Star Wars: Episode I* Actor Jake Lloyd Has Been through 'Living Hell,' according to Jake Lloyd," AV Club, March 6, 2012, https://www.avclub.com /star-wars-episode-i-actor-jake-lloyd-has-been-through-1798230213.

18. Cyberbullying was not limited to the prequels. Kelly Marie Tran, who played Rose in TLJ, left social media after a relentless barrage of racist and sexist comments drove her to therapy. See "Kelly Marie Tran: I Won't Be Marginalized by Online Harassment," *New York Times*, August 21, 2018. Tran's role in *The Rise of Skywalker* was cut down to a glorified cameo thanks to this backlash as well.

19. This is not to be confused with Genndy Tartakovsky's *Clone Wars* (2003), a microseries of animated shorts set and released between Episodes II and III. They were part of an extended multimedia experience for the prequels, an experiment with dubious success, but they are well worth watching on their own merit.

20. The major exception would be TLJ, but a full discussion of that movie and the controversies raging around it would be an essay unto itself. I will point out that even TLJ, which brought in the most original ideas of the sequel trilogy, still included recognizable story beats from both *The Empire Strikes Back* and *Return of the Jedi*.

21. Adam Chitwood, "J.J. Abrams Reflects on *Star Wars* and When It's Critical to Have a Plan," Collider, May 26, 2021, https://collider.com/jj-abrams-star-wars-sequel -trilogy-plan-comments/.

22. Jesse Hassinger, "The *Star Wars* Prequels Don't Deserve Your Hatred," AV Club, November 16, 2015, https://www.avclub.com/the-star-wars-prequels-don-t -deserve-your-hatred-1798286432.

23. Callum Russel, "Why the *Star Wars* Prequels Are Better Than the Sequels," *Far Out*, March 15, 2022, https://faroutmagazine.co.uk/why-star-wars-prequels-are -better-than-the-sequels/.

24. Neel Patel, "The *Star Wars* Prequels Are Finally Beloved Because They Were Made for the Internet," *Syfy Wire*, June 29, 2020, https://www.syfy.com/syfy-wire /star-wars-prequel-trilogy-memes.

25. Joel Davis, "How the Prequels Went from Hated to Loved in 10 Years," Culture Slate, September 1, 2021, https://www.cultureslate.com/news/how-the-prequels-went-from -hated-to-loved-in-10-years.

26. Richard Lawson and K. Austin Collins, "25 Scenes, 25 Years: The 25 Most Influential Movie Scenes of the Past 25 Years," *Vanity Fair*, January 25, 2019, https://www .vanityfair.com/hollywood/2019/01/25-best-movie-scenes.

27. Jon Favreau and Bryce Dallas Howard, *Disney Gallery, Star Wars: The Mandalorian*, season 1, episode 8, "Connections," December 27, 2019, 6:25–6:43.

28. See Mark McDermott, "The Menace of the Fans to the Franchise," in *Finding the Force of the "Star Wars" Franchise: Fans, Merchandise, and Critics*, ed. Matthew Wilhelm Kapell and John Shelton Lawrence (New York: Peter Lang, 2006), 243–78.

19

From Rebels to Emperors to Jedi Spirits

Walt Disney, George Lucas, and Their Fans

CRAIG SVONKIN

Joining Fandom, Not Once but Twice

Hello. My name is Craig. And I'm a Disney and Lucas fan.[1]

Nineteen seventy-seven was a profoundly important year in my life: I had my Bar Mitzvah and saw *Star Wars* for the first time, thereby becoming a "man" while sneakily meandering into what was to be an extended fan boyhood.[2] Entering my teenage years meant I was now officially part of the targeted audience for *Star Wars*, *Close Encounters of the Third Kind*, and teen comedies and horror films like *National Lampoon's Animal House*, *Grease*, and *Halloween*. That was also the year Walt Disney Productions released *The Littlest Horse Thieves*, *Pete's Dragon*, and *Candleshoe*, all of which I saw and publicly denied seeing. As a secret Disney apostle ten years after Walt's death, I'd tie myself in knots to privately embrace these post-Walt films, as well as mediocre Disney films made during his lifetime. However, when I ran into a classmate at a showing of *Herbie Goes to Monte Carlo*, the nadir of the Love Bug series, I claimed I was there as a favor to my six-year-old sister (in fact, I had had to bribe her with movie theater candy to convince her to go with me). I knew it was terminally unhip to obsessively buy a ticket for every Disney movie, spend Sunday nights watching the *Wonderful World of Disney* television show, read everything available about Disney, and keep a scrapbook of Disneyland theme park ads, news, and my own attraction ideas. So I hid my

271

shameful Disney obsession from my peers, with my younger sister recruited as the only other member of my two-person, unofficial Disney fan club.[3] On the other hand, my love for *Star Wars* and the megahit film culture it had unleashed was marginally acceptable.

Throughout my teens, my connections to two distinct fan communities grew: (1) teen fantasy and science fiction fans interested in *Star Wars*, *Close Encounters of the Third Kind*, *Star Trek*, the Rays (Bradbury and Harryhausen), superhero comics, and J. R. R. Tolkien and (2) an older and, to my judgmental teenage eyes, more embarrassing group of Disney fans. Upon receiving my driver's license, I joined the Mouse Club, Disney merchandise collectors who had created a club in 1979 and held the first unofficial "Disneyana Convention" in 1982, only to witness the great schism of 1984 when the National Fantasy Fan Club (NFFC) formed.[4] With both the Lucas and Disney fan communities, I unsuccessfully attempted to introduce new conversational topics: why Disney should be making movies more like *Star Wars*, why George Lucas or Steven Spielberg should be hired to run Disney, and why Disneyland needed to build *Star Wars* rides and attractions.

My burning desire for the Disney company to bring Lucas and his creations into the Disney fold was met with puzzlement by fellow teenage fantasy and science fiction fans, who considered "Disney" an anti-aphrodisiac. Likewise, the adults I interacted with at the Mouse Club and NFFC meetings were Disney purists uninterested, for the most part, in *Star Wars*. Instead, they would talk about the need for rides or shows based on *Mary Poppins*, Ichabod Crane, or post–Walt Disney flops like *The Black Hole*. I felt alone in my conviction that Walt Disney Productions needed a creative outsider like Lucas, or better yet Lucas himself, to replace Walt. My Disney fan isolation lasted until 1984, when Hollywood executives Michael Eisner and Frank Wells were hired to replace Disney CEO Ron Miller, Walt Disney's son-in-law; began producing films with greater teenage appeal; announced a deal with Lucas for attractions at Disney's parks. My immersion in these different fandoms gave me a front-row seat to the spiritual practices of two corporate American fan cultures, inspiring my interest in the intersection of capitalism and religion.

Cult(ural) Break: A Cross-ReligiCorp Analysis

So, what had I sensed at thirteen that only a few other Disney fans and employees sensed? Specifically, this: Lucas was somehow the logical successor to Walt Disney, even if we couldn't put our collective fan finger on the exact nature of the Disney-Lucas connection. One longtime, trusted Disney employee, James "Jim" Algar, who had begun animating Mickey Mouse cartoons in 1934 and worked closely with Walt on *Snow White and the Seven Dwarfs*, *Fantasia*, *Bambi*, the True-Life Adventure documentaries, and the New York World's Fair show, "Great Moments with Mr. Lincoln," stated in 1984 that there was indeed a logical successor to Walt, "but not at the Disney Studios."[5] That "other" Walt Disney was the young Lucas, "a new master storyteller" who, Algar argued, shared many of Disney's qualities, including his strong will, good taste, and tremendous determination: "He's low key, level headed, mature and, like Disney, he is a perfectionist."[6]

When Eisner and Wells took over management of Walt Disney Productions, beginning a dramatic cultural break from years of creative atrophy, they quickly forged a business connection with Lucas that resulted in building *Captain Eo*, *Star Tours*, and the *Indiana Jones Adventure*. But the decision to build non-Disney-themed rides based on Lucasfilm intellectual properties was not met with universal acclaim. Many now think of Lucas's creations as being a part of Disney, after Disney's purchase of Lucasfilm in 2012. But that wasn't always the case. At the 1985 Disney stockholders' meeting, I remember hearing boos and hurrahs alike when Eisner announced a deal with Lucas to build Lucas-themed rides at Disneyland. And as demonstrated by the mixed responses of many Disney fans to the 2019 addition of twin *Star Wars*: Galaxy's Edge lands to Disneyland in Anaheim and Disney's Hollywood Studios in Florida, even today not all Disney fans embrace *Star Wars*. And not all *Star Wars* fans are Disney fans. As a fan of both, I therefore faced moments of cognitive dissonance, having to hide my dedication to one messiah from devotees of the other.

Online Disney fans often complain that the Disney company devotes too much space and money to *Star Wars* and Marvel properties and not enough to the intellectual properties they deem Walt Disney–approved (even if those were sometimes made long after Walt Disney's death). Likewise, after the 2015 release of *The Force Awakens*, 2017 release of *The Last Jedi*, and 2018 release of the stand-alone *Solo: A "Star Wars" Story*, disappointed *Star Wars* fans complained that Disney was ruining *Star Wars*. These fans, many of whom had felt betrayed by their messiah for his prequel trilogy, were now calling for the sacrifice of Lucasfilm president Kathleen Kennedy. As Henry Jenkins explains about fan aesthetic judgment: "Aesthetic distaste brings with it the full force of moral excommunication and social rejection."[7] These responses reveal the quasi-religious nature of contemporary, capitalist, consumer fandom. They also demonstrate that hard-core Disney fans tend to be more loyal in their corporate worship, more cultish perhaps, than their Lucas fan counterparts.

Theorizing Corporate Fandom

It is not just sports fans who celebrate corporations as if they were religions and corporate leaders as if they were saints. After Walt Disney's death, the mantra of "What would Walt do?" was often heard in the halls of the Disney Corporation and its Imagineering design wing. The mantra continues, with its fascinating transmutation of the religious "What would Jesus do?" into the realm of corporate decision-making and, even more so, into the often-harsh fan judgments of Disney-branded and Lucasfilm-branded products. While I am discussing Disney and Lucas fandom as quasi-religious communities and experiences, it is important to note that not all scholars accept this interpretation.[8] But I side with those who use the term *religion* in regard to fandom. All religions have members with a range of commitments, from High Holiday Jews and twice-a-year Catholics to zealots. Disney and Lucas fans clearly experience or practice these forms of fandom:

- There are organizations for Disney worshippers to share their mutual obsessions: official and unofficial fan clubs, such as Disneyland social clubs with members sporting matching jackets, and conventions, like the D23 Expo, at which fans cosplay as their favorite Disney, Lucas, and Marvel characters, in a manner reminiscent of religious pageants like Mardi Gras, Carnival, or Purim.
- Disney fans, like sects of other religions, argue over how to interpret their prophet's holy utterances: Walt Disney's statement (likely written by Disney Imagineer Marty Sklar) that "Disneyland will never be completed, as long as there is imagination left in the world"[9] has been read by progressives as allowing for classic Disneyland rides to be revised or even replaced to better fit the changing culture, whereas originalists have argued that changes for political reasons are not what Walt was endorsing.
- Many Disney and Lucas fans observe various dogma: the Disney parks must be clean, as Uncle Walt demanded; midi-chlorians and Jar Jar Binks, for many Lucas fans, were signs that Lucas had lost his way.
- Fans argue over what is canon and what apocrypha: Lucas once said that "the movies are gospel, the rest is just gossip," but the

fans themselves argue over the merits and canonicity of the works; Lucasfilm eventually established the Lucasfilm Story Group to monitor the *Star Wars* Expanded Universe (EU) "transmedia megaseries of novels, comics, video games, and so forth" and has declared some canon and others apocrypha.[10]

- Disney and Lucas fans have holy sites they hope to someday visit, including Walt's Disneyland apartment; the Walt Disney Studios in Burbank, California; the Disney Family Museum in San Francisco; Industrial Light & Magic at the Presidio; Skywalker Ranch in Marin County; and the *Star Wars*: Galactic Starcruiser hotel/experience at Walt Disney World.
- Many fans can speak of their initial moment of being called to worship at the Disney or Lucas altar. My moment of calling happened when I saw *Pinocchio* for the first time. The imagery and narrative affected me so deeply that I had to have more.

Please indulge me as I share a few of my own experiences as ethnographic evidence of the quasi-religious or cultlike potential of Disney fandom. As a child prone to melancholy meditations, I searched for moments of happiness and meaning, spaces of beauty and transcendence to help me cope with the void. When I first saw Disney films and visited Disneyland, I discovered what I had been searching for. On my first visit to Walt Disney's Enchanted Tiki Room show, the lighting, music, animated mechanical birds, and personified tikis, flowers, and water moved me to tears, not out of fear but rather from an encounter with the sublime. Like some latter-day, Southern California Hegel, I found the designed world of Disneyland more spiritual than a forest.[11] I became obsessed with Disney, looking through a variety of Disney artifacts for reassurance. In my obsessive-compulsive way, I attempted to transform my growing collection of Disney books, collectibles, and maps into a source of higher meaning or comfort. I became a Disney true believer.

My family patiently endured the missionary zeal with which I approached Disney. I sang the songs, reviewed the movies, and pitched my attraction ideas to bored relatives. On a cross-country family trip, I harassed my parents into driving hundreds of miles out of their way to Walt Disney World, begging them to go into debt so we could stay at one of the expensive, official Walt Disney World hotels I had read all about. I've since taken my own Disney pilgrimages to Kansas City, Disneyland Paris, Tokyo Disneyland, and DisneySea, and, via the "Keys to the Kingdom" behind-the-scenes tour, to the semisecret

"Utilidor" tunnels hidden beneath the Magic Kingdom. I littered my parents' bookshelves and closets with Disney books, collectibles, and ephemera. I hope to culminate my Disney life with pilgrimages to Shanghai Disneyland, Hong Kong Disneyland, Marceline, MO, and Tivoli Gardens in Copenhagen. When you wish upon a corporate star, makes no difference who you are: you may enrich your chosen corporation, while your/their corporate dreams come true.

Once upon a Kingdom: Creating (and Toppling) Saints

So, assuming you accept my argument that many Disney and Lucas fans engage in a religious or quasi-religious cultural practice and, as part of that practice, turn favorite filmmakers and corporate leaders into saints, how did this transformation from human to holy come about? First, Disney and Lucas fans alchemically transubstantiated real human beings into mythic demigods. Via hagiography and hero worship, fans created commodified, spiritual, iconic saints out of old Walt and George. The Disney Company assisted in Walt Disney's canonization by literally erasing "un-Disney-like" practices, such as Walt's chain-smoking (the company consistently airbrushes the ever-present cigarette out of photos of Disney), his penchant for profanity, his fondness for an evening drink, and his unpredictable temper. As I've learned from years of attending Disney fan club and convention meetings, reading Disney websites and blogs, and chatting with fellow Disney fans, a significant percentage of diehard Disney devotees are either avowed Christians or believers in a popular secular religion we might call the "When You Wish upon a Star," happy endings do come true faith. Or both. And since Christian or Happily-Ever-After believers might be put off by the rougher edges of Saint Walt, the company polishes those rough edges off for fans' devotional convenience.

Given his assertion that "capitalism essentially serves to satisfy the same worries, anguish, and disquiet formerly answered by so-called religion," Walter Benjamin likely wouldn't have been surprised by the corporate religion created by Disney fans in tandem with the Disney company.[12] Indeed, both Disneyland—with its appeals to personal and national nostalgia, its appropriative Orientalism meant to bestow its suburban Californian visitors the gift of cosmopolitanism, and its repetitions of archetypes of threat and survival[13]—and the *Star Wars* films—with their nostalgic futurism and quasi-Eastern religious elements folded into a batter of countercultural pop spiritualism—work to provide consumers with quasi-religious symbols of reassurance and rebirth, alongside holy consumer totems (to be purchased at toy stores or at the ubiquitous after-ride gift shop).

Dedicated fans often experience Disney's and Lucas's respective films and associated merchandise, and Disneyland, as narratives, icons, or spaces of secular religious devotion. As Kip Redick argues, modern "desacralized" spaces "leave a void that 'secular' people fill with new manifestations of what they perceive to be sacred."[14] In theme parks we can see a "merging of capitalism and religious devotion."[15] Here, the "ultimate desires of people are transferred from previous icons to new images of consumption." Thus, princess dolls and hidden Mickeys replace older religious iconographies. Megan Ashley Franklin asserts that purchasing Disney collectibles or revisiting Disneyland can function as quasi-religious experiences:

> As fans begin to assign pins meaning, they take on sacred qualities such as memories, stories, or ideals. For example, one fan I met . . . was wearing a castle pin on her hat. The fan explained to me that she wore the pin as a reminder to herself of the Disney ideal "Happily Ever After"; even when times were tough, she could look at the pin and remember to think positively because dreams come true. This is an example of how even while the physical object itself might not be sacred, the memory that it represents may have sacred qualities.[16]

Disneyland is thus "transformed from a place of profane entertainment, an amusement park, to a quasi-sacred place where the participant may experience transcendental devotion" upon their purchase of an entrance ticket—and perhaps some very expensive "Lightning Lane" special front-of-the-line pilgrim upgrades.[17] Franklin concludes that "Disneyland and the other Disney parks are sacred to . . . many fans."[18]

In an earlier essay, I discussed my ecstatic, sublime responses to the dual synagogues of my youth, both suffused with stained-glass window lighting and mystery: Temple Beth Torah's sanctuary in Alhambra, California, and Walt Disney's Enchanted Tiki Room.[19] Yet in my Disney worship, I never feared I was replacing Adonai with a golden Walt. Believing that Disneyland would be empty, I once convinced my sister Jeanine and my friend Cheryl to go to Disneyland on Easter Sunday, only to be confronted by claustrophobia-inducing crowds. And, a Catholic friend assures me, many a mass has been skipped for a trip to Disneyland, only to be pardoned in the Disney-friendly Southern California confessional. In the syncretic ways of contemporary religious practice, Disney worship can coexist peacefully with other religious praxis.

From Walt to George: Childhood, Oedipal Struggles, and Other Fathers

While I experienced Disney fandom differently from Lucas fandom, I noticed early on many common traits between the actual Walt Disney and the actual George Lucas, as well as between their respective oeuvres. We can trace how Disney and Lucas, who lived through very different American eras, transformed from young film rebels hungry for experimentation into moguls overseeing their respective self-named corporate empires and then finally into force spirits or ghosts in the shell of corporations (for Disney, after his death; for Lucas, after his 2012 sale of Lucasfilm to the Disney Company). Marketing avatars of Disney and Lucas now appear in corporate Jedi-ghost form as the nonmouse, nonrobot corporate mascots of Lucasfilm and its mother ship, the Walt Disney Company, a megacorporation that has increasingly become a holding company of other creative companies and intellectual properties. Despite these uncanny transformations, it remains worthwhile to look back on the similarities and differences between these two creative artists. We can see the influence of the Disney company on Lucas, who modeled himself, to some extent, on Walt as a sort of spiritual other-father. Both of these small-town-raised American gentile filmmakers from very different eras experienced Hollywood as outsiders. And both created, or more accurately cocreated, iconic films and characters that then became the intellectual, mythic centers of increasingly large corporations and fan movements that spread beyond film into television, games, and licensed toys and collectibles, as well as theme parks, themed lands, and themed attractions.

Renowned critic Pauline Kael expressed concern regarding Steven Spielberg's statement that "the real movie-lovers are still children," ironically responding that "there's no doubt he means that in a congratulatory sense."[20] Kael viewed Lucas as "hooked on the crap of his childhood." Perhaps too harsh, Kael's critique is applicable to Lucas and Spielberg, as well as their fans and spiritual progeny, John Lasseter, Guillermo del Toro, and Jon Favreau. Kael's critique could likewise apply to Walt Disney, arguably Lucas and Spielberg's spiritual father, who built a studio and Disneyland so he could play with oversize versions of the toys he desired but was denied as a boy. In fact, Disney

and Lucas, and their fans, might accurately be called the Disneyland generation, given that Walt's playground also fits Kael's critique.

Kael argued that if Lucas were to bring "his resources to bear on some
projects with human beings in them—there's no imagining the result."[21] She
blamed Lucas's "temperament and tastes," and not a crass capitulation to the
marketplace, for his decision to make what she seems to read as boyish love
letters to wires and circuits and bolts. As she writes, "essentially, George Lucas
is in the toy business."[22]

Lucas commented on his love of comics, games, and toys in a 1977 interview: "I like comics and toys. I have a particular affection for games and toys;
there's no doubting that I haven't grown up."[23] Certainly, the same critique could
be leveled at Walt Disney, a man whose studio built such toys as the first sound
cartoon, the first Technicolor cartoon, the first feature-length animated film
made in the United States, and a theme park with a rocket ship to the moon,
a number of steam trains, a paddle-wheel steamboat, a fairy-tale castle, robot
birds and presidents and pirates, and other toys for the grown-up Walt Disney
to play with. Perhaps Disney and Lucas's common fixations on childhood
and on toys emanated from similar strained relationships with their fathers.
Joseph Zornado explains that both survived "painful, formative childhood
experiences with their fathers typified by detachment, emotional austerity,
and a general lack of faith in who and what their sons aspired to do and be."[24]
Disney experienced his father, Elias, as emotionally distant, financially frugal,
and prone to temper.[25] Lucas remembers feeling frequently angry with what
he perceived as his father's domineering tendencies, which left him with the
overriding goal of being "able to do something on his own, and have it be the
way I envision it. I've always had a basic dislike of authority figures."[26] Indeed,
Lucas's plot use of an Oedipal struggle in *Star Wars* may have been inspired
by his "strained relationship with his father."[27] So too his relationship to his
father might have been a cause of his rejection of the Hollywood studio system
and studio heads.

Lucas followed Disney in another important way when it comes to toys
and playthings: both Disney and Lucas used profits from branded toys to help
support their creative endeavors and to connect to young (and sometimes not
so young) fans beyond the movie theater and between film releases. In 2021,
the Walt Disney Company, now including Lucasfilm (acquired by Disney in
2012), earned $56.2 billion from retail sales of licensed merchandise. Walt
Disney, and his brother Roy, began using merchandise to increase profits
and to help create a fan culture even before the creation of Mickey Mouse.

Disney- and Lucas-branded toys, pins, dolls, games, and action figures help fans to form community connections and, like the sacred mementos brought home from holy sites by ancient pilgrims, allow fans to maintain quasi-religious connections to their beloved childhood memories of the films and the parks.

Where I think Pauline Kael gets Lucas, and by extension Disney, wrong is in her assumption that films inspired by "the crap of . . . childhood," films about nonhumans, or films, rides, or attractions that are also elaborate toys cannot be ideologically, aesthetically, or spiritually interesting. The most living, interesting thing in one of Disney's artistic productions may just be a series of "dead" drawings of a puppet transforming into a living boy that themselves somehow, when viewed at twenty-four frames a second, magically come alive. Or it may be protean animals changing form, talking pigs, a sentient Volkswagen, or animatronic dinosaurs, birds, or pirates. Likewise, the most living thing in one of Lucas's artistic productions may be the robots R2-D2 and C-3PO or the puppet Jedi master, Yoda. Disney and Lucas are recent members of a venerable society of magicians who have animated the inanimate, including Wolfgang von Kempelen, Robert-Houdin, Georges Méliès, Winsor McCay, George Pal, Ray Harryhausen, and Jim Henson. So while Disney and Lucas's common interest in animating, personifying, and transforming the nonliving may not be seen as serious work by Kael, I and others disagree. The great Soviet director and film theorist Sergei Eisenstein praised Disney for possessing just this prerational power to animate everything and anything, to stretch and shrink "beast, fish and birds," to "triumph over the fetters of form."[28] Eisenstein saw in Disney animation something primal: "[Disney] creates somewhere in the realm of the very purest and most primal depths. There, where we all are children of nature. He creates on the conceptual level of man not yet shackled by logic, reason, or experience."[29]

Nostalgia and Futurism, Technophobes and Technophiles

Fans may be fans in the first place because they sense some trait, fear, or desire in their idol that they feel stirring within themselves. We can read Lucas's attraction to Disney in this way. He follows in Disney's footsteps, sharing a paradoxical attraction to technology and nostalgic fixation on the past. Disneyland's layout—with its celebration of the faux-past of idyllic small-town, turn-of-the-century American life (Main Street, USA), the American West (Frontierland), the European fantasy village representing the visitor's own childhood past (Fantasyland), and the colonial wild (Adventureland), and its seemingly contradictory fixation on the wondrous promise of technology to cure all societal ills (Tomorrowland)—may be the best example of Walt Disney's ideological complexity. His obsession with new technologies, such as the multiplane animation camera and audio-animatronic robots, reveals his interest in the future. However, Disney often used innovative film technology to tell stories based on ancient folktales or set in a rosy past; likewise, Disney's earliest uses of animatronics were celebrations of the colonial past in the Enchanted Tiki Room's animatronic bird show and the patriotic recreation of Abraham Lincoln through robotics.

Lucas, like Disney, has a simultaneous penchant for nostalgia and love of technology. He uses cutting-edge technology in *Star Wars* to combine and remake the old-fashioned serial, western, Samurai film, Disney fantasy, and fighter pilot film and move them into space. It is important to note that *Star Wars* takes place "a long time ago in a galaxy far, far away," which situates it directly adjacent to the fairy-tale realm. Lucas includes folktale tropes such as a princess in need of saving, a boy on a quest, and a wise old man who presents the hero a magical swordlike talisman. He also includes classical Hollywood tropes—the villain in black and the hero in white from old westerns, comic-relief robot sidekicks à la Laurel and Hardy, and images and motifs borrowed from *The Wizard of Oz*, *Pinocchio*, and *Casablanca*.

Lucas mixes the cinematic past and future in *Star Wars* by juxtaposing an opening narrative crawl straight out of a *Flash Gordon* serial with a state-of-the-art space battle and initial exposition spoken by a robot, C-3PO, quickly followed by an old-fashioned wipe transition edit. Indeed, the most vibrant of Lucas's *Star Wars* characters are arguably his robot comedy duo, C-3PO and R2-D2, and the Jedi master Yoda, a low-tech puppet brilliantly performed by Muppeteer Frank Oz, the genius behind Miss Piggy, Fozzie Bear, Animal, Bert, and Grover. Lucas, like Disney, often used simple technologies to depict the future, or futuristic technologies to depict the past. Disney's and Lucas's paradoxical fusion of nostalgia and futurism may help us to understand their broad cult(ural) appeal. They understood and shared the modern fan's desire for escape, whether into a lost, idealized past or a promised, idealized future.

While Walt Disney's nostalgia never quite crossed into technophobia, Lucas's films demonstrate a doubleness or even anxiety concerning modernity. Lucas's technophilia is apparent in his establishment of Industrial Light & Magic (his special effects company), in his loving depiction of R2-D2 and C-3PO (arguably *Star Wars'* most appealing "live" characters), and in his love

281

of hot rods, fast bikes, and fighter planes (apparent in the various racing scenes found throughout the series). Lucas, however, also demonstrates technophobia. The emotional climax of *Star Wars*, for example, comes when Luke Skywalker, the film's protagonist, switches off his targeting computer and uses "the Force" to destroy the Death Star. Martin Kevorkian argues that "the *Star Wars* saga, through Darth Vader, recounts the horror of what happens to the white male body when it is technologized: it is reduced to a black voice, enslaved to the ghastly emperor."[30] Kevorkian reads the trilogy as a primer for anticorporate technophobia.[31] Undoubtedly he is largely correct, for Darth Vader, a man turned into a frightening machine, the white-shelled, nameless, faceless Imperial stormtroopers, and the Death Star, the ultimate technological weapon, all point to Lucas's concerns regarding high-tech, totalitarian militarism. Lucas's initial *Star Wars* trilogy is thus more thematically similar to his experimental student films, *Look at Life* and *Electronic Labyrinth: THX 1138 4EB*, than first meets the eye. His emphasis on the Force, a pseudo-Buddhist or New Age concept of radical interconnectedness, and on the Ewoks, a primitive group of savage teddy bear–like creatures who defeat the Empire (and who speak a language that contains some Tibetan words), point to his post-1960s anxieties of American technology and militarism run amok. The good characters in *Star Wars* tend to wear natural fabrics—like hippies on some sort of Eastern-philosophy-based commune—whereas the evil characters are part machine, like Darth Vader and General Grievous, or wear cold, plastic or metal techno-armor. In this way, Lucas seems warier of technology than Disney, whose techno-faith had its ultimate example in his late, unfinished plans for a utopian community, EPCOT, the Experimental Community of Tomorrow, which Disney envisioned working with the captains of American industry to build.

George Lucas: Fan Influences and Fan Service

It could be argued that Lucas was influenced in both his technophobia and technophilia by Disney and such Disney-branded, post-Walt movies as *The Love Bug* (1969), which imagined a sentient, sentimental, lovable, feisty Volkswagen—well before Lucas imagined R2-D2, a sentient, sentimental, lovable, feisty robot. Elements of *Star Wars* seem inspired by Disney parks and films. The Ewoks appear to be Lucas's mash-up of cute Disney stuffed animals and Cambodian guerilla fighters. Many of *Star Wars'* most iconic, kinetic scenes, including the space battles and Endor speeder bike chases, recall not only war films, racing movies, and afternoon adventure serials but also Disneyland rides, more specifically the park's trains, canoes, monorails, and bobsleds. Disneyland's immersive "lands" may have influenced Lucas's creation of various distinct, encompassing worlds in his *Star Wars* films. The Lucas family's annual trip to Disneyland, which opened when Lucas was eleven years old, undoubtedly made a large impression on him: "I loved Disneyland. . . . I wandered around, I'd go on the rides and the bumper cars, the steamboats, the shooting galleries, the jungle rides. I was in heaven."[32]

Like a Disney überfan attempting to take over as the new Disney once the former magician had exited the stage, Lucas often spoke of *Star Wars* as his attempt to make a Disney-style children's film: "I decided I wanted to make a children's movie, to go the Disney route," out of concern that "a whole generation was growing up without fairy tales."[33] Lucas envisioned the audience for *Star Wars* to be "fourteen and maybe even younger than that."[34] He wanted "to do a modern fairy tale, a myth" set "in an exotic, faraway land," with the goal of "getting children to believe there is more to life than garbage and killing."[35] However, he found that our world's exotic, fairy-tale locations had disappeared: "We no longer have the Mysterious East or treasure islands or going on strange adventures."[36] So, instead, Lucas created a new Adventureland in space, that "bigger, mysterious world in space that is more interesting than anything around here."[37]

Lucas's description of *Star Wars* as an Adventureland in outer space evokes Disney's description of Disneyland as found on its welcome plaque: a place to entertain both nostalgic desires and future hopes, where guests can relive "fond memories of the past" and "savor the challenge and promise of the future."[38] *Star Wars'* spatially and temporarily ambiguous opening title card, "A long time ago, in a galaxy far, far away," is a creative mishmash of the uninstalled plaque written for Adventureland, "Here is adventure. Here is romance. Here is mystery," and the Tomorrowland plaque, "Tomorrowland: A vista into a world of wondrous ideas. . . . Tomorrow offers new frontiers in science, adventure, and ideals."[39] In a 1980 interview, Lucas revealed that his then wife Marcia said he "either live[d] in the past or in the future, never in the present."[40] The same might have as easily been said of Disney.

Lucas's double vision, of past and future, parallels Disney's. As I stated previously concerning Disney, "Both nostalgia and utopianism . . . show evidence of a desire for transcendence, as well as an existential anxiety concerning mortality and the present. For the person . . . fixated on the past and the future, it is the present and the ineluctable reality of mortality that is the problem."[41] Disney's and Lucas's interest in bringing the inanimate to life may come out of these sorts of anxieties, although this desire to see the automaton live is shared by many. Pauline Kael's critique of Lucas for his interest in toys ignores this desire—the desire, to use Victoria Nelson's terms, to bring a seemingly lifeless object or modern electrical puppet to life in a way that may seem more "alive" than a human actor.[42]

While Lucas spoke of *Star Wars* as his Disneyesque children's film, he also wanted to be taken seriously as a director. His references to Disney, therefore, weren't always positive. At times he used Disney as a marker of failure, a form of self-flagellation. After a particularly troubling screening of a *Star Wars* rough cut, Lucas kept repeating, "Only kids—I've made a Walt Disney movie, a cross between *Willie Wonka and the Chocolate Factory* and *The Computer Wore Tennis Shoes*. It's gonna do maybe eight, ten million."[43] Lucas clearly felt some anxiety about being associated with Disney. But Lucas's anxiety was not a typical Harold Bloomian fear of sitting in the shadow of a greater artist. In his most optimistic moments, he seemed hopeful that he would surpass his idol. But like a teen fan afraid of judgment, he may have felt uneasy because Walt Disney Productions was then at its commercial, critical nadir and because his director friends thought he should be making important, serious cinema.

Lucas, like Spielberg, was torn between two desires: becoming a successful box office director/producer and being considered important, serious, and even avant-garde. As Peter Biskind explains, "Lucas wanted to be taken seriously as an artist, be paid the kind of attention the critics lavished on Coppola and Scorsese."[44] Lucas even tried to compare his *American Graffiti* to Fellini's *I Vitelloni*.[45] His director friends undoubtedly added to these anxieties: "When Lucas finished a draft [of *Star Wars*], he would show it to his friends. . . . No one was supportive." Lucas recalled them telling him, "George, you should be making more of an artistic statement."[46] This desire to be considered a serious artist rather than a director and producer of blockbusters has remained with Lucas, as can be seen in his recurring talk of once again making "a more abstract kind of movie, without characters and without plots," as he did back in his USC Film School days.[47] While Lucas demonstrated anxieties about being associated with Disney early in his career, he also acknowledged his debt to Disney. Lucas was and is nothing if not true to his aesthetic desires, and he desired to make revisionary versions of the sorts of *Flash Gordon*, Edgar Rice Burroughs pulp adventure serials he had watched as a boy on his favorite childhood television show, *Adventure Theater*.[48] Lucas wanted to make movies that played with his nostalgic memories, not art films like those his friends Scorsese and Coppola were making.

From Rebels to Emperors: Disney, Lucas, and the Will to Control

In the 1980s Lucas began to come to terms with Disney's many influences on his creative output. Their similarities, some already referenced, are worth noting. Disney and Lucas both were raised in small towns. Both viewed themselves as outsiders, disrespected and abused by the mainstream studios (although in his younger days Disney hobnobbed with many Hollywood directors and stars). Both took on entertainment genres that were derided, recreating and reviving them so as to transform them into huge, popular successes—Disney with the animated film and the amusement park, Lucas with the pulp space opera, the western, and the adventure serials he had watched in reruns on television as a young boy. Despite these similarities, it is important to note the ways the two differed. Lucas still aspired to be thought of as an intellectual, avant-garde filmmaker, even into the 1980s and 1990s after he had become a major movie mogul, whereas Disney, who undoubtedly enjoyed the brief period early in his career when many intellectuals and critics praised him as avant-garde, never made gaining their praise into a primary goal. Lucas flirted with countercultural beliefs, whereas Disney's patriotism and conservatism only grew as he aged.

One key similarity between Disney and Lucas was their common interest in owning and controlling their creative work. Both ensured that their names became the sole names widely associated with their products. And both Disney and Lucas attempted to create filmmaking kingdoms where they were the benevolent (and at times not-so-benevolent) dictators. While Lucas may have learned his habit of control from his careful father, Walt Disney might also have been a model for such tendencies.

Lucas and Disney's common interest in maintaining control over their products, their personae, and their filmmaking worlds may be attributable to similar formative experiences of conflict and betrayal. First, both grew up with demanding fathers, which may have encouraged each to struggle for autonomy. And later, both men felt betrayed by Hollywood producers or studios. Disney often spoke of the important and painful lessons he had learned when producer Charles Mintz signed his animators out from under him and took possession of Oswald the Lucky Rabbit, a character Disney mistakenly thought he owned. Disney explained: "You had to be careful whom you trusted[,] that you had to control what you had or it would be taken from you[, and] how duplicitous the business world could be."[49]

Lucas likewise spoke of painful formative experiences. In the authorized documentary *Empire of Dreams: The Story of the "Star Wars" Trilogy* (2004), Lucas speaks of his first two moviemaking experiences with studios as life lessons that taught him to maintain control: "My first film [the studio] didn't understand and they meddled with it after it was all finished. Same thing with my second film. The corporate entity came in and jerry-rigged it—cut five minutes out."[50] Lucas's use of the term "corporate entity" in reference to the movie studio is particularly interesting given its similarity to his filmic depiction of the evil Empire in *Star Wars*—a faceless, bureaucratic, dystopian power lacking all humanity or empathy. In an interview about his experience working with Hollywood studios on *THX 1138* and *American Graffiti*, Lucas's anger and distrust are clear: "They're rather sleazy, unscrupulous people. L.A. is where they make deals, do business in the class corporate way, which is screw everybody. . . . They're not filmmakers. I don't want to have anything to do with them."[51] Lucas's response to his encounter with the "corporate entity" was to run but also to learn similar lessons to those that Disney had learned: "I came up [to San Francisco and Zoetrope Studios] with no intention of actually becoming successful, but I did have a very strong feeling about being able to be in control of my work."[52]

Unlike his cursing and smoking, Disney's will to control made it into the studio's mythologizing of the man. As Michael Barrier states, "Disney was . . . absolute ruler of his studio."[53] Longtime Disney story man Joe Grant, a powerful creative force and head of the studio's influential, deceptively titled Character Model Department from 1937 to 1949, explained, "There was only one authority at the studio: Walt. That was the final signature on everything."[54] Similarly, editor Walter Murch seemed to believe that Lucas's success and his obsession with Lucasfilm wound "him tighter and tighter into a workaholic control-driven person."[55]

Walt's controlling tendencies affected the production and marketing of his films, with his name being the only one he wanted the public to see. Disney started this practice early on, changing the studio's name from the Disney Brothers Studio to the Walt Disney Studio in 1926, thereby making it clear to his brother Roy and the world which Disney brother was in charge.[56] Disney also made sure that his name—not that of Ubbe Iwerks, cocreator and original animator of Mickey Mouse—was the only name associated with the cartoon star. Whether Disney's desire to market only his name and persona came out of his savvy business and marketing sense or was related to his ego, it was a central part of his practice. Disney wanted everyone on staff to call him Walt, but he also wanted them to know that his name was the name that counted; if they wanted their names widely known, they were at the wrong studio. "'There's just one thing we're selling here,' [Disney] told [Disney artist] Ken Anderson . . . 'and that's the name 'Walt Disney.' If you can buy that and be happy to work for it, you're my man. But if you've got any ideas of selling the name 'Ken Anderson,' it's best for you to leave right now."[57] Disney reprimanded artists who dared to sign their drawings, and he refused his thousands of artists adequate screen, press, or verbal credit for their creative contributions. These practices may have added to the discontent that led to the Disney animators' strike of 1941: "The staff now began to voice another raw grievance: Walt never gave them credit."[58] One Disney artist complained of Walt, "He's a genius at using someone else's genius."[59] That complaint reveals the damage done to the studio and the bad feelings created by Disney's unwillingness to share credit and compliment his artists. Some of Disney's most talented artists, from Art Babbitt to Joe Grant to Bill Peet, were driven out, fired, or quit; the strongest personalities were usually the first to go.

Like Disney, Lucas also attempted to turn his name into a powerful, iconic brand. And, like Disney, as the years went on he experienced more and more difficulty working with his longtime collaborators. Delays and cost overruns on *The Empire Strikes Back* broke Lucas's long-standing relationship with his film school friend, producer Gary Kurtz.[60] After *Empire*, Kurtz never worked with Lucas again. The declining quality of *Return of the Jedi* and the *Star Wars* prequels as compared to *Empire* may have resulted from Lucas's difficulties in working with strong writers or artists. Marcia Lucas, Lucas's ex-wife, a film editor, and an important creative colleague early in their careers, also indicated that Lucas was far too sparing with compliments: "He never felt that I had any talent, he never felt I was very smart, he never gave me much credit."[61] Fellow USC film graduate John Milius likewise thought that Lucas became insular and surrounded by yes-men once *Star Wars* hit it big.[62]

Disney adapted European fairy tales, stamping them as Disney creations in both his and the American public's minds. He often spoke of "his" Cinderella, Sleeping Beauty, Alice in Wonderland, Mary Poppins, and Peter Pan, evidently forgetting that these were either folktale figures created by oral storytellers hundreds of years before his birth or characters created by authors such as Charles Dodgson, P. L. Travers, and J. M. Barrie. Disney television writer

Charles Shows describes Disney's idea for an opening to an episode of *Walt Disney's Wonderful World of Color* titled "Disneyland Goes to the World's Fair": "How about opening with a long shot of the New York World's Fair grounds. . . . I get out of the chopper, followed by all of my cartoon characters, like Snow White, Peter Pan, Little Red Riding Hood, the Big Bad Wolf."[63] Shows's comment on Disney's appropriation of these characters is interesting: "It was obvious that Walt considered every cartoon character he had ever filmed as his own personal creation. It didn't seem to bother Walt one bit that many of 'his' characters had been created hundreds of years before he was born!"[64] While Lucas didn't attempt to claim Snow White or Cinderella as his own, he did combine Flash Gordon with other influences, thereby creating Luke Starkiller, eventually renamed Luke Skywalker.

Pauline Kael criticizes Lucas for combining a variety of archetypal figures and marketing the results as his sole creation. She mocks Lucas for claiming that *Willow* was "a pure fantasy film that came out of [his] psyche": "Maybe only a movie mogul can believe that he's the source of the world's treasury of legends and movies. If you took Bible stories and *Peter Pan* and *Robin Hood* and the *Oz* books and the Grimm Brothers' fairy tales and *Gulliver's Travels* and *Lord of the Rings* and *Ran* and *Snow White and the Seven Dwarfs* (and the *Star Wars* trilogy) and put them in a hopper and spun it around until it was a whirring mess of porridge, you'd have the mythical-medieval *Willow*, or something close to it."[65]

While both Disney and Lucas may have had a common will to control, perhaps exacerbated by the inevitable isolation caused by their success, I am not arguing that their desire for control was an entirely negative force. As a result of their very impulse to create, major artists must have, it seems to me, some desire to control their creative product and creative surroundings. In more solitary creative arts, such as writing an essay that few may ever read, this will to control may not cause creative tensions. It is only for creators working in more communal art forms, such as movies or theme parks, that the will to control their artistic production, their persona, or their creative process can become problematic, divisive, or even destructive.

The Creator Has Left the Building: Let the Heretics Speak

Very few artists continue innovating throughout long, creative lives. And so Walt Disney and George Lucas fans are inevitably disappointed. There are no angrier people than hard-core devotees disappointed by their messiahs, whether that disappointment is marked by the messiah's creative failure or literal death. It isn't just Disney or Lucas who has a will to control. The Disney or Lucas fan, whether of the progressive or the originalist variety, desires to judge and control the holy works produced by their chosen corporate religion, especially after the prophet has left the building. After Walt Disney's death in 1966, it admittedly took fans some time to notice that his disciples lacked the old man's creative chops. But, eventually, notice they did, and their frustration became palpable. George Lucas's fans have been even more furious with him, and all while Lucas happily continues to breathe.

When Disney CEO Eisner began to make what many Disney fans felt were terrible creative decisions, or when recently deposed CEO Bob Chapek likewise disappointed, the calls for these failed leaders' expulsion came quick and loud. After the initial prophet grows fat and talentless, dies, or, as with Lucas, sells his company to a rival sect, hard-core fans get more and more frustrated as a bureaucratic caretaker almost inevitably desecrates the holy factory. Given the fans' growing disappointment and unlikely-to-be-satisfied desire for control (I have a recurring dream that I've been chosen to become CEO of the Disney Company, but I always wake up robbed of my rightful role), what exactly is to be done?

How are fan worshippers supposed to go on as their corporate religion moves further and further away from its beloved origins? When the ReligiCorp gains new management, what must happen for the apostles to be retained? Do the holy scriptures need to be reimagined in different forms or mediums, or does that dilute their power? Can a corporate religion retain its power long after the prophet has retired? What impact might the loss of corporate copyright over holy characters or texts have on the health and longevity of these objects of worship? Might that loss empower a wider range of fan reformers, heretics, or iconoclasts to share their own experiences and color? Or is fandom ultimately fraught at the root, given its tendency toward hero worship and thus the erasure of the communal nature of creation?

The only viable solution seems to be the fans creating their own alternative productions, whether their new scriptures be stories, plays, novels, songs, tweets, films, vlogs, comics, TikTok videos, websites, essays, or imaginary theme parks or rides. One can only hope that the most talented of Disney or Lucas fans will rise up and take over their holy factories or, barring that, become their own Disneys or Lucases, but less autocratic ones. Just as Disney replaced Felix the Cat with Mickey Mouse, we welcome fan heretics who will usurp Walt Disney's and George Lucas's holy seats by producing the popular art that we cannot yet quite imagine.

Notes

1. Paraphrase of Henry Jenkins, *Fans, Bloggers, and Gamers: Exploring Participatory Culture*, ed. Henry Jenkins (New York: New York University Press, 2006), 1.

2. This chapter develops elements found in a related essay, Craig Svonkin, "From Disneyland to Modesto: George Lucas and Walt Disney," in *Myth, Media, and Culture in "Star Wars": An Anthology*, ed. Douglas Brode and Leah Deyneka (Plymouth: Scarecrow, 2012), 21–30.

3. Thank you to my kind and supportive fellow Disney scholarship fan club members, Russell McDermott, Cynthia Kuhn, Richard Hishmeh, Stanley Orr, Jeanine Svonkin, Sonia Christensen, David John Boyd, Joseph T. Thomas Jr., and Jeremiah B.C. Axelrod.

4. Megan Ashley Franklin, *Following the Mouse: A Historical and Cultural Analysis of the Disney Fan Community* (master's thesis, California State University, 2012), 12.

5. Gerald Perry, "George Lucas another Disney?," *Modesto Bee*, September 27, 1978, 45.

6. Ibid.

7. Henry Jenkins, *Textual Poachers: Television Fans & Participatory Culture* (Oxfordshire: Routledge, 1992), 16.

8. For example, see Matt Hills, "Excerpts from 'Matt Hills Interviews Henry Jenkins,'" in Jenkins, *Fans, Bloggers, and Gamers*; Hills, *Fan Cultures* (London: Routledge, 2002), 86. On the other hand, a critic who agrees that fandom is akin to religion is David Giles, *Illusions of Immortality: A Psychology of Fame and Celebrity* (London: Macmillan, 2000), 135.

9. Marty Sklar, *Dream It! Do It! My Half-Century Creating Disney's Magic Kingdoms* (Glendale, CA: Disney Editions, 2013), 92.

10. William Proctor and Richard McCulloch, "Introduction: From the House That George Built to the House of Mouse," *Disney's "Star Wars": Forces of Production, Promotion, and Reception*, ed. William Proctor and Richard McCulloch (Iowa City: University of Iowa Press, 2019), 10.

11. G. W. F. Hegel, in *Aesthetics: Lectures on Fine Art*, trans. T. M. Knox (Oxford: Oxford University Press, 1975), 29, writes that "a work of art is only such because, originating from the spirit, it now belongs to the territory of the spirit; it has received the baptism of the spiritual. . . . Therefore the work of art stands higher than any natural product which has not made this journey through the spirit."

12. Walter Benjamin, "[Fragment 74]: Capitalism as Religion," trans. Chad Kautzer, in *Religion as Critique: The Frankfurt School's Critique of Religion*, ed. Eduardo Mendieta (Oxfordshire: Routledge, 2005), 259–62, 259.

13. Some obvious examples of the many Disneyland attractions that transport passengers from threats of death to finales of survival or resurrection include Mr. Toad, ending in hell and then life after the ride; the Storybook Land Canal Boats, with their

entrance into and out of Monstro the Whale; the Haunted Mansion, guiding riders into and out of the afterlife; and Pirates of the Caribbean, where surburbanites take ferry boats down a waterfall into a world of marauding pirates and their inevitable skeletons, only to ascend once more to the land of the living.

14. Kip Redick, "Profane Experience and Sacred Encounter: Journeys to Disney and the Camino de Santiago," *Environment, Space, Place* 5, no. 1 (2013): 46–72, 48.

15. Ibid., 53.

16. Franklin, *Following the Mouse*, 52–53.

17. Redick, "Profane Experience and Sacred Encounter," 53–54.

18. Franklin, *Following the Mouse*, 103.

19. Craig Svonkin, "A Southern California Boyhood in the Simu-Southland Shadows of Walt Disney's Enchanted Tiki Room," in *Disneyland and Culture: Essays on the Parks and Their Influence*, ed. Kathy Merlock Jackson and Mark West (Jefferson, NC: McFarland, 2010), 23–30.

20. Pauline Kael, *Taking It All In* (New York: Holt, Rinehart and Winston, 1984), 212.

21. Ibid.

22. Ibid.

23. Claire Clouzot, "The Morning of the Magician: George Lucas and *Star Wars*," in *George Lucas: Interviews*, ed. Sally Kline (Jackson: University Press of Mississippi, 1999), 59.

24. Joseph Zornado, *Disney and the Dialectic of Desire: Fantasy as Social Practice* (London: Palgrave MacMillan, 2017), 217.

25. Michael Barrier, *The Animated Man: A Life of Walt Disney* (Berkeley: University of California Press, 2007), 14, 20; Neal Gabler, *Walt Disney: The Triumph of the American Imagination* (New York: Knopf, 2006), 24–32.

26. Dale Pollock, *Skywalking: The Life and Films of George Lucas* (New York: Harmony Books, 1983), 36.

27. Ibid. Also see Zornado, *Disney and the Dialectic of Desire*, 216.

28. Sergei Eisenstein, "Screen: Sergei Eisenstein on Walt Disney—Movie masterclass," *Guardian*, December 14, 1992, 4.

29. Ibid.

30. Martin Kevorkian, *Color Monitors: The Black Face of Technology in America* (Ithaca, NY: Cornell University Press, 2006), 123.

31. Ibid.

32. Pollock, *Skywalking*, 21.

33. Stephen Zito, "George Lucas Goes Far Out," in Kline, *George Lucas*, 47, 53.

34. Ibid., 47.

35. Ibid., 53.

36. Ibid., 54.

37. Ibid.

38. Bruce Gordon and David Mumford, *Disneyland: The Nickel Tour* (Santa Clarita, CA: Camphor Tree, 1995), 17.

39. Ibid., 60, 64.

40. Jean Vallely, "*The Empire Strikes Back* and So Does Filmmaker George Lucas with His Sequel to *Star Wars*," in Kline, *George Lucas*, 97.

41. Svonkin, "Southern California Boyhood."

42. Victoria Nelson, *The Secret Life of Puppets* (Cambridge, MA: Harvard University Press, 2001), 249–50.

43. Peter Biskind, *Easy Riders, Raging Bulls: How the Sex-Drugs-and-Rock 'n' Roll Generation Saved Hollywood* (New York: Simon and Schuster, 1998), 334.

44. Biskind, *Easy Riders, Raging Bulls*, 319.

45. Ibid.

46. Ibid., 324.

47. Kerry O'Quinn, "The George Lucas Saga," in Kline, *George Lucas*, 126.

48. Pollock, *Skywalking*, 17, 142.

49. Gabler, *Walt Disney*, 108–10.

50. Edith Becker and Kevin Burns, dirs., *Empire of Dreams: The Story of the "Star Wars" Trilogy*, (Los Angeles: Prometheus Entertainment, 2004), DVD.

51. Vallely, "*Empire Strikes Back*," 93.

52. Ibid.

53. Michael Barrier, *The Animated Man: A Life of Walt Disney* (Berkeley: University of California Press, 2007), 197.

54. Ibid., 197.

55. Biskind, *Easy Riders, Raging Bulls*, 423.

56. Gabler, *Walt Disney*, 98.

57. Ibid., 206.

58. Ibid., 354.

59. Ibid., 355.

60. Biskind, *Easy Riders, Raging Bulls*, 380.

61. Ibid., 422.

62. Ibid., 340.

63. Charles Shows, *Walt: Backstage Adventures with Walt Disney* (La Jolla, CA: Communication Creativity, 1979), 125–26.

64. Ibid., 126.

65. Pauline Kael, *Hooked* (New York: E.P. Dutton, 1989), 473.

20

George Lucas in Museums

Kim Munson

Star Wars: Episode IV—A New Hope came out in 1977, the summer I graduated from high school. My best friend at the time was the assistant manager of the Vogue Theatre in my northern Michigan hometown, so I saw *New Hope* every time it was shown, two screenings a night for two weeks. I was a theater kid, and the film held me in rapt attention every time. I had never seen anything like it. I wanted to adventure with those characters in a galaxy far, far away from Manistee, Michigan. I read everything about the film I could get my hands on, and in 1979, I moved to Los Angeles, where I worked as a scenic artist for about ten years.

While researching this chapter on the exhibitions of Lucasfilm from 1988 to the new Lucas Museum of Narrative Art currently under construction in Los Angeles, I have heard and read similar stories from both fans and exhibition professionals. One fan, an amateur model maker, flew with his brother from Orange County to San Francisco three times to see the first US museum exhibit of *Star Wars* objects at the Yerba Buena Center for the Arts (YBCA) in 1994–1995. A design professional from New York told me of the huge impression *New Hope* made on him as a child and said that the concept art by Ralph McQuarrie influences his creative aesthetic to this day.[1] In general, many fans wrote about the emotional experience of seeing the real thing (objects actually used in the production of the films) on display in museums. They made multiple visits, which often involved traveling or sharing the experience with different sets of friends and family. Sometimes they came in cosplay or wore *Star Wars* T-shirts. They spoke of being in the same room with their favorite objects, like Princess Leia's hooded white robes from *New Hope* or the production model of the *Millennium Falcon* with such love and enthusiasm that it reminded me in some ways of people participating in a religious pilgrimage.

Fans are willing to invest in the success of Lucasfilm (now Disney) by purchasing endless numbers of movie tickets, streaming subscriptions, toys, games, merchandise, and yes, tickets to museum exhibits. Beginning with an exhibit at the Marin County Fair in 1988, which was a surprise sensation, the Lucasfilm Archives developed many exhibits that have drawn large and enthusiastic audiences worldwide, such as *The George Lucas Exhibition* (Japanese tour, 1993–1994), *The Art of "Star Wars"* (YBCA, San Francisco, 1994), *The Magic of Myth* (began at the National Air and Space Museum, Washington, DC, 1997), *The Art of "Star Wars"* (Barbican Centre, London, 2000), *Star Wars: Art of the Starfighter* (Smithsonian Institution, 2001), *Where Science Meets the Imagination* (tour began at the Boston Science Museum, 2006), *"Star Wars": The Exhibition* (Cité des Sciences, Paris, 2006), *"Star Wars: Identities"* (tour began at the Montreal Science Centre, 2012), *Rebel, Jedi, Princess, Queen: "Star Wars" and the Power of Costume* (tour began at the Museum of Pop Culture, Seattle, 2015), *An Art Odyssey* (Le Café Pixel, France, 2015), and *"Star Wars": Visions* (tour began at the Mori Arts Center, Tokyo, 2015).

While several early exhibits included material from a wide range of Lucasfilm/Industrial Light & Magic (ILM) projects (such as *Raiders of the Lost Ark, Star Trek IV: The Voyage Home,* and *Willow*), exhibitions exclusively focused on the *Star Wars* universe have been the most popular by far. Scholars Beatriz Bartolomé Herrera and Philipp Dominik Keidl, in an excellent essay about how *Star Wars*–themed exhibitions work as a transmedia storyworld vehicle (more on this later), point out that these exhibits bring large numbers of visitors into many different institutions. "For instance," they note, "throughout its fifteen-month run from October 1997 to January 1999, *The Magic of Myth* drew more than 900,000 visitors to the Smithsonian's National Air and Space Museum (NASM), becoming one of the most popular shows in the institution's history."[2] Herrera and Keidl continue, explaining that the benefits of presenting these exhibits have proved to outweigh the high cost of rental and production:

> For example, renting the Smithsonian's third *Star Wars* traveling exhibition *Rebel, Jedi, Princess, Queen: Star Wars and the Power of Costume* for a period of 22 weeks cost $US 400,000. However, this was still a profitable investment given the large crowds and media attention these shows attract. In March 2014—two weeks before its final run at the Tech Museum of Innovation (San José, California) and 20 venues and nine years into the exhibition's tour—3,000,000 people had visited *Where Science Meets the Imagination.* Moreover,

Princess Leia's original costume on display with the *Star Wars and the Power of Costume* traveling exhibit at the Detroit Institute of Arts in 2018. (courtesy Michael Barera/https://creativecommons.org/licenses/by-sa/4.0/deed.en)

an evaluation conducted for the Boston Museum of Science (MOS), which originally produced *Where Science Meets the Imagination*, indicated that interest in *Star Wars* exhibitions also impacted general admissions, and encouraged ticket sales to infrequent visitors at a higher rate than other exhibitions in the museum.[3]

Restoration and Rediscovery: Early Exhibits 1988–1995

Throughout the making of the first *Star Wars* trilogy, no one had any idea that the stuff of moviemaking—the models, creatures, props, costumes, matte paintings, and artwork—could be valuable or become the focus of popular museum exhibits worldwide. Then the urgent problem was storage. Objects were squirreled away in a giant warehouse in San Rafael, California, in hidden corners at ILM, and in cubby holes at Elstree Studios in England. Many of the objects were beginning to deteriorate because of rough handling on set and less than optimal storage conditions.

According to Deborah Fine, the first Director of Lucasfilm's archives, this all changed one day in 1983 when George Lucas arrived at ILM to pose for publicity photos for *Return of the Jedi*. "Someone had the idea to take a publicity shot of George Lucas amid a sea of models and miniatures used to make the trilogy," Fine recalls. "ILM then added a starfield with the ominous Death Star under construction hovering overhead. It wasn't until that day on the gigantic ILM soundstage that we had seen all these pieces in one place. We were stunned by the volume of it. George turned to me and said 'You know, we need to save all this stuff. We need to start an archive. You're in charge of it.'"[4]

With the change in focus from storage to preservation came a new appreciation for the significance of the artifacts. As the archive's staff worked at cataloging and photographing the collection (there were more than ten thousand pieces of artwork alone), another project came along that would change everything. *The Magic of Lucasfilm* was an exhibit displayed over the Fourth of July weekend at the 1988 Marin County Fair in the Marin Veterans Memorial Auditorium, which had fifteen thousand square feet of floor space. The *San Francisco Chronicle*'s longtime culture reporter John Stanley wrote a detailed account of the space organized into twelve themed areas, starting at the "hall of hits" in gallery one, where visitors were greeted by posters and artwork from Lucasfilm/ILM's many hit films. The second gallery was devoted to *Raiders of the Lost Ark*, including a model of the Pan Am clipper ship and the Ark of the Covenant.[5]

The heart of the exhibit were galleries three through six, which focused exclusively on *Star Wars*, including Darth Vader's costume and Imperial shuttle craft, the Death Star under construction, Luke's full-scale Landspeeder, Jabba the Hutt's barge, and the Jawa Sandcrawler, as well as many character busts and costumes. *The Empire Strikes Back* and the snow planet Hoth got their own room, featuring an Imperial AT-AT, a Rebel snowspeeder, an Imperial scout droid, the Tauntaun creature, Yoda, and Han Solo frozen in carbonite. The next room focused on models, such as the *Millenium Falcon*, the Rebel blockade runner, and a full-scale speeder bike.

Area seven was dedicated to *Tucker*, including a silver Tucker car, one of only fifty that were made. The focus shifted to *Star Trek IV: The Voyage Home* in gallery eight, which included a model of a Klingon Bird of Prey and a full-scale, radio-controlled replica of a humpback whale. Room nine contained props and costumes from *Willow*. Gallery ten was dominated by a full-size mine car from *Indiana Jones and the Temple of Doom*, including a short film explaining how the mine car chase scene was shot with models, miniature sets, and stop-motion animation. The rest of the space was filled out with objects from other ILM projects, like the DeLorean time machine from *Back to the Future* and the bicycle from *E.T.* Visitors could get their picture taken with R2-D2 and C-3PO and view a how-to film from ILM about the creation of special effects.

Two Marin County teenagers donned stormtrooper armor and walked around interacting with fairgoers who waited in line up to two and a half hours in the ninety-two-degree heat to get in. It was the largest crowd ever in the history of the fair, drawing over ten thousand people a day.[6] According to Peter Stack and Torri Minton, *San Francisco Chronicle* reporters who came out to interview people in the crowd, visitors came from all over California and as far away as Berlin, Chile, and Taiwan.[7] Stack recounts a conversation with exhibit visitors James Cornwell, eighteen, and Gordon Windcott, also eighteen, who drove seventy minutes from Sunnyvale to line up at 6:45 a.m. (the gates opened at 11:00 a.m.). "It's a show of great stuff," Cornwell said. "I came to check out the *Star Wars* stuff, because that was the movie of my generation. I was seven years old when I saw it the first time, now I'm 18, and I lost count after seeing *Star Wars* for the 150th time. For me, if there's magic here, it's the old *Star Wars* thing." Jim Farley, the Marin Fair operations manager, marveled at the crowd and said, "It's exciting, it's just incredible. It's his latest hit."[8]

Lucasfilm returned to the fair in 1989, with a film presentation and smaller-scale exhibit because many of the props and models either were being used in production or were on display in Japan and France. Lucasfilm traveled to Japan for their next significant show, *The George Lucas Exhibition*, which toured eight to ten cities from July 1993 to September 1994. Organized by Shinji Hata for Hata International, this show was another large overview of the best of Lucasfilm/ILM, with many of the same objects shown at the Marin Fair. Before sending all the objects on their way overseas, a large-scale restoration effort took place, led by archivist and model and creature maker Don Bies with a team of six model and creature makers.

In a detailed interview with Pamela E. Roller for the *Lucasfilm Fan Club Magazine*, Bies described the daunting task at hand. Before they were moved into the state-of-the-art archives building at Skywalker Ranch in 1991, careless storage contributed to the decay of many objects, which Bies said were stored in a "warehouse with no insulation, no heat, no air conditioning."[9] Most of the items were conceived and constructed with temporary use in mind, and they were used in extreme conditions on set in Tunisia and Hawaii. Restoring the starship models, such as the eight-foot Imperial Star Destroyer, to their original condition required a great deal of intricate work. Many small parts were lost, and some of the models had been modified and reused as background ships in other films. The puppets also needed a lot of restoration because the latex used in their heads and hands had decayed badly. The head of Yoda, for example, was recast from the original mold for the exhibit.

When asked why this huge exhibit was going to Japan instead of an American tour, Bies answered: "One reason is that the upcoming exhibit in Japan exemplifies the universal appeal of Lucas' work. His films are very popular in Japan, and he has become a veritable folk hero there. . . . However, the main reason for the exhibit going to Japan is funding." He explained that Lucasfilm had been open to the idea of other museum exhibitions but that the shows were expensive to organize and insure. This is where Hata International entered the picture, with a wish list of some six hundred items, plus artwork and storyboards, and funding to get all of it over to Japan. "The logistics involved—the restoring and the packing—is all very expensive."[10]

As evidence of Lucas's folk-hero status, the catalog for the Japanese tour used for its cover photo the 1983 shot mentioned earlier of Lucas surrounded by a sea of models with the Death Star hanging ominously in the background. In 1994, a translation of the Japanese catalog, *From "Star Wars" to "Indiana*

Jones": The Best of the Lucasfilm Archives, was published, with photos and detailed text about all the newly restored items that went on tour, their use, and their significance.[11]

Roller summarizes the challenges faced by the archives team in planning and assembling *The George Lucas Exhibition* for Hata and then goes on to describe the possible benefits: "Not only will a new culture of people be able to enjoy the magic and excitement that Lucasfilm has offered a generation of American audiences, but the exhibit has also renewed Lucasfilm's commitment to restoration and preservation, so its film history can be experienced by generations to come. Who knows, the Japan tour may even open the door for Lucas exhibits elsewhere."[12] She did not wait very long; almost as soon as the objects returned from Japan, work began on the first formal US museum exhibit, *The Art of Star Wars* (December 27, 1994–February 12, 1995), organized by Renny Pritikin, chief curator of the newly opened YBCA in San Francisco's downtown museum district.

In a reminiscence on the Northern California Arts blog *SquareCylinder,* Pritikin recalls the genesis of the *Star Wars* show. He wanted to curate an exhibit made up of an iconic film or TV set, like the cantina from *Star Wars,* the bridge set from *Star Trek,* or *Pee Wee's Playhouse.* The playhouse and the *Star Trek* set were unavailable, and he was about to give up when his boss happened to run into Lucas at a charity dinner, where he pitched the idea of the exhibit to him. "He graciously and readily agreed," Pritikin recalls. "It turned out that a Lucas exhibition had just returned from Japan and was set go. However, I actually had to start from scratch because the Japanese show was just a fan show, and we wanted something more ambitious."[13] In preparation, Pritikin and his team visited the archives and studied the history of military uniforms and theories of multiculturalism.

"On opening day, we had a line around the block, with many people in costume," Pritikin recalls.

SFMOMA was opening its new building at the same time across the street [the landmark Mario Botta–designed building on Third Street], and we had deliberately chosen to juxtapose the two forms of contemporary exhibition-making. . . . The difference between the art world and the world of Hollywood film was a revelation I have never forgotten; we had 120,000 visitors in six weeks, in contrast with our annual attendance of 50,000. From then on, I

always included a thread of popular culture in our exhibitions,
for I realized that the demographics of the audience was the most
diverse of any show we had mounted before.

Visitors to the exhibit were flanked by the Yoda puppet and the costume of
Darth Vader at the entry, which opened into a large room of starship models
and then a room of smaller props and weapons. The largest gallery featured
three tiers of costumes against a large window, followed by a room of busts,
puppets, and maquettes. Concept art was featured on the mezzanine, looking
out over the crowd and a cluster of hanging models. The huge model of the
Death Star under construction was showcased just off the lobby. Arriving at a
time considered by fans as the Dark Ages (when the first trilogy was over and
it looked as if there would be no new films or toys), the show had an emotional
impact on fans. Many of them documented their experiences seeing this show
in writing or on video. Here are short samples from three of them.

Communications consultant Jayne Cravers discusses seeing *The Art of
Star Wars* with a friend as a present to herself on her twenty-ninth birthday.
Characterizing the visit as a "religious experience," she describes what she
saw that day:

> A full-sized Yoda puppet stood by the entrance, in a glass case,
> but the light showing it didn't stay on but for a few seconds. It was
> the same for the Darth Vader costume. The sign said something
> about doing that because you only got a glimpse of them in the
> movies, never a long look, and they wanted a similar experience
> in the exhibit—indeed, viewing Vader's costume up close made
> it look cheaply made, definitely not intended for long closeups
> on screen. . . . But I cried when I came into the hall with all the
> costumes. I just burst into tears immediately and had to sit down
> on the couches in the middle of the room and just stare at them. . . .
> It was glorious. It was the best birthday of my life up to that point,
> and still in the top three.[14]

Summerlea Kashar, the current executive director of San Francisco's Cartoon
Art Museum, was working as an intern at the arts nonprofit ArtSpan in 1995.
"The *Star Wars* exhibit was stunning," she told me in an email interview. "As you
walked into the big main gallery, at the far wall was a large three-tiered display
of the costumes from *Star Wars*. The size and the volume were impressive, and

really showed the breadth of artistic development. One of the things that I wasn't aware of was the influence of Japanese samurai and soldier designs on the costuming. There were text panels that discussed this and showed examples of the Japanese designs, which really brought it home."[15]

The anonymous owner of the YouTube channel TheProjectWorkBench, who identifies himself as a model enthusiast, flew three times from Orange County with his brother to see the show. During their last trip, they visited the exhibit on two days and surreptitiously recorded a very detailed video tour. The video also included the text of the entry wall panel, which contains many concepts that would be repeated in future *Star Wars* exhibits, such as the tensions between high art and low art.[16] Such arguments have been bone of contention in the arts world since the modernist movement following World War II, when the arts establishment, including museums, generally shunned all representational or commercially made art in favor of abstract art. Popular art forms like original comic art, illustration, and other types of commercial arts began a return to the museums after the pop art movement of the 1960s. Here, Pritikin recognizes that at the end of the millennium the old high and low argument has run its course and that we can learn a lot about ourselves and our culture by studying other types of popular media.

The wall text contains a series of questions that show the curator's thought process: "We used the same analytical tools that we employ in similar retrospective projects. We explore those questions that may further explain the importance of these objects. What were the intentions of the creators and what were their assumptions about reality? How were these objects originally conceived and how do we see them today? What did we bring to our understanding of them and how are our own personal biases impacted by our social statuses and the larger society's conditions?"[17]

Some of these questions became the central thesis of future exhibitions. All Lucasfilm exhibitions, from the Marin County Fair to newer shows like *Rebel, Princess, Jedi, Queen: "Star Wars" and the Power of Costume* (begun in 2015), reinforce the role of Lucas as the creative visionary that has shaped the official *Star Wars* universe. *"Star Wars": Identities* (begun in 2012) invites visitors to consider the diverse cultures that coexist in the *Star Wars* universe and to create their own character within it. Pritikin's wall text contains a discussion of the trilogy's plot and sources, including Buddhist philosophy and the mystical writings of Carlos Castenda.

The last section of the wall panel recognizes the effect of 1990s-era advances in filmmaking technology and the fact that models like the ones on view are already historical artifacts: "In its time, *Star Wars* was at the forefront of technical innovation. It was one of the first films to exploit the possibilities of computer-generated filmmaking. Ironically, the items on display are themselves victims of technological advance, the next trilogy will not use such models to any significant extent, rather the new films will be created entirely on computers. High technology has rendered the objects in *The Art of Star Wars* relics of film's past, anachronisms from the 70s and thus even more historically significant."[18]

One does not have to look further than *"Star Wars": The Rise of Skywalker* (2019) or streaming series like *The Mandalorian* to see this technical progress in action. Technology in film production, distribution, and social media outreach have enabled the growth of the sprawling *Star Wars* universe from a risky low-budget film in 1977 into one of the most recognized transmedia storyworlds worldwide.

The Saga Continues: Exhibitions in a Transmedia Universe

In the opening pages of *"Star Wars" and the History of Transmedia Storytelling*, media scholar Henry Jenkins tells Dan Hassler-Forest (himself a well-known *Star Wars* fan and academic) about his foundational *Star Wars* experience. When *A New Hope* came out in 1977, he saw the first trailer for it while he was an undergrad at Georgia State University, and he was unimpressed, thinking it looked "laughably bad." "When I saw the film, I fell hard," Jenkins explained. "It totally excited my imagination. It had such a strong sense of fun and adventure; its reliance on the Hero's Journey would have been particularly resonant with me at the time since I was undergoing a period of undergraduate infatuation with the writings of Joseph Campbell."[19] He met his wife around that time, when he cornered her before a class and tried to convince her of the social significance of *Star Wars*. Soon after, they married, and Jenkins has continued on to study the fandoms of *Star Wars*, *Star Trek*, *Buffy the Vampire Slayer*, and other popular media.

The sprawling transmedia story of the *Star Wars* universe has inspired a connected galaxy of fan-created content, such as fan fiction and artwork, cosplay, novels, games, and videos. As a regular at San Diego Comic-Con, I can personally attest to the domination of *Star Wars* on the exhibit floor and the ongoing popularity of *Star Wars* in cosplay and in merchandise purchased. Lucasfilm both encourages this fan interaction and cautiously defends its intellectual properties, maintaining control of the official narrative and all public uses of their materials. Jenkins, now a professor at University of Southern California, addresses these conflicting desires in a discussion of fandom and cultural resistance (how fan communities find ways to challenge and critique commercial culture), where he explains, "There can be no easy separation between fans and producers; more and more, media producers embrace our participation as a means of increasing engagement in a highly competitive media system. Yet they also seek to shape and direct our participation into what they see as serving their own interests."[20]

Exhibits shown within the validating, educational authority of the museum space are the ideal way to reinforce Lucasfilm's official version of the transmedia *Star Wars* story and forge a personal connection with their legion of fans. Exhibition labels, audio tours, videos, catalogs, and related materials reaffirm Lucas as the creative visionary and ultimate authority on the *Star Wars* narrative, as well as establishing what is or is not part of the official canon. Nowhere is this idea expressed as strongly as in the 1997 Smithsonian touring exhibit *The Magic of Myth*, which is very much about the importance of storytelling through objects (touring the US and Australia through 2003). Unlike the YBCA show, which purposely displayed items without much commentary or references to the actors who played the characters, *The Magic of Myth* explicitly tied the props, costumes, paintings, and models of *Star Wars* to the myths, legends, and historical research that inspired the films. To this end, *The Magic of Myth* made much more use of stills from the films, film clips, and video interviews than the YBCA show.[21] This emphasis on storytelling and connection is the common theme between *Star Wars: Identities* (opened at the Montreal Science Centre, 2012), *Rebel, Princess, Jedi, Queen: "Star Wars" and the Power of Costume* (opened at the Museum of Popular Culture, Seattle, 2015), and the new Lucas Museum of Narrative Art in Los Angeles, set to open in 2025, which will feature not only *Star Wars* materials but Lucas's extensive art collection from Renaissance panels and Norman Rockwell paintings to comic art, children's book illustrations, and Mexican murals.

Audience connection was the real point of *"Star Wars": Identities*. Aside from showing a wide range of costumes, props, and models, *Identities* was an immersive experience. Visitors received a wristband at the exhibit entry that enabled them to select traits they admired in characters displayed throughout the galleries and create their own *Star Wars* avatar using those traits at the end. They were encouraged to share these avatars on social media, but only after acknowledging Lucasfilm's ownership of all *Star Wars* materials (including their avatar). After its launch in Canada, *Identities* traveled to Europe, to Australia, and throughout Asia, concluding at Singapore's ArtScience Museum, Marina Bay Sands (January 30–July 25, 2021). In an interview with Ms. Sam David of *Pelago*, archives director and curator Laela French explained the innovative audience interaction developed for *Identities*:

> We knew we wanted that interactive element to be strong in order to engage audiences. We had lots of discussions with all sorts of creative folks. We even had a scientific committee of 12, 13 people from different universities to help us focus on the psychology of human identity. All these experts were at the table, and my team came in from a branding perspective, trying to see how to fit the *Star Wars* archive in there. One day during a brainstorming session, someone shared how they were inspired by an article that talked about how people playing video games get so into the process of creating their alter ego. My team went, "Hmm . . . what if these people come to the exhibition to learn about human identity and they also make their own *Star Wars* identity? It's immersive. It's learning without learning." That's the spark we were looking for and that's what we went with.[22]

At a time when museums are reinventing themselves to be more responsive and relevant to their constantly plugged-in visitors and stimulate more interaction, Lucasfilm seems to have hit the sweet spot here. With the science of human identity as a theme, they were able to both enhance the audience's connection with their characters and involve them in a gamelike identity quest.

While *Identities* used this quest as part of the storytelling experience, the next major exhibit, *Rebel, Princess, Jedi, Queen: "Star Wars" and the Power of Costume* (which toured through the Smithsonian), emphasized character and storytelling through costume.[23] The costumes in the original trilogy, as described by visitors to the YBCA *Star Wars* show, may have been visually effective but cheaply made, but by the time of the prequel trilogy, money was not an obstacle, and the costumes were rich in design, fabric, and detail. Costumes in the original trilogy were mainly in stark black and white to show the conflict between the Empire and the Rebellion. In the prequel trilogy, the costumes reflected the rich diversity of the Republic's cultures. The title suggests an emphasis on the strong female heroines of the *Star Wars* universe, and the rich gowns worn by the queen and the robes of the senator took a central place in the exhibit. The exhibit included a special gallery containing design sketches and information about the historical influences that inspired the costumes. The costumes from both trilogies were impeccably arranged on thematic groupings on platforms and lit to their best advantage.

The exhibition made extensive use of film stills, clips, and, importantly, specially made documentary videos to tie the costumes into the *Star Wars* storyworld, show them in movement as they were meant to be seen, and explain the creative process from design to creation and on-set use. Interviews with Lucas, Trisha Biggar (costume designer), and cast members emphasized how the costumes helped the cast shape their characters and reinforced the role of Lucas as the genius creator of the *Star Wars* universe.

The Lucas Museum of Narrative Art: If You Build It, Will They Come?

In the *Perlago* interview, French talks about studying art history in college and seeing the *Star Wars* collection in art historical terms. "I like art history. It's where you study culture through the art of the people. And this is why I enjoy doing what I do." She ties this art historical thread to Lucas's style of storytelling, saying:

> OK, so, George Lucas is a storyteller. He tells stories through film. And to me, the *Star Wars* archives are really intriguing because people don't initially look at it as art. But I see it with art history in mind, and the collection we have tells a story about a time and a place in cinema history. There's also a big piece of cultural history here: *Star Wars* was born out of 1970s-America, and there George Lucas was absorbing various influences, from the films of Akira Kurosawa, comic books, as well as the Vietnam war. These things informed him, and he turned around and created *Star Wars*. *Star Wars* is woven into the cultural fabric of the world. Everyone has heard of it. Everyone can visually recognize the iconography of Darth Vader or a Stormtrooper. It's part of a language we all can speak, no matter where you are from, no matter if you're a *Star Wars* nerd or if you're not even a fan.[24]

The next major curatorial challenge French will face will be folding the *Star Wars* collection and its massive storyworld into the larger art historical framework that will be on display at the soon-to-open Lucas Museum of Narrative Arts, scheduled to open in Los Angeles in 2025. The museum's journey to LA's Exposition Park was long and arduous, with a string of proposals, rejections, and lawsuits in both San Francisco and Chicago before they finally broke ground on March 18, 2018, in Los Angeles right next to the University of Southern California, Lucas's alma mater.[25] The collection shown at the spaceship-like building designed by Ma Yansong of MAD Architects will emphasize storytelling through images, with a growing collection of art that represents historical eras from Greco-Roman to the present, including paintings, sculptures, murals, photography, comic art, book and magazine illustrations, the arts of filmmaking, and a large filmmaking archive.

As of this writing, the museum has been reluctant to share many details about their plans leading up to their grand opening in 2025. However, they made an exception for the 2019 San Diego Comic-Con, where three of the curators, Anastasia James, Ryan Linkof, and Erin Curtis, gave attendees a general overview of the museum's architecture and collection.[26] While it may be unusual to see a fine art museum making a presentation at Comic-Con, it was the best place to reach out to people who understand what narrative art is and, most importantly, to committed *Star Wars* fans. I was present that morning and saw many audience members in *Star Wars* cosplay responding enthusiastically to the idea of a permanent display of the *Star Wars* collection. Will *Star Wars* fans make a pilgrimage to LA's Exposition Park to celebrate the *Star Wars* universe they love? Only time will tell.

Notes

1. The model maker is the anonymous host of TheProjectWorkbench YouTube channel, who will be discussed later. The design professional is Jonathan Alger of C & G Partners, New York, who designed the exhibition *Star Wars: Power of Costume* for Running Subway Productions at Discovery Times Square. See S & G Partners for exhibition photos, n.d., accessed May 13, 2022, https://www.cgpartnersllc.com/projects/star-wars-and-power-costume/?set=exhibits-environments.

2. Beatriz Bartolomé Herrera and Philipp Dominik Keidl, "How *Star Wars* Became Museological: Transmedia Storytelling in the Exhibition Space," in *"Star Wars" and the History of Transmedia Storytelling*, ed. Sean Guynes and Dan Hassler-Forest (Amsterdam: Amsterdam University Press, 2017), 155–68.

3. Ibid., 156.

4. Mark Cotta Vaz and Shinji Hata, *From "Star Wars" to "Indiana Jones": The Best of the Lucasfilm Archives* (San Francisco: Chronicle Books, 1994).

5. John Stanley, "Lucas Shares His Fantasy Treasures: Major Exhibit of Memorabilia from *Star Wars* to *Willow* at Fair," *San Francisco Chronicle*, June 28, 1988, 21–22,

Marin County Library, Anne T. Kent California Room, Moving Pictures: Lucasfilm Clippings 1985–1989 folder, San Rafael, California (hereafter LC 85–89 folder).

6. Brad Breithaupt, "Lucasfilm Will Return to County Fair with New Exhibit," *Marin Independent Journal*, March 11, 1989, LC 85–89 folder.

7. Torri Minton, "Thousands Mob Marin Fair's Lucas Exhibit," *San Francisco Chronicle*, July 21, 1988, A3; Peter Stack, "The Toys in George Lucas' Attic," *San Francisco Chronicle*, July 1, 1988, E1.

8. Minton. "Thousands Mob Marin Fair's Lucas Exhibit."

9. Pamela E. Roller, "Welcome to the George Lucas Exhibit," *Lucasfilm Fan Club Magazine*, Summer 1993, 6, 27–29.

10. Ibid.

11. Although it is not explicitly stated in the text of Vaz and Hata's *Archives* book, in a February 3, 2022, email, Laela French, the current director of the Lucasfilm Archives, confirmed that it is a translation of the Japanese catalog.

12. Roller, "Welcome to the George Lucas Exhibit."

13. Renny Pritikin, "Renny Pritikin Remembers: Part 4," *SquareCylinder* (blog), May 3, 2020, https://www.squarecylinder.com/2020/05/renny-pritikin-remembers-part-4/.

14. Jane Cravers, "A Visitor's Account of *The Art of Star Wars*, an Exhibit at the Center for the Arts in Yerba Buena Gardens in San Francisco, California, December 27, 1994–March 12, 1995," Coyote Communications, accessed May 13, 2022, https://www.coyotecommunications.com/starwars/index.html.

15. Summerlea Kashar, "*Star Wars*," email interview with author, February 2, 2020.

16. TheProjectWorkBench, "The Art of Star Wars: Exhibit at Yerba Buena Gardens," YouTube, December 6, 2016, https://youtu.be/U8BueLgLmJk.

17. Ibid.

18. Ibid.

19. Henry Jenkins and Dan Hassler-Forest, "I Have a Bad Feeling about This: A Conversation about Star Wars and the History of Transmedia," in Guynes and Hassler-Forest, *"Star Wars" and the History of Transmedia Storytelling*, 15–31.

20. Henry Jenkins, Mizuko Ito, and danah boyd, *Participatory Culture in a Networked Era* (Malden, MA: Polity, 2016).

21. Mary Henderson, *"Star Wars": The Magic of Myth* (New York: Bantam Books, 1997). See also *Magic of Myth* online exhibit, 1999, accessed May 13, 2022, https://airandspace.si.edu/exhibitions/star-wars/online/guide.htm.

22. Sam David, "What Force Shapes You? A *Star Wars* Special with Laela French," *Pelago Magazine*, May 4, 2021.

23. *Rebel, Princess, Jedi, Queen: Star Wars and the Power of Costume*, Lucasfilm and Smithsonian Institution Traveling Exhibit Service, 2017, http://powerofcostume.si.edu /abouttheExhibition.html.

24. David, "What Force Shapes You?"

25. The museum was first proposed as a new Tudor-style building on the edge of San Francisco's Presidio district facing the newly restored Crissy Field waterfront park. The Presidio of San Francisco is a former military base on the San Francisco Bay near the Golden Gate Bridge. Although it is a strictly regulated historical site, Lucas had

success in building a new campus for ILM nearby, on the site of the former Letterman Military Hospital. There were community complaints about both the location and the architecture. After four years of unsuccessful negotiation with the Presidio Trust, Lucas announced that the project would move to a location on the edge of Lake Michigan near Soldier Field in downtown Chicago. This effort was met with a lawsuit by a group called Friends of the Parks. In 2015, District Judge John Darrah ruled that the land intended for the museum was held in public trust, blocking construction. Shortly after giving up on the Chicago location, the museum project was welcomed in Los Angeles by 2017. The Lucas Museum of Narrative Art's Wikipedia page has a surprisingly thorough section of links to all aspects of this story. The *Chicago Tribune* also posted a date-by-date summary of events. See Kyle Bentle, Jonathon Berlin, and Jemal R. Brinson, "The Saga of the Lucas Museum," *Chicago Tribune*, June 15, 2016, https://www .chicagotribune.com/news/breaking/ct-lucas-museum-timeline-20160610-htmlstory .html.

26. The Comic-Con presentation was on Thursday morning, July 18, 2019. At the time of this preview, the museum's opening may have been in sight, but it subsequently shifted to 2023 because of delays due to the COVID-19 pandemic. For coverage of the presentation, see Todd Martens, "Lucas Museum of Narrative Art Gives the Comic-Con Crowd a Sneak Peek," *Los Angeles Times*, July 18, 2019, https://www.latimes .com/entertainment-arts/story/2019-07-18/lucas-museum-narrative-art-comic-con.

Postscript

Richard Ravalli

With the publication of Peter Krämer's long-awaited book on *American Graffiti* in 2023, George Lucas may finally be garnering the type of academic focus that his filmmaking career deserves. He is certainly beloved by numerous fans, but scholars have generally remained distant. Granting the many obstacles facing the Lucas researcher, the fact that it took so long for the first monograph dedicated to a creation other than *Star Wars* to appear is still surprising. As the contributors to this volume have successfully demonstrated, there are numerous opportunities to examine the interrelated yet distinct contributions that Lucas has made to the history of American cinema.

Various questions will guide future analyses and build upon the work of this collection. For example, can fresh approaches to biographical material offer insight into Lucas's life and work before the conclusion of the original *Star Wars* trilogy? The transcription and publication of Dale Pollock's interview tapes may hold the key here, but as of this writing they are unavailable. Lucas's early film career has been receiving some attention as of late, yet a book-length study of *THX 1138* seems not only possible but long overdue. What effect has Disney ownership had on the telling of *Star Wars* and Lucasfilm history more broadly? Julie Turnock's experiences in recent years as a nonauthorized researcher of Industrial Light & Magic suggest the usefulness of a comparative analysis of Lucas's engagement with academic and critical communities over time versus Disney's.

What precisely was the financial impact of the Lucas divorce on his company during the 1980s, and how might Lucasfilm have evolved differently had it not occurred? Counterfactual consideration might also be given to the business history of Skywalker Ranch and the ways in which pushback from Marin County interests stymied developments of particular industrial infrastructures in Northern California. How Lucasfilm's various divisions were affected by leadership changes and corporate reorganizations into the 1990s should also be explored in more detail. Interviews of key officials in the history of computer animation could help elucidate Lucas's creative influence in Pixar's early film work.

As Kathy Merlock Jackson demonstrates in this volume, Lucas's work as a producer prior to his return to the *Star Wars* franchise and its relevance to high-concept moviemaking offers rich ground for analysis. His overtly negative reputation among critics and academics notwithstanding, Lucas went from being hailed as an "American Master" at the end of the twentieth century to having "raped the childhoods" of his fans by the millennium. This evolving and complex popular reception during the period, in conjunction with his eventual though partial scholarly rehabilitation, needs closer scrutiny.

Finally, historians should not neglect Lucas's own role in the reshaping of his legacy over the course of his career. Despite artistic and personal attempts to counter long-standing criticisms of him as a Reagan-era retrograde and purveyor of lowbrow entertainment, elite political interests of two major American cities rejected his philanthropic donation of an art museum in the early twenty-first century. The tragic biographical chords struck by this late-life moment for the boy from Modesto and the future reimaginings of his historical and cultural contributions are stories that have yet to be told.

Acknowledgments

Thanks to the following individuals for their support of and assistance with this project: Tyler Alexander, Annalie Bywaters, Jordan Lieser, Audrey Lokteff, Ashley Runyon, Haley Seaman, Eva Wohlwend, and Ryan Wong.

Contributors

Stephen Andriano-Moore is assistant professor of media industries studies at Xi'an Jiaotong–Liverpool University.

Joseph J. Darowski teaches English at Brigham Young University.

Shanti Fader-Whitesides is the author of two previous essays on *Star Wars* and is senior administrative assistant at Yale University.

Valerie Estelle Frankel is the author of numerous books on popular culture and is an instructor at San Jose City College.

Stefan Hall is associate professor of game design at High Point University.

Christopher Holliday teaches film studies and liberal arts at King's College London, specializing in Hollywood cinema, animation history, and contemporary digital media.

Kenneth Hough is lecturer in history at University of California, Santa Barbara, and a former California State Parks Historic Guide at Hearst Castle.

Andrew Howe is professor of history at La Sierra University and the author of numerous chapters in film and cultural studies anthologies.

Kathy Merlock Jackson is professor of communication at Virginia Wesleyan University and the current president of the Popular Culture Association.

Michael Kaminski is independent scholar and author of *The Secret History of "Star Wars."*

Contributors

Jim Kendrick is professor in Film & Digital Media at Baylor University and the author of *Darkness in the Bliss-Out: A Reconsideration of the Films of Steven Spielberg*.

Peter Krämer is senior research fellow in Cinema & TV in the Leicester Media School at De Montfort University (Leicester, UK).

Janice Liedl is professor of history at Laurentian University and coauthor of *"Star Wars" and History*.

Patti McCarthy is assistant professor of film studies at Whittier College and the author of *The Lucas Effect: George Lucas and the New Hollywood*.

John C. McDowell is professor of philosophy, systematic theology and ethics at University of Divinity and the author of *The Gospel according to "Star Wars": Faith, Hope and the Force*.

Kim Munson is independent scholar and curator and the author of the edited collection *Comic Art in Museums*.

Chris Pallant is the author of *Demystifying Disney* (2011), *Storyboarding: A Critical History* (2015), *Animated Landscapes: History, Form and Function* (2015), and *"Snow White and the Seven Dwarfs": New Perspectives on Production, Reception, Legacy* (2021).

Dale Pollock is interim dean of filmmaking at University of North Carolina School of the Arts and the author of *Skywalking: The Life and Films of George Lucas*.

Christine Sprengler is professor of art history at Western University and the author of *Screening Nostalgia* (2009) and *Hitchcock and Contemporary Art* (2014).

Craig Svonkin is associate professor of English at Metropolitan State University of Denver.

Julie Turnock is associate professor of Media & Cinema Studies at University of Illinois, Urbana-Champaign, and the author of *The Empire of Effects: Industrial Light and Magic and the Rendering of Realism* (2022).

Index

Note: Entries in italics denote films unless otherwise clarified in parentheses

315

Index

Index

Index

Index

Index

Index

Index

Index

Wolfe, Thomas, 13
Woman under the Influence, A, 148
Wonderful World of Disney
  (TV show), 271
Wood, Aylish, 181
Wood, Robin, 82, 138, 141, 142–45,
  147, 149
Woolley, Leonard, 100
Worrell, Denise, 23–24
Wydler, Christopher, 38

X-Wing (video game), 211

Yansong, Ma, 306
Yates, JoAnne, 127
YBCA show, 303

You Can't Go Home Again
  (Wolfe), 13
Youngblood, Gene, 29
Young Frankenstein, 64, 67
Young Indiana Jones Chronicles, The
  (TV series), 6, 161, 163, 215, *220;*
  edutainment programming and,
  221–25
Young Sherlock Holmes, 176
youthfulness, idea of, 147

*Zak McKracken and the Alien
  Mindbenders* (video game), 209
Zeitlin, Benh, 193
Zemeckis, Robert, 192, 193
Zornado, Joseph, 279